The Body

BLACKWELL READINGS IN CONTINENTAL PHILOSOPHY

Series Editor: Simon Critchley, University of Essex

Each volume in this superb new series provides a detailed introduction to and overview of a central philosophical topic in the Continental tradition. In contrast to the author-based model that has hitherto dominated the reception of the Continental philosophical tradition in the English-speaking world, this series presents the central issues of that tradition, topics that should be of interest to anyone concerned with philosophy. Cutting across the stagnant ideological boundaries that mark the analytic/Continental divide, the series will initiate discussions that reflect the growing dissatisfaction with the organization of the English-speaking philosophical world. Edited by a distinguished international forum of philosophers, each volume provides a critical overview of a distinct topic in Continental philosophy through a mix of both classic and newly-commissioned essays from both philosophical traditions.

The Body
Edited by Donn Welton

Forthcoming

Race
Edited by Robert Bernasconi

The Religious
Edited by John Caputo

The Body

Classic and Contemporary Readings

Edited and introduced by

Donn Welton

BLACKWELL
Publishers

Copyright © Blackwell Publishers Ltd 1999; editorial matter and organization copyright © Donn Welton 1999

First published 1999
Reprinted 1999

Blackwell Publishers Inc.
350 Main Street
Malden, Massachusetts 02148
USA

Blackwell Publishers Ltd
108 Cowley Road
Oxford OX4 1JF
UK

Library of Congress Cataloging-in-Publication Data

LOC data applied for

ISBN 0631211845 (hardback)
ISBN 0631211853 (paperback)

British Library Cataloguing in Publication Data

A CIP catalogue record for this book is available from the British Library.

Typeset in Bembo on 11/13.5 pt
By Pure Tech India Ltd, Pondicherry
http://www.puretech.com
Printed in Great Britain by M.P.G. Books Ltd, Bodmin, Cornwall

For Arthur F. Holmes,
who taught us to "walk in truth"

CONTENTS

ACKNOWLEDGMENTS

The editor and publishers gratefully acknowledge the following for permission to reprint copyright material:

Bonner, Charles W., "The Status and Significance of the Body in Lacan's Imaginary and Symbolic Orders."

Butler, Judith, "Foucault and the Paradox of Bodily Inscriptions," *The Journal of Philosophy*, 86 (November, 1989). Reprinted by permission of the author.

Chanter, Tina, "Beyond Sex and Gender: On Luce Irigaray's *This Sex Which Is Not One*."

Foucault, Michel, *Discipline and Punish*, trans. Alan Sheridan (Vintage Books, New York, 1979). Copyright © 1975 by Éditions Gallimard. Reprinted by permission of Georges Borchardt, Inc. for the author. Copyright © 1992 Penguin Books UK.

Foucault, Michel, *The History of Sexuality, Volume 1: An Introduction*, trans. Robert Hurley (Vintage Books, New York, 1980). Copyright © 1976 by Éditions Gallimard, Reprinted by permission of Georges Borchardt, Inc. for the author. Copyright © 1990 Penguin Books UK.

Heidegger, Martin, specified excerpts from *Early Greek Thinking*, trans. David Farrell Krell and Frank A. Capuzzi (Harper and Row, New York, 1975). English translation copyright © 1975, 1985 by Harper & Row, Publishers, Inc. Reprinted by permission of Harper Collins Publishers, Inc.

Heidegger, Martin, *Parmenides*, trans. Andre Schuwer and Richard Rojcewicz (Indiana University Press, Bloomington, 1992).

Heidegger, Martin, specified excerpts from *Being and Time*, trans. John Macquarrie and Edward Robinson (Harper and Row, New York, 1962). Copyright © 1962 by SCM Press Ltd. Reprinted by permission of Harper Collins Publishers, Inc.

Heidegger, Martin, specified excerpts from *What is Called Thinking?*, trans. F. Wieck and J. G. Gray (Harper and Row, New York, 1968). English translation copyright © 1968 by Harper & Row, Publishers, Inc. Reprinted by permission of Harper Collins Publishers, Inc.

Holenstein, Elmar, "The Zero Point of Orientation: Placing the I in Perceived Space," new translation by Lanei Rodemeyer and Sebastian Luft of "Der Nullpunkt der Orientierung," *Menschliches Selbstverstandnis* (Suhrkamp, Frankfurt am Main, 1985).

Husserl, Edmund, *Ideas Pertaining to a Pure Phenomenology and to a Phenomenological Philosophy*, Book 2: *Studies in the Phenomenology of Constitution*, trans. Richard Rojcewicz and Andre Schuwer, *Collected Works*, Vol. 3 (Kluwer Academic Publishers, Dordrecht, 1989). These pages are included with permission of Prof. Rudolf Bernet, Director Husserl-Archives Leuven.

Irigaray, Luce, "This Sex Which Is Not One," translation reprinted from *New French Feminisms*, eds. Elaine Marks and Isabelle de Courtivron (Amherst: The University of Massachusetts Press, 1980). Copyright © 1980 by The University of Massachusetts Press. © Les Éditions de Minuit, Paris.

Kristeva, Julia, *New Maladies of the Soul*, trans. Ross Buberman. Copyright © 1995, Columbia University Press. Reprinted with permission of the publisher.

Kristeva, Julia, *Revolutions in Poetic Language*, trans. Margaret Waller. Copyright © 1984, Columbia University Press. Reprinted with permission of the publisher.

Lacan, Jacques, *The Four Fundamental Concepts of Psycho-Analysis*, ed. Jacques-Alain Miller, trans. Alan Sheridan (Hogarth Press, London, 1977). Reprinted by permission of Random House, London and W. W. Norton & Company Inc., New York.

Lacan, Jacques, from *The Seminar of Jacques Lacan: Book I*: Freud's Papers on Technique 1953–1954 by Jacques Lacan, translated by John Forrester. Copyright © 1975 by Les Éditions du Seuil. English translation © 1988 by Cambridge University Press. Reprinted by permission of W. W. Norton & Company Inc., New York.

Lacan, Jacques, from *The Seminar of Jacques Lacan: Book II*: The Ego in Freud's Theory and in the Technique of Psychoanalysis by Jacques Lacan, translated by Sylvia Tomaselli. Copyright © 1978 by Les Éditions du Seuil. English translation copyright © 1988 by Cambridge University Press. Reprinted by permission of W. W. Norton & Company Inc., New York.

Lacan, Jacques, "Some Reflections of the Ego," *The International Journal of Psycho-Analysis*, Vol. 34 (1953).

Leder, Drew, "Flesh and Blood: A Proposed Supplement to Merleau-Ponty," *Human Studies*, 13 (1990).

Levin, David, "The Ontological Dimension of Embodiment: Heidegger's Thinking of Being."

Lingis, Alphonso, "The Subjectification of the Body," *Foreign Bodies* (Routledge, New York, 1994).

Merleau-Ponty, Maurice, *Phenomenology of Perception*, trans. Colin Smith (Routledge & Kegan Paul, London, 1962, Éditions Gallimard, Paris).

Oliver, Kelly, "The Flesh Become Word: The Body in Kristeva's Theory."

Steinbock, Anthony J., "Saturated Intentionality."

The publishers apologize for any errors or omissions in the above list, and would be grateful to be notified of any corrections that should be incorporated in the next edition or reprint of this book.

There were a number of people who contributed to the design and execution of this project but none more than Gina Zavota. I would especially like to thank her for her insightful suggestions as well as long hours of hard labor on this volume.

INTRODUCTION: FOUNDATIONS OF A THEORY OF THE BODY

With the rise of Modern philosophy in the seventeenth century, there came into being the question of how one can develop a rigorous theory of the nature of persons or, to put it more accurately, of what could be admitted into such a theory if one employed a philosophical method incorporating the precision found in the newly emerging mathematical and natural sciences. Descartes almost single-handedly set the parameters for all subsequent attempts to answer this question over the course of the next 300 years. From where we stand today, however, we can see that Descartes' method of framing the question introduced an epistemological reduction that produced two other interconnected ontological reductions.

In his efforts to shake free from reliance upon either the speculative, logical analysis of the new Aristotelians or the special theological content garnered in the Catholic church, two strands that had been intertwined to form a holy alliance in the schools of his day, Descartes introduced a reduction of truth to what can be clearly and distinctly apprehended by mind, employing a method that it constructs from its own resources exclusively. Mathematics met these requirements in that its objects are transparent and their generation the result of rules that are clearly and distinctly intuited. Such intuitive insight is itself secure, because it is the product of a self-referential mode of cognition that does not rely on anything other than itself, namely, thinking. The result was not only a grounding of the unity of math in a thinking subject but, with this, an elevation of the mind, in contrast to the body, to what is most essential to us as persons. Notice how Descartes moves from his epistemological criterion of clarity to a specification of our natures:

> For if we, who are supposing that everything which is distinct from us is false, examine what we are, we see very clearly that neither extension nor shape nor

local motion, nor anything of this kind which is attributable to a body, belongs to our nature, but that thought alone belongs to it.[1]

With mathematics firmly established, Descartes secures its connection to nature by arguing that "the distinction between quantity or number and the thing that has quantity or number is merely a conceptual difference" and not a "real difference."[2] With the extension of an epistemic into an ontic characterization, the things of science become cast in a form that allows them to be known with certainty.

> For I freely acknowledge that I recognize no matter in corporeal things apart from that which the geometers call quantity, and take as the object of their demonstrations, i.e., that to which every kind of division, shape and motion is applicable.[3]

As a result a certain closure is achieved: mathematics becomes the language of truths about the world. When Descartes applied this approach to the study of the human body, which he undertook with devotion and enthusiasm some six or seven years before he published his *Meditations*, he not only gave a purely mechanical explanation to several functions that were previously attributed to the soul (motion, digestion, circulation, etc.), but also reduced the body to what is extended in time and space and, thereby, what is measurable.[4] The body becomes an object whose true being is disclosed only by those natural sciences that attend to it.

The result of this program was not a unified account of the person but a theory torn in two directions.

(1)   The nature of the mind is such that it has an existence that is completely independent of the body. For Descartes this means not only that it is the unassailable foundation of all that can be known but also that what is known must itself be understood using a method that is consistent with those criteria that allow the mind to become self-evident to itself, i.e., clear and distinct ideas. Descartes' characterization of the mind as a unique substance (not extended in space and time) should not misguide us. The mind, as he understood it, was not primarily a stream of individual experiences but the ego, directly known because of the self-reflexive structure of consciousness, that grasps what is given in its essential truth. In short, it was that proto-mathematical starting point that allowed for the enframing of all that is as mathematics. Descartes' characterization of mind in contrast to everything material (substances extended in time and space) secured that difference, for one cannot use the ruler that sets the standard to measure itself; one cannot measure the rules of measurement.

(2)   By contrast, Descartes' "Treatise on Man," his book on human physiology, was a systematic attempt to reduce various types of human experience to

the mechanical interactions of the body, i.e., ultimately to physics. As this work progresses, Descartes shows how the whole range of human passions and moods, as well as determinations of the will, are nothing more than effects of the mechanical interactions of the fluids and parts of the body. It invites the next step, which some have suggested that Descartes himself intended subversively, of reducing thinking itself to the body, a step that has been taken without hesitation by various materialist theories since Descartes, as well as behaviorist and artificial intelligence models in this century.

In these accounts the focus of attention was on the nature of mind, the assumption being that what we mean by the body is settled. So effective was Descartes' placing of the body that it became the unproblematic term in efforts to understand the mind-body relation over the next three centuries. But this is precisely the term that the thinkers in this collection want to call into question. Each will challenge the treatment of the body throughout the era of modern philosophy and then the extension of that treatment in analytic philosophy, arguing that it renders impossible an account of embodiment – of corporeality understood in terms of human actions upon, and involvement with, the world – and, thereby, of mind, of our intentional cognition of that world. In place of the normal procedure of attempting to define what is or is not meant by the mind and then asking how it is connected to the body, this anthology takes the opposite approach by reconsidering what is meant by the body and then using this as the key to unlocking the concept of the mind, and then that of personhood.

Of course, there were forerunners in the nineteenth century. Hegel, Marx, Kierkegaard, and Nietzsche each employed concepts of the body to subvert Cartesian dualism. But only with the rise of phenomenology in this century (Husserl, Heidegger, Sartre, Merleau-Ponty) did an effective counter-tradition arise to what is still the dominant way of asking the question in much of analytic philosophy of mind, cognitive psychology and artificial intelligence programs. These ideas were then reworked and extended by a second cluster of thinkers (Lacan, Foucault, Kristeva and Irigaray). The purpose of this collection is to make some of these works available.

I will not attempt to review or recount the main ideas of the thinkers featured in this collection. There is no need in this introduction to clarify their theories, difficult as some are, simply because each opening selection is followed by an essay or two that attempts this or, at least, in its efforts to appropriate certain ideas, sheds light on what is significant about the selection. Rather, in what follows I will provide only a brief suggestion as to how we might place our thinkers in relation to each other and thereby find a certain historical flow to the problematics of the body through twentieth-century Continental philosophy. One should be careful not to think of a strict linear development as these very independent thinkers pursued creative lines of their own and do not in any sense form a school. Instead, I will describe three clusters of theories, the later building upon the earlier.

Though we do find the contrast in Scheler[5] about the same time, it was Edmund Husserl's untiring pen that first developed the notion of *Leib*, of lived-body, and set it in opposition to *Körper*, the body under a strict physical or physicalistic description. This contrast, extensively treated in manuscripts from around 1912 (*Ideas II*), and well known to all the thinkers in this collection, set the ground work for the phenomenological approach to the issue of the body, precisely that term that the whole movement of modern philosophy thought most unproblematic. When brought together with the theory of intentionality, which Husserl had published in 1901,[6] a whole new understanding of subjectivity was framed, though it was those who followed in his wake who understood this better than the master himself. The distinction between physical and lived-body still leaves open the question of how they are related, which I address in my essay by focusing on the issue of how Husserl understands the materiality of the lived-body. Elmar Holenstein's essay, which is translated into English for the first time here, critically challenges the lingering solipsism in Husserl's characterization of the body and uses results in psychology to develop a much more dynamic and situated concept.

Martin Heidegger was convinced that Husserl had decisively refuted the theory of psychologism in logic but was concerned, as Husserl himself worried, that it returned at the level of his method in a transcendental register. To put it programmatically, in *Being and Time* (1928)[7] Heidegger wanted to develop phenomenology into an ontology, into a discipline that thought of itself as governed not by the question of the relationship between subjectivity and world, but by the question of the *being* in the world. The result was to replace the notion of subjectivity with that of *Dasein*, of human existence, and to unfold it through the notion of modalities rather than clusters of syntheses. As a consequence, Heidegger turns from the question of the body to the question of embodiment. The body, in the final analysis, functions adverbially: "We do not 'have' a body; rather, we 'are' bodily."[8] Because of this, David Levin argues, we can and should approach the issue ontologically, which means that we must think embodiment in its relationship to being or, better, in terms of the various dimensions of its "disclosive responsiveness to the presencing of being." What Levin adds to the analysis that goes well beyond Heidegger's own formulations is a narrative of the "seasons" of embodiment, of the learning processes that are part of the very structures of embodiment that constitute Dasein.

The limitations of space preclude selections from Jean-Paul Sartre. Had we been able to include them, they would show that Sartre, living under the long shadow of Descartes, was not convinced that the notion of consciousness could be dispensed with as quickly as Heidegger thought, at the same time that he used Heidegger's notion of Dasein to correct and expand what he means by consciousness. The story is further complicated by the fact that his *Being and Nothingness* (1943)[9] escalates Husserl's static phenomenological difference between subjectivity and world into an ontological difference between consciousness (the for-itself, Nothingness) and world (the in–itself, Being). As a result, the notion of the body is left suspended between the two, with Sartre, like Heidegger, concentrating on the structures of embodiment. Sartre's later work, however, replaced the earlier characterization of consciousness as lucid with one that understands its contingency and opacity; this allowed for a richer integration of the body into his theory.[10]

Maurice Merleau-Ponty, always uneasy with Sartre's theory, stayed with, as he developed, the concept of the body first proposed by Husserl, using light from Heidegger's notion of being-in-the-world to dispel finally what remained of Descartes' shadow and to illuminate the internal connection between the body, actions and perception. This also allows for a rich theory of the inter-relationship among intentionality, the body and the earth, as suggested by Anthony Steinbock. Merleau-Ponty's reflections on the body did not stop with his *Phenomenology of Perception* (1945);[11] his last work, *The Visible and the Invisible* (1964),[12] attempts to extend its phenomenology into an ontology. Much like Heidegger thought of Dasein as provisional, providing a privileged point of access to the question of Being, so Merleau-Ponty comes to see his theory of the body as requiring deeper roots. In place of Heidegger's notion of Being or, perhaps, as its counterpart, Merleau-Ponty introduces his notion of the flesh, a crucial development that Drew Leder brings to analysis and then uses to reflect back upon and enrich the original theory of the body.

This first cluster of theories, the handiwork of philosophers moving beyond the limitations of Modern philosophy, is supplemented by a second, in which we see new appropriations and insights coming from psychoanalysis, social history, literary theory, and gender theory.

Jacques Lacan, whose fragmentary writings are unusually difficult, attempts to integrate, like Paul Schilder before him, a psychoanalytic account of the formation of the ego with an account of the body. Reworking Sartre's emphasis upon the gaze, Lacan tracks the early months of childhood through his now famous mirror stage. Charles Bonner shows how the body and its imaging are involved in the early development of the ego (with its internal connection to others) and thus essential to Lacan's mirror stage.

Michel Foucault, as much an intellectual and social historian as a philosopher, has a theory of the body grown in the soil of Nietzsche's thought but with roots in Merleau-Ponty's shift from the concept of the body to that of the flesh. For Merleau-Ponty the flesh is understood as an intertwining of structures and forces that interact without the dominance of one above all others or the agency of a controlling center. Similarly, Foucault looks to constellations of different nexuses of power (hospitals, political regimes, schools, prisons, etc.) as applied to the body to account for its constitution. Such nexuses employ normalizing practices that effectively discipline the body and configure not just its appearance in different eras but even its very materiality. Alphonso Lingis tracks several of these constellations as described in Foucault's account of torture and prisons, and then connects them to his account of sexuality.

Conspicuously missing from the analysis of the body thus far, are the questions of language and of gender. Each is taken up in different ways in part three of this collection.

Julia Kristeva is especially interested in the roots of signification, in the semiotic sources from which meaning and symbolic systems come, and in the way the symbolic reshapes those sources. Her interpretation of drives not as blind forces but as biological and semiotic structures means that they already carry meaning and a relation to other persons that is not just the result of internalizing symbols (language) and social norms. The grip of "linguistic imperialism" is broken and, in principle, the diversity of types of psychic representations, interacting in various ways, is recognized. With this, as Kelly Oliver shows, an internal connection between the body and language is established.

Luce Irigaray's theory of gender is sometimes understood as a return to essentialism because of a failure to appreciate the fact that it attempts to articulate semiotic structures in Kristeva's sense. In contrast to the phallic, centered nature of masculine sexuality, Irigaray uses the plurality of erotogenic zones and the multiple lips of the labia, simultaneously touching and touched, to speak of the polyvalent and decentered nature of feminine sexuality. Tina Chanter argues, however, that her theory moves beyond any rigid distinction between sex and gender at the same time that it shows that the sexes are not symmetrical.

The third cluster of theories are anticipated by each of the essays that follow the primary selections, for the very process of discussing the theory of another already envisions its strengths and suggests alternatives to its weaknesses. Others have thought through these issues, too, and then moved into systematic theories of their own. This volume has a companion, *Body and Flesh* (Blackwell Publishers, 1998), that contains some of the most recent and important work in this area by English-speaking writers who take their bearings from the theories represented here. That anthology looks at this field in more of a systematic than an historical fashion. This is one of the most active areas of philosophical reflection at the present, and so I conclude this brief introduction with an invitation to take up *Body and Flesh* after one has finished this collection.

Donn Welton
Stony Brook, New York

Notes

1 Rene Descartes, "Principles of Philosophy," *The Philosophical Writings of Descartes*, trans. by John Cottingham, Robert Stoothoff, Dugald Murdoch, vol. 1 (Cambridge: Cambridge University Press, 1984), Part One, Section 8, p. 195.

2 Ibid., Part Two, Section 8, p. 226.

3 Ibid., Part Two, Section 64, p. 247.

4 For his work on human physiology see his "Treatise on Man," ibid., 1, 99–108 or the full texts in *Treatise of Man*, trans. by Thomas Stelle Hall (Cambridge, Mass.: Harvard University Press, 1972). His "Meditations on First Philosophy" are published in *Philosophical Writings*, vol. II, pp. 1–62.

5 We first find the concept of the lived-body in Max Scheler in his "Die Idole der Selbsterkenntnis," *Vom Umsturz der Werte*, 4th edn (Bern: Franche Verlag, 1955), pp. 242–5; "Idols of Self-Knowledge," *Selected Philosophical Essays*, trans. by David Lachtermann (Evanston, Ill.: Northwestern University Press, 1973), pp. 37–41. The essay was first published in 1911 under the title "Über Selbsttäuschungen" in the *Zeitschrift für Psychopathologie*. His theory of the body, however, is elaborated in *Der Formalismus in der Ethik und die Materiale Wertethik*, 4th edn (Bern: Franche Verlag, 1954), pp. 408–32; *Formalism in Ethics and Non-Formal Ethics of Values*, trans. by Manfried Frings and Roger Funk (Evanston, Ill.: Northwestern University Press, 1973), pp. 398–424. This was initially published in two parts, the first appearing in Husserl's *Jahrbuch für Philosophie und phänomenologische Forschung* in 1913, the second in 1916, though Scheler notes that it was ready for press in 1913 (p. 9; Eng. trans., p. xvii).

6 *Logische Untersuchungen*, 2 vols (Halle: Max Niemeyer, 1900–1). The second edition is translated as *Logical Investigations*, trans. by J. N. Findlay, 2 vols (New York: Humanities Press, 1971).

7 Martin Heidegger, *Sein und Zeit* [1928] (Tübingen: Max Niemeyer, 1967); *Being and Time*, trans. by John Macquarrie and Edward Robinson (New York: Harper and Row, 1962).

8 Martin Heidegger, *The Will to Power as Art*, vol. 1, *Nietzsche* (New York: Harper & Row, 1979), pp. 99.

9 Sartre, Jean-Paul, *L'Être et le néant* (Paris: Librairie Gallimard, 1943); *Being and Nothingness: An Essay on Phenomenological Ontology*, trans. by Hazel Barnes (New York: Philosophical Library, 1956). On the notion of the body as developed in *Being and Nothingness* see pp. 303–10; 318–30. See also Sartre, "Faces," *Essays in Phenomenology*, ed. by Maurice Natanson (The Hague: Martinus Nijhoff, 1966), pp. 158–63.

10 On this see Hubert Dreyfus and Piotr Hoffman, "Sartre's Changed Conception of Consciousness: From Lucidity to Opacity," *The Philosophy of Jean-Paul Sartre*, ed. by Paul Schilpp, *The Library of Living Philosophers*, vol. 16 (La Salle, Ill.: Open Court, 1981), 229–45.

11   Maurice Merleau-Ponty, *Phénoménologie de la perception* (Paris: Gallimard, 1945);
      Phenomenology of Perception, trans. by Colin Smith (London: Routledge and Keegan
      Paul, 1962).

12   Maurice Merleau-Ponty, *Le Visible et l'invisible* (Paris: Gallimard, 1964); *The Visible
      and the Invisible*, trans. by Alphonso Lingis (Evanston, Ill.: Northwestern University
      Press, 1964).

PART I

PHENOMENOLOGICAL
FORMULATIONS

EDMUND HUSSERL

Material Things in Their Relation to the Aesthetic Body

The aestheta in their relation to the aesthetic body[1]

§18 The subjectively conditioned factors of the constitution of the thing; the constitution of the Objective material thing

Our entire analysis has been moving in a determinate narrow frame, the limits of which we must fix. The real unity, which was constituted for us in levels, has nevertheless, with all these levels, not reached the ultimate one, the level on which the Objective material thing is actually constituted. What it is that we have described is the thing constituted in the continuous-unitary manifold of the sense intuitions of an experiencing Ego or in the manifold of "sense-things" of various levels: multiplicities of schematic unities, of real states and real unities on various levels. It is the *thing for the solitary subject*, the subject thought of ideally as isolated, except that this subject in a certain sense remains forgotten to itself and equally forgotten by the one who is doing the analysis.

§a) The intuitive qualities of the material thing in their dependencies on the experiencing subject-Body

Nevertheless, this self-forgetfulness is hardly appropriate for the restoration of the full givenness of a thing, a givenness in which the thing exhibits its actual reality. We need only consider how a thing exhibits itself as such, according to its essence, in order to recognize that such an apprehension must contain, at the

From Edmund Husserl, *Ideas Pertaining to a Pure Phenomenology and to a Phenomenological Philosophy*, Book 2: *Studies in the Phenomenology of Constitution*, trans. by Richard Rojcewicz and Andre Schuwer, *Collected Works*, Vol. 3. (Dordrecht: Kluwer, 1989), pp. 60–70, 82–9, 151–69.

very outset, components which refer back to the subject, specifically the human (or, better: animal) subject in a fixed sense.

The qualities of material things as aestheta, such as they present themselves to me intuitively, prove to be dependent on my qualities, *the make-up of the experiencing subject*, and to be related to *my Body and my "normal sensibility."*

The Body is, in the first place, the *medium of all perception*; it is the *organ of perception* and is *necessarily* involved in all perception. In seeing, the eyes are directed upon the seen and run over its edges, surfaces, etc. When it touches objects, the hand slides over them. Moving myself, I bring my ear closer in order to hear. Perceptual apprehension presupposes sensation-contents, which play their necessary role for the constitution of the schemata and, so, for the constitution of the appearances of the real things themselves. *To the possibility of experience there pertains, however, the spontaneity of the courses* of presenting acts of sensation, which are accompanied by series of kinesthetic sensations and are dependent on them as motivated: *given with the localization of the kinesthetic series in the relevant moving member of the Body is the fact that in all perception and perceptual exhibition (experience) the Body is involved as freely moved sense organ, as freely moved totality of sense organs*, and hence there is also given the fact that, on this original foundation, all that is thingly-real in the surrounding world of the Ego has its relation to the Body.

Furthermore, obviously connected with this is the distinction the Body acquires as the bearer of the zero point of orientation, the bearer of the here and the now, out of which the pure Ego intuits space and the whole world of the senses. Thus each thing that appears has *eo ipso* an orienting relation to the Body, and this refers not only to what actually appears but to each thing that is supposed to be able to appear. If I am imagining a centaur I cannot help but imagine it as in a certain orientation and in a particular relation to my sense organs: it is "to the right" of me; it is "approaching" me or "moving away;" it is "revolving," turning toward or away from "me" − from me, i.e., from my Body, from my eye, which is directed at it. In phantasy, I do look at the centaur; i.e., my eye, freely moved, goes back and forth, accommodating itself in this or that way, and the visual "appearances," the schemata, succeed one another in motivated "appropriate" order, whereby they produce the consciousness of an experience of an existing centaur–object viewed in various ways.

Besides its distinction as a center of orientation, the Body, in virtue of the constitutive role of the sensations, is of *significance for the construction of the spatial world*. In all constitution of spatial thinghood, two kinds of sensations, with totally different constituting functions, are involved, and necessarily so, if representations of the spatial are to be possible. The first kind are the sensations which *constitute*, by means of the apprehensions allotted to them, corresponding *features of the thing* as such by way of adumbration. For example, the sensation-colors with their sensation-expansions: it is in the apprehension of these that the corporeal colorations appear together with the corporeal extension of these colorations. Likewise, in the tactual sphere, thingly roughness appears in the apprehension of the roughness-sensations, and corporeal warmth appears in relation to the sensation of warmth, etc.

The second kind are the "sensations" which do not undergo such apprehensions but which, on the other hand, are necessarily involved in all those apprehensions of the sensations of the first kind, insofar as, in a certain way, they *motivate* those apprehensions and thereby themselves undergo an apprehension of a completely different type, an apprehension which thus belongs correlatively to every constituting apprehension. In all constitution and on all levels, we have, by necessity, "circumstances," related one to the other, and "that which is dependent on" all the circumstances: everywhere, we find the "if-then" or the "because-therefore." Those sensations which undergo extensional apprehension (leading to the extended features of the thing) are motivated as regards the courses they take either actually or possibly and are apperceptively *related to motivating series, to systems, of kinesthetic sensations*, which freely unfold in the nexus of their familiar order in such a way that if a free unfolding of one series of this system occurs (e.g., any movement of the eyes or fingers), then from the interwoven manifold as motive, the corresponding series must unfold as motivated. In this way, from the ordered system of sensations in eye movement, in head movement freely moved, etc., there unfold such and such series in vision. That is, while this is happening, there unfold, *in motivated order*, "images" of the thing that was perceptually apprehended to begin the eye movement and, likewise, the visual sensations pertaining to the thing in each case. An apprehension of a thing as situated at such a distance, as oriented in such a way, as having such a color, etc., is unthinkable, as can be seen, without these sorts of relations of motivation. In the essence of the apprehension itself there resides the possibility of letting the perception disperse into "*possible*" series of perceptions, all of which are of the following type: *if* the eye turns in a certain way, *then* so does the "image;" if it turns differently in some definite fashion, then so does the image alter differently, in correspondence. We constantly find here this two-fold articulation: kinesthetic sensations on the one side, the motivating; and the sensations of features on the other, the motivated. The like holds, obviously, for touch and, similarly, everywhere. Perception is without exception a *unitary accomplishment* which arises essentially out of the playing together of two *correlatively related functions*. At the same time, it follows that *functions of spontaneity* belong to every perception. The processes of the kinesthetic sensations are *free processes* here, and this freedom in the consciousness of their unfolding is an essential part of the constitution of spatiality.

§b) The significance of *normal* perceptual conditions for the constitution of
the intuited thing and the significance of abnormalities (change of the
Body, change in the thing)

Now the processes of perception, in virtue of which one and the same external
world is present to me, do not always exhibit the same style; instead, there are
distinctions which make themselves noticeable. At first, the same unchanged
Objects appear, according to the changing circumstances, now this way, now in
another way. The same unchanged form has a *changing appearance*, according to
its position in relation to my Body; the form appears in *changing aspects*, which
present "it itself" more or less "advantageously." If we disregard this and instead
consider real properties, then we find that one and the same Object, maintaining
one identical form, does have different color appearances (the form as filled),
according to its position relative to an illuminating body; furthermore, the color
appearances are different when it stands under different illuminating bodies, but
all this happens in an ordered fashion, one which may be determined more
precisely in regard to appearances. At the same time, certain conditions prove to
be the "*normal*" ones: seeing in sunlight, on a clear day, without the influence of
other bodies which might affect the color-appearance. The "optimum" which is
thereby attained then counts as the *color itself*, in opposition, for example, to the
red light of the sunset which "outshines" all proper colors. All other color
properties are "*aspects of*," "appearances of," this pre-eminent color-appearance
(which latter is called "appearance" only in an *other* sense: namely, with respect
to a higher level, the physicalistic thing, still to be discussed). Yet it is inherent in
the thing that its normal color keeps changing, precisely in dependence on
whatever illuminating bodies are involved, whether the day is one of clear light
or is hazy, etc., and it is only with the return of the normal circumstances that
the normal color reappears. "In itself" there belongs to a body a color as being in
itself, and this color is grasped in seeing, but it ever appears differently, and the
aspect it presents depends thoroughly on the Objective circumstances, and it can
be distinguished there either more or less easily (with the limit case of complete
invisibility). And the degree of visibility affects the form, too.

It should also be examined whether from the very start all Objective circumstances are apperceived *as causal*, as emanating from things. Certain circumstances exhibit periodic changes – e.g., the relations of night and day – and
correspondingly the things which otherwise are experienced as unchanged, for
instance things given as unchanged for the sense of touch, undergo periodic
changes in the unfolding of their visual characters. With regard to the visual
mode of givenness, which brings out the color characteristics as well as the form
characteristics that become visible along with them, a privilege attaches to *clear
daylight*, such that there not only does the form become visible in a particularly

favorable way up to its finer details, but also in this light such global characteristics are visible through which properties of other sense spheres are co-
announced at the same time, properties given in the nexus of these experiences
as not affected by the change of color (e.g., the material attributes, which are
disclosed when the surface structure become visible). Therefore in the series of
possible appearances a certain givenness of the thing is privileged in that with it
is given, *of the thing as a whole, what is relatively the best*, and this acquires the
character of what is *especially intended*: it is the predominating focus of the
"interest," what the *experience is tending toward, terminates in*, is fulfilled in; and
the other modes of givenness become intentionally related to this "optimal"
one.

Included *in the normal experience*, in which the world is *originally* constituted as
world, "*the way it is*," are still other *conditions of normal experience*: e.g., seeing in
air – which counts as immediate seeing, seeing without any mediating things –
touching by immediate contact, etc. If I interpose a foreign *medium* between my
eye and the things seen, then all things undergo a change in appearance; more
precisely, all phantom-unities undergo a change. It will be said: the same thing is
seen, but through different media. The thing has no dependency on such
changes; it remains the same. Only the "mode of appearance" of the thing (in
this case, the appearance of the phantom) depends on whether this or that
medium is mediating between the eye and the thing. Transparent glass is indeed
a medium that can be seen through, but it changes the images of things in
different ways according to its different curvatures, and, if it is colored, it
transmits its color to them – all that belongs in the realm of experience. Finally,
if I put on colored lenses, then everything looks changed in color. If I knew
nothing of this medium, then for me all things would be colored. Insofar as I
have experiential knowledge of it, this judgment does not arise. The givenness
of sense-things counts, with regard to the color, as *seemingly* given, and semblance again means a mode of givenness which could possibly also occur in this
way within the system of normal givenness, under the appropriate circumstances, and which would induce an *Objectively false* apprehension where there
are motives prompting a mixup, something those circumstances are very likely
to bring about. The "false" lies in the contradiction with the normal system of
experience. (The change of appearance is a uniform one for all the things,
recognizable as a uniform change according to type.)

The case is the same if we take, instead of an interposition of a medium
between organ and thing, an *abnormal change of an organ itself*. If I am touching
something with a blister on my finger, or if my hand has been abraded, then all
the tactual properties of the thing are given differently. If I cross my eyes, or if I
cross my fingers, then I have two "things of sight" or two "things of touch,"
though I maintain that only one actual thing is present. This belongs to the
general question of the constitution of a thingly unity as an *apperceptive unity of a*

manifold of different levels which themselves are already apperceived as unities of multiplicities. The apperception acquired in relation to usual perceptual conditions obtains a new apperceptive stratum by taking into consideration the new "experience" of the dispersion of the one thing of sight into a pair and of the fusion of the pair in the form of a continuous overlapping and convergence in the regular return to the former perceptual conditions. The doubled things of sight are indeed completely analogous with the other things of sight, but only *the latter* have the additional meaning of "things;" and the lived experience has the meaning of a *lived experience of perception only as related to a certain "position of the two eyes,"* the *homologous* one or one from the system of normal eye positions. If a *heterology* now occurs, then I indeed have analogous images, but they *mean* things only in *contradiction* to all normal motivations. The images now once again obtain the apprehension, "actual thing," precisely through the constitutive nexus, i.e., the *motivation which puts them in a concordant relation to the system of motivated perceptual manifolds.* If I take my eyes out of a normal position into a disparate *crossed position*, then two semblant images arise; "semblant images:" i.e., images which would, each for itself, present "the thing" only if I lent them normal motivations.

A further important consideration deals with other groups of abnormalities. If I ingest santonin, then the whole world "seems" to change; e.g., it "alters" its color. The "alteration" is a "seeming." Afterwards, as is the case with every change of colored lighting, etc., I once again have a world which matches the normal: everything is then concordant and changes or does not change, moves or is at rest, as usual, and it displays the same systems of aspects as before.

But here it must be observed that rest and motion, change and permanence, get their sense by means of the constitution of thinghood as reality, in which such occurrences, especially the limit cases of rest and permanence, play an essential role.

Therefore the global coloring of all seen things can easily "change," for example when a body emits rays of light which "cast their shine" over all things. There is more to the constitution of the "change of things according to color" than just a change of the filled schemata with respect to color: *change of things is, from the very outset, constituted as causal change* in relation to causal circumstances, as, for example, each advent of an illuminating body. I can apprehend the change without seeing such an illuminating body, but in that case the causal circumstance is, in an indeterminate way, co-apperceived. These causal circumstances, however, are of the order of things. *The relativity of the spatial things with reference to other ones determines the sense of the change in things. But the psychophysical conditionalities do not belong here in the least.* This must be kept in mind. It goes without saying, however, that my Body is indeed involved in the causal nexuses: if it is apprehended *as a thing in space*, it is certainly not apprehended as mere schema but instead as the point of intersection of real causalities in the real (exclusively spatio-thingly) nexus. Belonging to this sphere is, for example, the fact that a stroke of my hand (considered purely as the striking of a corporeal thing, i.e., excluding the lived experience of the "I strike") acts exactly the same as a stroke of any other material thing, and, similarly, the fall of my Corporeal body is like any other fall, etc.[2]

Now concerning the intake of santonin, this too is therefore, abstracting from all "concomitant psychic facts," a *material process*, one which could very well, if required by the constitution of the world of experience, or by the further elaboration of the constitution of the experience of this world in the course of new experiences, enter into a real relation with the optical change of the rest of the material world. In itself it is thus thinkable that I would find experiential motives for seeing a general change in the color of the entire visible world and for regarding the change, in this apprehension, as a real-causal consequence of the material process of ingesting santonin (with its Bodily-material consequences). It would be a normal perception just like any other. As long as, and whenever, I experience the change of all visible colors as an optical change of the *things*, I must assume a causal relation between whatever causing thinghoods there might be; it is *only* in the *causal* nexus that a change is precisely a change of a *thing*. As soon as experiential motives arise in opposition, then there must necessarily take place a *transformation in the apprehension*, in virtue of which the "change" that is seen loses the sense of a change and forthwith acquires the *character of "seeming."* A semblant change is a schematic transformation apprehended as a change under normal conditions, thus in relation to experiences constitutive of causality. But now it is given in a way which cancels the causal apprehension. The causal apprehension is suggested by the given schematic transformation: it is as if it would present a change, but this is, under the given circumstances, excluded. The intake of santonin is not, with respect to the general "change in color," a process which is or which could be apprehended as a cause. The shift in color of all seen things is such that there is not even an incentive to regard it at all as a real change of the illumination (e.g., in the manner of a light source emitting colored rays). It is therefore that it presents itself as a semblant change; everything looks "as though" there were a new source of light shining, or "as if," in some other way, real causes were there effecting a general optical change (even if these causes were undetermined, unknown). But such causes may not now be presupposed; they are, given the total experiential situation, excluded.

We have to ask: what can, *on the basis of a transformation in the sense-thing, totally cancel the apperception of real change* in this way, in opposition to the cases in which such an apperception, already accomplished, merely undergoes a modification (by the fact that a different causal nexus is substituted for the one that had been supposed, that is, the assumed cause abandoned but another cause accepted)?

The answer is a modification in the sphere of *psychophysical "causality"* or, rather, *"conditionality,"* to say it better. (For a *causa* in the proper sense is precisely a *real* cause. The subjective, however, is, in opposition to reality, an irreality. Reality and irreality belong together essentially in the form of reality and subjectivity, which on the one hand mutually exclude one another and on the other hand, as is said, essentially require one another.) Besides the relations of the real to the real, which belong to the essence of everything real as spatial, temporal, and causal relations, there also belong to this essence relations of psychophysical conditionality in possible experience. Things are "experienced," are "intuitively given" to the subject, necessarily as unities of a spatio-temporal-causal nexus, and necessarily pertaining to this nexus is a pre-eminent thing, "my Body," as the place where, and always by essential necessity, a system of subjective conditionality is interwoven with this system of causality and indeed in such a way that in the transition from the *natural attitude* (the regard directed in experience to nature and life) to the *subjective attitude* (the regard directed to the subject and to moments of the subjective sphere), real existence, and manifold real changes as well, are given as in conditional connection with subjective being, with a state of being in the subjective sphere. Something thingly is experienced (perceptually apperceived, to give privilege to the originary experience) in such a way that, through a mere shift of focus, there emerge relations of dependency of the apperceived state of the thing on the sphere of sensation and on the rest of the subjective sphere. Here we have the *primordial state of psychophysical conditionality* (under this heading are included *all conditional* relations which run back and forth between thingly and subjective being). To every psychophysical conditionality there necessarily appertains *somatological causality*, which immediately always concerns the relations of the irreal, of an event in the subjective sphere, with something real, the Body: then mediately the relations with an external real thing which is in a real, hence causal, connection with the Body. . . .

§e) Possibility of the constitution of an "Objective nature" on the solipsistic level

We have pursued the constitution of material nature through various strata and have seen that already for the "solipsistic" subject – the subject in isolation – there exist motives for the distinction between an "appearing" thing, whose qualitative content is relative to my subjectivity, and the "Objective" thing, which remains what it is even if changes occur in my subjectivity and, dependent on it, in the "appearances" of the thing. Thereby we have to understand under the heading "true" or "Objective" thing still something double:

(1) the thing as it presents itself to me under *"normal" conditions*, in opposition to all other thing-like unities which, constituted under "abnormal" conditions, are degraded to "mere semblance."

(2) the identical content of qualities which, *abstraction made from all relativity*, can be worked out and fixed logico-mathematically: i.e., the physicalistic thing. Once this is known and once we have, in addition, Objective knowledge of the psychophysical character of experiencing subjects, as well as of the existing conditionalities between thing and subject, then from that it can be determined Objectively how the thing in question must be intuitively characterized for the respective subjectivity – the normal or the abnormal.[3]

The question now, however, is whether or not the motives for the necessary distinction between the subjectively conditioned thing and the Objective thing, motives which do present themselves in solipsistic experience, are sufficient or have to be there at all. As long as we take cases in which changes of the external world, feigned for us by an abnormal perceptual organ, are shown up as "semblances" by the testimony of the other organs, to that extent the distinction between "seeming" and what actually is is always given, even if it may remain undecided in particular cases *what* is semblant and *what* is actual. But if we assume for once that a subject would always have only normal perceptions and would never undergo a modification of any of its organs, or on the other hand would undergo a modification, but one that allowed for no possibility of correction (loss of the entire field of touch, or mental diseases which alter the entire typical character of perception), then the motives of the distinction between "semblance" and "actuality," assumed up to now, would be eliminated, and the level of "Objective nature" could not be attained by such a subject. But the danger, that under the assumed conditions the constitution of Objective nature could not be attained, is removed as soon as we lift the abstraction we have maintained up to now and take into account the conditions under which constitution takes place *de facto*: namely, that the experiencing subject is, in truth, *not a solipsistic subject* but is instead one among many.

§f) Transition from solipsistic to intersubjective experience

Let us consider a little more closely the possibility of a *solipsistic world*, something we have assumed up to now. I (everybody should substitute here his own "I") would experience a world, and it would be exactly the same as the one I actually do experience; everything would be the same, with the only exception that in my field of experience there would be no Bodies I could apprehend as Bodies of *other* psychic subjects. If this apperceptive domain is lacking, then it neither determines my apprehensions of things, and insofar as it does usually determine these apprehensions in my actual experience, then its influence would be absent from my world-image as now modified. Moreover, I now have the same manifolds of sensation; and the "same" real things, with the same properties, appear to me and, if everything is in harmony, exhibit themselves as "actually being," or otherwise, if discrepancies of a known kind occur as exceptional, the things show themselves as being "different" or as not being at all. Seemingly, nothing essential has changed; seemingly, only a fragment of my world of experience is missing, the world of animalia, as well as the group of causalities precisely involved with it in a world-nexus. Let us then imagine, however, that at a point of time within the time co-constituted along with the solipsistic world, suddenly in my domain of experience Bodies show up, things understandable as, and understood as, human Bodies. Now all of a sudden and for the first time human beings are there for me, with whom I can come to an understanding. And I come to an understanding with them about the things which are there for us in common in this new segment of time. Something very remarkable now comes out: extensive complexes of assertions about things, which *I* made in earlier periods of time on the ground of earlier experiences, experiences which were perfectly concordant throughout, are *not corroborated* by my current companions, and this not because these experiences are simply lacking to them (after all, one does not need to have seen everything others have seen, and vice versa) but because they thoroughly conflict[4] with what the others experience in experiences, we may suppose, that necessarily are harmonious and that go on being progressively confirmed. Then what about the actuality exhibited in the first period of time? And what about myself, the empirical subject of this actuality? The answer is clear. As I communicate to my companions my earlier lived experiences and they become aware of how much these conflict with their world, constituted intersubjectively and continuously exhibited by means of a harmonious exchange of experiences, then I become for them an interesting *pathological* Object, and they call my actuality, so beautifully manifest to me, the hallucination of someone who up to this point in time has been mentally ill. One may imagine perfection in the exhibition of my solipsistic world and raise that perfection to any height, still the described state of affairs as an a *priori* one, the ideal possibility of which is beyond question, would not change at all.

Light must now be shed on a certain problem: the relation to a multiplicity of people who have dealings with one another – how does that enter into the apprehension of a thing and come to be constitutive for the apprehension of a thing as "Objective and actual"? This "how" is at first very puzzling, because when we carry out an apprehension of a thing we do not, it *seems*, always co-posit a number of fellow men and, specifically, co-posit them as ones who are to be, as it were, invoked. One might also wonder if we are not entangled here in a circle, for surely the apprehension of one's fellow man presupposes the apprehension of the Body and consequently also presupposes thing-apprehension. There is only one way to solve this problem, the way prescribed for us by phenomenology. We must interrogate the thing-apprehension itself, there where it is an experience of an "Objectively actual" thing, and we must interrogate the experience which is not yet exhibiting, but is in want of exhibition, as to what, inherent in it, is in need of exhibition, what components of unfulfilled intentions it harbors. (In this regard it must be observed that we have in fact described the constitution of the thing incompletely by investigating only the manifolds of sensation, the adumbrations, schemata, and, in general, visual things in all their levels. We must overcome in a decisive point the Ego's self-forgetfulness we touched upon previously.) Each thing of my experience belongs to my "environment," and that means first of all that *my Body* is part of it precisely as Body. It is not that we have here a matter of essential necessity in any sense. That is precisely what our solipsistic thought-experiment has taught us. Strictly speaking, the *solus ipse* is unaware of the *Objective Body* in the full and proper sense, even if the *solus ipse* might possess the *phenomenon* of its Body and the corresponding system of experiential manifolds and know them in just as perfect a way as the social man. In other words, the *solus ipse* does not truly merit its name. The abstraction we carried out, for justifiable theoretical reasons, does not yield the isolated *man*, the isolated human person. This abstraction does obviously not consist in our arranging for a mass murder of the people and animals of our surrounding world, sparing one human subject alone. For in that case the remaining subject, though one and unique, would still be a human subject, i.e., still an intersubjective object, still apprehending and positing himself as such. But, on the contrary, the subject we constructed knows nothing of a human environment, knows nothing of the reality or even just the real possibility of "other" Bodies, understood in the sense of an apprehension of the human, and thus knows nothing of his own Body as understandable by others. This subject does not know that others can gaze upon the same world, one that simply appears differently to different subjects, such that the appearances are always relative to "their" Bodies, etc. It is clear that *the apprehension of the Body plays a special role for the intersubjectivity* in which all objects are apprehended "Objectively" as things in the one *Objective* time and one *Objective* space of the one Objective world. (In every case the exhibition of any apprehended Object-ivity whatsoever requires a relation to the apprehension of a multiplicity of subjects sharing a mutual understanding.) The thing which is constituted for the individual subject in regulated manifolds of harmonious experiences and which, as one for sense intuition, stands continuously over and against the Ego in the course of perception, obtains in that way the character of a merely subjective "appearance" of the "Objectively real" thing. Each of the subjects who are intersubjectively related in mutual understanding in regard to the same world and, within that, in regard to the same things, has his own perceptions of them, i.e., his own perceptual appearances, and in them he finds a unity in the appearances, which itself is only an appearance in a higher sense, with predicates of appearance that may not, without any further ado, count as predicates of the appearing "true thing."

Thus we come here, in considering mutual understanding, to the same distinction we already demonstrated as possible on the solipsistic level. The "true thing" is then the Object that maintains its identity within the manifolds of appearances belonging to a multiplicity of subjects, and specifically, again, it is the *intuited* Object, related to a community of normal subjects, or, abstraction made from this relativity, it is the *physicalistic* thing, determined logico-mathematically. This physicalistic thing is obviously the same, whether it is constituted solipsistically or intersubjectively. For logical Objectivity is *eo ipso* Objectivity in the intersubjective sense as well. What a cognizing subject comes to know in logical Objectivity (hence in such a way that this presents no index of a dependency of its truth-content upon the subject or upon anything subjective) can be similarly known by any cognizing subject as long as he fulfills the conditions *any* subject must satisfy to know such Objects. That is, he must experience the things and the *very same things*, and he must, if he is also to know this identity, stand in a relation of empathy to the other cognizing subjects, and for that he must have Corporeality and belong to the same world, etc.

It pertains to *perception's very sense*, as well as to that of *experience* in general, that things come to presence there which are to be determined in themselves and distinguished from all other things. And it pertains to the sense of experiential *judgment* to make a claim to Objective validity. If a thing is determined in itself and distinct from every other, then it has to allow for judgmental, therefore predicative, determination in such a way that its distinctiveness as regards all other things stands out.

The thing given in perception and experience is, in accordance with perception's very sense, something *spatio-temporal* from the first, having form and duration and also having a position in space and time. So we have to distinguish between the *appearing* form and the *form itself*, between the appearing spatial magnitude, the appearing location, and the magnitude and location themselves. Everything that we experience of the thing, even the form, has reference to the experiencing subject. All these appear in changing aspects, in the change of which the things are present as sensibly changed also. In addition, the space between things and the form of this space appear under different aspects according to the subjective circumstances. Always and necessarily, however, the one and the same space "appears" as the form of all possible things, a form that cannot be multiplied or altered. Every subject has his "space of orientation," his "here" and his possible "there," this "there" being determined according to the directional system of right-left, above-below, front-back. But the basic form of all identification of the intersubjective givennesses of a sensuous content is of such a kind that they necessarily belong to one and the same *system of location*, whose Objectivity is manifest in that every "here" is identifiable with every relative "there" as regards every new "here" resulting from the subject's "moving on" and so also as regards every "here" from the viewpoint of another subject. This is an ideal necessity and constitutes an Objective system of location, one that does not allow of being grasped by the vision of the eyes but only by the understanding; that is, it is "visible," in a higher kind of intuition, founded on change of location and on empathy. In this way is solved the problem of the "form of intuition" and of spatial intuition. It is not a matter of the senses, although in another respect it is. The primary intuitive space is sensuously given though this is not yet space itself. Objective space is not sensuous, although it is still intuited on a higher level, and it comes to givenness by means of an identification within a change of orientation, but exclusively one the subject itself carries out freely. Oriented space (and along with it, *eo ipso* Objective space) and all appearing spatial forms already admit of idealization; they are to be grasped in geometrical purity and determined "exactly."

The *Objective form* is Objective as ordered within *Objective space*. Everything *else* about a thing that is Objective (detached from all relativisms) is so through a connection with what is fundamentally Objective, viz., space, time, motion. Real properties manifest themselves as real substantial-causal unities in the motion and deformation of the spatial form. These are the *mechanical properties* which express the causal-lawful dependencies of the spatial determinations of bodies. The thing is always *form* in a *situation*. The form is, however, in every situation a *qualified* one. Qualities are what fills, they extend over the surface and through the corporeality of the form. *Qualifications*, however, extend from the things into empty space: *rays of light, radiations of heat*, etc. That means that thingly qualities condition qualities and qualitative changes in other things and indeed do so in such a way that the effect is a constant function of the situation: to every change of situation there corresponds a change of effect. In virtue of such a subordination to spatial relations which may be determined with exactitude, even the sense qualities become amenable to exact determination. Thus we come to an understanding of the physicalistic world-view or world-structure, i.e., to an understanding of the method of physics as a method which pursues the sense of an intersubjectively-Objectively (i.e., non-relative and thereby at once intersubjective) determinable sensible world.

The constitution of psychic reality through the body

§35 Transition to the study of the constitution of "man as nature"

Now, the theme of the following considerations is to be the constitution of the *natural reality, man* (or animal being), i.e., the constitution of man as he presents himself to a naturalistic point of view: as material body upon which are constructed new strata of being, the Bodily-psychic. It is possible that in this constitutive consideration much will have to be included that subsequent investigation will show as belonging to the personal or spiritual Ego. It will be possible to provide the ultimate distinction between "man as nature" and "man as spirit," as well as the establishment of their reciprocal relations, only when both these Objectivities have been subject to constitutive study.

If we now look for a point of departure for our constitutive analysis, then we must take into account what came to light for us as regards the constitution of material nature, namely, that it, with its entire intuitive content, is related to animal subjects. Hence when we approach the constitution of the natural Object, "man," we may not already presuppose his Body as a fully constituted material thing but instead must at first pursue what is already constituted prior to, or correlative with, material nature, as regards the psychophysical subject. And here, as before, let us first try to see how far we can advance in a solipsistic consideration.

§36 Constitution of the Body as bearer of localized sensations (sensings)

We have seen that in all experience of spatio-thingly Objects, *the Body* "is involved" as the perceptual organ of the experiencing subject, and now we must investigate the constitution of this Corporeality. We can thereby choose immediately the special case in which the spatially experienced body, perceived by means of the Body, is the Corporeal body itself. For this too is perceived from the outside, although within certain limits, preventing it from being considered, without qualification, as a thing like any other in a thingly nexus. Thus there are parts of this body which can indeed be perceived by touch but cannot be seen. At first, however, we may disregard these and begin instead with parts that we can both touch and see. I can look at them and feel them, just like other things, and in this respect the appearances have entirely the same nexus as do other appearance of things. But now there is a distinction between the *visual* appearances and the *tactual* regarding, e.g., a hand. Touching my left hand, I have touch-appearances, that is to say, I do not just sense, but I perceive and have appearances of a soft, smooth hand, with such a form. The indicational sensations of movement and the representational sensations of touch, which are Objectified as features of the thing, "left hand," belong in fact to my right hand. But when I touch the left hand I also find in it, too, series of touch-sensations, which are "*localized*" in it, though these are not constitutive of properties (such as roughness or smoothness of the hand, of this physical thing). If I speak of the *physical* thing, "left hand," then I am abstracting from these sensations (a ball of lead has nothing like them and likewise for every "merely" physical thing, every thing that is not my Body). If I do include them, then it is not that the physical thing is now richer, but instead *it becomes Body, it senses*. "Touch"-sensations belong to every appearing Objective spatial position on the touched hand, when it is touched precisely at those places. The hand that is touching, which for its part again appears as a thing, likewise has its touch-sensations at the place on its corporeal surface where it touches (or is touched by the other). Similarly, if the hand is pinched, pressed, pushed, stung, etc., touched by external bodies or touching them, then it has its sensations of contact, of being stung, of pain, etc. And if this happens by means of some other part of one's Body, then the sensation is *doubled* in the two parts of the Body, since each is then precisely for the other an external thing that is touching and acting upon it, and each is at the same time Body. All the sensations thus produced have their *localization*, i.e., they are distinguished by means of their place on the appearing Corporeality, and they belong phenomenally to it. Hence the Body is originally constituted in a double way: first, it is a physical thing, *matter*, it has its extension, in which are included its real properties, its color, smoothness, hardness, warmth, and whatever other material qualities of that kind there are. Secondly, I find on it, and I *sense* "on" it and "in" it: warmth on the back of the hand, coldness in the feet, sensations of touch in the fingertips. I sense, extended over larger Bodily areas, the pressure and pull of my clothes. Moving my fingers, I have motion-sensations, whereby a sensation in an ever changing way extends itself over and traverses the surface of the fingers, but within this sensation-complex there is at the same time a content having its localization in the interior of the digital space. My hand is lying on the table. I experience the table as something solid, cold, and smooth. Moving my hand over the table, I get an experience of it and its thingly determinations. At the same time, I can at any moment pay attention to my hand and find on it touch-sensations, sensations of smoothness and coldness, etc. In the interior of the hand, running parallel to the experienced movement, I find motion-sensations, etc. Lifting a thing, I experience its weight, but at the same time I have weight-sensations localized in my Body. And thus, my Body's entering into physical relations (by striking, pressing, pushing, etc.) with other material things provides in general not only the experience of physical occurrences, related to the Body and to things, but also the experience of specifically Bodily occurrences of the type we call *sensings*. Such occurrences are missing in "merely" material things.

The localized sensations are not properties of the Body *as* a physical thing, but on the other hand, they *are* properties of the thing, Body, and indeed they are effect-properties. They arise *when* the Body is touched, pressed, stung, etc., and they arise there *where* it is touched and at the time *when* it is touched: only under certain circumstances do they still endure after the touching takes place. Touching refers here to a physical event. Even two lifeless things can touch one another, but the touching of the Body provides sensations on it or in it.

We must now give heed to the following: in order to bring to perception here the tactual thing, paperweight, I touch it, with my fingers, for example. I then experience tactually the smooth surface of the glass and the delicate crystal edges. But if I attend to the hand and finger, then they have touch sensations which still linger when the hand is withdrawn. Likewise, my finger and hand have kinesthetic sensations, and precisely the same sensations which function as indicational or presentational with respect to the thing, paperweight, function as touch-*effects* of the paperweight on the hand and as sensings produced in it. In the case of the hand lying on the table, the same sensation of pressure is apprehended at one time as perception of the table's surface (of a small part of it, properly speaking) and at another time produces, with a "different direction of attention," in the actualization of an other stratum of apprehension, sensations of digital pressure. In the same way are related the coldness of the surface of a thing and the sensation of cold in the finger. In the case of one hand touching the other, it is again the same, only more complicated, for we have then two sensations, and each is apprehendable or experienceable in a double way.

Necessarily bound to the tactual perception of the table (this perceptual apprehension) is a perception of the Body, along with its concomitant sensation of touch. This nexus is a necessary connection between two possible apprehensions: pertaining correlatively to that, however, is a connection between two thinghoods that are being constituted. It is shown empirically by the possibility of a representation of the world in those blind from birth that everything can come into play in the extra-visual sphere and that here the apperceptions have to be ordered in such a way that these correlations can be constituted.

§37 Differences between the visual and tactual realms

We find now a striking difference between the sphere of the visual and that of the tactual. In the tactual realm we have the *external Object*, tactually constituted, and a second Object, the *Body*, likewise tactually constituted, e.g., the touching finger, and, in addition, there are fingers touching fingers. So here we have that double apprehension: the same touch-sensation is apprehended as a feature of the "external" Object and is apprehended as a sensation of the Body as Object. And in the case in which a part of the Body becomes equally an external Object of an other part, we have the double sensation (each part has its own sensations) and the double apprehension as feature of the one or of the other Bodily part as a physical object. But in the case of an *Object constituted purely visually* we have *nothing* comparable. To be sure, sometimes it is said that the eye is, as it were, in touch with the Object by casting its glance over it. But we immediately sense the difference. An eye does not appear to one's own vision, and it is not the case that the colors which would appear visually on the eye as localized sensations (and indeed visually localized corresponding to the various parts of its visual appearance) would be the same as those attributed to the object in the appre-hension of the seen external thing and Objectified in it as features. And similarly, we do not have a kind of extended occularity such that, by moving, one eye could rub past the other and produce the phenomenon of double sensation. Neither can we see the seen thing as gliding over the seeing eye, continually in contact with it, as we can, in the case of a real organ of touch, e.g., the palm of the hand, glide over the object or have the object slip past the hand. I do not see myself, my Body, the way I touch myself. What I call the seen Body is not something seeing which is seen, the way my Body as touched Body is some-thing touching which is touched.[5] A visual appearance of an object that sees, i.e., one in which the sensation of light could be intuited just as it is in it – that is denied us. Thus what we are denied is an analogon to the touch sensation, which is actually grasped along with the touching hand. The role of the visual sensations in the correlative constitution of the Body and external things is thus different from that of the sensations of touch. All that we can say here is that if no eye is open there are no visual appearances, etc. If, ultimately, the eye as organ and, along with it, the visual sensations are in fact attributed to the Body, then that happens indirectly by means of the properly localized sensations.

Actually, the eye, *too*, is a field of localization but *only for touch sensations*, and, like every organ "freely moved" by the subject, it is a field of localized muscle sensations. It is an Object of touch for the hand; it belongs originally to the merely touched, and not seen, Objects. "Originally" is not used here in a temporal-causal sense; it has to do with a primal group of Objects constituted directly in intuition. The eye can be touched, and it itself provides touch and kinetic sensations; that is why it is necessarily apperceived as belonging to the Body. All this is said from the standpoint of straightforward empirical intuition. The relation of the seen color of the thing to the seeing eye, the eye "with which" we see, the "being directed" of the open eye onto the seen thing, the reference back to this direction of the eye which is part of having visual appearances, and, furthermore, growing out of this, the relation of the color sensations to the eye – all that will not be confused with the givenness of these sensations in the manner of localized "sensings."

The same applies to *hearing*. The ear is "involved," but the sensed tone is not localized in the ear. (I would not even say that the case of the "buzzing" in the ears and similar tones subjectively sensed in the ear are exceptions. They are in the ear just as tones of a violin are outside in space, but, for all that, they do not yet have the proper character of sensings and the localization proper to them.) It would be an important task to thoroughly examine in this regard the groups of sensations of the various senses. However important that would be for a completely elaborated theory of the phenomenological constitution of material thinghood, on the one hand, and of the Body, on the other hand, for us now the broad distinctions will suffice. To make ourselves sure of them, we must be perfectly clear on the fact that *localization of sensings* is in fact something *in principle different from the extension of all material determinations of a thing*. The sensings do indeed spread out in space, cover, in their way, spatial surfaces, run through them, etc. But this *spreading out* and spreading into are precisely something that differs essentially from *extension* in the sense of all the determinations that characterize the *res extensa*. The sensing which spreads over the surface of the hand and extends into it is not a real quality of a thing (speaking always within the frame of intuitions and their givenness) such as, for example, the roughness of the hand, its color, etc. These real properties of a thing are constituted through a sensuous schema and manifolds of adumbrations. To speak in a similar way of sensings would be quite absurd. If I turn my hand, bring it closer or take it away, then, for one, the unchanged color of the hand is given to me as constantly different. Yet the color itself presents itself, and the color constituted first (that of the sensuous schema) manifests a real optical property of the hand. Roughness, too, presents itself and does so tactually in manifolds of touch sensations which constantly flow into one another and to each of which a spreading-out belongs. The touch-sensings, however, the sensations which, constantly varying, lie on the surface of the touching finger, are, such as they are lying there spread out over the surface, nothing given through adumbration and schematization. They have nothing at all to do with the sensuous schema. The touch-sensing is not a *state* of the material thing, hand, but is precisely the *hand itself*, which for us is more than a material thing, and the way in which it is mine entails that I, the "subject of the Body," can say that what belongs to the material thing is its, not mine. All sensings pertain to my soul; everything extended to the material thing. *On* this surface of the hand I sense the sensations of touch, etc. And it is precisely thereby that this surface manifests itself immediately as my Body. One can add here as well: if I convince myself that a perceived thing does not exist, that I am subject to an illusion, then, along with the thing, everything extended in its extension is stricken out too. But the sensings do not disappear. Only what is *real* vanishes from being.

Connected to the privilege of the localization of the touch sensations are differences in the complexion of the visual-tactual apprehensions. Each thing that we see is touchable and, as such, points to an immediate relation to the Body, though it does not do so in virtue of its visibility. *A subject whose only sense was the sense of vision could not at all have an appearing Body;* in the play of kinesthetic motivations (which he could not apprehend Bodily) this subject would have appearances of things, he would see real things. It cannot be said that this subject who only sees sees his Body, for its specific distinctive feature as Body would be lacking him, and even the free movement of this "Body," which goes hand in hand with the freedom of the kinesthetic processes, would not make it a Body. In that case, it would only be as if the Ego, in unity with

this freedom in the kinesthetic, could immediately and freely move the material
thing, Body.

The Body as such can be constituted originally only in tactuality and in
everything that is localized with the sensations of touch: for example, warmth,
coldness, pain, etc. Furthermore, the kinetic sensations play an important role. I
see how my hand moves, and without it touching anything while moving, I
sense kinetic sensations, though as one with sensations of tension and sensations
of touch, and I localize them in the moving hand. And the same holds for all the
members of the Body. If, while moving, I do touch something, then the touch
sensation immediately acquires localization in the touching surface of the hand.
At bottom, it is owing only to their constant interlacing with these primarily
localized sensations that the kinetic sensations receive localization. But because
there obtains here no parallelism which is exactly stratified as there is between
temperature sensations and touch sensations, so the kinesthetic sensations do not
spread out in a stratified way over the appearing extension, and they receive
only a rather indeterminate localization. Yet this is indeed not without significance; it makes the unity between the Body and the freely moveable thing more
intimate.

Obviously, the Body is also to be seen just like any other thing, but it
becomes a *Body* only by incorporating tactile sensations, pain sensations, etc. –
in short, by the localization of the sensations as sensations. In that case the visual
Body also participates in the localization, because it coincides with the tactual
Body, just as other things (or phantoms) coincide, ones which are constituted
both visually and tactually, and thus there arises the idea of a sensing thing which
"has" and which can have, under certain circumstances, certain sensations
(sensations of touch, pressure, warmth, coldness, pain, etc.) and, in particular,
have them as localized in itself primarily and properly. This is then a precondition for the existence of all sensations (and appearances) whatsoever, the visual
and acoustic included, though these do not have a primary localization in the
Body.

§38 The Body as organ of the will and as seat of free movement

The distinctive feature of the Body as a field of localization is the presupposition
for its further distinctive features setting it off from all material things. In
particular, it is the precondition for the fact that it, already taken as Body
(namely, as the thing that has a stratum of localized sensations) is an *organ of
the will*, the *one and only Object* which, for the will of my pure Ego, is *moveable
immediately and spontaneously* and is a means for producing a mediate spontaneous
movement in other things, in, e.g., things struck by my immediately spontaneously moved hand, grasped by it, lifted, etc. *Sheer material things are only
moveable mechanically and only partake of spontaneous movement in a mediate way.*

Only Bodies are immediately spontaneously ("freely") moveable, and they are so, specifically, by means of the free Ego and its will which belong to them. It is in virtue of these free acts that, as we saw earlier, there can be constituted for this Ego, in manifold series of perceptions, an Object-world, a world of spatial-corporeal things (the Body as thing included). The subject, constituted as counter-member of material nature, is (as far as we have seen up to now) an Ego, to which a Body belongs as field of localization of its sensations. The Ego has the "faculty" (the "I can") to freely move this Body – i.e., the organ in which it is articulated – and to perceive an external world by means of it.

§39 Significance of the Body for the constitution of higher Objectivities

Now, besides this, the Body is involved in all other "conscious functions," and that has its various sources. Not only the sensations which exercise a constitutive function as regards the constitution of sense-things, appearing spatial Objects, not only these sensations have a localization given in immediate intuition along with the relation to a Body grounded therein, but that is also true of *sensations belonging to totally different groups*, e.g., the "sensuous" feelings, the sensations of pleasure and pain, the sense of well-being that permeates and fills the whole Body, the general malaise of "corporeal indisposition," etc. Thus here belong groups of *sensations which, for the acts of valuing*, i.e., for intentional lived experiences in the sphere of feeling, or *for the constitution of values* as their intentional correlates, *play a role, as matter, analogous to that played by the primary sensations for what is intentionally lived in the sphere of experience*, or for the constitution of Objects as spatial things. Moreover, all kinds of sensations, difficult to analyze and discuss, belong here as well, ones that form the material substrate for the life of desire and will, sensations of energetic tension and relaxation, sensations of inner restraint, paralysis, liberation, etc. All these groups of sensations, as *sensings*, have an immediate Bodily localization. Thus, for every human being, they *belong, in a way that is immediately intuitable, to the Body as to his particular Body*, i.e., as a subjective objectivity distinguished from the Body as a mere material thing by means of this whole stratum of localized sensations. *The intentional functions, however, are bound to this stratum*; the matter receives a spiritual forming, just as, discussed above, the primary sensations undergo *apprehension*, are taken up in perceptions, upon which, then, perceptual judgments are built, etc. Hence in this way a *human being's total consciousness is in a certain sense, by means of its hyletic substrate, bound to the Body*, though, to be sure, the intentional lived experiences themselves are *no longer directly and properly localized*; they no longer form a stratum on the Body. Perception, as the touching apprehension of form, does not have its seat in the touching finger in which the touch sensation is localized; thinking is not actually localized intuitively in the head, the way the impressions of tension are, etc. That we very often speak as if it were so is no proof that we actually apprehend it that way in intuition. The co-intertwined contents of sensation have a localization which is actually intuitively given, but the intentionalities do not, and only metaphorically are they said to be related to the Body or to be in the Body.

§40 More precision concerning the localization of the sensings and concerning the non-thingly properties of the Body

Now, if all that belongs to the matter is Bodily localized or is, by means of localization, related to the Body and is constitutive, therewith, for the Body in the Objectivity proper to it, then we need to ask how this constitution is to be understood and *what it is that institutes unity here*. The physical Body is, of course, a constituted unity, and only to it does the stratum of the sensings belong. How is the content of the sensation connected to what is constituted, and how does the Body, which is equally a material thing, have in itself and on itself the contents of sensation? It is certainly not in the way in which the sensation-content, tone quality, and the sensation-content, intensity, have an essential unity, nor is it the way in which the sensation-content, color, is unified with the moment of spread (we do not mean here spatial extension, talk of which makes no sense with regard to sensation-contents). Here we have on the one side not sensation-contents but constituted real unities instead, and is it really the case that we have mere sensation-contents on the other side? Let us reflect. If an object moves mechanically over the surface of my skin, touching it, then I obviously have a succession of sensings ordered in a determinate way. If it always moves in the same way, with the same pressure, touching the same parts of the Body at the same pace, then the result is obviously always the same. All this is "obvious," it is there in the apprehension; precisely under such circumstances this Corporeal body behaves in such a way that it is not to be stimulated in just any way but is stimulatable in a definite way under definite circumstances, and such that all effects of stimulation have their system, and to the system of thingly bodies appearing in it there correspond distinctions as to place, whereby, however, to each such place pertains a definite, dependent on the type of the stimulation-effect, further dimension of possible distinctions. To the place in the extension corresponds a place-moment in the sensation, and to the degrees of stimulation and kinds of stimulation correspond definite moments which render the sensation concrete and modifiable according to more or less known ways. Thus there lies in the sensations an order which "coincides" with the appearing extension; but that is already implicit in the apprehension from the outset, in such a way that the stimulation-effects do not appear as something alien and as just an effect, but rather as something *pertaining* to the appearing Corporeal body and to the extensive order, and as something ordered in a *coincident* order. In each Bodily sensation, the mere sensation is not grasped, but it is apprehended as belonging to a system of possible functional consequences which corresponds exactly to the extensive order, consequences that the material real must undergo in consistent parallels with possible material effects. We must also note that the fields of sensation in question here are always completely filled, and each new stimulation does not provoke a sensation as if for the first time, but rather, it provokes in the sensation-field a corresponding change in the sensation. Hence the field undergoes an apprehension as something changeable in manifold ways and as dependent on extension in the type of its changeableness. The field receives localization, and in the field each new change receives localization as a consequence of the particular stimulating circumstances. The new stratum the thing has received by means of the localization of the field acquires, with respect to the constancy of the field, the character of a kind of real property. The Body, we can say, always has states of sensation, and which particular ones it has depends on the concomitant system of real circumstances under which it senses. Under the real circumstances of the "sting" in this or that part of the Body, there emerges in the sensation field (as a field of states) the state of sensation, "sting-sensation." Under the real circumstances we call entrance into a hot room, a change occurs in the total localized field with respect to its total stratum of warmth sensation in the sense of rising temperature, etc. The sensitiveness of the Body thus is constituted throughout as a "conditional" or psychophysical property. And that enters into the apprehension of the Body, as it is perceived "externally." To the apprehension of Corporeality as such belongs not only the apprehension of a thing but also the *co*-apprehension of the sensation fields, and indeed these are given as belonging, in the mode of localization, to the appearing Corporeal body. "Belonging": phenomenologically, this term expresses relations of the phenomenal "if-then": if my hand is touched or struck, then I sense it. We do not here have the hand as physical body and, connected with it, an extra-physical consequence. From the very outset it is apperceptively characterized as a hand *with* its field of sensation, with its constantly co-apprehended state of sensation which changes in consequence of the external actions on it, i.e., as a *physical-aesthesiological unity*. In the abstract, I can separate the physical and aesthesiological strata but can do so precisely only in the abstract. In the concrete perception, the Body is there as a new sort of unity of apprehension. It is constituted as an Objectivity in its own right, which fits under the formal-universal concept of reality, as a thing that preserves its identical properties over against changing external circumstances. The relations of dependency under which it stands toward external nature are thereby, however, other than the ones material things have amongst themselves. (It has already been mentioned, and it will be discussed with more precision in what follows, that the Body, in addition, as a material thing like all others, is fit within the nexus of reality in a more strict sense, namely, the one of causal regulation.)

It pertains in general to the intuition of something real to leave open, in this intuition's apprehension, further real dependencies which do not yet belong to the content of the executed apprehension in a determinate way (although they may be determinate in their specific nature). The real can therefore be related, in new apprehensions and in extensions of old ones, to new circumstances as something dependent on them, whereby real properties of the same real object are constituted. The sense of the expanded apprehension then prescribes the type which the course of experience has to bear out and determine more precisely. With this more precise determination the apprehension itself then necessarily takes on fuller form.

In this way, even the Body is apprehended not only as dependent with respect to the primary stratum of sensation, its properly localized one, but also with respect to the fields of sensation and groups of sensation that pertain to it mediately and are not properly localized, thus, e.g., with respect to the field of vision. How the visual field of sensation is filled, which motivations can occur therein, and consequently what in the visual field can be experienced by the subject, and in which modes of appearance it must be exhibited, this all depends on certain qualities of the Body, especially on those of the eye, and, furthermore, on the eye's Bodily connections, especially its connections with the central nervous system, and even more particularly it depends on this system itself and, on the other hand, on the concomitant external stimulations. Along with that, hence, are constituted new real properties of the Body, which, thereby, is obviously involved as already constituted from elsewhere. So the capacity to be stimulated in general becomes a universal title for a class of real properties which have quite another source than the properly extensive (and therewith material) properties of the thing and which in fact pertain to a quite different dimension. For through this stratum, through this new group of real properties which display themselves as real insofar as they are constituted through a relation to real circumstances within the real, the material Body is intertwined with the soul. What can be apprehended as localized stratum of the Body as well as what can be apprehended as dependent on the Body (in the full sense of Body, including this stratum already) and on the "sense organs," all this forms, under the heading of the matter of consciousness, an underlying basis of consciousness and undergoes its realizing apprehension in unity with this consciousness as soul and psychic Ego. To say that this Ego, or the soul, "has" a Body does not merely mean that there exists a physical-material thing which would, through its material processes, present real preconditions for "conscious events" or even, conversely, that in its processes there occur dependencies on conscious events within a "stream of consciousness." Causality belongs, if the word is to retain its pregnant sense, to reality, and conscious events participate in reality only as psychic states or as states of a psychic Ego. Soul and psychic Ego "have" a Body; there exists a material thing, of a certain nature, which is not merely a material thing but is a Body, i.e., a material thing which, as localization field for sensations and for stirrings of feelings, as complex of sense organs, and as phenomenal partner and counterpart of all perceptions of things (along with whatever else could be said about it, based on the above), makes up a fundamental component of the real givenness of the soul and the Ego.

§41 Constitution of the Body as material thing in contrast to other material things

We have seen how, correlative to the material world, a subject of Bodily-psychic faculties (sense faculties, faculties of free movement, of apperception, etc.) is constituted, whereby the Body comes to light, at one and the same time, as Body and as material thing. In this regard, however, we made the restriction that the Body emerges as a thing of a particular type, so that one cannot, without qualification, assign it to nature as a part just like any other part. This is what we must discuss somewhat more precisely.

(a) The Body as center of orientation

If we consider the characteristic way in which the Body presents itself and do the same for things, then we find the following situation: each Ego has its own domain of perceptual things and necessarily perceives the things in a certain orientation. The things appear and do so from this or that side, and in this mode of appearing is included irrevocably a relation to a here and its basic directions. All spatial being necessarily appears in such a way that it appears either nearer or farther, above or below, right or left. This holds with regard to all points of the appearing corporeality, which then have their differences in relation to one another as regards this nearness, this above and below, etc., among which there are hereby peculiar qualities of appearance, stratified like dimensions. The Body then has, for its particular Ego, the unique distinction of bearing in itself the *zero point* of all these orientations. One of its spatial points, even if not an actually seen one, is always characterized in the mode of the ultimate central here: that is, a here which has no other here outside of itself, in relation to which it would be a "there." It is thus that all things of the surrounding world possess an orientation to the Body, just as, accordingly, all expressions of orientation imply this relation. The "far" is far from me, from my Body; the "to the right" refers back to the right side of my Body, e.g., to my right hand. In virtue of its faculty of free mobility, the subject can now induce the flow of the system of its appearances and, along with that, the orientations. These changes do not have the significance of changes of the things of the environment themselves, and specifically, they do not signify a movement of the things. The Body of the subject "alters its position" in space; the things appearing in the environment are constantly oriented thereby; all appearances of things preserve their fixed system according to form. The form of intuition, the lawful character of the adumbrations, and, therewith, the form of the order of orientation around a center, all this is necessarily preserved. But whereas the subject is always, at every now, in the center, in the here, whence it sees the things and penetrates into the world by vision, on the other hand the Objective place, the spatial position, of the Ego, or of its Body, is a changing one.

Nevertheless, at the present stage of our investigation we are not at all so advanced that we could assign to the Ego such an "Objective place." Provisionally, we must say: I have all things over and against me; they are all "there" – with the exception of one and only one, namely the Body, which is always "here."

(b) Peculiarity of the manifolds of appearance of the Body

Other peculiar properties of the Body are conjoined with its distinctive character as we have described it. Whereas, with regard to all other things, I have the freedom to change at will my position in relation to them and thereby at the same time vary at will the manifolds of appearance in which they come to givenness for me, on the other hand I do not have the possibility of distancing myself from my Body, or my Body from me, and accordingly the manifolds of appearance of the Body are restricted in a definite way: certain of my corporeal parts can be seen by me only in a peculiar perspectival foreshortening, and others (e.g., the head) are altogether invisible to me. The same Body which serves me as means for all my perception obstructs me in the perception of it itself and is a remarkably imperfectly constituted thing.

(c) The Body as integral part of the causal nexus

If, despite all this, we apprehend the Body as a real thing, it is because we find it integrated into the causal nexus of material nature. We spoke of the peculiarity the Body has (as Body) of being moved "spontaneously" or "freely" by the will of the Ego. Besides these free kinesthetic processes, others emerge which, instead of being "done by," are characterized as being "done to," i.e., as passive processes in which spontaneity plays no part. In that case, we have at the same time an experiencing of the mechanical process of the movement of the Body and a givenness of this process with the "psychic" character of enduring something – not as if it were something painful or repugnant but simply in the sense that "my hand is moved, my foot is struck, pushed," etc. Similarly, I experience the mechanical movement of the Body as the movement of a material thing like any other thing even in the case of spontaneity, and I find it characterized at the same time as a spontaneous movement in the sense, "I move my hand," etc.

Thus movements of my Body are apprehended as mechanical processes like those of external things, and the Body itself is apprehended as a thing which affects others and upon which the others have effects. All the cases mentioned earlier of conditional relations between things and the Body also admit of changes in apprehension, thanks to which the processes in question appear as merely physical ones. If a heavy body is resting on my hand (or perhaps the one hand on the other) then I have, abstracting from the resultant sensation of pressure or pain, the physical phenomenon of one body pressing on another, perhaps deforming it by its pressure. If I cut my finger with a knife, then a physical body is split by the driving into it of a wedge, the fluid contained in it trickles out, etc. Likewise, the physical thing, "my Body," is heated or cooled through contact with hot or cold bodies; it can become electrically charged through contact with an electric current; it assumes different colors under changing illumination; and one can elicit noises from it by striking it. The last two cases, however, are different from the earlier ones where there was a psychophysical process that could be split apart abstractively into a physical process and its "psychical" consequence (or vice versa). But the physical process, "red illumination of my hand," is not followed by the sensation of red in the same way that the sensation of warmth follows the heating of my hand, and the physical process to which the sensation of the color is linked – red light rays striking my eyes – is not given to me at all. The "turning point," which lies in the Body, the point of the transformation from causal to conditional process, is hidden from me.

§42 Character of the Body as constituted solipsistically

If we now try, in a short summary, to characterize the way a Body is constituted for the solipsistic subject, then we find that:

(1) viewed from "within" – in the "inner attitude" – it appears as a freely moving organ (or system of such organs) by means of which the subject experiences the external world. Furthermore, the Body appears as a bearer of sensations, and, thanks to their intertwining with the rest of psychic life in its totality, it appears as forming, with the soul, a concrete unity.

(2) Approached from the outside – in the "outer attitude" – it presents itself as a reality *sui generis*. That is: on the one hand, as a material thing of special modes of appearance, a thing "inserted" between the rest of the material world and the "subjective" sphere (the subject together with what was just mentioned in 1), as a center around which the rest of the spatial world is arranged, and as being in causal relationship with the real external world. On the other hand, the Body appears here at the same time as a "turning point" where the causal relations are transformed into conditional relations between the external world and the Bodily-psychic subject. And in virtue of that, the Body appears as pertaining integrally to this subject and its properties, both the specifically Corporeal and the psychic ones bound up with them. That which is constituted in the outer attitude is there co-present together with what is constituted in the inner attitude.

In solipsistic experience, however, we do not attain the givenness of our self as a spatial thing like all others (a givenness which certainly is manifest in our factual experience) nor that of the natural Object, "man" (animal being), which we came to know as correlate of the "naturalistic attitude," a material thing upon which the higher strata of what is specifically animal are built and into which they are, in a certain way, inserted, "introjected." In order to attain that, a different path has to be followed; one must go beyond his own subjectivity and turn to the animalia encountered in the external world.

Notes

1 Aestheta refers here to material things as such in their aesthetic structure.
2 To be sure, it still remains to be discussed to what extent the solitary subject has the possibility of apprehending his Body as a material body like any other.
3 Thus are determined, as will later be shown in full, the tasks of physics, psycho-physics, and psychology.
4 Of course, this conflict should not be considered total. For a basic store of *communal* experiences is presupposed in order for mutual understanding to take place at all.
5 Obviously, it cannot be said that I see my eye in the mirror, for my eye, that which sees *qua* seeing, I do not perceive. I see something, of which I judge indirectly, by way of "empathy," that it is identical with my eye as a thing (the one constituted by touch, for example) in the same way that I see the eye of an other.

2

SOFT, SMOOTH HANDS: HUSSERL'S PHENOMENOLOGY OF THE LIVED-BODY

Donn Welton

One must, as far as possible, make science ocular.

M. A. Petit (1797)

Ein bloss augenhaftes Subjekt könnte gar keinen erscheinenden Leib haben.

Husserl (1912–16)[1]

We are often amused, sometimes saddened, by what posterity does with the works of a great philosopher. Many times the appropriations are faithful to the intentions of the original thinker, or at least we can recognize the architectonic of the original in the reconstructions of those who follow. In other cases they are nothing short of a total distortion. But often what we find are appropriations of *parts* of a philosopher's thought, often those parts that were not central to the thinker's own vision of philosophy. The mark of a great philosopher, we realize, is that in forging a new path he or she sets the surrounding world ablaze, and we come to see much that, while marginal to his or her concerns, nevertheless remained in darkness until sparks flew from his or her pen.

No doubt Husserl worked on the idea of the body[2] in several different texts. The first place seems to be his 1907 lectures entitled "Ding und Raum."[3] After writing *Ideen I*, Husserl returns to the question in 1912 in his efforts to work out regional ontologies. What we now have as *Ideen II*, a text we will concentrate on in this study, contains his most fruitful insights on the body.[4] Finally there are what is known as the D manuscripts, scattered texts that were composed after 1920 and as late as 1932.[5] Given the central vision of Husserl's thought, however, all these texts are "margins" – margins as only Husserl could write them, running to several hundred pages.

Husserl is not, it must be said, a philosopher of the body but a philosopher of consciousness. Moreover, the long-range goal of his work is not to describe the sensuous texture of incarnate existence, but to establish the autonomy and efficacy of reason. Yet in his effort to ground reason, he discovers its horizonal character and its dependency on types of constitution that exceed, and thereby escape, its closure; his relentless pursuit of these types sheds so much light on what would have otherwise remained concealed. Thus while Husserl is not a philosopher of the body, his phenomenology of the body, that hidden source of not only the presence but also the meaning that the perceptual world has for consciousness, envisions what no other philosophy had previously seen.

Given this fact and given the tremendous importance of this concept for phenomenologists like Sartre, Merleau-Ponty, Gurwitch, and Erwin Strauss, it comes as no small surprise to realize that Husserl's concept of the body has received little direct analysis in English. While everywhere assumed and often appropriated, the extensive critical analysis necessary to assess its value has been lacking.[6] This is all the more surprising since his most important text on the body, *Ideen II*, has been available for consultation in the Husserl Archives in Louvain for some 55 years and was used and noted extensively in Merleau-Ponty's groundbreaking *Phenomenology of Perception*, published in 1945.[7] It was also one of the first of Husserl's texts published in his collected works, appearing some 45 years ago. This essay, and the one following by Elmar Holenstein, can thus be thought of as two attempts to remedy the situation.

At the same time, I do not think of this essay as primarily an historical study. Rather, I am after a rather nasty philosophical issue, at least for phenomenologists: how does one understand the relationship between a natural scientific description of the body and a phenomenological characterization of the body? Is there a point at which these descriptions, or these bodies, if it turns out that we have two, intersect? Are we left with an irreconcilable difference in grammars, or even a confrontation of kinds of beings that calls upon us to reject one and affirm the other? This statement of the issue is quite provisional, for part of the problem is to show how the issue is generated. I propose to do this in the first part of this essay by tracing Husserl's own effort to characterize the body from within what he calls the "natural attitude," by placing this characterization in relation to Descartes, and by asking how the presence of things indicates the presence of the body as lived-body. The second part will raise the question of access: what "phenomena" give us a point of entry into a description of the lived-body in its own terms, and how are we then to envision such a body? The third part, returning to our problem, will ask if there is a sense in which we can see the lived-body as a part of nature and if we can place it in relation to an "objective" description of the body. Finally, I will conclude by briefly returning to our starting point in the nature of things and deepening our first descriptions.

1 The Presence of Things

Things of nature, first of all, are things of and for perception. Nature, in turn, is a "sphere of mere things [*blosse Sachen*]."[8] In describing their essential features, Husserl reaches for that very idea that first gave rise to modern science and sets the physical thing in contrast to another kind of object, an object that can be thought of only as outside the realm of nature:

> Descartes designates extension as the essential attribute of material things – accordingly, it is also simply called corporeal – over against psychic or spiritual being, which, in its spirituality as such, has no extension and, indeed, essentially excludes it.[9]

When thought of as extended in time and space, material in composition, and governed by rigid laws of causality, things bow and finally assume a posture that allows us to become the true "lords and masters of nature" as Descartes put it.[10] The essences of things become reduced to their mathematizable features, their measurable spatio-temporal extension, their geometric configurations; this means that they are reducible to quantity, for, as Descartes was the first to show, geometry can be reconstructed as algebra. At least Descartes was clear as to the implications of this approach: the body, as one of these things, is brought under the "rules in medicine."[11] It is taken in hand as a "corpse."[12]

But in what sense are such things actually seen in perception? Does a physical characterization describe the only legitimate, or the most basic, way in which things are present to us? When I look at a blooming rose or hear the plaint of an Indian funeral song, do I see electromagnetic waves 650 nanometers in length or listen to compression waves between 27 and 1,000 cycles per second? Do I not rather see a blooming rose and sometimes a velvet red, alive with passion? Do I not rather hear a funeral song, and perhaps a wail tremoring with lost love?

Husserl is quite clear that the Cartesian analysis of nature takes things as though they were free of values and void of "practical predicates."[13] This analysis must assume what does not exist, namely, a free-standing, constituting agent beneath the practical agent engaged with nature, "a pure, 'objectivating ego-subject' that does not carry out value judgments [*Wertungen*] of any kind."[14] Instead of seeing it as the correlate of a "pure" mind or agent – assumed to be free of human values only so that its products, understood as they "really" are, might assume them – Husserl thinks of nature physically characterized as the correlate of a particular *interest* brought to it by the subject. The perceiver is "indifferent" towards the objects that appear; "it" has no interest in their value or in practically changing them. To put it positively, "this subject values the knowledge of appearing being."[15] This is not a matter of bald construction for we are still speaking of experience, even a form of vision. But this experience, which Husserl boldly calls "theoretical experience,"[16] introduces its own value, the value of knowing something "as it is" and "how it is," and its own praxis, the experimental procedure.[17]

Let me pause to set up an idea to which we will return in the third part. If the physical body, projected by the canons of physical science, were a manifest given to which we could correlate an independent objectivating ego, or an independent level of constitution, then its presence would be not only concrete but also absolute, and its relation to other entities describable only in its own terms. But if not, if the body as probed by the gloved hand of science arises only in correlation with a specific interest, then we can open the question of how it is related to other entities given through other interests. But for now let me return to an inventory of the things of nature.

With the correlation between physical thing and interest established, we, in turning our attention to the range of such things, do find an object that is peculiar, an object that is indeed a thing and yet something more, an object that in the very style of its visibility suggests a certain invisibility. It is this surplus, this excess, that requires us to introduce a second order to nature:

> The objects of nature in a second, broader sense are, when taken in their full concretion, animal realities. We may characterize them as ensouled bodies. Here we have founded realities, which in themselves presuppose material realities, the so-called material bodies as their founding stratum. These have, and this is what is new, besides their specifically material determinations, yet new systems of proper-ties, psychic [properties].... In experience the new properties in question are given as *belonging* to the body under consideration, and it is precisely because of them that it is called lived-body [*Leib*].[18]

Having discovered a unique set of objects among the objects of nature, Husserl first attempts to clarify them in terms of nature:

> Insofar as men and animals *have* material bodies, they have spatiality and materi-ality. But according to what is specifically human and animal, i.e., according to what is psychic, [men and animals] *are* not material, and, accordingly, they, taken as *concrete wholes*, are *not material* realities in the proper sense.[19]

The lived body then is that concrete whole which is simultaneously material and not material. This characterization of the lived-body strains traditional categories and is quite unsatisfactory, for here the concept is but an amalgam of incompa-tible elements. Husserl does attempt to explain himself:

> Material things are divisible parallel to the extension belonging to their essence. Men and animals are not divisible. Men and animals are *spatially localized;* even

what is psychic for them, at least by virtue of its essential foundation in what is bodily [*Leiblichen*], can be ordered in relation to what is spatial. We would even say that much of what is counted as psychic, unclear as that title is, has something like extension [*Ausbreitung*] (although it is not extension [*Verbreitung*] in space). But in principle *nothing* on this side is extended in the proper sense, in the specific sense of extension we have described.[20]

This explanation is itself wrought with tension: the lived-body is a peculiar blend of what is not extended and what is spatially localized, what is not extended yet ordered into space. It has something like an extension that is not extension, or at least not an extension in space. How can what is in principle not extended ever achieve a connection with what is extended, let alone go on to gain a location in the extended by virtue of this connection? As Kant constantly reminds us, putting two worlds in the same book does not make them one. Is not the concept of lived-body nothing more than the admission of a failure, not only by Husserl but by a whole tradition?

It took the rest of *Ideen II* for Husserl to rethink this issue and, in effect, to displace his first set of contrasts by other, more basic ones. In fact, his analysis there may be the first clear example of what he comes to call depth-history in *The Crisis*,[21] for what he does is not to discard the initial formulation but to show its origins, to discover those transformations or articulations of the basic structure making it possible. What is most suggestive about Husserl's account, then, is that it asks us, first of all, to carry out the analysis of materiality from within the natural attitude. He does not attribute such an analysis to philosophical prejudices and then leap, as if by magic, into a realm beyond. Rather, it is a further interrogation of the object as material that will provide the *Leitfaden*, the thread guiding us to a phenomenological analysis of the body from *within* the natural attitude.[22] Let me show how an analysis of the materiality of things requires the introduction of the notion of the lived-body.

Remember that we began by suggesting that things of nature are things of and for perception. If one envisions perception as a simple passive process in which the things of nature are replicated in the mind as images or ideas, then the body functions, as in Descartes, only as a conduit or transmitter of such ideas and does not directly contribute to the configuration or the content of what is perceived. But, as the history of modern philosophy endlessly reminds us, this leaves us with a *phenomenal* object and the tedious alternatives of realism, which attempts to locate it in nature, and idealism or conceptualism, which argues that such objects are found only in the mind. In *Ideen II* Husserl undercuts these alternatives in a very suggestive way by asking what we would have to do with perception to create such a phenomenal object. If we take the thing, first of all, in isolation from other things and from the circumstances in which it is found, and if we fix it before our eye, then we would have something approaching what is usually meant by a phenomenon. We would be presented with a spatial Gestalt filled out with various qualities. But if this is what we begin with, Husserl argues, then we will never be able to build up a real object out of such phenomena. There might even be "a synthetic unity of many strata of 'sensuous appearances' of different senses,"[23] but what would be missing is precisely the materiality of the thing, for this is not a phenomenal feature that can be found in any of the appearances so given. Thus we will never know if the experienced thing is real or a mere illusion,[24] real or conceptual. To discover this we must lift the methodological abstraction in play and reinsert the thing into its environment:

> Reality in the proper sense, what we are calling here materiality, does not lie in the simple sensuous [i.e., the filled out Gestalt], not in what is at hand in the perceived. . .; rather it lies in its relation [to circumstances] and the manner of apprehension corresponding to this relation.[25]

Husserl, then, understands the material presence of things to be a *relational* presence. Without their web of conditional dependence on other things and other dimensions of the environment, things would be but "phantoms" floating at a distance somewhere between world and mind. But kept in this web, the thing takes on its flesh. Changes in lighting affect the radiant appearance of a blue sky, fluctuations in temperature the consistency of maple syrup, changes in ingredients the taste of a plate of spaghetti. All of this follows a formal rule: "Under the same circumstances we get the same results."[26]

What Husserl realizes, as he presses the analysis, is that the lived-body is the third item making it all possible, that the lived-body is constitutive of the flesh of perceived things. Things have a relation to other things because they are perceptually situated, and they are perceptually situated because of the orientation they have to our perceiving and moving bodies. This orientation is constitutive of the thick space that things have. If the body were reducible to just another thing in space, it could not be the source of that space. Even if the body were a "fixed eye," it would give us a space lacking all depth, all thickness, all paths. Thus in order to account for the materiality of things, a new way of envisioning the body must come into play. The body that constitutes the space of perceived things, then, is not simply that center in terms of which all things are situated but also the lived-body of free movement, of approaching and distancing, of grasping and repelling, of resisting and penetrating. These movements of the body are experienced not like the movement of ever so many things, but from within. Husserl calls them kinaesthetic sensations. "The courses of kinaesthetic sensations are here free courses and this freedom in our consciousness of their transpiring is an essential part of the constitution of spatiality."[27]

What this leaves us with, then, is the idea that the materiality of perceived things requires that they be situated spatially and the idea that the space of perceived things exists by virtue of the body as a center of motility and of action. It is the very materiality of experienced things that demands that the body be characterized not as physical body but as lived-body. In fact, this bond between the lived-body and perceived things is primary and underlies the later interpretation of them using the mathematical notion of extension.

If we return to our initial bewilderment about how the body could be both extended and non-extended, we have a first answer: the primary correlation between material things and bodily experiences undergoes an interpretation in which it is construed as a relationship between physical (extended) and psychological (non-extended):

> This entire system of conditionality, binding sensible things and subjective events in lawful fashion, is the basis of a higher stratum of apperception built on it; it becomes [interpreted as] the psycho-physical conditionality between my lived-body and its causal intertwining in nature outside the lived-body, on the one hand, and subjective courses of sensations, aspects, etc., on the other.[28]

Of course, this is only a first answer, for we do not yet have a clue as to how the lived-body is itself spatial, how it not only orients the things of perception but is also itself one of the things oriented. There are other problems as well: saying that the lived-body belongs to a second order of nature means that the scientific methods of description appropriate to the first order may not apply. How can we both secure the presence of the lived-body as lived-body and then introduce an analysis appropriate to it? What we have in this section is a clue that required the introduction of the lived-body but nothing more. We do not yet have a full description of the "evidence" Husserl would require. Securing this requires another approach.

2 The Presence of the Body

The analyses until now have this in common: they treat the body as a thematic object. The characteristics that Husserl attributes to it – kinaesthetic sensations, its role in constituting the spatiality, and thus materiality, of things, its function of bearing the soul – clearly go beyond traditional theories in that the *correlation* between body and world is understood as a whole with interdependent moments. Even for our initial analysis, the body is something more than a mechanism; as "ensouled" or, better, as living, its involvement with things runs much deeper than Descartes could imagine.[29] Yet the lived-body is still viewed from the perspective of another person, the phenomenologist, and thus it is viewed as *phenomenon* in correlation to other phenomena.

This approach changes when we ask how the lived-body comes to know itself. A second moment in the dialectic of our analysis emerges, for now it is a question not of how we discover a *Körper* as *Leib*, as in the first moment, but of how we can know the *Leib* as *Leib*. Since this is not a categorical act but an aesthetic synthesis, the question becomes one of understanding how the lived-body senses, feels, has a "sensation" of itself or, better, lives itself. In this analysis the lived-body is not a "theme" as in the first moment, nor a referent of an act of understanding, nor is our experience of it gained through an act of reflection upon it (though our phenomenology *of* that experience is so gained). Rather it is now a question of how, in our awareness of things, we come to experience the lived-body *as* experiencing.

Let us focus on what our initial analysis described as the correlation between sensations of motility and sensations through which features of material things are given. What Husserl discovers is that the very process of touching is *reflexive*; in touching an object I become aware of the fact that I am being touched by it:

> The hand lies on the table. I experience the table as solid, cold, smooth. Moving it over the table I experience it and its determinations as a thing. At the same time, however, I can always pay attention to the hand and find on it tactile sensations, sensations of smoothness and coldness, etc. In the interior of the hand, running parallel to the experienced movement, I [also] find sensations of motion, etc. Lifting a thing I experience its weight, but at the same time I have sensations, related to the weight, located in my lived-body. And thus, in general, my lived-body, coming into physical contact (striking, pressing, pushing, etc.) with other material things offers not only the experience of physical events relating the lived-body to things, but also specific lived-bodily events of the kind that we call *sensings* [*Empfindnisse*]. Such events are missing in "merely" material things.[30]

Thus the very process of touching something establishes a new kind of experience. It is rare to find Husserl constructing neologisms, but in this case he introduces the term *Empfindnisse*, a lived experience (*Erlebnis*) that is not an experience-of (*Erfahrung*), a sensorial event (*Empfindung*) that is not a perception (*Wahrnehmung*), a finding *of* oneself (*sich befinden*) that is not a finding of something. *Empfindnisse* are those peculiar sensorial events that offer the body as lived to itself in the very process of being offered to the world. They arise at the intersection of tactile sensations and kinaesthetic sensations and, at precisely that juncture where all distance is traversed, undergird the flesh of things with the flesh of the lived-body.

Notice that *Empfindnisse* offer the body to itself in a way fundamentally different than those tactile sensations presenting the world. The lived-body is present but not yet visible, or is present only as invisible. This all changes when the lived-body itself is one of the things that we come to experience. The text where Husserl first brings this out is sufficiently important to merit quoting it at length:

> Let us choose the special case where the spatially experienced body perceived by means of the lived-body is itself the physical lived-body [*Leibkörper*].... Touching the left hand I have tactile appearances, i.e., I not only sense [*empfinde*] but I perceive and have appearances of a soft, smooth hand formed in a certain way. The indicating sensations of movement and the representing tactile sensations, which are objectivated as features in the thing "left hand," belong to the right hand. But also in the left hand being touched I find a series of tactile sensations; they are "*localized*" in it but do not constitute properties (such as roughness and smoothness of the hand, of this physical thing). If I speak of the *physical* thing "left hand," I abstract from these sensations "in the left hand" (a bullet does not have these sensations, nor does any "mere" physical thing that is not my lived-body). But if I include these sensations it is not that the physical thing becomes enlarged; rather it becomes lived-body, it senses [*es empfindet*]. The tactile sensations belong to each appearing, objective spatial position on the touched hand as it is touched precisely at that particular place. In like manner the touching hand, which for its part appears as thing, has its tactile sensations on the spatial surface where it touches (or is touched by the other).[31]

In the very process of touching the lived-body something new enters: the object touched also becomes the object touching. It is this unique structure of touching while being touched, of being touched while touching, that makes the lived-body palpable to itself and comes to constitute it as an object. Thus there is a circuit running not only between the world and the lived-body but also between the lived-body and itself. In this circuit there is a doubling of touch: the touching is touched and the touched is touching. There seems to be a blending of what is felt and what is perceived, such that I come to perceive the lived-body as it is feeling. We will leave open until the next section the question of whether this account is sufficient to place the lived-body in the same order as things. For now we at least have secured not just the "felt" presence but also the "experienced" presence of the lived-body to itself. It is the latter that guarantees that, contrary to Sartre,[32] the lived-body also belongs to the order of the in-itself, that it is an object, though of a special order, at least to itself, and that it comes to build up not just those sets of lived coordinates (over – under, back – front and left – right) that give things their spatial orientation, as in the first moment, but also locations "in" it and "on" it that constitute its own spatiality, its own extension.[33]

Keep in mind, too, that the lived-body is not stationary but in constant movement. The process of touching is a process of moving the touching hand, and thus the *Empfindnisse* convey a unity between "lived-body and [the lived-body as a] freely moving thing."[34] In this way the lived body acquires various possibilities of spontaneous movement or, as Piaget will call it, various schemata of appropriation and accommodation.[35]

While this dimension of Husserl's analysis is clearly the most creative and innovative inasmuch as it integrates body and conscious life in a way never envisioned by the tradition of Western philosophy, I do not want to tarry here but to go on to the problem we have set for ourselves in this essay. Before doing so let me summarize the course of our considerations thus far.

Our first attempt to characterize the body, in short, discovered a *Körper* as *Leib*. Among the multiplicity of things there is one set that stands out from the rest and has the singular determinations we mentioned in section 1. Yet we also saw in this context that Husserl, although he does not embrace, at least reinscribes Descartes' mapping. These considerations, however, were undergirded by a certain *Einstellung*, a type of categorial analysis inhabiting the natural attitude and treating its themes as objects, for it looks at the body as manifest phenomena and not as self-constituting presence.

In section 2 this attitude is replaced by a phenomenological analysis that treats the *Leib* as *Leib*. In a certain sense this remains within the framework of the natural attitude, for persons as part of nature[36] are in view. Yet the lived-body is given not as the theme of an objectivating act but rather as a proto-thematic presence enlived. We suggested that this self-presencing can be taken apart into three interweaving moments.

In the process of touching an object, the lived-body senses itself as the one touching. It knows itself not as object, for the object is what is touched, but as the non-object doing the touching. I have spoken of this as a *reflexive* sensing by the lived-body.

This changes when, in the second moment, the lived-body touches itself, for then the one touching is the object touched, and the object touched, in turn, senses itself as the one being touched. Moreover, the hand being touched can in this case become the touching hand. In this circuit of exchanges, this self-referentiality that in fact involves no act of referring at all, the body is offered to itself as lived. The reflexive but preconscious (in Freud's sense) sensing *by* the body which we discover in the first moment is now enriched into the body's *reflective* and conscious sensing *of* itself in this second moment: the one sensing is sensible *as* sensing, the experiencing can be experienced *as* invisible.

The third moment makes a decisive advance in the analysis by seeing the hand that touches as a hand that *moves*. In a certain sense this third moment cuts across the first two. To say that the lived-body reflexively senses itself, as we find in the first moment, means that the lived-body moves itself in the ongoing course of perception. In exploring an object we move closer, pick it up, and turn it over in our hands. The determinations we come to find, the tactual qualities of smooth, hard, and cold, arise in correlation with the various move-ments of the hand and the lived-body. When the lived-body touches itself, as in the second moment, its very touching is a function of its moving. The one sensing is sensible as sensing because the one moving is sensible as moving. The enlived-body, accordingly, is present to itself not only as nexus of sensing but also as locus of movement, even as a system of movements.

3 The Flesh of the Body

It is tempting to stop the story here. All the accounts that I have seen do. In fact, one could ask whether Merleau-Ponty did not rest content with these results in *Phenomenology of Perception*.[37] Certainly Sartre did, at least in *Being and Nothingness*. To conclude our account here, however, would be to bypass what is most problematic about any account of the lived-body. For as the analysis stands, we have not just another perspective on the phenomena with which we began, but also another object, another body. The physical body is an extended thing which can be penetrated by the usual weapons of scientific analysis and medical technology. If one places the lived-body in this mapping of things, nothing seems to change. For in Husserl's own terms, the lived-body is a *Nullpunkt*, a point that may have a place but no extension, or, better, a point in terms of which all position, and thus extension, is defined, but which does not itself have that place or extension characteristic of the things it perceives.

Even when we take into consideration the way in which the lived-body comes to know itself as an object, we still have the nasty question of whether its spatiality and its extension are the *same* as those possessed by things. To argue that the lived-body simply becomes manifest, becomes visible much like other objects, will not suffice, for the fact that it is necessarily given in a way that things are not might entail that it is not a thing, is not something that can have extension and location in the same way that they do. It could very well belong to a second order of nature, but not to the first; it could very well be an object, but not a thing. Thus while the lived-body not only is constitutive of the presence of the world but also possesses a unique self-presence and even its own objecthood, it still seems displaced, a shade shimmering on the edge of existence. If this is so, then it seems that all we have is a replication of Cartesian dualism in another register, for now it becomes not so much the mind-body problem as the body-body problem.

What I find most intriguing about Husserl's analysis is that he attempts to handle this problem in two ways: first, the initial analysis of sensing is extended into an account of localization; second, the description of movement is inserted into an analysis of "motivational" interdependency.[38] These ideas are somewhat fragmented in Husserl's text but they show promise.

Unlike acts of perception that depend upon it, the activity of touching an object involves certain feelings that are localized in the lived-body. In touching a glass there are feelings in the fingers, in sensing the cool waters of the ocean there are sensations in the feet, while in perceiving the glass as smooth or the water as cold the intentional act cannot be placed in any part of the lived-body. "The co-intertwined contents of sensation . . . do have a localization that is actually intuitively given while the intentionalities do not."[39] Localization, Husserl wants to argue, is constitutive of the "objectivity," albeit "appropriate objectivity" (*eigene Objectivität*) of the lived-body. But how? How can localization bridge body as lived and body as physical object?

Interestingly enough, Husserl rejects the idea that sensations (as lived) and locations in the physical body are related as two dependent moments: "It is not like the sensorial content tone-quality and the sensorial content intensity having an essential unity, nor like the sensorial content color [being united] with the moment of expanse."[40] We could take this to mean that it might be possible to have sensations for which there is no location on the real body (phantom limb) or to have changes in the receptors for which there are no feelings (holding a hand in ice-water during hypnosis). The moments in these examples could not be dependent because sensations and stimulation of the physical body can exist without each other. But I think that Husserl is emphasizing the fact that localized sensations do belong to a different order than locations on the body under a physical description. In a special sense of the term, they are causally tied and not, at this level, interdependent. We can describe stimuli applied to the body as causing local sensations but we cannot speak of color qualities as causing their extensions (or vice versa). Because they belong to a different order of analysis, they cannot be dependent moments. But this only aggravates the problem. How can we understand this relationship?

At this point Husserl undertakes a significant shift in emphasis. Instead of concentrating on how the lived-body gives rise to the determinations and places of things, he thinks about what happens when the lived-body is affected by something, when things, in a certain sense, place the body. If an object is rubbed "mechanically" on the skin of my hand I obviously

> have a series of sensings ordered determinately: if it always moves in the same manner, with the same pressure, touching the same places on the lived-body with the same speed, then the result is always the same. All this is obvious. What is important is the interpretation: this lived, physical body behaves in such a way that under such circumstances it not only is stimulated in general but in a determinate manner under determinate circumstances, that all effects of

stimuli have their system, that differences in location correspond to the appearing
thing-body. . . . To the localization in extension there corresponds a locale-
moment in sensation, and to the strength and manner of the stimulation there
correspond determinate moments that make the sensation concrete and modifiable.[41]

With this shift in emphasis, then, Husserl begins to study the way in which the
sensations that I experience neither come one by one nor simply arise from
within; rather they are ordered series dependent upon circumstances. It is in
terms of certain properties in the physical stimuli that our sensations are
changed along certain lines. Thus the experiential order of sensations, their
functional dependence upon circumstances, and the manner in which they
are modified all arise as a result of what happens to and with the physical
body.

> Effects of stimuli appear not as something foreign and only [externally] effective
> [*Bewirktes*] but as something *belonging* to the appearing lived, physical body and its
> order of extension [*extensive Ordnung*] . . . . In each sensation of the lived-body the
> mere sensation is not grasped but it is apprehended as belonging to a system of
> possible functional consequences corresponding exactly to the order of exten-
> sion.[42]

Husserl's point, then, is not only that there is a functional correlation between
locations on the body as material and those locations accompanying all tactile
sensations, but also that such sensations are themselves presentational, exhibiting
an order of antecedent and consequent that is not of their own making but
belongs to the world of material things and events. Notice that Husserl is
working with a modified form of the constancy hypothesis only in the sense
that he resists collapsing the difference between sensorial events and physical
events. Instead he displays a dependency that crosses the two orders, one which
he can only call a motivational dependency, such that at this level of *Empfind-
samkeit*, the material body carries the sensorial, the lived, and the order of
extension determines the order of felt locations.

Since these ideas are somewhat complex, let me suggest that there are four
steps to an Husserlian analysis of the materiality of the lived-body:

1   In our direct and immediate awareness of the body we know it primarily
    through the various *tactile sensations* involved in any activity of touching some-
    thing. In fact, Husserl's argument is that a subject that had only vision would
    never know the body as lived-body.[43]
2   One of the unique traits of tactile sensations is that they are given as having a
    location in the lived-body. Their location is not a series of discrete points but a
    field.

3   The field of sensations is experienced as functionally dependent upon a *real order* of circumstances and events. Each significant change in things and the actions of things upon the surface of the physical body produces a change in the field of sensations according to a scheme of *conditional dependency*, an "if-then" scheme.

4   Since changes on the surface of the body are experienced as changes in the field of sensations having that location, the lived-body is manifested as material.

Let me quote Husserl's own summary of this discussion. It elaborates on the perceptions involved in our apprehension of the lived body, and it gives us a clue to the last point I want to make in this section:

> Thus the sensitivity [or receptivity, *Empfindsamkeit*] of the lived-body is constituted throughout a "conditional" or psycho-physical property. And this is ingredient in the apperception of the lived-body as it is "externally" perceived. To the apprehension of corporeality as such there belongs not only an apprehension of a thing [i.e., of the body as a thing] but the co-apprehension of the sensorial fields and, indeed, they are given as belonging to the appearing, lived physical body [*Leibkörper*] in the mode of localization. "Belonging to": phenomenologically that expresses relations of the phenomenal "if-so." When the hand is touched, bumped etc., I undergo sensations. In this case the hand does not stand there as a physical body to which there is linked an extra-physical body to which there is linked an extra-physical effect [i.e., sensations]; from the very outset it is apperceptively characterized as a hand *with* its field of sensations, with a continuously co-apprehended sensorial state that changes as a result of external actions, i.e., [it is apperceived] as a *physical, aesthesiological unity*. In the abstract I can sunder physical and aesthesiological strata but, indeed, only in the abstract. In concrete perception the lived-body stands there as a new kind of unity of apprehension. It is constituted as an objectivity in its own right, which can be ordered under the formal and general concept of reality, which preserves its identical properties over against changing external circumstances. But even here the relations of dependency in which it stands to external nature are different than those of material things among themselves.[44]

One does not find Husserl adding much light to the question of the materiality of the body in his other writings but there is a very suggestive late text, written in January 1934, that addresses this issue. In it Husserl repeats his claim that the lived-body is not to be treated simply as a physical body among other physical things. There is a "pure" difference to be made between "outer bodies" and my own physical body as an "inner body." The inner body is "a unity of organs, kinaesthetically and sensibly moved," whose "directions of activity" make possible various "courses of appearances."[45] He adds: "*The lived-body is at one with the physical body*, membered thus and so, and, through the actual and potential kinaestheses belonging [to it] in their special way, [it is] precisely organ and system of organs."[46] This analysis of the lived-body as organ rejoins the account of touching-touched:

> If the lived-body becomes an object as physical body, if some particular part that otherwise functions as an organ becomes objective, then this is preceded by a kinaesthesis that is itself localized in the physicality [*Körperlichen*] of what, functioning by virtue of this, is called an organ.[47]

With the notions of conditionality and receptivity, Husserl comes to understand the lived-body not just as "null point" but also as a thick ensemble of organs. This is the notion he uses to preserve its essential unity with its material existence. This, however, is as far as Husserl goes in the direction of treating the body as flesh.

4 The Flesh of Things

When Husserl reminds us, as he just did, that the relationship between body and things is not identical to that between physical things, the question of what is meant by a thing is reopened. Throughout this essay we have assumed that the characterization of things by modern science best describes the things we experience. But Husserl, even in these texts written some 20 years before *The Crisis*, is cautious. Objectivity does require that a given be determined or determinable "by each researcher in absolutely identical fashion."[48] In this sense the descriptions we have undertaken and the contrast between lived-body and physical body are all objective. But Husserl recognizes that the physical body should figure as an item in "the natural world" before its further elaboration by one of the natural sciences. He even speaks of its description as "a universal morphology of the natural world as the shared, common world of a people, of a society."[49] The analysis of the body as lived-body, more than any other study Husserl undertook before the 1920s, opened up the analysis of physical objects as well, and we discover that they are, first and foremost, lived objects before they become objects of the physical sciences proper. The natural sciences, in fact, begin with such a world but then "construe" or reconstruct it in a particular way.

> The physical thing of the natural sciences has only a formal essence; it only has its formula [or its rule]; in fact, its essence is simply that it is an intentional unity of an infinite manifold of appearances "to all men" regulated by this formula [or rule].[50]

When one adds mathematics as the basic language of such formulas or rules, then we have the Cartesian characterization of the thing as extended. Since Descartes, the gaze of science has always seen such things and has found only what Foucault sometimes calls "a world of constant visibility."

This modern scientific characterization of extension and things, supported by an interest that has neutralized practical and ethical concerns, should not be confused with the underlying basis from which, through a series of methodically controlled abstractions, it is derived, with the ringing surfaces of the cobblestones on which I walk, with the rough board I am planing, with the supple face I embrace and hold in my hands. Surfaces that support, boards that are planed, faces that are embraced: they have an "aesthetic" extension and then a flesh, one that our perceptions enfold, that is not yet the result of a categorial synthesis, of an act of cognition or, better, interpretation. It is this sense of extension that is in play for physical bodies, and it is in this sense of the physical body that the lived body, in tactual experience, begins to discover itself as flesh.

Notes

A special word of thanks to Forest Williams for critical comments on an earlier draft of this essay, to Tom Brockelman and Gina Zavota for their assistance in editing, and to Virginia Massaro and Letitia Dunn for their assistance in typing.

1   The quote from Petit is found in Michel Foucault, *The Birth of the Clinic* (New York: Vintage Books, 1975), p. 88, and the Husserl quote is from Edmund Husserl, *Ideen zu einer reinen Phänomenologie und phänomenologischen Philosophie*, Book II: *Phänomenologische Untersuchungen zur Konstitution*, ed. by Marly Biemel, *Husserliana*, vol. 4 (The Hague: Martinus Nijhoff, 1952), p. 150; cf. *Ideas Pertaining to a Pure Phenomenology and to a Phenomenological Philosophy*, Book 2: *Studies in the Phenomenology of Constitution*, trans. by Richard Rojcewicz and Andre Schuwer, *Collected Works*, vol. 3 (Dordrecht: Kluwer, 1989), p. 158.

2   We are immediately faced with the problem of faithfully rendering Husserl's different terms for body into English. When the context requires something more specific than the general term "body" I will render Husserl's notion of *Körper* as "physical body," *Leib* as "lived-body," *Leiblichkeit* as "corporeality," and his peculiar *Leibkörper* somewhat awkwardly as "lived physical body." I use the last term in order to preserve the inner tension in the German. Rojcewicz and Schuwer translate these terms, respectively, as "body," "Body," "Corporeality" and "Corporeal body."

3   Edmund Husserl, *Ding und Raum: Vorlesungen 1907*, ed. by U. Claesges, *Husserliana*, vol. 16 (The Hague: Martinus Nijhoff, 1974). In this work the role of the kinaesthetic syntheses in perception is highlighted much more than the body per se.

4   They are found in both the first and second parts of this work.

5   The manuscripts are housed in the Husserl Archives in Louvain, Belgium.

6   Three notable exceptions to this general rule are Alphonso Lingis, "Intentionality and Corporeity," *Analectica Husserliana*, vol. 1 (1971), 75–90; Shaun Gallagher, "Hyletic Experience and the Lived Body," *Husserl Studies*, vol. 3 (1986), 131–66;

and an article by Ricoeur that reviews *Ideen II* as a whole. See Paul Ricoeur, "Husserl's Ideas II: Analysis and Problems," in *Husserl: An Analysis of His Phenomenology*, trans. by Edward Ballard and Lester Embree (Evanston, Ill.: Northwestern University Press, 1967), pp. 35–81. There is also a very helpful analysis in German in Ulrich Claesges, *Edmund Husserls Theorie der Raumkonstitution, Phaenomenologica*, vol. 19 (The Hague: Martinus Nijhoff, 1964), pp. 90–144. The best analysis in German on this concept, Elmar Holenstein's "Nullpunkt der Orientierung," has been translated into English for the first time and follows this essay.

7   Maurice Merleau-Ponty, *Phénoménologie de la perception* (Paris: Gallimard, 1945); *Phenomenology of Perception*, trans. by Colin Smith (London: Routledge and Keegan Paul, 1962).

8   Husserl, *Ideen II*, 25; Eng. trans., p. 27. While references to the excellent English translation in addition to the German original will be given, the translations are my own.

9   *Ideen II*, pp. 28–9; Eng. trans., p. 31.

10   Rene Descartes, "Discourse on Method," *The Philosophical Writings of Descartes*, trans. by John Cottingham, Robert Stoothoff, Dugald Murdoch, vol. I (Cambridge: Cambridge University Press, 1984), pp. 142–3.

11   Descartes, "Discourse," p. 151.

12   In his Second Meditation, Descartes employs a strict, objective characterization of the body which has the effect of reducing it to a corpse, i.e., a physical thing without the power of its own movements. Thus he says: "The first thought to come to mind was that I had a face, hands, arms and the whole mechanical structure of limbs which can be seen in a corpse, and which I call the body." To this first thought a second is added: "The next thought was that I was nourished, that I moved about, and that I engaged in sense-perception and thinking; and these actions I attributed to the soul." While his extensive study of human physiology, complete only some six or seven years before he wrote the "Meditations," will contest this received understanding of the functions of the soul, the description of the body remains. Thus the "Meditations" immediately adds this clarification: "by a body I understand whatever has a determinable shape and a definable location and can occupy a space in such a way as to exclude any other body; it can be perceived by touch, sight, hearing, taste or smell, and can be moved in various ways, not by itself but by whatever else comes into contact with it. For, according to my judgement, the power of self-movement, like the power of sensation or of thought, was quite foreign to the nature of a body." Descartes, "Meditations on First Philosophy," *The Philosophical Writings of Descartes*, trans. by John Cottingham, Robert Stoothoff, Dugald Murdoch, vol. II (Cambridge: Cambridge University Press, 1984), p. 17. For his work on human physiology see his "Treatise on Man," ibid., I, 99–108 or the full texts in *Treatise of Man*, trans. by Thomas Stelle Hall (Cambridge, Mass.: Harvard University Press, 1972).

13   Husserl, *Ideen II*, 25; Eng. trans., p. 27.

14   Husserl, *Ideen II*, 26; Eng. trans., p. 28.

15   Husserl, *Ideen II*, 26; Eng. trans., p. 28. Italics removed.

16   Husserl, *Ideen II*, 26; Eng. trans., p. 28. But cf. *Ideen zu einer reinen Phänomenologie und phänomenologischen Philosophie*, Band 3: *Die Phänomenologie und die Fundamente*

der Wissenschaften, ed. by M. Biemel, *Husserliana*, vol. 5 (The Hague: Martinus Nijhoff, 1952), p. 2; *Ideas Pertaining to a Pure Phenomenology and to a Phenomenological Philosophy*, Book 3: *Phenomenology and the Foundations of the Sciences*, trans. by Ted Klein and William Pohl, *Collected Works*, vol. 1 (The Hague: Martinus Nijhoff, 1980), p. 2.

17 Husserl, *Ideen II*, 26; Eng. trans., p. 28.

18 Husserl, *Ideen II*, 32–3; Eng. trans., pp. 35–6.

19 Husserl, *Ideen II*, 33; Eng. trans., p. 36.

20 Husserl, *Ideen II*, 33; Eng. trans., p. 36.

21 Edmund Husserl, *Die Krisis der europäischen Wissenschaften und die transzendentale Phänomenologie*, ed. by Walter Biemel, *Husserliana*, vol. 6 (The Hague: Martinus Nijhoff, 1954), pp. 15–17, 57–9, 379–80; *The Crisis of European Science and Transcendental Phenomenology*, trans. by David Carr (Evanston, Ill.: Northwestern University Press, 1970), pp. 17–18, 56–8, 371–2. Cf. *Ideen III*, 93–105; Eng. trans., pp. 80–90.

22 Speaking of a phenomenological analysis of materiality from within the natural attitude needs some further clarification. The analysis upon which we are drawing is found mainly in sections 14 to 18. Notice that it is only in section 34 of *Ideen II* that Husserl speaks of going beyond the natural attitude, although he does not actually do it for some pages after that. The confusion can be solved by seeing that there are at least two different oppositions defining the natural attitude:

1 In *Ideen I* the contrast between the natural and phenomenological attitudes is found at the level of *philosophical* method, and Husserl's sustained argument is that the first needs to be rejected in favor of the second. Thus the phenenological reduction always involves a rejection of the natural attitude.

2 In *Ideen II*, however, the contrast is between the natural and the "personalistic" attitudes (pp. 139–43; Eng. trans., pp. 147–50) and they are understood as *regional* methods (the method of either the ontology or the science appropriate to a given domain) within a larger phenomenological analysis.

Armed with this distinction, our analysis of materiality in this section operates from within the natural attitude as a regional method but not as a philosophical method. We must speak of a natural attitude within the scope of a phenomenological analysis, i.e., of a method of describing materiality *phenomenologically*.

23 Husserl, *Ideen II*, 39; Eng. trans., pp. 42–3.

24 Husserl, *Ideen II*, 40; Eng. trans., p. 43.

25 Husserl, *Ideen II*, 41; Eng. trans., p. 44.

26 Husserl, *Ideen II*, 46; Eng. trans., p. 50.

27 Husserl, *Ideen II*, 58; Eng. trans., p. 63.

28 Husserl, *Ideen II*, 66; Eng. trans., p. 71.

29 To put it more accurately, the second book of *Ideen* introduces the essential breakthrough in spite of periodic lapses back into classical formulations. Even after suggesting that the Cartesian analyses are the result of an interpretation based on a deeper-lying system of perceptual experience, section 33, for example,

interprets my sensations, perception, and recollections as moments of my subjective stream of experience, as states of my soul, in unity with physical events or states in the body. The body, in turn, is seen as "a bearer of the relationships of psycho-physical dependency." Thus Husserl concludes: "The unity of the soul is a real unity in that it, as unity of the soulish life, is coupled with the body as unity of the bodily stream of being, which, for its part, is a member of nature" (p. 139). Descartes nods.

30   Husserl, *Ideen II*, 146; Eng. trans., p. 153. I am following the Rojcewicz and Schuwer translation of *Empfindnisse* as "sensings." It might also be rendered "sensorial event."

31   Husserl, *Ideen II*, 144–5; Eng. trans., pp. 152–3.

32   Jean-Paul Sartre, *Being and Nothingness: An Essay on Phenomenological Ontology*, trans. by Hazel Barnes (New York: Philosophical Library, 1956), pp. 329–30.

33   Husserl, *Ideen II*, 145; Eng. trans., p. 153.

34   Husserl, *Ideen II*, 151; Eng. trans., p. 158.

35   See Jean Piaget, *The Mechanisms of Perception*, trans. by G. N. Seagrim (New York: Basic Books, 1969), pp. 353–4 for the application of this idea to perception.

36   Cf. Husserl, *Ideen II*, 143; Eng. trans., p. 150.

37   I will put to the side the question of how Merleau-Ponty's analysis in *Phenomenology of Perception* is related to his *Le Visible et l'invisible* (Paris: Gallimard, 1964); *The Visible and the Invisible*, trans. by Alphonso Lingis (Evanston, Ill.: Northwestern University Press, 1964).

38   I find both of these ideas in section 40 of *Ideen II*, one of the most difficult texts penned by Husserl.

39   Husserl, *Ideen II*, 153; Eng. trans., p. 161.

40   Husserl, *Ideen II*, 154; Eng. trans., p. 161. For an analysis of the concept of dependent moments see the Third Investigation, sections 3 and 4 in Edmund Husserl, *Logische Untersuchungen*, vol. II, Part I: *Untersuchungen zur Phänomenologie und Theorie der Erkenntnis*, 2nd revd edn (Halle: Max Niemeyer, 1913); *Logical Investigations*, trans. by J. N. Findlay, vol. I (New York: Humanities Press, 1970).

41   Husserl, *Ideen II*, 154; Eng. trans., pp. 161–2.

42   Husserl, *Ideen II*, 154; Eng. trans., p. 162.

43   Husserl, *Ideen II*, 150; Eng. trans., p. 158.

44   Husserl, *Ideen II*, 155–6; Eng. trans., p. 163.

45   Edmund Husserl, *Zur Phänomenologie der Intersubjektivität*, Dritter Teil: 1929–1935, ed. by Iso Kern, *Husserliana*, vol. 15 (The Hague: Martinus Nijhoff, 1973), p. 643.

46   *Intersubjektivität*, III, 643.

47   *Intersubjektivität*, III, 643.

48   Husserl, *Ideen II*, 389; Eng. trans., p. 398.

49   Husserl, *Ideen II*, 376; Eng. trans., p. 385. Notice that this appendix is from the third part of *Ideen II* and thus probably was written between 1920 and 1925.

50   Husserl, *Ideen II*, 376–7; Eng. trans., p. 286. Italics removed.

3

THE ZERO-POINT OF ORIENTATION: THE PLACEMENT OF THE I IN PERCEIVED SPACE

Elmar Holenstein

1 The Traditional Phenomenological Thesis

In Husserl's descriptions of perceived space, the perceiver's own lived-body [*Leib*] is proclaimed as the zero-point of orientation. Accordingly, everything, be it spatially perceived or even imagined and fantasized, is given in such a way that it is oriented towards one's lived-body. The various spatial determinations, directions, qualities, and valences – near and far, over and under, right and left, and so forth – have their pole of reference in this lived-body (1952: 56, 109ff., 158ff.; 1966: 297ff., etc.).

Husserl never called this thesis (that the lived-body is the zero-point of orientation) into question – for either methodical or thematic reasons. To him, it appears immediately self-evident from "the thing itself," from the perceived situation. Opposing observations are not registered. Likewise, he neglects to reflect upon the possible theoretical or dogmatic background of this thesis, although the application of this thesis beyond the region of bare perception would have to produce suspicion. Finally, Husserl also does not worry about intersubjective confirmation, i.e., in this case, interdisciplinary confirmation.

Husserl's thesis was, with one exception,[1] taken over by the entire phenomenological movement: by its philosophical representatives, Heidegger (1927), Sartre (1943), Merleau-Ponty (1945), as by its psychological followers, Binswanger (1932) and Graumann (1960). At the same time, though – even during Husserl's lifetime – the absolute claims of this thesis would be descriptively as

New translation by Lanei Rodemeyer and Sebastian Luft of Elmar Holenstein, "Der Nullpunkt der Orientierung," *Menschliches Selbstverständnis* (Frankfurt am Main: Suhrkamp, 1985), pp. 14–58.

well as experimentally challenged as untenable. Counterpositions were formed in the area of gestalt psychology, and, at the latest, through the careful investigations of Kleint (1936–40). The lived-body of the perceiving subject behaves no differently than any perceived object, as far as its localization is concerned.

Given the present state of research, the goal of this work is the motivational elucidation of orientation in various perceived situations (sections 3–8), as well as to uncover unreflected presuppositions in the Husserlian thesis (section 9). After indicating that the origin of the constitution of objectivity is based upon a divergence in every perception between subject-related and objectively founded orientations, the last section (10) will briefly summarize the results.

2 Clarifications of Method

The following investigations are based upon everyday experience, experiences that anyone can have, as well as experiments run in cognitive psychology. Just as a theory, through its translation into another form of theory, can be confirmed, expanded, and corrected, so too an experience through its translation into another type of experience. The unveiling of the secret biases of empirical psychology, which praises itself for being without assumptions, led many practitioners of phenomenology to hold contempt for the experimental method. They attempted to rehabilitate everyday experience as the original locus of revelation, one which was not falsified by theories. A more exact view, however, shows that long stretches of everyday experience are no less influenced by externally acquired and unjustifiably extrapolated assumptions, prematurely fixed, than many a scientific experimentation.

One ought to attempt to track down unprejudiced orientation by holding and playing out both modes of experience against one another in varying perceived situations. Abstract experiments, especially, cause schemes of experience, which have often become habit and are distinguished as original, to collapse; these experiments offer an occasion to pursue the acquisition of such schemes of experiences step by step. On the other hand, a comparison of both modes of experience shows that experimental experience corresponds to a specific type of experience – one which is linked to other types in everyday life. Artificially arranged experimental situations produce, almost necessarily, a contemplative, disengaged attitude in test subjects. For the observer, the experimental purpose of constructed devices and, even more so, objects projected on a TV screen lack practical meaning. That which is played out in the experiment is inconsequential for him/her. "Played out" is the correct term. Usually, test subjects experience experiments as they would a game. The world of experiments is understood to be as separate from the "real" world – with all of its vital implications – as the world of games.

This limitation of experimental experience must be taken into account when an experiment's results are evaluated. But this limitation should not at all be rated as only negative. In a (theatrical) play, things are possible that would not be counted as valid in everyday life. Many test persons, therefore, encounter experimental demonstrations much more freely, without bringing the expectation of what is "correct" to what are "impossible" occurrences. Practical disengagement can be further interpreted as a reduction, which, as in every reduction, can be incorporated into an analysis directed at different attitudes of consciousness.

The reduction of practical engagements is especially interesting for our problem. It is often assigned a decisive roll in the centering of perception. Excluding this reduction therefore promises to disclose motivations for orientation, those which in concrete experience become easily covered up; such motivations have their source not in the meaning of objects for the observer, nor in their practical function, but rather in the formal structures and relations of the perceived object. Such formal structures and relations are, for example, resemblance and contrast, size and shape, in short, associative and figurative factors. In their subjective genesis, these formal factors essentially differentiate themselves from the actual sense-factors with which they compete in complex ways in their constitution.[2]

3 The Dominating Formation of Perception [*Wahrnehmungsgefüge*] as Center of Orientation

After these preliminary methodological remarks, let us introduce the circumstances of our problem through plain observation.

If I walk with a friend, side by side, I involuntarily feel myself to be the member of a pair, i.e., of a whole. The whole assigns me a subordinate position, as one of its parts. If I am walking in a longer column, my experience of the assignment of place is even more pronounced. The column is given to me in such a way that it is a dominating whole, whose center, from which it partitions itself, at best accidentally coincides with my position. I can just as easily find myself in front or in back, on the left or right side, as in the middle. The column, for example, is not around me to my left, rather, I am standing inside it to the right.

An orthodox Husserlian would object that there are multi-staged processes of appresentation, of the experience of the Other [*Fremderfahrung*], at play here. He might say that I appresent or presentiate my partner with each of his own individual zero-points of orientation. With the spontaneous intention to bring the different zero-points into coincidence, the constitution of a common center (one which coincides with the center of the group) emerges secondarily. It could also be argued that the group is personified, comprehended as a sort of collective quasi-person, from which each individual is seen as centered. In any case, the group-center and the ordering towards it would be a derivative, and not a primordial, datum [*Gegebenheit*]. Originally, each individual formed its own center for itself.

Such processes of intersubjective experience, or similarly conceivable ones, are without doubt co-involved in the establishment [*Instauration*] of the zero-point. But at the same time we are dealing with secondary processes whose paths have been cleared and preconstituted through motivations, which decentralize the individual I already at the primordial level, before any experiences of the other. This can be seen in situations where no other subjects appear.

If I stand in the marketplace of an old city, which is surrounded by houses, then I am oriented towards that place, towards its center, which may even be additionally accentuated by a monument, and not it towards me. If I walk along a two-lane avenue, I feel just as little that I am the zero-point of orientation. The two rows of trees dominate the space. It is their arrangement that determines its center. If one takes the trees, and maybe also the houses, as objects upon which we impose an interpretation of them as persons – and they, accordingly, like real persons would entail the appresentation of a trans-individual center – then one can choose a situation that makes such a personification improbable, for example, a perception dominated by a railway or a bare stretch of wall.

In concrete perception, as we experienced in the above situations, the formation that dominates perception – a column, a marketplace, an avenue – determines the centralization of the space and thereby the localization of individual objects. The lived-body of the perceiving subject is no exception. There can be no talk of a privileged localization of one's lived-body, nor of a function of this body in constituting spatial orientation, at least for the time being. The objectively appearing formation of the perceived world erects its own center for itself.

Of course, we can also find situations in which one's own lived-body does appear as centralizing space – in other words, situations that at first glance appear to support Husserl's thesis. If investigated more closely, however, they confirm the opposing thesis. The lived-body alone centralizes only when, by chance, it happens to function as the dominating figure of perception. The lived-body can behave not only as a subordinate figure of perception [*untergeordnetes Wahrnehmungsgebilde*], like any corporeal thing, but also as the outstanding figure of perception [*hervorragendes Wahrnehmungsgebilde*]. In the first case it appears centered towards others, in the second, on the other hand, as centering the others. Let me supply two examples that may serve as an introduction to both factors of motivation in orientation and, moreover, that may reveal certain presuppositions of his thesis which Husserl did not take into consideration. The following section is devoted to a comparison of these two examples.

The first example is supplied by experimental psychology. In a dark room, in which no objects are perceivable, a vertical line is projected onto the wall. If the test person tilts his/her head to one side, this induces the objectively vertical line to lean to the opposite side. In this situation, the individual lived-body functions as determining the direction. The line subordinates itself to the lived-body, receiving the assignment of its position from it.

In the evaluation of this experiment, one must consider that the observer does not have a complex structure of perception in front of him/her, but instead has an isolated line in an empty, undivided, homogeneous space. In such a specially furnished, or rather emptied, room – one which natural experience offers us rather infrequently – the single lived-body, of course, establishes itself as the outstanding figure of perception, and, as such, determines the orientation of the isolated lit-up object of perception. The same effect as is produced by one's lived-body can be brought forth by a larger, stronger line, which is projected at a slant next to the first, smaller and weaker line. Every line brings about an induction to every other line. The extent of the induction depends upon the difference in size between the two lines.

The second example comes from everyday experience. At a festively decked table, certain guests move their plates so that they are aligned to them on the table. Other guests, in comparison, align themselves and, if necessary, even their chairs, in order to place themselves directly in front of the setting. For the first, they themselves, and their position, predominate; for the second, the arrangement of the setting already found there sets the norm. Intuitively, one would look to the psychical constitution of such persons in order to find the reasons for this difference in behavior, and take advantage of situations like these for tests. A strong and self-confident personality would more likely see him/herself in the center, and thus as the point of departure of orientation, than a weak and obsequious person.

4 Gestalt- and Sense-Factors

In the penultimate example, size suggested itself as the significant, dominating factor, and thus as the factor that has a centralizing effect on certain figures of perception. "The larger object subordinates the smaller one to itself." It seems that this is how one must formulate the claim derived from this example. In the last example, however, we also ascertained that the meaning that one assigns to the I, independent of a person's bodily size, has a centralizing effect. If one studies the literature on our topic more closely, one quickly realizes that the size and the meaning of the I merely depict two especially noticeable variants of the main categories of space-orientating factors, gestalt and sense.

Along with size, for example, solidity and enclosure can be traced as further gestalt-factors in spatial orientation. An airy object like a balloon appears to lay or float "next to" the massive figure of a body of metal, even though its volume surpasses that of the body of metal. If they have the same quality, an enclosed figure localizes itself inside the enclosing one. If the enclosed figure appears more colorful and denser than the enclosing one, however, then the enclosed figure makes the latter appear as oriented towards itself. These examples already clearly establish that the different gestalt-factors cannot be considered as having the same value. They call for an ordering based upon their weight.

As regards sense-factors, the last example of the former section readily showed that one's own I in no way plays the dominating role in all circumstances. Any objective data that have a greater practical or affective meaning for the perceiver can just as well draw the orientation to themselves.

How do gestalt- and sense-factors relate to one another? Gestalt psychology and phenomenology are themselves in controversy over their relation. Gestalt psychology tends to subordinate the problem of sense to that of gestalt. Sense-fulness [*Sinnhaftigkeit*] is tied down to claims of gestalt, and interconnections of sense, even logical relationships, are derived from the dynamically conceived gestalt-structure of the phenomena in question.

This conception is opposed by phenomenological psychology in essentially two ways. First, it insists upon the underivable character and originality of sense and meaning, with rules of their own. Perceptions give themselves to us as sense-laden, as if from some vital, practical, or aesthetic meaning, and often already before their gestalt has been crystallized. Colorful objects appear to us as attractive or repellent, friendly or frightening, even before we grasp them in their visible quality and structure. It is not just the case that a certain gestalt insinuates a certain sense. Often it is exactly vice versa. It is a certain sense-expectation that leads towards the gestalt of a perception. If we speak of a meaningful perception, we do well to differentiate between the "sense-fulness" that lies in the way gestalt behaves, in its composition, in opposition to the factors of "pregnant gestalt" [*prägnante Gestalt*] as presented by gestalt psychology, and the sense-fulness that, for example, lies in its practical function.

Moreover, phenomenology claims that sense-fulness always only exists for a subject: that is, sense-fulness not only in the specific phenomenological meaning of the word, but also sense-fulness in the form of a good or pregnant gestalt. A thing is only a tool if it is conceived as such. It is likewise a pregnant gestalt only for a perceiving subject. But the subject, according to the phenomenological complaint, is not thematized as such in gestalt psychology's investigations. It is only treated as one object among the others. The relation of our perception of objects to the perceiving subject, which in phenomenological opinion also belongs to perception, is suppressed (Merleau-Ponty 1945: 23ff., 117; Linschoten 1952: 40ff., 71; Graumann 1960: 103).

In its critical controversy with gestalt psychology, phenomenologically oriented psychology, unfortunately, fell to the opposite extreme (in an all too well-known reaction). In this way, Merleau-Ponty and Graumann ousted figural no less than classical associative factors, which partially coincide in phenomenological analysis with the figural, in favor of sense-motivations that are acknowledged alone.[3] Being slightly more careful, Linschoten (1952) concerned himself with an exactly defined subordination and degradation of gestalt factors. He formulated his critique using his investigations of so-called induced movement. His investigations can thus serve to demonstrate the inadmissibility not only of ignoring but also of subordinating, in one-sided fashion, gestalt factors under sense factors in the clarification of phenomena of perception, like orientation and the distribution of two phenomena, rest and movement, that are closely connected.[4]

In a series of experiments, Linschoten came to the conclusion that it is not the gestalt of perceived objects that is decisive; instead it is their "content," their function, attributed to them by the observers, that is decisive for the distribution of rest and movement. If a dark point next to a rectangular, frame-like form is seen as a nail, then in an experiment, where one of the figures (point or rectangle) is set in a vertical motion to the other, the much more spacious rectangle moves along with the small point. According to Linschoten, the movement of the rectangle must be interpreted as "contrary to law" by gestalt psychology. It contradicts the law of gestalt, according to which the smaller object subordinates itself to the larger, and according to which the smaller object should show itself in motion relative to the larger, and not the other way around. But the movement is in no way "contrary to sense," if one conceives the point as a fixed nail, pounded into the wall, and the rectangle as a moveable frame (ibid.: 41).

By taking the subjective bestowal of sense [Sinngebung] into consideration in his efforts to clarify the phenomena being investigated, Linschoten, without a doubt, puts his finger on a correct and important factor. Nevertheless, the choice of his experiments is open to critique. After discovering that perceptions "contrary to sense" do indeed turn up every once in a while, he should have increased his search for counterexamples, in order to be able to clarify the area of motivation in a more differentiated way. In this case, counterexamples do not even have to be experientially constructed. "Natural experience" offers enough of them. Most likely, the phenomenon of induced movement became a preferred object of research not only because of the fact that, in certain situations, objects appear to be at rest or moving which in fact are not (a train starting off next to a standing one, in which we sit), but especially because, to our bewilderment, those objects which according to their sense ought to be at rest or moving appear as their opposite. We see in the night sky, for example, the moon at great speed going along behind fields of clouds. This perception contradicts our sense-apprehension, that the moon stands still, and instead the wind drives the clouds in front of it. Here the gestalt factors are clearly stronger than the "sense-model" quoted by Linschoten.

But above all, Linschoten's theoretical evaluation of the results of his experiments is insufficient, even partially false. I mean especially the following theses which his investigation, it seems, from the onset intended to prove: (1) Perception cannot be described as a play of psychological vectors or factors (ibid.: 41, 71); (2) The gestalt laws are not proper laws which possess an absolute and necessary character. They supply only a "statistical norm" that, *ex post*, is acquired inductively (ibid.: 40ff., 64). (3) The figural factor is "not a determining factor of the distribution of movement, but rather is a measure of distribution of a distribution of movement" (ibid.: 64).

Perception is not something complete and pregiven, as phenomenological analysis suggests; it is rather an event that plays itself out all the time "before our eyes." Perception is in the most literal sense a (theatrical) play. New affections continually come into the scene all the time. They can slow up, suppress, and overturn, as well as confirm and enforce the already formed connections and already founded apprehensions (relations of orientation). All the time, motivation rises up against motivation, whereby the stronger and the one confirmed in the course of perception finally triumphs. By virtue of this play of partly coinciding, partly clashing motivations, different forms of modalization arise – modes of certainty, possibility, doubtfulness, and those of negation or cancellation – by which our perceptive data are marked (Husserl 1966: 25ff.). What phenomenology denies is not the assertion that each relatively fixed perception is "the result of a play of factors," but rather (1) that the play of factors is not carried out only in perception itself – on the phenomenological level – but is also carried out in a physiological field, functioning as substrate, whose results then are mirrored isomorphically on the plane of perception, and (2) that we are dealing solely with a play between gestalt factors. Both gestalt-and sense-factors participate in the genesis of concrete perception.

Linschoten's sin of omission consists in the fact that, in the cases where the test-subjects hesitated in their responses – because the distribution of rest and movement at first seemed unstable and ambiguous, or even absurd to them – he looks for the reason for this exclusively in the their psychical structure, i.e., in the character trait of indecision, and not in the components of the developing perception itself (Linschoten 1952: 76ff.).

From the undeniable fact that certain distributions of rest and movement do not follow the laws of gestalt, Linschoten concludes that these laws lack the character of necessity claimed before. If he had let himself get involved in unstable and ambiguous perceptions, he would have by necessity come across the fact that gestalt-factors in these cases are indeed very effective, but that they become inhibited in effectiveness by superior sense-factors. In cases in which such an inhibited effectiveness cannot, however, be established, one would still need to clarify whether the gestalt which can be found from an objective, i.e., the physical standpoint, is also given subjectively to the observer. In fact it is perfectly possible that in a certain sense-apprehension, a gestalt is there which, as far as the physical stimuli are concerned, will not be seen. Only that which is seen can be motivationally effective. The fact that a perception does not follow gestalt laws does not automatically contradict the necessity of the effectual working of a gestalt. It only tells us about the strength and the force of impact of gestalt-factors as opposed to other possible factors.

The effectiveness of gestalt-factors is just as phenomenally demonstrable as that of sense-factors. "In principle the analysis of one single case" is likewise enough to present this effectiveness (ibid.: 64). In addition, it remains uncontested that the percentile probability of a specific distribution of rest and movement can be statistically registered when given specific gestalt qualities for specific individuals or groups. We dispute only that it is gestalt-factors alone that can be statistically elicited, whereas sense-factors elude every statistical registration. Statistical calculation of the sense-distribution of certain "stimuli-words" for specific individuals or groups has already been successful (Osgood 1957). Why should not it also be possible to calculate and subsequently predict "the special relation of the subject to the world," the apprehension of sense that is manifested in the distribution of rest and motion for different people and types given certain pregiven "stimuli-constellations" [Reizlage]?

The fact that at least for the factors of the main dimension [Haupterstrecktheit] and intensity – as investigated by the gestaltists – a 65 percent confirmation could be established is interpreted by Linschoten to mean that the figural factors do indeed render a measure for the distribution of rest and movement. What remained unclear was how something can serve as a measure for something else if it is not standing in a formative, causal or motivational connection with the latter.

When Linschoten in conclusion writes about figural properties that they "are not effective as causal factors, but rather only as motives" (ibid.: 91), one must respond to him with the same reproach that he held against the gestaltists: "confusing the concepts" (ibid.: 63). After just having denied the gestalts any determining effect, gestalts are here again acknowledged as motives. What is a motivational relation, if not a causal relation between phenomenal data?

If one acknowledges that different factors intervene in the orientation of spatial perception, the question arises about the hierarchy of these factors, about their rank and order as it relates to their temporal structure and their strength. The answer to this question exceeds the capacity of a single researcher interested in exploiting his or her own experience purely phenomenologically. His or her field of experience is limited. It is the "natural experience" of an adult, which, viewed developmentally [*in genetischer Hinsicht*], is the consolidated product of long training. Likewise, one's method of experience is limited. It is only self-observation, too well known for all its trickiness and limitations. In order to uncover complex relationships, such as the percentage of a single factor's participation in a specific centralization, one requires scientific aids, experiments, the running of tests, and the like.

There are varying experimental investigations concerning the hierarchy of gestalt-factors, especially regarding what role they play in the distribution of rest and motion. A critical examination of hierarchies established to that end was precisely the concern of Linschoten's aforementioned investigations. Linschoten came to the conclusion that the factors of main dimension and intensity presented the strongest power [*Mächtigkeit*], whereas precisely those factors emphasized by gestalt psychology, those of fixation and enclosure, revealed a much more restricted influence. For our problem of orientation that, as we said, was related to the distribution of rest and motion, and for our specific inquiry about the meaning of the I, it may be especially worth noting that fixation, i.e., a factor that is subjectively controlled, appears to have significantly less potency than was expected and estimated.

Led by his desire to demonstrate the importance of the subject, in contrast to gestalt psychology's doctrine of perception, Merleau-Ponty had assigned the decisive role to this subjective factor in his analysis of the relativity of motion, following Duncker's emphasis on fixation. He interpreted fixation as the all-carrying and orientating anchor of the subject in its world, i.e., as the fundamental and transcendental condition of the possibility of spatial perception as such (Merleau-Ponty 1945: 320ff.).

Contrary to this interpretation, it can be shown that the orientational anchor of the subject and its objects in the most original perception is not left to "our own power." We obtain our position before we have had the opportunity to get a grasp on ourselves and our psychic abilities. It is assigned by a world that constitutes itself in our sense-perception before any activity of the I. The axle upon which the world is anchored and around which it turns together with us, its anonymous designers, is not fixed by us, not [the result of] a subject-guided fixation originating with us, the perceivers. Rather the axle is an objectively guided referential structure [*Verweisung*] that has congealed and crystallized itself as the main axle in the living formation of our sensual affections.

Concerning the hierarchy of sense-factors, one must respect the fact already emphasized that the meaning of the I does not simply and absolutely subordinate all objective meaning to itself. The dominance of a specific meaning depends upon the various needs, interests, and attitudes of the perceiver. Since these are, as is well known, relative, unstable, and polyvalent, it is to be expected that the orientation that depends on them likewise has a relative, unstable and polyvalent nature (cf. section 8).

What can we say about the mutual relation of the two groups, the gestalt- and sense-factors? It would best correspond to the classical interpretation of order, if gestalt-motivations were pre- and subordinated to sense-motivations in a genetic respect as well as with respect to strength. A genetic priority of gestalt-motivations, however, contradicts the discovery according to which our perceptions, even before they have formed an optical gestalt, are already sense-laden, are pregnant with some immediate, vitally appealing and always highly emotional meaning. As to the question of whether gestalt-motivations are subordinate to sense-motivations with respect to strength, this is contradicted by everyday experience in which a specific arrangement or formation of perceived objects is able to overturn, "tangibly" disturb, or even no longer let surface a sense taken as objectively valid or just traditionally handed down.

The orientation of the earth towards the sun as postulated by Copernican astronomy could not get its way in our sensible perception. If we see a grade-school pupil talking with his teacher, the teacher forms the reference point of orientation, as it were. We see the student standing "in front of" or "by" his teacher, not the other way around. If, however, the pupil considerably surpasses his teacher in size, then this localization undergoes a noticeable disturbance. The superordinance of the teacher now disrupted through the gestalt relation, appears incredible, and in some circumstances ridiculous.

We visibly experience the reversal of orientation provoked by gestalt-factors when we replace an unremarkable, narrow picture-frame with a splendidly colored, broad one. The apprehension "frame around the picture" easily flips over in this case to the apprehension "picture in the frame." If a house is surrounded by a narrow strip of garden, then the house forms the reference point for orientation. The garden seems to be laid out either symmetrically or asymmetrically around the house. On the other hand, if the house stands in a giant park, then the latter becomes the dominating system of reference, allowing the house to appear placed either in its middle or in some other part of it.[5]

The common denominator which we can find for the orienting gestalt- and sense-factors is called "dominance" [Mächtigkeit]. The dominance of an object may be founded in its gestalt as well as in its sense [Sinn] or meaning [Bedeutung]. It is not by accident that the word "meaning" contains the connotation "importance." Dominance is to be addressed as the actual principle of orientation of spatial perception.

5 The Space of Action contra Intuited Space?

Up until now, have we not unjustly limited ourselves exclusively to intuited space [Anschauungsraum], and neglected action-space [Handlungsraum]? Is not the action-space of engaged persons prior to the pure visual space of the con-templative observer? And is not at least this genetically earlier space essentially I-oriented? In seeing, my own lived-body remains alien to me. We learned from Sartre that the Look objectifies – even one's own lived-body. It would thus be understandable that the lived-body ranks itself as a thing among other things in visual perception. On the other hand, in action, in touching and grasping, the organs of my lived-body become present [to me] in a distinct way. I experience them as "mine" (Straus 1935: 391).

It appears that one could call upon Heidegger regarding the thesis of I-orientation in action-space. In *Being and Time* (1927: 101ff.) Heidegger undertook a derivation of the categories of spatiality through the circumspect, concernful doing of *Dasein*, the subject. That which is immediately ready-to-hand for the subject has the character of nearness. It refers one to more distant equipment that must first be brought into proximity, so that one can actively use it. Heidegger designates this bringing-into-nearness with a play on such words as *Ent-fernung* [re-moval or de-distancing].[6]

Re-moval, understood in an active and transitive sense, means as much as to-make-vanish, sublating the distance. In active re-moval, the subject discovers the spatial determinations of de-severance and of distance. This re-moval is the first mode of the constitution of space. A second is orientation-towards, which results from the first. Every re-moval opens up a direction from which the removed thing comes nearer. In this way, the primal directions of right and left originate in re-moval.

The nexus of involvement, which assigns to the ready-to-hand, the equip-ment, its own sense, has its origin and its goal in the person, which in its being [*Sein*] cares for itself. Its actions are oriented towards itself and so also is space, which originates from this action as a re-moval. In its activity, the subject takes re-moval and orientation-towards, which are nothing else but its manners of being, with it constantly. The world appears as an environment [*Um-welt*] oriented towards the caring structure of the activity [*Handhabung*] of the I.

But Heidegger is too careful a phenomenologist to overlook the relativity of the subjective here and simply to describe it as anchored in itself and as the absolute source of orientation – as happens in a rather nearsighted way in his followers (cf. Binswanger 1932: 173ff.):

> Dasein understands its here in terms of its environmental there. . . . Dasein, in accordance with its spatiality, is proximally never here but there; from this There it comes back to its Here, and it comes back to its here only in the manner that it interprets its concernful Being-towards . . . in terms of what is ready-to-hand over there. (Heidegger 1927: 107ff.)

Of course, Heidegger neglects to account for the basic consequences that result from these findings – at least in *Being and Time* – consequences for the analytic of the subject and its "being-in-the-world."

If the understanding of the current Here comes from a There, then what is first in the way spatiality constitutes itself is not a de-distancing of equipment, but rather is a finding-oneself-distanced from that which I need for my existence – re-moved from a source of nourishment, a place of housing, a place of refuge and the like – and then a self-de-distancing (drawing closer) in the direction of such strived-for centers. The freeing of the nexus of involvement as a whole is not of the same origin as "a re-moving-orienting-letting-be" of the ready-to-hand in a region, but instead is a self-re-moving, self-orienting towards these regions. The subject always already finds itself stretched inside a network of needs that attracts it soon over here and then over there.

The practical situations and usable goods disclosed by my needs and interests, and toward which my doings and strivings are oriented, form the centers from which space erects itself; it is not I from whom the doings and strivings proceed. Spurred on by the interpretation of the subjective Here out of the surrounding There in Heidegger, Zutt described in striking analysis the origin of spatial formation from the objective pole of perceiving and action (Zutt 1953: 347ff.):

> Rather there, on the place on which my gaze rests, the "middle" originates.... Middle means that there, on the place on which my gaze rests, a spatial organization originates, a three-dimensional spatial organization, with a front-back, right-left, over-under.... However, the three-dimensional spatial organization as such is not something like the effect of a supplementary, secondary act of judgment; rather this spatial organization is co-given in the perception, just like external qualities are.... From there, I experience space, and not out of the dark interior of my lived-body. It is because I am there, outside, with the seen things, that I do not experience things as if I were peering out from my dark lived-body like a lighthouse guard. Rather I am in space open to all side, I am presently where my gaze rests.[7]

An example: if I want to jump over a brook, then either the landing on the other bank, which I definitely must reach, or the landing from which I have to push off becomes the center in terms of which my action-space is partitioned and toward which my present position and the stretch I choose for a running start are oriented.

Naturally, we could find situations in which the I alone forms the center of its activity; for example, if one is fearfully snatching up one's personal effects under the threat of losing them. It is only important to admit that also in action-space the I does not exclusively and necessarily embody the zero-point of orientation.

Does the origin of spatial constitution rest in praxis at all, in active involve-ment with the ready-to-hand? Before making a final judgment, one must here take several points into account.

We should not forget that, according to Heidegger's own analysis, intuitable space in immediate involvement with objects of use still remains undisclosed. Space as such only becomes explicit if the project of calculating and measuring practical orientation is taken on by circumspective activity. As long as the subject is absorbed in praxis, then: "The 'above' is 'on the ceiling,' the 'below' is 'on the floor,' the 'behind' is 'at the door'" (Heidegger 1927: 103). One could continue in the subjective perspective: "left" is what, comparatively, I feel as "left-like" or "awkward" [linkisch], and "right" is what suits me as "right" [richtig]. In plane activity, orientations reduce themselves to the subjec-tive qualities of doings and to the thematic relations of objects. A spatial form as such is not perceived.

If I enter an unfamiliar building, or if, while I'm traveling, a new landscape suddenly opens up before me, then the first thing that I notice is not the practical or impractical setup of the building, nor the commercial utility of the new region. My first impressions are rather those of narrowness and width, height and depth, in short, spatial qualities of an emotional and aesthetic type. Possibly these qualities imply practical values. At least, such values are easy to induce from them. But these qualities definitely do not let themselves be reduced to practical aspects.

The first is "attuned space" [gestimmter Raum, i.e., space qualified by an affect or a mood]. According to Straus, who introduced this term (Straus 1930: 25), such a space is not characterized by measurable dimensions, but rather by qualities in the manner mentioned above. But it appears to me that just as these qualities, easily and almost by themselves, induce practical values, they will also induce formal determinations that invite measurements, determinations such as direction, size, distance. Vertical direction spontaneously dominates a tall building. It draws a measured gaze upwards. Analogously, while standing in a narrow, cylindrical tunnel, we would come to feel the effect of suction [induced] by the length, with which it constitutes itself. In the case of colors, whose mood-quality can hardly be avoided, their space-orienting is especially noticeable. In the choir front of the Fraumünster church in Zurich there are three new stained-glass windows by Chagall; the left one is made in a deep blue. It draws the gaze irresistibly towards itself and away from the other two, which are light yellow and green. Its imposing centralizing effect disturbs the panels' architectonic symmetry.

It has been suggested that spatial abilities do not necessarily rest upon a visual presentation of space. So-called spatially blind people are able to execute complicated activities even though any kind of presentative spatial orientation escapes them (Cassirer 1929: 3. 179, 185; Merleau-Ponty 1945: 119ff.). But a space that is not perceived is no space. In the case of those who are spatially blind, one can speak of action-space only from an external, objective point of view.

Köhler's famous intelligence tests on primates suggest that at least low level reasonable achievements presuppose a perceived spatial organization. If a chimpanzee is to conceive of something as a suitable tool, the object must visually stand out from the chimpanzee's surroundings. Each optical structuring, however, also implies *ipso facto* a primary orientation. One might object that the decisive motivation for such a coming forth is the intention of the action. Is it not a common experience that we, searching for a certain tool, discover objects that we never would have noticed otherwise? But here one could respond that Köhler feels it justified to maintain that, given the intelligence level of chimpanzees, a certain visual organization has to be presupposed in order to account for the fact of finding an article of use (Köhler 1917: 78ff.). The adult person, on the other hand, with his or her highly developed ability for abstraction, is capable of deciphering at will optically compact clusters at any random point distinguished just by an abstract spatial position. In case of discovering new tools, chimpanzees and humans, each in their own way, rely on the perception of an optical-spatial ordering, and on a visual-spatial overview of their surroundings – an overview which, in a practical respect, is relatively free and not absorbed by a goal of the action.

According to Merleau-Ponty, the anchor of the world of perceptions is to be ascribed to an active and engaged lived-body. "My lived-body as a system of possible actions" establishes the founding "spatial level" to which each material order and orientation finally relates (Merleau-Ponty 1945: 287ff.). But this tendency to find an anchor for the world of my perception in myself [as the null point of orientation] finds itself in chronic tension with the sensible materials of perception that are formed into wholes according to their immanent factors – assuming, of course, that the tension in fact perdures and the tendency to take myself as null-point does not just lazily adapt to what is objectively given and the factors immanent to them. According to Merleau-Ponty's own description, a test person will adapt when the room he or she is in can only be seen through the reflection in a mirror that is bent at a 45° angle. The reflected room affects the engaged person in a way that instead of feeling his or her own arms and legs, [the person] feels those arms and legs that he or she would need in order to move around and be active in the reflected room. The subsequent conclusion, however, is not sound: that it is only by virtue of this "practically" required adaptation that the spatial level becomes unsteady and [re]establishes itself in the new situation. When a line dominating perception, like that of the famous "leaning tower," which is objectively slanted, is vertically oriented, the subject spontaneously adopts to this dominant direction, shifting into a tilted position that is in no way "practical." The person nearly falls over, and finds it difficult to act in this new position. In this case, the foundational spatial level is obviously founded in the living play [*Schauspiel*] of perception itself, and not in the intention-in-action of the subject.

Spatial orientation is the result of a play of phenomenal vectors, that of sensible perception forming itself according to its own laws and that of intention-in-action springing forth from the lived-body. If the latter is not able to assert itself, then it must act according to the space of perception. Here again, as has been often experimentally confirmed (Kleint 1936–40: 149, 40; Schilder 1950: 106ff.), visual impressions dominate. All the other sensory experiences, not excluding those in which one's own "body image" [*Körperbild*] specifically constitutes itself, subordinate themselves to them. Giving activity priority over intuition in the question of spatial constitution, as has become common, can no longer be upheld.

6 The Body-schema

Perspective

With the help of Cézanne on the artistic side and gestalt psychology on the scientific side, we have again come to realize that we see most things perceptivally "incorrectly." In Cézanne's paintings, the table is placed "not quite right" in horizontal depth, as it should be in proper perspective. The apples that are further away do not appear smaller and paler than those that are closer. The cupped part of the glasses, and the inner parts of the plate, lay almost flat on the objects portrayed in perspective, so that their contents become seen as if we were seeing them simultaneously from above.

Does our body behave any differently than Cézanne's wineglasses and fruit bowls? Do we, of all things, see it "perspectively correct," as it should appear according to the geometric calculation of the visual fields radiating from our eyes? Why has it not occurred to any artist – neither a naturalist nor a surrealist! – to draw a "self-portrait" like and insofar as (according to classical psychological understanding) he or she actually sees him or herself: from the chest and upper arms downwards?[8] Why do they all draw themselves from the outside, most often from the front, sometimes in profile, rarely from behind?

There are psychic conditions in which someone, through hallucination, can come face-to-face with him or herself in the flesh. Two variations are distinguished in this condition, called heautoscopy. In the first, one's own bodily image is projected into external space. The affected person sees him or herself, for example, suddenly striding toward him or herself. In the second, it is as if the patient had eyes outside of the lived-body, with which he or she gazes back upon him or herself. Such an affected person sees him or herself, for example, from the room's ceiling downwards, as he or she actually is lying in bed. This hallucinatory self-perception is probably triggered through a pathologically heightened occupation with oneself and one's own situation. Also in this case, one sees oneself most often from the outside, and likewise most often from the front (Menninger-Lerchenthal 1946).

Aside from artists and patients, how do "ordinary and normal" people fare? Experimental investigations show that most of them see themselves spontaneously in a "normal" position and manner, i.e., largely from outside themselves, if they are occupied with themselves in imagination. Tactile and internal sensations of the lived-body follow, as already mentioned, the visual image.

> When the individual puts his head in another unusual position, for example, bending it forward to an extreme degree, he very often feels his face in the horizontal plane although it is not completely in the horizontal plane. The horizontal plane of the face affords a simple opportunity of correlating the impressions. Some subjects have the feeling that they are observing themselves from above and can somehow see through the skull. Others see their face shortened, as it might appear to an observer opposite them. We can generally say that in the perception of our own body we try to maintain normal positions and observe ourselves as if we were outside objects. This is true not only when we see, but also when we imagine. (Schilder 1950: 84)

There are excellent psychological analyses of the so-called body-schema, i.e., of the gestalt-like and dynamic presence of our lived-body, at our disposal. Obviously, the body-schema is neither purely visual, nor a pure condition of vision. Schilder divides the factors which participate in its constitution into three groups: physiological factors, i.e., sensible and perceptual manners; libidinal factors, i.e., in the manner of drives and feelings; and sociological factors, i.e., influences which underlie our interpersonal experience.

However, the first group especially requires a differentiated analysis. The experience, in which both our motor impulses and their kinaesthetic achievement steering perception and activity proceed from our own lived-body, easily leads us to regard that lived-body, without further consideration, as the zero-point of orientation of all perception and activity. In doing so, one overlooks the connection between the objectively oriented intention of this impulsive and kinaesthetic experience, and the intention of the whole perceptive and practical project of the world guiding it. It is the telos of the experience that has an immediate centralizing effect, not the point of departure of the experience. It is only in view of this goal that one's own lived-body is experienced in the corresponding perspectives.

Here-Qualification

It is not the lived-body as a whole, which, of course, is itself spatially extended, but, according to Husserl, only one of its points that is "always characterized in the mode of the ultimate central Here, namely, in one Here that has no other outside of itself in relation to which it would be a There" (Husserl 1952: 158). The qualification of the absolute Here depends, according to Husserl, on the function of the zero-point of the place in question. He leaves it open as to where this place is exactly located. The zero-point, according to him, is not given originally, rather only approximately as limit [*Limes*].

To this it can be said that (1) the zero-position can be concretized in a way that goes beyond Husserl's general and formal analyses, and that (2) in no way is a single position constantly and exclusively able to preserve the qualification of being the zero-point. The zero-point changes with changing situations. Not only do different people hold different bodily portions to be the "seat of the I," and thereby the center of their own lived-body; intellectuals have a preference toward the head, others rather the navel, and even within individual people themselves, the central point varies according to attitude, mood, activity. According to Balzac, the I, which normally resides in the head (on the bridge of the nose, between the eyes), sinks downward into the torso when one is dancing (Straus 1930: 167). According to Schilder's investigations, the specific body zone, belonging to a desire which increasingly makes itself noticeable, becomes itself the center of the bodily schema (Schilder 1950: 124). The lived-body is treated no differently than any randomly perceived object. Its centralization depends on its gestalt structure and its meaning, the weight of which shifts around regularly in living perception.

The expressions "here" and "there" fulfill a referential function. The Here-qualification belongs primarily to the referential organ itself. If the whole lived-body functions as this referential organ, then it and its immediate surroundings appear as Here. By the way, the scope of "here" varies enormously. "Here" can extend to my room in which I work, and reach as far as the city in which I live. If only a single limb of the lived-body functions as referential organ in relation to its parts, then it attains the absolute qualification of Here. A paralyzed person who can only move one finger is able to characterize everything that it can point to as "here." In case this person is able to draw attention to him or herself with this finger, the finger itself will always exclusively be characterized as "here" and never "there" from his or her own perspective. If she or he is also able to move yet another finger on the other hand, she or he will qualify the first finger as "there" and take the pointing finger as "here", using the latter as an organ of reference.

The absolute Here-qualification, which is bestowed upon the lived-body in contrast to all other things, is not due to a general and absolute zero-point function for the orientation of perceived space, but rather to the lived-body's specific function as a referential organ. As such, the lived-body cannot be entirely replaced by nothing whatsoever.

Origin and Anchoring of Spatial Determinations

Up to this point, we have concentrated on the zero-point of orientation as such, how it can be identified in various perceptual formations. Let us now turn to pairs of spatial directions, which all radiate from a zero-point, and to spatial qualities, which are anchored in such a zero-point. According to Husserl, the lived-body functions as the carrier of the zero-point of these spatial determinations: everything that appears *eo ipso* has an orientational relation to my lived-body. "If I imagine a centaur, then I cannot imagine it in any other way than with a certain orientation and a certain relation to my sense organs: it stands 'on my right', comes 'closer' or 'distances' itself, 'turns' itself, turns 'towards me' or away" (Husserl 1952: 56).

On the other hand, we can establish that such orientation toward my lived-body is not realized in many, if not most, perceptions. It may be the case that this orientation-towards is virtually present and can principally be actualized; however, it only takes place in very specific motivational situations. The phenomenological interest in providing evidence for the principal subject-relatedness of every perception deforms its factual structuring by making a relation conscious, accentuating such a relation normally not accentuated (section 9).

Objective and subjective systems of orientation overlap one another in our language. There seem to be languages that only have an objective system. The Yurok, a tribe of California Indians,

> for example, have two main directions: "downstream" and "upstream". Right and left of these two directions are called "toward the other bank" and "away from the stream," whereby the person in question is thought of on the one side of the stream. These directions, which are related entirely to the momentary situation, control the thinking of the Yurok in such a way, e.g., that a door is not on the west but on the "downstream" side of a house – or that a man lifts something up that lies not on his left but "upstream" from him. . . . The constant change of this locationally determined direction, when we compare it to solar orientation, is not noticed by the Yurok. They use the English word "east" only as a translation for their "upstream" direction, whether or not it applies correctly to their specific position. (Jensen 1947: 41)

The Yurok's orientation is objectively fixed like our solar orientation, and at the same time, given the running and winding of the stream, it changes in the way our right-left orientation does.

Is the lived-body, at least, the originary site of the directional pairs of "over" and "under," "front" and "behind" and above all "right" and "left" – the pairs that can be anchored in the lived-body as well as in some objects? We do not know whether this is factually the case, excepting right-left orientation. Only empirical psychology can elicit that. However, one can certainly assert that this does not have to be the case – without excepting right-left orientation! A child can learn what "over" and "under," "front" and "behind," "right" and "left" are from any objects – a house, a mountain, a stream – and in the same way that the child projects this understanding over to other things, it can project it into its own lived-body. Whether we relate these expressions to our lived-body, once we have learned them, or anchor them in an object, depends on the specific situation. They adjust themselves according to the dominant figure of perception. In a valley, we call one village the front one and the other the one behind, one the village above and the other the one below, independent of where we ourselves are standing – in one of the villages, somewhere outside, or by chance in the middle between the two.

Piaget ascertained with tests that the majority of children over five years old are able to differentiate their own right and left side. As of eight years old, they can successfully apply this differentiation to a conversational partner. Only after age eleven, taking their point of departure solely from objects and their situated relations [Lageverhältnissen], without considering a subject, are they capable of using right and left completely relative [to each other]. From these results, Piaget concludes that the development of a child's spatial orientation occurs in three stages, going from pure egocentrism, through socialization, to complete object-ivation (Piaget 1925: 90ff.). If one, however, reads these tests just cited more closely, one finds that a child's perception only appears egocentric from an adult perspective, where an adult's own egocentric view is projected onto the child on the basis of external correlations. Here we have a confusion similar to that which occurs when the color-blind learn colors. The teacher points to a spot of color and calls it red. The color-blind person does not relate the expression "red" to the color, but rather to the degree of brightness or some other characteristic of the spot. The teacher points to the right hand of the child and designates it as such because of its specific relation to the subject. The child, on the other hand, links the designators "right" to some type of qualitative feature found on its right side. For the child, the designators "right" and "left" are like the expressions "brother" and "sister," they are not initially I-, or subject-related, but rather are qualitatively determined. The child does not learn them any differently than it would expressions like "house," "boy," and so on, i.e., through their qualitative or functional characteristics. What the adult understands as concepts of relation are for the child originally qualitative concepts.

Once the child grasps these concepts as concepts of relation, they are still, in the first phase, objective rather than subjective concepts. The first phase of orientation is obviously not one of subjective, egocentric orientation; rather it is an orientation of objective visual things to one another (cf. Bischof 1966: 315). The child orients the things she or he sees in terms of one another, and this in an absolute manner. In this process, one's own lived-body functions as one such visual object among others. When that which has the same relation to an outstanding thing as another thing has to it which already has taken on a spatial characterization, then the former takes on that same characterization. If the child has learned that a radio, which has been placed in the cellar, is "below" in contrast to the one found in the apartment, then it carries this designation over to all other things that are deposited there. The same goes for "right" and "left." That which holds the same relationship as the right hand, compared to the torso, is also called "right," thus also the left hand of the person sitting across from the child. In this phase, the child does not yet know of subjective relationships. The distinction between egocentric orientation and that of foreign subjects is still beyond the child.

This first phase of orientation determined by objects must not be equated with the phase of "complete objectification," which the child, according to Piaget's tests, only reaches after age eleven. This second phase is distinguished by mastery over the relativity of relationships. Relationships are no longer bound absolutely to a certain object, nor anymore to a subjective viewpoint. Things can now be oriented towards each other reciprocally in any manner whatsoever.

Kant assigns a fundamental and absolute role in orientation to the "feeling of difference concerning my own subject, namely concerning the right and left hand." If we were not able to distinguish the movement of left to right from that of its opposite, we would not know, according to Kant's interpretation, on which side of the horizon we, taking our bearing from the south point, would have to place the west (Kant 1786: 134ff.). Experience shows us, however, that the subjective feeling of the right-left distinction cannot protect us any more from illusions of orientation than the spatial direction received from the difference of two objects. If all of the objects in a room, which according to our memory ought to be on the left side, are now on the right, there are no clues had by us which can tell us whether our memory is deluding us or the furniture has been changed around. Do we not occasionally lose our orientation in a new city after a guided tour, and then think that the main street, which should lead to the next city, is going off in the wrong direction; or that the train, that should be taking us to a certain town, to our bewilderment is coming into the station exactly from that direction in which we imagine it to be?

Right-left orientation is absolutely secure not even for our own lived-body, for the simple reason that visual and tactile experiences do not necessarily coincide. Through experiments, we can diametrically oppose these two types of experience by putting on glasses that turn visual perception upside-down.[9] As a rule we can say that in such situations, visual experience triumphs (as we have seen earlier); tactile experience adapts itself to the visual. Also the positional relations of parts of our lived-body that are sensibly perceptible or merely representational, relations upon which we orient ourselves in space, can fall apart. If I encounter a picture of myself after a long period of time, I am bewildered by the fact that the part in my hair is on the left side. I take the photograph, along with all duplicated objects, to be backwards. According to my own conception, the part is where I see it every day in the mirror – on the right. If I touch my head, or imagine combing my hair, then the "true" position becomes clear.

If one direction takes preference, then it is not the direction of right-left, but rather of the vertical. The directional system of the predominant figure of perception tends toward a vertical orientation. This fact is clearly confirmed in the experiments involving a turning house. The turning house, which is an enclosed shell of a house in which a test subject is placed, can be turned in various directions without the subject's being able to observe the operation of the mechanisms. If the turning house is brought to an objectively slanted position, the whole space (i.e., in this case, the inner part of the shell) realigns itself for the subject – after awhile and after some initial opposition – and appears vertical, as it did before. A rod that is hanging objectively perpendicular from the ceiling (in the line of gravity) consequently appears, according to the arrangement of the whole room, to be hanging off-balance. The lived-body does not behave any differently if a test subject takes a seat in a hanging, movable swing. Similarly, one can show through experiments in a dark room how images projected as slanted on the wall have a tendency to appear vertical. This tendency is so strong that even the floor, upon which the observer is standing, seems to be slanted contrary to the tilted images (Kleint 1936–40: 138, 9ff.). When figures with a pronounced main axis are presented to test-persons in a tilted position, they are regularly reproduced as upright. Sometimes this even happens with figures that are laid horizontally before the test-persons. Figures shown vertically are always reproduced correctly (Howard and Templeton 1966: 301).

This privileged position of the vertical, which has been well known for a long time, has been justified in classical literature, by recourse to one's own lived-bodily experience – an upright gait and the lived experience of the force of gravity (Bollnow 1963: 44ff.). But especially Kleint's aforementioned observations force one to relativize here as well. One could object to the traditional thesis – that man sets things upright, orienting them vertically, because he himself has an upright stance – that man rather sets himself erect because (apart from practical reasons) he was obviously impressed by the vertical orientation of certain significant perceptual formations which led him to adopt it.

Husserl also links the spatial distinctions of nearness and distance, along with spatial directions, to the lived-body of the subject. An unbiased consideration will show that these determinations, as well, have no unequivocal and absolute dependence upon one's own lived-body. Their range varies considerably in a manner similar to that of "here" and "there," according to the gestalt and sense of the structure in which we immediately locate ourselves. What we already assess as "distant" and "far" in a room, we would still classify as "near" in an open field. In addition, we can learn and apply these expressions just as well in relation to any object. The expression "the distant" [die Ferne] has, like the expression "the stranger" [die Fremde], a subjective connotation in our use of language, although not in an individually subjective sense but an intersubjective one, related to a community or a shared good. If I stay in a foreign country, that which is subjectively close for me is at the same time "in the distance" in an intersubjective sense. Two differently oriented determinations of nearness and distance intersect here.

A primary concern of Merleau-Ponty's phenomenology, with its existential philosophical character, was to provide an existential, subjective definition for all forms of perception. Accordingly, he states, a thing is large "if my gaze is not able to encompass it, small, if my gaze effortlessly encloses it" (Merleau-Ponty 1945: 350).

It is an objective fact that the differentiated perception of large and small is correlative to a specific manner of gazing. It is questionable, however, whether the different manner of gazing is also always a phenomenal datum – an actual one and not just a virtual one – a datum that is constitutive for the apprehension of the seen object. It appears to me that the original indication for the differentiation between "large" and "small" will be found where this differentiation appears, and where the indication should thus first be sought, i.e., on the noematic side of consciousness, in the seen itself, not on the noetic side, in the lived-experience of seeing.

How forms of perception are determined by their respective contexts is immediate, intuitive, experiencable. A large church that towers over and dominates the two-and three-story houses that surround it would be swallowed up, as it were, by the skyscrapers in New York. It visibly loses weight, reality, meaning. This is because the surroundings of the church are determinate of its size: in one context it appears large and in another it appears as small as a hand-made model. The famous Müller-Lyer deception illustrates in a striking manner that the environment does not merely take a datum remaining constant in its material content and cover it over, in a purely external manner, with interchangeable, relational determinations. Rather it shows that it is able to alter the sensible contents themselves. Different arrangements of supplemental lines are able to visibly shorten and lengthen a straight one.

The following sentence from Husserl's *Nachlaß* (1966: 299) expresses what has now become the conventional phenomenological teaching on perception, the thesis that the lived-body holds a privileged position: "The movement of an external thing does not necessarily influence the manners of appearance of other things; the movement of the lived-body revolutionizes the manner of appearance of everything." Contrary to this position, one should endorse the position of gestalt theory: the movement of a thing revolutionizes the manner of appearance of surrounding things just as well as the movement of one's own lived-body. Let's draw two parallel lines. The two lines not only constitute themselves according to a specific aspect and in a specific position in relation to us, to the right or left or straight in front of us. They also constitute themselves just as originally in relation to each other. They appear to be next to one another, parallel, and for them an inside and outside develop out of their relation to each other. They do not just change if we switch our position, seeing them, if it is possible, from behind or from the left instead of from where we were on the right. They change just as well if they are themselves rearranged. What was formerly seen as the inner side now becomes the outer side, and vice versa. If one is removed and drawn through a circle, then it divides the circle into two equal or unequal halves, while the other seems "lost" and "off to the side," etc.

8 The Results

Relativity, lability and plurality of orientation

The spatial orientation of perception proves to be utterly relative. Each dominant formation of perception draws toward itself the zero-point of orientation. One's own lived-body neither occupies the orienting dominance in the world of perception constantly nor does it do so even originally. The person is neither the absolute center of all things, nor does he or she function as their one and only measure. The range of spatial dimensions like "near" and "far," and "large" and "small," are not determined by the person alone.

The instability of orientation is linked with its relativity. Perception is not a pregiven structure, neither according to its gestalt nor according to its sense, the two determining the dominance factors. It is constantly in the state of developing and changing. One reason for this is that the manner in which sensible objects of perception are given is inadequate. Every phenomenon implies horizons that are empty and undetermined, and that strive toward concrete fulfillment and arrangement. In this way, sensory consciousness is constantly held in motion by tensions that provoke regroupings on the objective side and new attitudes on the subjective side. Whatever comes into view and is weighed as new also, *ipso facto*, affects orientation, which now also comes to change.

This transposition and its resulting re-centralization is not always radical and complete. If we are sitting in a closed room, the zero-point is determined by its gestalt and the arrangement of its furniture. If we walk to the window and see a marketplace, the zero-point leaps from the room into the middle of the market-place. If we happen to know that this marketplace is second to another that can be found in the middle of the city, the zero-point again leaps even further. If, however, the place in front of our house is one of the city's two dominant squares which are laid out symmetrically, the orientation vacillates. The two places hold each other in check, as it were, finally coordinating into a double-poled system of relation. The tension and the division of orientation is not only sensed in cases where two formations are equal, but also in cases where one is subordinate or dominant. Orientation vacillates between orientation-towards our quarter and the whole city. As a rule, we will see our quarter in relation to the whole city, as sloping toward and adjoining it. Other times we might succeed in concentrating on our quarter, thereby orienting the city to it as its center and attributing a derivative position to the city.

Every figure of perception has its own center. Accordingly, a complex perception gives itself polycentrically.

The tendency towards establishing a single dominant zero-point

There could be no worse mistake than making the established relativity, lability, and plurality of orientation absolute. Nothing could be less adequate than paying homage to an absolute relativism and a simple perspectivism. Concrete, complex perception reveals equal orientations just as little as it insinuates equal perceptions.

The special correlation of perspectival aspects and horizon found in percep-tion of [material] things is taken as a preferred model in the phenomenological theory of perception. A thing is directly intuited by us only from one side. But this intuited side remains in a reciprocal, functioning interrelation within a network of referential implications [*Verweisungsgeflecht*] with the side of the thing that is turned away from our gaze and is not directly intuitive. The seen aspect not only carries the more or less empty and undepicted presentations of the back side, but the latter also supports that which is presently in view. Without reference to what is not directly viewable, the intuitively given aspect of a house is simply not as it purports to be. Cut off from its referential implication, the [viewable] aspect loses the gestalt and the sense that it had. It loses its three-dimensionality and equilibrium, both of which depend on this intentional relationship between the different aspects. It also loses that which gives it sense. It no longer functions as the side view of a house. Now it only presents a two-dimensional plane.

We can only perceive perspectivally. Each perspective intentionally implies an infinite series of other perspectives. We experience this implicit intentional implication of other perspectives as a motivational invitation to change our position, so that the other profiles of an object can likewise be brought to intuition.

These perspectives do not have equal value compared to one another. In an art gallery, we spontaneously search out the position from which a painting best presents itself. We are led by our first snatched glances, which hint at a more precise view in their very unclearness and inner lack of balance. Every thing gives itself as a system of series of perspectives, advancing toward what is ever better and finally optimal. We yield ourselves to one of these hierarchical sequences, depending on the gestalt and the sense which is either insinuated in our first glance or brought to the perception from somewhere else. We soon realize that, in the case of viewing a building, we have to go to a specific side in order to better conjure up the idea of a tent which guided the architect, to another side in order to bring out more clearly the function of the building, and yet to a third in order to realize in an optimal way how the architecture takes up and continues the main lines of the landscape.

Depending on the sense that we pursue, certain series of perspectives will have a stronger attraction. These series characterize themselves as ascending, culminating in an optimal perspective. Such an ascending series is a gestalt phenomenon, in which a datum continually and consequently changes in a certain respect and by which the whole series constitutes itself as a unity. For example, a band of colors that darkens itself successively in one direction.

The optimal perspective, even if it is not intuitively given but rather merely prospectively anticipated, tends to establish itself as absolute, making the rest of the perspectives appear to be oriented towards it. This perspective is linked with the apprehension that this perspective gives the object as it is "in itself," whereas all the preceding, less than optimal manners of appearance are apprehended as deficient appearances of this objective gestalt.[10]

A similar phenomenon of attraction and absolutizing is observable in orientation: in a complex perception, the predominant center reveals a tendency to draw the other centers and, respectively, their centralizing functions towards itself, constituting itself as the optimal and absolute center. The attraction here is even more distinct, as it not only orients the other centers towards itself but also actually absorbs them into itself.

Due to its dominating height, a city or countryside is most likely to be chosen as a political or religious center. Conversely, one expects the most important building in a city, the city hall or the cathedral, also to dominate the city through its size. If the orientation of gestalt is pregiven, then it draws the sensible orientation towards it, and vice versa.

If the unification of different centers of orientation is achieved, it strikes us as satisfactory. The tension in our perception dissolves. Or rather: it reduces itself. If such a unification is not possible, we can easily experience it as disturbing. As a child I found it pleasant that the city of Lucerne, in whose vicinity we lived, is located more or less in the center of Switzerland, and Switzerland for its part in the center of Western Europe. But then I was disturbed to find that Europe does not in one way or another figure as the central continent of the whole planet, either through its gestalt or position, but on the contrary coincides with some discarded tip of the Eurasian land mass. Similarly, it made me think that the capital of Switzerland neither lies in the country's geographical middle, nor is it the biggest city of the country, nor, finally, does it function as the religious center, the seat of the bishop. The decentralization of the world in the most different ways obviously contradicted my desire for an absolute zero-point of orientation.

East-Asian maps of the world show the Eurasian land mass and Africa on the right, and the two Americas on the left, so that the East-Asian countries come close to the center of the map. Astonishingly, no one on the Southern hemisphere seems to have thought of printing world maps upside down, with the South on top and North on the bottom. Such a map would be conductive to our global consciousness of space.

The tendency to let the subjective center of perception coincide with the objective subordinates itself to the general law that the stronger center seeks to absorb the weaker. We tend either to adapt ourselves to the objective center of our world or to draw all of the criteria of orientation towards ourselves, depending on the weight we assign to ourselves as the subject of perceiving and actions and to our own lived-body as the organon of this perceiving and action.

A conceited person constantly carries the zero-point of orientation along with him or herself. Such a person is much like the Achilpa Indians who always carry their holy post – which for them represents the *axis mundi* – along with them on their travels. The motives of these Indians, however, differ from those of the conceited individual; they do not wish to distance themselves from the center which connects them with the supernatural world (Eliade 1957: 26). This is quite different from the person whose thinking has been influenced with the structures of the world proper. This person resembles the pilgrim who goes on a search for the center of the world, which he might find at the top of the country's highest mountain or in some "holy city." Eliade concluded in his investigations in religious phenomenology "that the religious person wants to live as close as possible to the center of the world." This is probably a tendency that is far from limited only to the *homo religiosus*. In watching tourists one can observe their childlike efforts to reach the center of an architectural construction or landscape, in order to subjectively feel one with the objective orientation of the world.

We can always experience our world from two centers: first, directly and intuitively from our subjective position, and second, prospectively from the objective zero-point of the perceived world. Thanks to this double orientation of our perception, we are just as little delivered over to an unending chain of orientations as to perspectives, which (1) would be altogether of equal value and thus indifferent, and (2) would be judged as being purely subjective.

One might object that the world of perception, in which we contrast our subjective position with an objective center, is itself again as a whole subjective. The historical fact that every people saw its country's highest mountain or its capital as the world's navel seems to support this opposition.

Here are two things we must distinguish: (1) the fact that each respective zero-point of orientation sets itself as absolute, a tendency that continually offers, yet even imposes itself; and (2) a possible confusion that stems from the equivocation of the concepts "subjective" and "objective."

We notice how every segment of our perception (our room, our quarter), on the one hand, strives to support itself on enclosing and more powerful systems of perception (our city, our country), and on the other hand, exhibits a certain resistance against these systems. Each perception is unfolded between its own contradictory tendencies, the tendency to constitute itself as a whole as an enclosed unity, and the tendency to reach beyond its own borders. That which holds for an enclosed part of our perception, holds equally for our world of perception, whose borders are marked for us through our factual means of moving around. Here, too, we find the same tension between the tendency to enclose oneself within oneself, to absolutize one's own center, and the tendency to push forward to new horizons. Which of the two tendencies outweighs the other depends, aside from the structure of the perceived world, also on the degree of the development of consciousness.

We call the center of a figure of perception objective insofar as it stems from the tendency, belonging to this figure, to constitute itself as a unity and, in so doing, to set the subjective pole – from which the I-experiences of perception stem as centered – in opposition to itself. This center belongs, along with the noematic intentions carrying it, on the noematic side of perception, the object-ive side turned away from consciousness. The virtual orientation of each figure of perception upon a more encompassing "world" and, finally, upon the all-embracing world – which we are not able to realize intuitively but rather to conceive only *idealiter* – can principally keep us from taking the concrete, and in this sense objective, center of an actually given structure of perception to be more than it actually is, and from hastily equating it with the absolute center of the all-embracing world.

9 Unreflected Presuppositions of the Husserlian Thesis

The refutation of a thesis is not complete if it is falsified through contradictory findings. An integral, complete critique must uncover the false or one-sided assumptions which lead to a thesis, or which lead to an insufficient selection of research materials which support the thesis.

Husserl's intention is to build the world up, phase by phase, step by step, from a secure point of departure. To this purpose, he reduces complex, pregiven reality to his own consciousness, which remains for him absolutely given. He then constructs the world anew as a correlate to consciousness, at first according to the pure temporal and spatial form of consciousness, and then, based on this, according to its inner plenitude. In doing so, Husserl does not set up at the outset, as we find in gestalt psychology, a diffused, self-differentiating totality; instead, he starts out, in a way comparable to sensualist psychology, with single affections which grow together through syntheses to become complex formations. As long as the I is given only empty time and equally empty space, it will obviously find itself in the center of its (empty) world. In a purely formally constructed world, the constituting I sets up the dominating structure of perception and thereby the zero-point of orientation, according to the basic law of orientation, as we have seen.

If one were to bring individual objects into this empty space, then these as well would show an orientation towards the subject, especially if these objects are minor things like writing utensils or similar articles of use. These single objects which Husserl imagined into an empty, pure space behave like those "isolated lines" that were projected on the dark-room wall in experimental psychology. They have too little weight to draw the centering of space away from the perceiving subject and onto themselves.

The point of departure of Husserl's investigations of spatial orientation is no different from either classical, idealistic philosophy, with its pure space, or classical, empirical psychology, with its dark rooms, i.e., an abstract, artificially constructed space, without reflecting on the possibility that an orientation which is found in empty space might not continue to be valid in a concretely filled-out space. Indeed, things which one introduced into a space do not simply fill up this space, following pregiven, formal structures; rather they form it anew with new lines, i.e., with utterly striking lines "bound to things" [dingfest]. They do not just fill out the empty space, they also transform it. New, stronger figures of perception come before the I, making it difficult for the I to anchor the orientation in the I, perhaps even shifting the orientation completely away from the I.

Husserl connects the centering of the perception of things in one's own lived-body with their kinaesthetic dependence, with the fact that the lived-body is implied in all transcendent perception as a mobile, and, in this mobility, as a kinaesthetically experienced organ of perception.

In fact, there is a peculiar motivational relation between the kinaesthetic experience of one's own lived-body and the series of perceptions. In Husserl the insistence upon this coupling, and at the same time the nearly constant one-sided view of this principally mutual motivational relation, is conspicuous. Not only does the kinaesthetic bodily experience – or, for that matter, already the pure consciousness of the mastery of this experience – motivate and anticipate, as Husserl mainly describes it, the further expansion of transcendent perception, but also, vice versa. The horizonal referential implication immanent in the experiential world is also able to provoke new kinaesthetic attitudes of the lived-body or of individual organs. Kinaesthesis is not necessarily an active process launched from the I. It can also be set in motion before an intention of the I or even, from the opposite direction, come from transcendent perception, which is full of intentional implications.

The presentation [*Vergegenwärtigung*] in reflection of this coupling between transcendent perception and one's lived-body and consciousness naturally aligns the orientation of the perceptive world to the subject, and to its organon, especially if this presentation is so laden with meaning as it is with Husserl. According to Husserl, part of the essence of spatio-objective experience is the fact that the body is not only presupposed objectively, as it is for a realistic philosophy, but that it is also phenomenally "co-present" [*mit dabei*] (Husserl 1952: 56, 81, 144; 1966: 298).[11] Merleau-Ponty adopted this thesis in his critique of gestalt psychology: "One's own lived-body is the constantly co-present third moment in the structure of figure-background" (Merleau-Ponty 1945: 117).

Is the lived-body really co-present in every figural and thingly experience? Over large stretches of experience, the subject is actually "self-forgotten," as Husserl himself originally claims, and, one can add, "lived-bodily-forgotten." Kinaesthetic processes are hardly noticed as they run their course. Accordingly, their centripetal force is not noticeable either. There are, of course, specific types of experience in which the perceiving subject together with the transcendent object comes to consciousness. In this way the sensing subject constitutes itself simultaneously along with the transcendent object in a touching experience as opposed to in visual perception. In the same way, emotional qualities, in contrast to simply natural and purely material qualities, point back in their sense to a value-taking subject. But we do not live in such experiences continually, and thus we need an additional motivation in order to bring this subjective, retroactive coupling of all transcendent perception to our consciousness.[12]

Husserl's *Ideas II* (1952: 55ff.) discloses his motivation. Not until he began working – according to his phenomenological ideal of making pregiven phenomena fully evident – on "the production [!] of a full givenness of a material thing," did the fundamental fact that external perception is related to the subject and the lived-body become acutely clear to him. Given such purpose, it soon became clear that it belongs to the essence of a thing to refer back to a subject endowed with a lived-body from which the thing is being experienced. Husserl subsequently forgot that in natural experience oftentimes even essential and fundamental things are merely virtually given; they do not need to be present and accentuated in the way it would be necessary for a reflective attitude.

As a result, his phenomenological ideal became a trap. He allows himself to be guided by an ideal and idealized perception in developing his thesis of the lived-body as the zero-point of orientation. Even Merleau-Ponty, whose main philosophical preoccupation was developed from the later Husserl's demand to return to natural experience, followed him in this.[13] Obviously, one should reject as abstract an analysis of perceived space that, like gestalt psychology, only considers figures and points alone, and neglects their horizon, which encompasses the lived-body of the perceiver (Merleau-Ponty 1945: 117). But one can also distort perception by going in the other direction, by fixating, overestimating and assigning them the same weight as the directly perceived. Sartre, of all the phenomenologists, shows himself here to be more careful and restrained, i.e., not in the thesis of the subjective zero-point of orientation itself, but rather in the presuppositions that Husserl provides for his thesis. According to Sartre's analysis (1943: 388ff.), it is the lived-body, although it can be identified in the analysis as the underlying center of the mundane nexus of referential implication, which is always "the already crossed," the "silently happened" in the execution of perception and action. Sartre appropriately compares that consciousness which we have of our own lived-body to the consciousness of the sign, which, in a similar way, is passed over for its meaning and neglected in favor of its sense.[14]

Although there is a philosophical interest in explicating all the implications of a perception, this interest is not the only subjective factor which can be made responsible for a multifaceted predominance of the I-relationedness of perception. We have also come upon less thematically oriented interests, as we noted in the case of a deliberate and self-assured personality that prefers to see itself in the center of its small and large world. A pronounced self-confidence can have a cultural–historical or an individual–psychological reason. Husserl neglected the question of both the possible psychological and sociological dependence of the structuring and orientation of the world. He considered neither his own self-confident personality nor the decidedly egologically oriented tradition of European philosophy since Descartes and Kant.

Every science is jeopardized by assumptions that appear obvious and that are hardly ever formulated explicitly – at the earliest in secondary literature – and thus whose validity is also not critically examined, assumptions which nevertheless are continually at work. A famous example for such an implicit presupposition is the constancy hypothesis of sensualistic psychology, which was unmasked by gestalt psychology. The constancy hypothesis is the assumption of a constant correspondence between stimulus and sensation, i.e., the constant nature of a sensation, whether that sensation remains isolated or is integrated in different complex gestalts and wholes of sense.

Such an "obvious" assumption is hidden also in Husserl's thesis of the zero-point of orientation. It can be formulated as such: the origin and center of constitution coincide. The source-point [*Quellpunkt*] of constitution is also its midpoint [*Mittepunkt*]. We will not find this assumption formulated directly like this anywhere by Husserl himself. However, it gives itself away fairly clearly in *Ideas II* (Husserl 1952: 56, 109ff.). It can be found explicitly formulated in Bollnow (1963: 23ff.): "As the being which shapes and expands space, a person is essentially not only the origin, but also, at the same time, the perduring middle of his or her space."

A rigorous parallelism is postulated here between the transcendental, consti-tuting inner world and the transcendent, constituted outer world. From the assumption that "the pure I [is] the center of all intentionality," Husserl directly concludes that also "the empirical I in the form of the I-person functions as the phenomenal-real central member for the constitution in appearances of the entire spatial-temporal world" (Husserl 1952: 109ff.). The dialectic between *naturans* and *naturatum*, *constituens* and *constitutum* or noesis and noema, which disjoints this one-sided and clearly determined parallelism, is overlooked.[15]

The I-consciousness, or the egological lived-body, does indeed function well as the point of departure and the ultimate carrier of all perception. However, the continuation and composition of perception is determined mostly by its own material. The intended, for its part, turns out to be intending, the constituted for its part to be constituting, the instituted sense for its part to be the instituting sense. Intentional rays do not just go out from the subject; objects by themselves insinuate relationships to one another, relationships to which the subject can only turn subsequently. Apart from noetic intentions, which stem from the I-consciousness, we find noematic referential implications which *ipso facto* have their origin in consciousness and which are likewise to be understood as intentional relationships (Husserl 1966: 76, 429). They determine the physio-gnomy of the world no less than noetic intentions.

10 Conclusion

It turns out that perception has a privileged position compared to other modes of consciousness, in genetic as well as in exemplary respect – and not just according to phenomenological interpretation. Its structuration also has effects on these other modes. Thus we can speak of perspectives not only in perception, but also in thinking, and just as well of orientation. A thoughtful analysis of the orientation of perception, therefore, is of central philosophical relevance.

Before we summarize our results, we shall quickly take note of one important consequence which results from the possible splitting of orientation into a subjective and an objective relational pole, and the tension which thus arises in perception as a consequence. This tension is also found beyond the sphere of perception and its immediate domain. It pertains to the constitution of object-ivity, of something being-in-itself, and is crucial for a philosophical science.

According to Husserl, a thing is constituted actually as objective, and correlat-ively, my experience of things is constituted actually as subjective in intersub-jective experience. There belongs to the complete evidence of the object not only its relationship to me, the subject which constitutes it – this alone has been discussed so far – but also its relationship to other appresented or appresentable subjects, in short, the co-appearing of people experiencing the object. Object-ivity constitutes itself in experience along with this in such a way that that which is seen by me also faces others in varied manners of appearance. The thing establishes itself as such by maintaining itself as something that is viewed at the same time by myself and by others. By virtue of the fact that there is something that perdures as identical through temporally, spatially and, finally, (inter)subjec-tively different appearances, a standing and abiding in-itself is constituted, to which we can return time and again.[16]

The later Husserl, however, overvalues the principal relevance of intersub-jective experience – not the factual one, which one could really not evaluate highly enough. Already in an individual subjective experience, which lacks any intersubjective interference, a thing is perceived in terms of multiple relational poles. Already at this point, the thing obtains an objectivating identification as it is represented in differently arranged appearances. This is not just a private anticipation of multipolar intersubjective experience. In intersubjective experi-ence, as it is described by Husserl, none of the many present and appresented manners of appearance render the thing better or more objective than any other. They are principally of the same value. Each is relative. On the other hand, we can show that the perceived thing already is disclosed as having different values in its appearances and orientations in private perception. An optimal view links itself intentionally (prospectively) with my actual view, and an orientation upon a center which a dominant structure of perception has drawn towards itself can compete with the possible orientation upon myself. Only in ideal cases do actual and optimal aspects, the subjective and objective orientations, coincide. It is intrinsic to optimal appearance that it be conceived as the "normal" and objective appearance that presents the thing as it is in itself (Husserl 1952: 59ff., 75), and it is intrinsic in the same way to the orientation connected to the perceived itself that it be conceived as objective and in itself valid. This means that a thing does not just constitute itself pole-like (as an identical relational pole of appearances) as objective and existing in itself in individual subjective experience with its ever only relative manners of appearance, but also that the manners of appearance of this thing constitute themselves in intersubjective experience.[17] Of course, one must not misunderstand this objectivity of a thing-pole, and especially not the objectivity of an appearance of a thing. Phenomenology abstains from the question of whether things and their qualities exist independently of consciousness; it even objects to it as absurd. Phenomenology only cares about the clarification of how things are apprehended in consciousness as things in themselves.

Summary

The most powerful figure in each context functions as the zero-point of orientation of a perception. Its power is founded in gestalt and sense factors. In order for one's own lived-body to obtain the role of the zero-point, it must dominate the rest of the perception by virtue of its gestalt or special meaning that is attributed to it no differently than to objective things. In our perceiving and likewise in our activities, we are most often completely given to the things which face us and thus our own lived-body, in its transcendental, constituting function, most often does not come to consciousness. Accordingly, it does not make itself motivationally noticeable in the competition for the dominance of perception. We can relate the various pairs of spatial directions like "over" and "under," even "right" and "left," and spatial qualities like "near" and "far" just as well to our own lived-body as we can to some objects grasped visually. In the struggle between objective and subjective orientation, the constitution of an object of perception as something that is in-itself and exists objectively comes into being.

Husserl's thesis of one's lived-body as the zero-point of orientation is plagued by multiple idealizations. (1) He derived his thesis from an abstraction, pure space, overlooking the fact that when the contents of this space are filled in, new motivations come into play for orientation. (2) He comes to this thesis through his purpose of uncovering all, and especially the subjective, relationships in which a thing constitutes itself, and, subsequently, overlooks that these relationships, whose explication, of course, affects the orientation of perception, are not consciously present, or at least are not accentuated, in natural experience, and therefore do not become motivationally effective to the same extent. (3) In his thesis he follows the "self-evident" assumption, which in reality however has never been proved, that the origin of constitution also functions as the center of the constituted; in doing so, he overlooks the dialectic that, time and again, breaks out between *naturans* and *naturatum* and that draws orientation into its very movement.

Translated by Lanei Rodemeyer and Sebastian Luft

Notes

1   Bollnow (1963: e.g. 56). However much Bollnow's realizations in his meditations on space are apt, he does not follow them through to their consequences. He also fails to question the motivations behind the different orientations of space.

2   For the difference between associative and sense-motivations, cf. Holenstein 1972a: 315ff.

3   Graumann argues that "it cannot at all be part of the "nature" of points to "belong to" other points. Only if a point gains a specific (functional) meaning, whether it be as a part of a pair of points, as the center of a circle, or part of a dotted page or a facial contour, can one speak of "belongingness," namely, of the "encompassing sense-gestalt" (Graumann 1960: 101). Phenomenological analysis produces the opposite conclusion, that a black point on a white piece of paper constitutes itself precisely in such a way that it (1) contrasts itself from its background and (2) intentionally refers to other actual and possible figures near to it, which in some way seem similar to it, and blends with them into a configuration. It belongs to the "essence" of a point to "belong to" a surrounding, independent of whether it gains a sense or function in the eyes of the perceiver. This surrounding differentiates itself (1) as background and (2) as other figures similar and near to it.

4   Normally, the centering object seems to be at rest and the centered object in motion. It has been discovered, however, that the onset of motion sometimes turns the centering or localizing upside down. The distribution of rest and motion, for its part, also appears to be a factor of orientation. However, one ought to research whether such a disturbance of orientation, where one institutes motion, does not just appear in the case of already ambivalent, unstable relations of orientation, in cases where the centering object is only able to maintain its function as zero-point with effort, as opposed to another figure which likewise has centralizing effective qualities. We know in the case of picture-puzzles that often only a minor shift in one's perception will motivate the flipping of the pictures.

5   The orienting function of gestalts reveals itself most vividly through its entire dynamic in the planning and developing of historical cities. According to Bacon (1968: 174ff.) "such a meaningless thing, like the form of a garden," namely that of Tuileries in Paris, is able to motivate the plan of such an imposing structure like the Champs-Elysées.

6   As in the Macquarrie and Robinson translation.

7   Zutt takes his foundational determinations to be the clarification of the pathological phenomenon of heautoscopy.

8   The "positivist" Ernst Mach had such a self-portrait drawn. "*My* lived-body differentiates itself from other human bodies . . . through the fact that it is only seen partially, and especially without a head" (Mach 1906: 15, with sketch).

9   Cf. the Stratton experiments (Merleau-Ponty 1945: 282ff.; Schilder 1950: 106ff.).

10   The tendency toward the optimal attitude is only marginally noticed in the phenomenological literature to date (e.g. Husserl 1966: 22ff.; Merleau-Ponty

1945: 348ff.) and its principal meaning is unfortunately not evaluated at all. Graumann's (1960) investigation of perspectivity completely lacks any such observation. Cf. in addition to this the linguistic arrangement in prototypical experiences (Holenstein 1980: 71ff.).

11   Husserl employs the same formula of "co-presence" or "co-participating with" for the I in relation to intentional acts founding and establishing sense.

12   Existential phenomenology following Husserl overvalues the engagement of the I in perception, as if it were no more than a "struggle for Dasein." Cf. De Waelhens (1951: 192): "Pour la perception réelle, *voir* équivaut à un engagement du corps tout entier et n'a rien d'un jeu." [In real perception, *seeing* is equivalent to an engagement of the lived-body in its entirety, and has nothing in common with a game.] In Merleau-Ponty, the playful character of perception keeps breaking through, in spite of all his emphasis on existential engagement, in their descriptions as a kind of theatre.

13   Likewise Graumann (1960: 84): "We find the fundamental poles of all perspectivity already at the most unfulfilled (!) level of sensible awareness; it is descriptively grounding and functionally ground-giving even before all objective differentiation: a sensually felt I-here facing a sensually felt something-there, a polarity that, descriptively-psychologically, 'accompanies all of my presentations'." The complete citation from Kant would be more appropriate: The polarity "must be able to accompany all of my representations;" it can be actualized in principle, but in no way does it need always to exist or even predominantly exist. This makes a big difference!

14   In a similar way, Sartre distances himself from Husserl's thesis of the presence of the I as a unifying pole in the execution of intentional acts, which is presented from *Ideas I* (1913) onward.

15   Merleau-Ponty (1945: 56, 278, etc.) repeatedly insisted upon this dialectic. A consequence, however, would be an even more radical displacement of the ego in phenomenological psychology, as we find in Merleau-Ponty himself.

16   Cf. Holenstein 1972a: 68ff.

17   Intersubjective experience, however, could be set up in such a way that a person distinguishes him or herself from among the appresented others in the way that he or she sees all things immediately in an optimal view and from their objective center, and thus perceives them objectively in an ideal manner. We cannot get into the foundational problematic of Husserl's teaching on intersubjectivity here, which in its own way is also characterized through an egocentric orientation, i.e., the other is only appresentative before me, experienced according to my self-experience. It will only be noted that, according to psychoanalytic theory, intersubjective experience goes precisely in the opposite direction. That which I perceive from the other in an original and direct way, I can take over and internalize. In psychoanalysis, the fundamental concept of the experience of the other is not appresentation, but rather identification.

References

Bacon, Edmund N. (1968) *Stadtplanung* (Zürich: Artemis).

Binswanger, Ludwig (1932) "Das Raumproblem in der Psychopathologie," *Augeswählte Vorträge und Aufsätze* (Bern: Francke 1955), 174–223.

Bischof, Norbert (1966) "Psychophysik der Raumwahrnehmung, *Handbuch der Psychologie*, 171, ed. by W. Metzger and H. Erke (Göttingen: Verlag für Psychologie), 307–408.

Bollnow, Otto Friedrich (1963) *Mensch und Raum* (Stuttgart: Kohlhammer).

Cassirer, Ernst (1929) *Philosophie der symbolischen Formen* 1 and 3 (Darmstadt: Wissenschaftliche Buchgesellschaft, 1964).

De Waelhens, Alphonse (1951) *Une Philosophie de l'ambiguité* (Leuven: Nauwelaerts, 1967).

Eliade, Mircea (1957) *Das Heilige und das Profane* (Hamburg: Rowohlt).

Graumann, Carl Friedrich (1960) *Grundlagen einer Phänomenologie und Psychologie der Perspektivität* (Berlin: de Gruyter).

Heidegger, Martin (1927) *Sein und Zeit* (Tübingen: Neimeyer, 1957).

Holenstein, Elmar (1972a) *Phänomenologie der Assoziation* (The Hague: Nijhoff).

—— (1972b) "Der Nullpunkt der Orientierung," *Tijdschrift voor Filosofie* 34, 28–78; reprinted in *Menschliches Selbstverständnis*.

—— (1980) *Von der Hintergehbarkeit der Sprache* (Frankfurt: Suhrkamp).

Howard, I. P. and Templeton, W. B. (1966) *Human Spatial Orientation* (London: Wiley).

Husserl, Edmund (1913) *Ideen zu einer reinen Phänomenologie und phänomenologischen Philosophie I: Husserliana* 3, (The Hague: Nijhoff, 1976).

—— (1966) *Analysen zur passiven Synthesis* (1918–26): *Husserliana* 11 (The Hague: Nijhoff).

Jensen, Ad. E. (1947) "Wettkampf-Parteien, Zweiklassen-Systeme und geographische Orientierung," *Studium Generale* 1, 38–48.

Kant, Immaneul (1786) "Was heißt: Sich im Denken orientieren?" *Werke* (Akademie-Textausgabe) VIII (Berlin: de Gruyter, 1968), 131–48.

Kleint, Herbert (1936–40) *Versuche über die Wahrnehmung* (Leipzig: Barth) (Sonderdruck einer siebenteiligen Artikelserie aus der *Zeitschrift für Psychologie* 138 (1936), 149 (1940)).

Köhler, Wolfgang (1917) *Intelligenzprüfungen an Menschenaffen* (Berlin: Springer, 1921).

Linschoten, J. (1952) "Experimentelle Untersuchung der sog. induzierten Bewegung," *Psychologische Forschung* 24, 34–92.

Mach, Ernst (1906) *Die Analyse der Empfindungen* (Jena: Fischer 1911).

Menninger-Lerchenthal, E. (1946) *Der eigene Doppelgänger*, Beiheft zur *Schweizerischen Zeitschrift für Psychologie* 11 (Bern: Huber).

Merleau-Ponty, Maurice (1945) *Phénoménologie de la perception* (Paris: Gallimard); German, *Phänomenologie der Wahrnehmung* (Berlin: de Gruyter 1966).

Osgood, Charles Egerton (1957) *The Measurement of Meaning* (Urbana, University of Illinois Press).

Piaget, Jean (1925) *Le Jugement et le raisonnement chez l'enfant* (Neuchâtel: Delachaux et Niestlé, 1963).

Sartre, Jean-Paul (1943) *L'être et le néant* (Paris: Gallimard); German, *Das Sein und das Nichts* (Hamburg: Rowohlt 1962).

Schilder, Paul (1950) *The Image and Appearance of the Human Body* (New York: International Universities Press).

Straus, Erwin (1930) "Die Formen des Räumlichen," *Psychologie der menschlichen Welt. Gesammelte Schriften* (Berlin: Springer, 1960), 141–78.

—— (1935) *Vom Sinn der Sinne* (Berlin: Springer, 1956).

Zutt, J. (1953) "'Außersichsein' und 'auf sich selbst Zurückblicken' als Ausnahmezustand: Zur Psychopathologie des Raumerlebens," *Gesammelte Aufsätze* (Berlin: Springer, 1963), 342–52.

MARTIN HEIDEGGER

Introduction to *Being and Time*

If the question about Being is to be explicitly formulated and carried through in such a manner as to be completely transparent to itself, then any treatment of it in line with the elucidations we have given requires us to explain how Being is to be looked at, how its meaning is to be understood and conceptually grasped; it requires us to prepare the way for choosing the right entity for our example, and to work out the genuine way of access to it. Looking at something, understanding and conceiving it, choosing, access to it – all these ways of behaving are constitutive for our inquiry, and therefore are modes of Being for those particular entities which we, the inquirers, are ourselves. Thus to work out the question of Being adequately, we must make an entity – the inquirer – transparent in his own Being. The very asking of this question is an entity's mode of *Being*; and as such it gets its essential character from what is inquired about – namely, Being. This entity which each of us is himself and which includes inquiring as one of the possibilities of its Being, we shall denote by the term *"Dasein."*[1] If we are to formulate our question explicitly and transparently, we must first give a proper explication of an entity (Dasein), with regard to its Being. . . .

The ontical priority of the question of Being

Science in general may be defined as the totality established through an interconnection of true propositions.[2] This definition is not complete, nor does it reach the meaning of science. As ways in which man behaves, sciences have the manner of Being which this entity – man himself – possesses. This entity we

From Martin Heidegger, *Selections from Being and Time*, trans. by John Macquarrie and Edward Robinson (New York: Harper and Row, 1962), pp. 26–7, 32–5, 98–9, 101–4, 142–3, 171–7, 186–9, 206–8 denote by the term "*Dasein.*" Scientific research is not the only manner of Being which this entity can have, nor is it the one which lies closest. Moreover, Dasein itself has a special distinctiveness as compared with other entities, and it is worth our while to bring this to view in a provisional way. Here our discussion must anticipate later analyses, in which our results will be authentically exhibited for the first time.

Dasein is an entity which does not just occur among other entities. Rather it is ontically distinguished by the fact that, in its very Being, that Being is an *issue* for it. But in that case, this is a constitutive state of Dasein's Being, and this implies that Dasein, in its Being, has a relationship towards that Being – a relationship which itself is one of Being.[3] And this means further that there is some way in which Dasein understands itself in its Being, and that to some degree it does so explicitly. It is peculiar to this entity that with and through its Being, this Being is disclosed to it. *Understanding of Being is itself a definite characteristic of Dasein's Being.* Dasein is ontically distinctive in that it *is* ontological.[4]

Here "Being-ontological" is not yet tantamount to "developing an ontology." So if we should reserve the term "ontology" for that theoretical inquiry which is explicitly devoted to the meaning of entities, then what we have had in mind in speaking of Dasein's "Being-ontological" is to be designated as something "pre-ontological." It does not signify simply "being-ontical," however, but rather "being in such a way that one has an understanding of Being."

That kind of Being towards which Dasein can comport itself in one way or another, and always does comport itself somehow, we call "*existence*" [*Existenz*]. And because we cannot define Dasein's essence by citing a "what" of the kind that pertains to a subject-matter [eines sachhaltigen Was], and because its essence lies rather in the fact that in each case it has its Being to be, and has it as its own,[5] we have chosen to designate this entity as "Dasein," a term which is purely an expression of its Being [als reiner Seinsausdruck].

Dasein always understands itself in terms of its existence – in terms of a possibility of itself: to be itself or not itself. Dasein has either chosen these possibilities itself, or got itself into them, or grown up in them already. Only the particular Dasein decides its existence, whether it does so by taking hold or by neglecting. The question of existence never gets straightened out except through existing itself. The understanding of oneself which leads *along this way* we call "*existentiell.*"[6] The question of existence is one of Dasein's ontical "affairs." This does not require that the ontological structure of existence should be theoretically transparent. The question about that structure aims at the analysis [Auseinanderlegung] of what constitutes existence. The context [Zusammenhang] of such structures we call "*existentiality.*" Its analytic has the character of an understanding which is not existentiell, but rather *existential*. The task of an existential analytic of Dasein has been delineated in advance, as regards both its possibility and its necessity, in Dasein's ontical constitution.

So far as existence is the determining character of Dasein, the ontological analytic of this entity always requires that existentiality be considered beforehand. By "existentiality" we understand the state of Being that is constitutive for those entities that exist. But in the idea of such a constitutive state of Being, the idea of Being is already included. And thus even the possibility of carrying through the analytic of Dasein depends on working out beforehand the question about the meaning of Being in general.

Sciences are ways of Being in which Dasein comports itself towards entities which it need not be itself. But to Dasein, Being in a world is something that belongs essentially. Thus Dasein's understanding of Being pertains with equal primordiality both to an understanding of something like a "world," and to the understanding of the Being of those entities which become accessible within the world.[7] So whenever an ontology takes for its theme entities whose character of Being is other than that of Dasein, it has its own foundation and motivation in Dasein's own ontical structure, in which a pre-ontological understanding of Being is comprised as a definite characteristic.

Therefore *fundamental ontology*, from which alone all other ontologies can take their rise, must be sought in the *existential analytic of Dasein*.

Dasein accordingly takes priority over all other entities in several ways. The first priority is an *ontical* one: Dasein is an entity whose Being has the determinate character of existence. The second priority is an *ontological* one: Dasein is in itself "ontological," because existence is thus determinative for it. But with equal primordiality Dasein also possesses – as constitutive for its understanding of existence – an understanding of the Being of all entities of a character other than its own. Dasein has therefore a third priority as providing the ontico-ontological condition for the possibility of any ontologies. Thus Dasein has turned out to be, more than any other entity, the one which must first be interrogated ontologically. . . .

If to Interpret the meaning of Being becomes our task, Dasein is not only the primary entity to be interrogated; it is also that entity which already comports itself, in its Being, towards what we are asking about when we ask this question. But in that case the question of Being is nothing other than the radicalization of an essential tendency-of-Being which belongs to Dasein itself – the pre-ontological understanding of Being.

Equipment, Action, and the World

Equipment can genuinely show itself only in dealings cut to its own measure (hammering with a hammer, for example); but in such dealings an entity of this kind is not *grasped* thematically as an occurring Thing, nor is the equipment-structure known as such even in the using. The hammering does not simply have knowledge about [um] the hammer's character as equipment, but it has appropriated this equipment in a way which could not possibly be more suitable. In dealings such as this, where something is put to use, our concern subordinates itself to the "in-order-to" which is constitutive for the equipment we are employing at the time; the less we just stare at the hammer-Thing, and the more we seize hold of it and use it, the more primordial does our relationship to it become, and the more unveiledly is it encountered as that which it is – as equipment. The hammering itself uncovers the specific "manipulability" ["Handlichkeit"] of the hammer. The kind of Being which equipment possesses – in which it manifests itself in its own right – we call *"readiness-to-hand"* [*Zuhandenheit*].[8] Only because equipment has *this* "Being-in-itself" and does not merely occur, is it manipulable in the broadest sense and at our disposal. No matter how sharply we just *look* [Nur-noch-*hinsehen*] at the "outward appearance" ["Aussehen"] of Things in whatever form this takes, we cannot discover anything ready-to-hand. If we look at Things just "theoretically," we can get along without understanding readiness-to-hand. But when we deal with them by using them and manipulating them, this activity is not a blind one; it has its own kind of sight, by which our manipulation is guided and from which it acquires its specific Thingly character. Dealings with equipment subordinate themselves to the manifold assignments of the "in-order-to." And the sight with which they thus accommodate themselves is *circumspection*.[9]

"Practical" behaviour is not "atheoretical" in the sense of "sightlessness."[10] The way it differs from theoretical behaviour does not lie simply in the fact that in theoretical behaviour one observes, while in practical behaviour one *acts* [*gehandelt* wird], and that action must employ theoretical cognition if it is not to remain blind; for the fact that observation is a kind of concern is just as primordial as the fact that action has *its own* kind of sight. Theoretical behaviour is just looking, without circumspection. But the fact that this looking is non-circumspective does not mean that it follows no rules: it constructs a canon for itself in the form of *method*.

The ready-to-hand is not grasped theoretically at all, nor is it itself the sort of thing that circumspection takes proximally as a circumspective theme. The peculiarity of what is proximally ready-to-hand is that, in its readiness-to-hand, it must, as it were, withdraw [zurückzuziehen] in order to be ready-to-hand quite authentically. That with which our everyday dealings proximally dwell is not the tools themselves [die Werkzeuge selbst]. On the contrary, that with which we concern ourselves primarily is the work – that which is to be produced at the time; and this is accordingly ready-to-hand too. The work bears with it that referential totality within which the equipment is encountered.[11]

The work to be produced, as the *"towards-which"* of such things as the hammer, the plane, and the needle, likewise has the kind of Being that belongs to equipment. The shoe which is to be produced is for wearing (footgear) [Schuhzeug]; the clock is manufactured for telling the time. The work which we chiefly encounter in our concernful dealings – the work that is to be found when one is "at work" on something [das in Arbeit befindliche] – has a usability which belongs to it essentially; in this usability it lets us encounter already the "towards-which" for which *it* is usable. A work that someone has ordered [das bestellte Werk] is only by reason of its use and the assignment-context of entities which is discovered in using it. . . .

Our concernful absorption in whatever work-world lies closest to us, has a function of discovering; and it is essential to this function that, depending upon the way in which we are absorbed, those entities within-the-world which are brought along [beigebrachte] in the work and with it (that is to say, in the assignments or references which are constitutive for it) remain discoverable in varying degrees of explicitness and with a varying circumspective penetration.

The kind of Being which belongs to these entities is readiness-to-hand. But this characteristic is not to be understood as merely a way of taking them, as if we were taking such "aspects" into the "entities" which we proximally en-counter, or as if some world-stuff which is proximally present-at-hand in itself[12] were "given subjective colouring" in this way. Such an Interpretation would overlook the fact that in this case these entities would have to be understood and discovered beforehand as something purely present-at-hand, and must have priority and take the lead in the sequence of those dealings with the "world" in which something is discovered and made one's own. But this already runs counter to the ontological meaning of cognition, which we have exhibited as a *founded* mode of Being-in-the-world. To lay bare what is just present-at-hand and no more, cognition must first penetrate *beyond* what is ready-to-hand in our concern. *Readiness-to-hand is the way in which entities as they are "in themselves" are defined ontologico-categorially.* Yet only by reason of something present-at-hand, "is there" anything ready-to-hand. Does it follow, however, granting this thesis for the nonce, that readiness-to-hand is ontologically founded upon presence-at-hand?. . .

How the worldly character of the environment announces itself in entities within-the-world[13]

The world itself is not an entity within-the-world; and yet it is so determinative for such entities that only in so far as "there is" a world can they be encountered and show themselves, in their Being, as entities which have been discovered. But in what way "is there" a world? If Dasein is ontically constituted by Being-in-the-World, and if an understanding of the Being of its Self belongs just as essentially to its Being, no matter how indefinite that understanding may be, then does not Dasein have an understanding of the world – a pre-ontological understanding, which indeed can and does get along without explicit ontolog-ical insights? With those entities which are encountered within-the-world – that is to say, with their character as within-the-world – does not something like the world show itself for concernful Being-in-the-world? Do we not have a pre-phenomenological glimpse of this phenomenon? Do we not always have such a glimpse of it, without having to take it as a theme for ontological Interpretation? Has Dasein itself, in the range of its concernful absorption in equipment ready-to-hand, a possibility of Being in which the worldhood of those entities within-the-world with which it is concerned is, in a certain way, lit up for it, *along with* those entities themselves?

If such possibilities of Being for Dasein can be exhibited within its concernful dealings, then the way lies open for studying the phenomenon which is thus lit up, and for attempting to "hold it at bay", as it were, and to interrogate it as to those structures which show themselves therein.

To the everydayness of Being-in-the-world there belong certain modes of concern. These permit the entities with which we concern ourselves to be encountered in such a way that the worldly character of what is within-the-world comes to the fore. When we concern ourselves with something, the entities which are most closely ready-to-hand may be met as something un-usable, not properly adapted for the use we have decided upon. The tool turns out to be damaged, or the material unsuitable. In each of these cases *equipment* is here, ready-to-hand. We discover its unusability, however, not by looking at it and establishing its properties, but rather by the circumspection of the dealings in which we use it. When its unusability is thus discovered, equipment becomes conspicuous. This *conspicuousness* presents the ready-to-hand equipment as in a certain un-readiness-to-hand. But this implies that what cannot be used just lies there; it shows itself as an equipmental Thing which looks so and so, and which, in its readiness-to-hand as looking that way, has constantly been present-at-hand too. Pure presence-at-hand announces itself in such equipment, but only to withdraw to the readiness-to-hand of something with which one concerns oneself – that is to say, of the sort of thing we find when we put it back into repair. This presence-at-hand of something that cannot be used is still not devoid of all readiness-to-hand whatsoever; equipment which is present-at-hand *in this way* is still not just a Thing which occurs somewhere. The damage to the equipment is still not a mere alteration of a Thing – not a change of properties which just occurs in something present-at-hand.

In our concernful dealings, however, we not only come up against unusable things *within* what is ready-to-hand already: we also find things which are missing – which not only are not "handy" ["handlich"] but are not "to hand" ["zur Hand"] at all. Again, to miss something in this way amounts to coming across something un-ready-to-hand. When we notice what is un-ready-to-hand, that which is ready-to-hand enters the mode of *obtrusiveness*. The more urgently [Je dringlicher] we need what is missing, and the more authentically it is encountered in its un-readiness-to-hand, all the more obtrusive [um so aufdringlicher] does that which is ready-to-hand become – so much so, indeed, that it seems to lose its character of readiness-to-hand. It reveals itself as something just present-at-hand and no more, which cannot be budged without the thing that is missing. The helpless way in which we stand before it is a deficient mode of concern, and as such it uncovers the Being-just-present-at-hand-and-no-more of something ready-to-hand.

In our dealings with the world[14] of our concern, the un-ready-to-hand can be encountered not only in the sense of that which is unusable or simply missing, but as something un-ready-to-hand which is *not* missing at all and *not* unusable, but which "stands in the way" of our concern. That to which our concern refuses to turn, that for which it has "no time", is something *un*-ready-to-hand in the manner of what does not belong here, of what has not as yet been attended to. Anything which is un-ready-to-hand in this way is disturbing to us, and enables us to see the *obstinacy* of that with which we must concern ourselves in the first instance before we do anything else. With this obstinacy, the presence-at-hand of the ready-to-hand makes itself known in a new way as the Being of that which still lies before us and calls for our attending to it.[15]

The modes of conspicuousness, obtrusiveness, and obstinacy all have the function of bringing to the fore the characteristic of presence-at-hand in what is ready-to-hand. But the ready-to-hand is not thereby just *observed* and stared at as something present-at-hand; the presence-at-hand which makes itself known is still bound up in the readiness-to-hand of equipment. Such equipment still does not veil itself in the guise of mere Things. It becomes "equipment" in the sense of something which one would like to shove out of the way.[16] But in such a Tendency to shove things aside, the ready-to-hand shows itself as still ready-to-hand in its unswerving presence-at-hand. . . .

If Dasein, in its concern, brings something close by, this does not signify that it fixes something at a spatial position with a minimal distance from some point of the body. When something is close by, this means that it is within the range of what is proximally ready-to-hand for circumspection. Bringing-close is not oriented towards the I-Thing encumbered with a body, but towards concernful Being-in-the-world – that is, towards whatever is proximally encountered in such Being. It follows, moreover, that Dasein's spatiality is not to be defined by citing the position at which some corporeal Thing is present-at-hand. Of course we say that even Dasein always occupies a place. But this "occupying" must be distinguished in principle from Being-ready-to-hand at a place in some particular region. Occupying a place must be conceived as a de-severing of the environmentally ready-to-hand into a region which has been circumspectively discovered in advance. Dasein understands its "here" [Hier] in terms of its environmental "yonder." The "here" does not mean the "where" of something present-at-hand, but rather the "whereat" [Wobei] of a de-severant Being-alongside, together with this de-severance. Dasein, in accordance with its spatiality, is proximally never here but yonder; from this "yonder" it comes back to its "here;" and it comes back to its "here" only in the way in which it interprets its concernful Being-towards in terms of what is ready-to-hand yonder. This becomes quite plain if we consider a certain phenomenal pecu-liarity of the de-severance structure of Being-in.

As Being-in-the-world, Dasein maintains itself essentially in a de-severing. This de-severance – the farness of the ready-to-hand from Dasein itself – is something that Dasein can *never cross over*. Of course the remoteness of some-thing ready-to-hand from Dasein can show up as a distance from it,[17] if this remoteness is determined by a relation to some Thing which gets thought of as present-at-hand at the place Dasein has formerly occupied. Dasein can sub-sequently traverse the "between" of this distance, but only in such a way that the distance itself becomes one which has been deseveed. So little has Dasein crossed over its de-severance that it has rather taken it along with it and keeps doing so constantly; for *Dasein is essentially de-severance – that is, it is spatial*. It cannot wander about within the current range of its de-severances; it can never do more than change them. Dasein is spatial in that it discovers space circum-spectively, so that indeed it constantly comports itself de-severantly towards the entities thus spatially encountered.

As de-severant Being-in, Dasein has likewise the character of *directionality*. Every bringing-close [Näherung] has already taken in advance a direction towards a region out of which what is de-severed brings itself close [sich nähert], so that one can come across it with regard to its place. Circumspective concern is de-severing which gives directionality. In this concern – that is, in the Being-in-the-world of Dasein itself – a supply of "signs" is presented. Signs, as equipment, take over the giving of directions in a way which is explicit and easily manipulable. They keep explicitly open those regions which have been used circumspectively – the particular "whithers" to which something belongs or goes, or gets brought or fetched. If Dasein *is*, it already has, as directing and de-severing, its own discovered region. Both directionality and de-severance, as modes of Being-in-the-world, are guided beforehand *by the circumspection* of concern.

Out of this directionality arise the fixed directions of right and left. Dasein constantly takes these directions along with it, just as it does its de-severances. Dasein's spatialization in its "bodily nature" is likewise marked out in accord-ance with these directions. (This "bodily nature" hides a whole problematic of its own, though we shall not treat it here.) Thus things which are ready-to-hand and used for the body – like gloves, for example, which are to move with the hands – must be given directionality towards right and left. A craftsman's tools, however, which are held in the hand and are moved with it, do not share the hand's specifically "manual" ["handliche"] movements. So although hammers are handled just as much with the hand as gloves are, there are no right-or left-handed hammers.

One must notice, however, that the directionality which belongs to deseverance is founded upon Being-in-the-world. Left and right are not something "subjective" for which the subject has a feeling; they are directions of one's directedness into a world that is ready-to-hand already. "By the mere feeling of a difference between my two sides" I could never find my way about in a world. The subject with a "mere feeling" of this difference is a construct posited in disregard of the state that is truly constitutive for any subject – namely, that whenever Dasein has such a "mere feeling," it is in a world already *and must be* in it to be able to orient itself at all. . . .

Dasein as Affective Responsiveness and as Understanding

In *understanding* and *state-of-mind*, we shall see the two constitutive ways of being the "there;" and these are equiprimordial. If these are to be analysed, some phenomenal confirmation is necessary; in both cases this will be attained by Interpreting some concrete mode which is important for the subsequent problematic. State-of-mind and understanding are characterized equiprimordially by *discourse*. . . .

The analysis of the characteristics of the Being of Being-there is an existential one. This means that the characteristics are not properties of something present-at-hand, but essentially existential ways to be. We must therefore set forth their kind of Being in everydayness.

Seeing and Sight

What we indicate *ontologically* by the term "state-of-mind"[18] [Befindlichkeit, or affective responsiveness] is *ontically* the most familiar and everyday sort of thing; our mood, our Being-attuned.[19] Prior to all psychology of moods, a field which in any case still lies fallow, it is necessary to see this phenomenon as a fundamental *existentiale*, and to outline its structure.

Both the undisturbed equanimity and the inhibited ill-humour of our everyday concern, the way we slip over from one to the other, or slip off into bad moods, are by no means nothing ontologically,[20] even if these phenomena are left unheeded as supposedly the most indifferent and fleeting in Dasein. The fact that moods can deteriorate [verdorben werden] and change over means simply that in every case Dasein always has some mood [gestimmt ist]. The pallid, evenly balanced lack of mood [Ungestimmtheit], which is often persistent and which is not to be mistaken for a bad mood, is far from nothing at all. Rather, it is in this that Dasein becomes satiated with itself. Being has become manifest as a burden. Why that should be, one does not *know*. And Dasein cannot know anything of the sort because the possibilities of disclosure which belong to cognition reach far too short a way compared with the primordial disclosure belonging to moods, in which Dasein is brought before its Being as "there." Furthermore, a mood of elation can alleviate the manifest burden of Being; that such a mood is possible also discloses the burdensome character of Dasein, even while it alleviates the burden. A mood makes manifest "how one is, and how one is faring" ["wie einem ist und wird"]. In this "how one is," having a mood brings Being to its "there."

In having a mood, Dasein is always disclosed moodwise as that entity to which it has been delivered over in its Being; and in this way it has been delivered over to the Being which, in existing, it has to be. "To be disclosed" does not mean "to be known as this sort of thing." And even in the most indifferent and inoffensive everydayness the Being of Dasein can burst forth as a naked "that it is and has to be" [als nacktes "Dass es es ist und zu sein hat"]. The pure "that it is" shows itself, but the "whence" and the "whither" remain in darkness. The fact that it is just as everyday a matter for Dasein not to "give in" ["nachgibt"] to such moods – in other words, not to follow up [nachgeht] their disclosure and allow itself to be brought before that which is disclosed – is no evidence *against* the phenomenal facts of the case, in which the Being of the "there" is disclosed moodwise in its "that-it-is;"[21] it is rather evidence for it. In an *ontico*-existentiell sense, Dasein for the most part evades the Being which is disclosed in the mood. In an *ontologico*-existential sense, this means that even in that to which such a mood pays no attention, Dasein is unveiled in its Being-delivered-over to the "there." In the evasion itself the "there" *is* something disclosed.

This characteristic of Dasein's Being – this "that it is" – is veiled in its "whence" and "whither," yet disclosed in itself all the more unveiledly; we call it the "*thrownness*"[22] of this entity into its "there"; indeed, it is thrown in such a way that, as Being-in-the-world, it is the "there."...

An entity of the character of Dasein is its "there" in such a way that, whether explicitly or not, it finds itself [sich befindet] in its thrownness. In a state-of-mind Dasein is always brought before itself, and has always found itself, not in the sense of coming across itself by perceiving itself, but in the sense of finding itself in the mood that it has.[23] As an entity which has been delivered over to its Being, it remains also delivered over to the fact that it must always have found itself – but found itself in a way of finding which arises not so much from a direct seeking as rather from a fleeing. The way in which the mood discloses is not one in which we look at thrownness, but one in which we turn towards or turn away [An-und Abkehr]. For the most part the mood does not turn towards the burdensome character of Dasein which is manifest in it, and least of all does it do so in the mood of elation when this burden has been alleviated. It is always by way of a state-of-mind that this turning-away is what it is.

Phenomenally, we would wholly fail to recognize both *what* mood discloses and *how* it discloses, if that which is disclosed were to be compared with what Dasein is acquainted with, knows, and believes "at the same time" when it has such a mood. Even if Dasein is "assured" in its belief about its "whither," or if, in rational enlightenment, it supposes itself to know about its "whence," all this counts for nothing as against the phenomenal facts of the case: for the mood brings Dasein before the "that-it-is" of its "there," which, as such, stares it in the face with the inexorability of an enigma.[24] From the existential-ontological point of view, there is not the slightest justification for minimizing what is "evident" in states-of-mind, by measuring it against the apodictic certainty of a theoretical cognition of something which is purely present-at-hand. However the phenomena are no less falsified when they are banished to the sanctuary of the irrational. When irrationalism, as the counterplay of rationalism, talks about the things to which rationalism is blind, it does so only with a squint.

Factically, Dasein can, should, and must, through knowledge and will, become master of its moods; in certain possible ways of existing, this may signify a priority of volition and cognition. Only we must not be misled by this into denying that ontologically mood is a primordial kind of Being for Dasein, in which Dasein is disclosed to itself *prior to* all cognition and volition, and *beyond* their range of disclosure. And furthermore, when we master a mood, we do so by way of a counter-mood; we are never free of moods. Ontologically, we thus obtain as the *first* essential characteristic of states-of-mind that *they disclose Dasein in its thrownness, and – proximally and for the most part – in the manner of an evasive turning-away.*

From what has been said we can see already that a state-of-mind is very remote from anything like coming across a psychical condition by the kind of apprehending which first turns round and then back. Indeed it is so far from this, that only because the "there" has already been disclosed in a state-of-mind can immanent reflection come across "Experiences" at all. The "bare mood" discloses the "there" more primordially, but correspondingly it *closes* it *off* more stubbornly than any *not*-perceiving.

This is shown by *bad moods*. In these, Dasein becomes blind to itself, the environment with which it is concerned veils itself, the circumspection of concern gets led astray. States-of-mind are so far from being reflected upon, that precisely what they do is to assail Dasein in its unreflecting devotion to the "world" with which it is concerned and on which it expends itself. A mood assails us. It comes neither from "outside" nor from "inside," but arises out of Being-in-the-world, as a way of such Being. But with the negative distinction between state-of-mind and the reflective apprehending of something "within," we have thus reached a positive insight into their character as disclosure. *The mood has already disclosed, in every case, Being-in-the-world as a whole, and makes it possible first of all to direct oneself towards something.* Having a mood is not related to the psychical in the first instance, and is not itself an inner condition which then reaches forth in an enigmatical way and puts its mark on Things and persons. It is in this that the *second* essential characteristic of states-of-mind shows itself. We have seen that the world, Dasein-with, and existence are *equiprimordially disclosed*; and state-of-mind is a basic existential species of their disclosedness, because this disclosedness itself is essentially Being-in-the-world.[25]

Besides these two essential characteristics of states-of-mind which have been explained – the disclosing of thrownness and the current disclosing of Being-in-the-world as a whole – we have to notice a *third*, which contributes above all towards a more penetrating understanding of the worldhood of the world. As we have said earlier, the world which has already been disclosed beforehand permits what is within-the-world to be encountered. This prior disclosedness of the world belongs to Being-in and is partly constituted by one's state-of-mind. Letting something be encountered is primarily *circumspective*; it is not just sensing something, or staring at it. It implies circumspective concern, and has the character of becoming affected in some way [Betroffenwerdens]; we can see this more precisely from the standpoint of state-of-mind. But to be affected by the unserviceable, resistant, or threatening character [Bedrohlichkeit] of that which is ready-to-hand, becomes ontologically possible only in so far as Being-in as such has been determined existentially beforehand in such a manner that what it encounters within-the-world can "*matter*" to it in this way. The fact that this sort of thing can "matter" to it is grounded in one's state-of-mind; and as a state-of-mind it has already disclosed the world – as something by which it can be threatened, for instance.[26] Only something which is in the state-of-mind of fearing (or fearlessness) can discover that what is environmentally ready-to-hand is threatening. Dasein's openness to the world is constituted existentially by the attunement of a state-of-mind.

And only because the "senses" [die "Sinne"] belong ontologically to an entity whose kind of Being is Being-in-the-world with a state-of mind,[27] can they be "touched" by anything or "have a sense for" ["Sinn haben für"] something in such a way that what touches them shows itself in an affect.[28] Under the strongest pressure and resistance, nothing like an affect would come about, and the resistance itself would remain essentially undiscovered, if Being-in-the-world, with its state-of-mind, had not already submitted itself [sich schon angewiesen] to having entities within-the-world "matter" to it in a way which its moods have outlined in advance. *Existentially, a state-of-mind implies a disclosive submission to the world, out of which we can encounter something that matters to us.* Indeed *from the ontological point of view* we must as a general principle leave the primary discovery of the world to "bare mood." Pure beholding, even if it were to penetrate to the innermost core of the Being of something present-at-hand, could never discover anything like that which is threatening.

The fact that, even though states-of-mind are primarily disclosive, everyday circumspection goes wrong and to a large extent succumbs to delusion because of them, is a μὴ ὄν [non-being] when measured against the idea of knowing the "world" absolutely. But if we make evaluations which are so unjustified onto-logically, we shall completely fail to recognize the existentially positive character of the capacity for delusion. It is precisely when we see the "world" unsteadily and fitfully in accordance with our moods, that the ready-to-hand shows itself in its specific worldhood, which is never the same from day to day. By looking at the world theoretically, we have already dimmed it down to the uniformity of what is purely present-at-hand, though admittedly this uniformity comprises a new abundance of things which can be discovered by simply characterizing them. Yet even the purest θεωρία [theory] has not left all moods behind it; even when we look theoretically at what is just present-at-hand, it does not show itself purely as it looks unless this θεωρία lets it come towards us in a *tranquil* tarrying alongside ..., in ραστώνη and διαγωγή. Any cognitive determining has its existential-ontological Constitution in the state-of-mind of Being-in-the-world; but pointing this out is not to be confused with attempting to surrender science ontically to "feeling." ...

Projection always pertains to the full disclosedness of Being-in-the-world; as potentiality-for-Being, understanding has itself possibilities, which are sketched out beforehand within the range of what is essentially disclosable in it. Under-standing *can* devote itself primarily to the disclosedness of the world; that is, Dasein can, proximally and for the most part, understand itself in terms of its world. Or else understanding throws itself primarily into the "for-the-sake-of-which;" that is, Dasein exists as itself. Understanding is either authentic, arising out of one's own Self as such, or inauthentic. The "in-" of "inauthentic" does not mean that Dasein cuts itself off from its Self and understands "only" the world. The world belongs to Being-one's-Self as Being-in-the-world. On the other hand, authentic understanding, no less than that which is inauthentic, *can* be either genuine or not genuine. As potentiality-for-Being, understanding is altogether permeated with possibility. When one is diverted into [Sichverlegen in] one of these basic possibilities of understanding, the other is not laid aside [legt ... nicht ab]. *Because understanding, in every case, pertains rather to Dasein's full disclosedness as Being-in-the-world, this diversion of the understanding is an existential modification of projection as a whole.* In understanding the world, Being-in is always understood along with it, while understanding of existence as such is always an understanding of the world.

As factical Dasein, any Dasein has already diverted its potentiality-for-Being into a possibility of understanding.

In its projective character, understanding goes to make up existentially what we call Dasein's "*sight*" [*Sicht*]. With the disclosedness of the "there," this sight is existentially [existenzial seiende]; and Dasein *is* this sight equiprimordially in each of those basic ways of its Being which we have already noted: as the circumspection [Umsicht] of concern, as the considerateness [Rücksicht] of solicitude, and as that sight which is directed upon Being as such [Sicht auf das Sein als solches], for the sake of which any Dasein is as it is. The sight which is related primarily and on the whole to existence we call "*transparency*" [*Durchsichtigkeit*]. We choose this term to designate "knowledge of the Self"[29] in a sense which is well understood, so as to indicate that here it is not a matter of perceptually tracking down and inspecting a point called the "Self," but rather one of seizing upon the full disclosedness of Being-in-the-world *throughout all* the constitutive items which are essential to it, and doing so with understanding. In existing, entities sight "themselves" [sichtet "sich"] only in so far as they have become transparent to themselves with equal primordiality in those items which are constitutive for their existence: their Being-alongside the world and their Being-with Others.

On the other hand, Dasein's opaqueness [Undurchsichtigkeit] is not rooted primarily and solely in "egocentric" self-deceptions; it is rooted just as much in lack of acquaintance with the world.

We must, to be sure, guard against a misunderstanding of the expression "sight." It corresponds to the "clearedness" [Gelichtetheit] which we took as characterizing the disclosedness of the "there." "Seeing" does not mean just perceiving with the bodily eyes, but neither does it mean pure non-sensory awareness of something present-at-hand in its presence-at-hand. In giving an existential signification to "sight," we have merely drawn upon the peculiar feature of seeing, that it lets entities which are accessible to it be encountered unconcealedly in themselves. Of course, every "sense" does this within that domain of discovery which is genuinely its own. But from the beginning onwards the tradition of philosophy has been oriented primarily towards "seeing" as a way of access to entities *and to Being*. To keep the connection with this tradition, we may formalize "sight" and "seeing" enough to obtain therewith a universal term for characterizing any access to entities or to Being, as access in general.

By showing how all sight is grounded primarily in understanding (the circumspection of concern is understanding as *common sense* [*Verständigkeit*]), we have deprived pure intuition [Anschauen] of its priority, which corresponds noetically to the priority of the present-at-hand in traditional ontology. "Intuition" and "thinking" are both derivatives of understanding, and already rather remote ones. Even the phenomenological "intuition of essences" ["Wesensschau"] is grounded in existential understanding. We can decide about this kind of seeing only if we have obtained explicit conceptions of

Being and of the structure of Being, such as only phenomena in the phenomenological sense can become. . . .

Understanding and interpretation[30]

As understanding, Dasein projects its Being upon possibilities. This *Being-towards-possibilities* which understands is itself a potentiality-for-Being, and it is so because of the way these possibilities, as disclosed, exert their counter-thrust [Rückschlag] upon Dasein. The projecting of the understanding has its own possibility – that of developing itself [sich auszubilden]. This development of the understanding we call "interpretation."[31] In it the understanding appropriates understandingly that which is understood by it. In interpretation, understanding does not become something different. It becomes itself. Such interpretation is grounded existentially in understanding; the latter does not arise from the former. Nor is interpretation the acquiring of information about what is understood; it is rather the working-out of possibilities projected in understanding. In accordance with the trend of these preparatory analyses of everyday Dasein, we shall pursue the phenomenon of interpretation in understanding the world – that is, in inauthentic understanding, and indeed in the mode of its genuineness.

In terms of the significance which is disclosed in understanding the world, concernful Being-alongside the ready-to-hand gives itself to understand what-ever involvement that which is encountered can have.[32] To say that "circum-spection discovers" means that the "world" which has already been understood comes to be interpreted. The ready-to-hand comes *explicitly* into the sight which understands. All preparing, putting to rights, repairing, improving, rounding-out, are accomplished in the following way: we take apart[33] in its "in-order-to" that which is circumspectively ready-to-hand, and we concern ourselves with it in accordance with what becomes visible through this process. That which has been circumspectively taken apart with regard to its "in-order-to," and taken apart as such – that which is *explicitly* understood – has the structure of *something as something*. The circumspective question as to what this particular thing that is ready-to-hand may be, receives the circumspectively interpretative answer that it is for such and such a purpose [es ist zum . . .]. If we tell what it is for [des Wozu], we are not simply designating something; but that which is designated is understood *as* that *as* which we are to take the thing in question. That which is disclosed in understanding – that which is understood – is already accessible in such a way that its "as which" can be made to stand out explicitly. The "as" makes up the structure of the explicitness of something that is understood. It constitutes the interpretation. In dealing with what is envir-onmentally ready-to-hand by interpreting it circumspectively, we "see" it *as* a table, a door, a carriage, or a bridge; but what we have thus interpreted

[Ausgelegte] need not necessarily be also taken apart [auseinander zu legen] by making an assertion which definitely characterizes it. Any mere pre-predicative seeing of the ready-to-hand is, in itself, something which already understands and interprets. But does not the absence of such an "as" make up the mereness of any pure perception of something? Whenever we see with this kind of sight, we already do so understandingly and interpretatively. In the mere encountering of something, it is understood in terms of a totality of involvements; and such seeing hides in itself the explicitness of the assignment-relations (of the "in-order-to") which belong to that totality.

Hearing, Discourse, and the Call of Care

We can make clear the connection of discourse with understanding and intelligibility by considering an existential possibility which belongs to talking itself – hearing. If we have not heard "aright," it is not by accident that we say we have not "understood." Hearing is constitutive for discourse. And just as linguistic utterance is based on discourse, so is acoustic perception on hearing. Listening to ... is Dasein's existential way of Being-open as Being-with for Others. Indeed, hearing constitutes the primary and authentic way in which Dasein is open for its ownmost potentiality-for-Being – as in hearing the voice of the friend whom every Dasein carries with it. Dasein hears, because it understands. As a Being-in-the-world with Others, a Being which understands, Dasein is "in thrall" to Dasein-with and to itself; and in this thraldom it "belongs" to these.[34] Being-with develops in listening to one another [Aufeinander-hören], which can be done in several possible ways: following,[35] going along with, and the privative modes of not-hearing, resisting, defying, and turning away.

It is on the basis of this potentiality for hearing, which is existentially primary, that anything like *hearkening* [*Horchen*] becomes possible. Hearkening is phenomenally still more primordial than what is defined "in the first instance" as "hearing" in psychology – the sensing of tones and the perception of sounds. Hearkening too has the kind of Being of the hearing which understands. What we "first" hear is never noises or complexes of sounds, but the creaking waggon, the motor-cycle. We hear the column on the march, the north wind, the woodpecker tapping, the fire crackling.

It requires a very artificial and complicated frame of mind to "hear" a "pure noise." The fact that motor-cycles and waggons are what we proximally hear is the phenomenal evidence that in every case Dasein, as Being-in-the-world, already dwells *alongside* what is ready-to-hand within-the-world; it certainly does not dwell proximally alongside "sensations;" nor would it first have to give shape to the swirl of sensations to provide the springboard from which the subject leaps off and finally arrives at a "world." Dasein, as essentially under-standing, is proximally alongside what is understood.

Likewise, when we are explicitly hearing the discourse of another, we proximally understand what is said, or – to put it more exactly – we are already with him, in advance, alongside the entity which the discourse is about. On the other hand, what we proximally hear is *not* what is expressed in the utterance. Even in cases where the speech is indistinct or in a foreign language, what we proximally hear is *unintelligible* words, and not a multiplicity of tone-data.[36]

Admittedly, when what the discourse is about is heard "naturally," we can at the same time hear the "diction," the way in which it is said [die Weise des Gesagtseins], but only if there is some co-understanding beforehand of what is said-in-the-talk; for only so is there a possibility of estimating whether the way in which it is said is appropriate to what the discourse is about thematically.

In the same way, any answering counter-discourse arises proximally and directly from understanding what the discourse is about, which is already "shared" in Being-with.

Only where talking and hearing are existentially possible, can anyone hear-ken. The person who "cannot hear" and "must feel"[37] may perhaps be one who is able to hearken very well, and precisely because of this. Just hearing some-thing "all around" [Das Nur-herum-hören] is a privation of the hearing which understands. Both talking and hearing are based upon understanding. And understanding arises neither through talking at length [vieles Reden] nor through busily hearing something "all around." Only he who already under-stands can listen [zuhören].

Hands

We are here attempting to learn thinking. . . .

A cabinetmaker's apprentice, someone who is learning to build cabinets and the like, will serve as an example. His learning is not mere practice, to gain facility in the use of tools. Nor does he merely gather knowledge about the customary forms of the things he is to build. If he is to become a true cabinet-maker, he makes himself answer and respond above all to the different kinds of wood and to the shapes slumbering within wood – to wood as it enters into man's dwelling with all the hidden riches of its nature. In fact, this relatedness to wood is what maintains the whole craft. Without that relatedness, the craft will never be anything but empty busywork, any occupation with it will be deter-mined exclusively by business concerns. Every handicraft, all human dealings are

From Martin Heidegger, *What is Called Thinking?*, intro. by J. Glenn Gray (New York: Harper and Row, 1968), pp. 14.6–16, 23–5, and *Parmenides*, trans. by André Schuwer and Richard Rojcewicz (Bloomington, Indiana: Indiana University Press, 1992), pp. 80–1, 84–5 constantly in that danger. The writing of poetry is no more exempt from it than is thinking.

Whether or not a cabinetmaker's apprentice, while he is learning, will come to respond to wood and wooden things, depends obviously on the presence of some teacher who can make the apprentice comprehend. . . .

We are trying to learn thinking. Perhaps thinking, too, is just something like building a cabinet. At any rate, it is a craft, a "handicraft." "Craft" literally means the strength and skill in our hands. The hand is a peculiar thing. In the common view, the hand is part of our bodily organism. But the hand's essence can never be determined, or explained, by its being an organ which can grasp. Apes, too, have organs that can grasp, but they do not have hands. The hand is infinitely different from all grasping organs – paws, claws, or fangs – different by an abyss of essence. Only a being who can speak, that is, think, can have hands and can be handy in achieving works of handicraft.

But the craft of the hand is richer than we commonly imagine. The hand does not only grasp and catch, or push and pull. The hand reaches and extends, receives and welcomes – and not just things: the hand extends itself, and receives its own welcome in the hands of others. The hand holds. The hand carries. The hand designs and signs, presumably because man is a sign. Two hands fold into one, a gesture meant to carry man into the great oneness. The hand is all this, and this is the true handicraft. Everything is rooted here that is commonly known as handicraft, and commonly we go no further. But the hand's gestures run everywhere through language, in their most perfect purity precisely when man speaks by being silent. And only when man speaks, does he think – not the other way around, as metaphysics still believes. Every motion of the hand in every one of its works carries itself through the element of thinking, every bearing of the hand bears itself in that element. All the work of the hand is rooted in thinking. . . . We have called thinking the handicraft *par excellence*.

Thinking guides and sustains every gesture of the hand.

We were talking about the cabinetmaker's craft. It could be objected that even the village cabinetmaker works with machines nowadays. It could be pointed out that today gigantic industrial factories have risen alongside the craftsmen's workshops, and have in fact been there for quite some time. Inside the factories, working men pull the same lever day and night for eight to ten hours at a stretch, and working women push the same button. The point is correct. But in this case, and in this form, it has not yet been thought out. The objection falls flat, because it has heard only half of what the discussion has to say about handicraft. We chose the cabinetmaker's craft as our example, assuming it would not occur to anybody that this choice indicated any expectation that the state of our planet could in the foreseeable future, or indeed ever, be changed back into a rustic idyll. The cabinetmaker's craft was proposed as an example for our thinking because the common usage of the word "craft" is restricted to human activities of that sort. However – it was specifically noted that what maintains and sustains even this handicraft is not the mere manipulation of tools, but the relatedness to wood. But where in the manipulations of the industrial worker is there any relatedness to such things as the shapes slumbering within wood? This is the question you were meant to run up against, though not to stop there. For as long as we raise questions only in this way, we are still questioning from the standpoint of the familiar and previously customary handicraft. . . .

Our age is not a technological age because it is the age of the machine; it is an age of the machine because it is the technological age. But so long as the essence of technology does not closely concern us, in our thought, we shall never be able to know what the machine is. We shall not be able to tell what it is to which the industrial worker's hand is related. We shall not be able to make out what kind of manual work, of handicraft, these manipulations are. And yet – merely to be able to ask such questions, we must already have caught sight of what is commonly meant by handicraft in the light of its essential references. Neither the industrial workman nor the engineers, let alone the factory proprietor and least of all the state, can know at all where modern man "lives" when he stands in some relatedness or other to the machine and machine parts. None of us know as yet what handicraft modern man in the technological world must carry on, must carry on even if he is not a worker in the sense of the worker at the machine. . . .

What is most thought-provoking is even closer to us than the most palpable closeness of our everyday handiwork – and yet it withdraws. Hence our need and necessity first of all to hear the appeal of what is most thought-provoking. But if we are to perceive what gives us food for thought, we must for our part get underway to learn thinking.

Whether, by way of this learning though never by means of it, we shall attain relatedness to what is most thought-provoking, is something altogether out of the hands of those who practice the craft of thinking.

What we can do in our present case, or anyway can learn, is to listen closely. To learn listening, too, is the common concern of student and teacher. No one is to be blamed, then, if he is not yet capable of listening. . . .

Man himself acts [handelt] through the hand [Hand]; for the hand is, together with the word, the essential distinction of man. Only a being which, like man, "has" the word (μῦθος, λόγος), can and must "have" "the hand." Through the hand occur both prayer and murder, greeting and thanks, oath and signal, and also the "work" of the hand, the "hand-work," and the tool. The handshake seals the covenant. The hand brings about the "work" of destruction. The hand exists as hand only where there is disclosure and concealment. No animal has a hand, and a hand never originates from a paw or a claw or talon. Even the hand of one in desperation (it least of all) is never a talon, with which a person clutches wildly. The hand sprang forth only out of the word and together with the word. Man does not "have" hands, but the hand holds the essence of man, because the word as the essential realm of the hand is the ground of the essence of man. The word as what is inscribed and what appears to the regard is the written word, i.e., script. And the word as script is handwriting.

It is not accidental that modern man writes "with" the typewriter and "dictates" [*diktiert*] (the same word as "poetize" [*Dichten*]) "into" a machine. This "history" of the kinds of writing is one of the main reasons for the increasing destruction of the word. The latter no longer comes and goes by means of the writing hand, the properly acting hand, but by means of the mechanical forces it releases. The typewriter tears writing from the essential realm of the hand, i.e., the realm of the word. The word itself turns into something "typed." Where typewriting, on the contrary, is only a transcription and serves to preserve the writing, or turns into print something already written, there it has a proper, though limited, significance. In the time of the first dominance of the typewriter, a letter written on this machine still stood for a breach of good manners. Today a hand-written letter is an antiquated and undesired thing; it disturbs speed reading. Mechanical writing deprives the hand of its rank in the realm of the written word and degrades the word to a means of communication. In addition, mechanical writing provides this "advantage," that it conceals the handwriting and thereby the character. The typewriter makes everyone look the same. . . .

The hand in its essence secures the reciprocal relation between "beings" and man. There is a "hand" only where beings as such appear in unconcealedness and man comports himself in a disclosing way toward beings. The hand entrusts to the word the relation of Being to man and, thereby, the relation of man to beings. The hand acts [*Die Hand handelt*]. The hand holds in its care the handling, the acting, the acted, and the manipulated. Where the essential is secured in an essential way, we therefore say it is "in good hands," even if handles and manipulations are not actually necessary. The essential correlation of the hand and the word as the essential distinguishing mark of man is revealed in the fact that the hand indicates and by indicating discloses what was concealed, and thereby marks off, and while marking off forms the indicating marks into formations [*indem sie zeigt und zeigend zeichnet und zeichnend die zeigenden Zeichen zu Gebilden bildet*]. These formations are called, following the "verb" γράφειν, γράμματα. The word indicated by the hand and appearing in such marking is writing. We still call the theory of the structure of language "grammar."

Writing, from its originating essence, is hand-writing. We call the disclosive taking up and perceiving of the written word "reading" or "lection" ["*Lesen*"], i.e., col-lection, gathering – ("gleaning" ["*Ähren lesen*"]), in Greek λέγειν – λόγος; and this latter, among the primordial thinkers, is the name for Being itself. Being, word, gathering, writing denote an original essential nexus, to which the indicating-writing hand belongs. In handwriting the relation of Being to man, namely the word, is inscribed in beings themselves. The origin and the way of dealing with writing is already in itself a decision about the relation of Being and of the word to man and consequently a decision about the comportment of man to beings and about the way both, man and thing, stand in unconcealedness or are withdrawn from it.

Therefore when writing was withdrawn from the origin of its essence, i.e., from the hand, and was transferred to the machine, a transformation occurred in the relation of Being to man. It is of little importance for this transformation how many people actually use the typewriter and whether there are some who shun it. The typewriter veils the essence of writing and of the script. It withdraws from man the essential rank of the hand, without man's experiencing this withdrawal appropriately and recognizing that it has transformed the relation of Being to his essence.

On Hearing the Logos

Saying is a letting-lie-together-before which gathers and is gathered. If such is the essence of speaking, then what is hearing? As λέγειν, speaking is not characterized as a reverberation which expresses meaning. If saying is not characterized by vocalization, then neither can the hearing which corresponds to it occur as a reverberation meeting the ear and getting picked up, as sounds troubling the auditory sense and being transmitted. Were our hearing primarily and always only this picking up and transmitting of sounds, conjoined by several other processes, the result would be that the reverberation would go in one ear and out the other. That happens in fact when we are not gathered to what is addressed. But the addressed is itself that which lies before us, as gathered and laid before us. Hearing is actually this gathering of oneself which composes itself on hearing the pronouncement and its claim. Hearing is primarily gathered hearkening. What is heard comes to presence in hearkening. We hear when we are "all ears." But "ear" does not here mean the acoustical sense apparatus. The anatomically and physiologically identifiable ears, as the tools of sensation, never bring about a hearing, not even if we take this solely as an apprehending of noises, sounds, and tones. Such apprehending can neither be anatomically established nor physiologically demonstrated, nor in any way grasped as a biological process at work within the organism – although apprehension lives only so long as it is embodied. So long as we think of hearing along the lines of acoustical science, everything is made to stand on its head. We wrongly think that the activation of the body's audio equipment is hearing proper. But then

From Martin Heidegger, *Early Greek Thinking*, trans. by David Krell and Frank Capuzzi (New York: Harper and Row, 1975), pp. 64–8 hearing in the sense of hearkening and heeding is supposed to be a transposition of hearing proper into the realm of the spiritual [*das Geistige*]. In the domain of scientific research one can establish many useful findings. One can demonstrate that periodic oscillations in air pressure of a certain frequency are experienced as tones. From such kinds of determinations concerning what is heard, an investigation can be launched which eventually only specialists in the physiology of the senses can conduct.

In contrast to this, perhaps only a little can be said concerning proper hearing, which nevertheless concerns everyone directly. Here it is not so much a matter for research, but rather of paying thoughtful attention to simple things. Thus, precisely this belongs to proper hearing: that man can hear wrongly insofar as he does not catch what is essential. If the ears do not belong directly to proper hearing, in the sense of hearkening, then hearing and the ears are in a special situation. We do not hear because we have ears. We have ears, i.e., our bodies are equipped with ears, because we hear. Mortals hear the thunder of the heavens, the rustling of woods, the gurgling of fountains, the ringing of plucked strings, the rumbling of motors, the noises of the city – only and only so far as they always already in some way belong to them and yet do not belong to them.

We are all ears when our gathering devotes itself entirely to hearkening, the ears and the mere invasion of sounds being completely forgotten. So long as we only listen to the sound of a word, as the expression of a speaker, we are not yet even listening at all. Thus, in this way we never succeed in having genuinely heard anything at all. But when does hearing succeed? We have heard [*gehört*] when we *belong to* [*gehören*] the matter addressed. The speaking of that which is spoken to is λέγειν, letting-lie-together-before. To belong to speech – this is nothing else than in each case letting whatever a letting-lie-before lays down before us lie gathered in its entirety. Such a letting-lie establishes whatever lies before us as lying-before. It establishes this as itself. It lays one and the Same in one. It lays one as the Same. Such λέγειν lays one and the same, the ὁμόν. Such λέγειν is ὁμολογεῖν: One as the Same, i.e., a letting-lie-before of what does lie before us, gathered in the selfsameness of its lying-before.

Proper hearing occurs essentially in λέγειν as ὁμολογεῖν. This is consequently a λέγειν which lets lie before us whatever already lies together before us; which indeed lies there by virtue of a laying which concerns everything that lies together before us of itself. This exceptional laying is the λέγειν which comes to pass as the Λόγος.

Thus is Λόγος named without qualification: ὁ Λόγος, the Laying: the pure letting-lie-together-before of that which of itself comes to lie before us, in its lying there. In this fashion Λόγος occurs essentially as the pure laying which gathers and assembles. Λόγος is the original assemblage of the primordial gathering from the primordial Laying. ὉΛόγος is the Laying that gathers [*die lesende Lege*], and only this.

However, is all this no more than an arbitrary interpretation and an all-too-alien translation with respect to the usual understanding which takes Λόγος as meaning and reason? At first it does sound strange, and it may remain so for a long time – calling Λόγος "the Laying that gathers." But how can anyone decide whether what this translation implies concerning the essence of Λόγος remains appropriate, if only in the most remote way, to what Heraclitus named and thought in the name ὁ Λόγος?

The only way to decide is to consider what Heraclitus himself says in the fragment cited. The saying begins: οὐκ ἐμοῦ. . . It begins with a strict, prohibiting "Not . . ." It refers to the saying and talking of Heraclitus himself. It concerns the hearing of mortals. "Not to me," i.e., not to this one who is talking; you are not to heed the vocalization of his talk. You never hear properly so long as your ears hang upon the sound and flow of a human voice in order to snatch up for yourselves a manner of speaking. Heraclitus begins the saying with a rejection of hearing as nothing but the passion of the ears. But this rejection is founded on a reference to proper hearing.

Οὐκ ἐμοῦ ἀλλὰ . . . Not to me should you listen (as though gaping), but rather . . . mortal hearing must attend to something else. To what? 'Αλλὰ τοῦ Λόγου. The way of proper hearing is determined by the Λόγος. But inasmuch as the Λόγος is named without qualification it cannot be just any customary thing. Therefore, the hearing appropriate to *it* cannot proceed casually toward it, only to pass it by once again. If there is to be proper hearing, mortals must have already heard the Λόγος with an attention [*Gehör*] which implies nothing less than their belonging to the Λόγος.

Οὐκ ἐμοῦ ἀλλὰ τοῦ Λόγου ἀκούσαντας. "When you have listened, not merely to me (the speaker), but rather when you maintain yourselves in hearkening attunement [*Gehören*], then there is proper hearing."

What happens, then, when such hearing occurs? When there is such proper hearing there is ὁμολογεῖν, which can only be what it is as a λέγειν. Proper hearing belongs to the Λόγος. Therefore this hearing is itself a λέγειν. As such, the proper hearing of mortals is in a certain way the Same as the Λόγος. At the same time, however, precisely as ὁμολογεῖν, it is not the Same at all. It is not the same as the Λόγος itself. Rather, ὁμολογεῖν remains a λέγειν which always and only lays or lets lie whatever is already, as ὁμόν, gathered together and lying before us; this lying never springs from the ὁμολογεῖν but rather rests in the Laying that gathers, i.e., in the Λόγος.

But what occurs when there is proper hearing, as ὁμολογεῖν? Heraclitus says: σοφόν ἔστιν. When ὁμολογεῖν occurs, then σοφόν comes to pass. We read: σοφόν ἔστιν. One translates σοφόν correctly as "wise." But what does "wise" mean? Does it mean simply to know in the way old "wise men" know things? What do we know of such knowing? If it remains a having-seen whose seeing is not of the eyes of the senses, just as the having-heard is not hearing with the auditory equipment, then having–seen and having–heard presumably coincide. They do not refer to a mere grasping, but to a certain kind of behavior. Of what sort? Of the sort that maintains itself in the abode of mortals. This abiding holds to what the Laying that gathers lets lie before us, which in each case already lies before us. Thus σοφόν signifies that which can adhere to whatever has been indicated, can devote itself to it, and can dispatch itself toward it (get under way toward it). Because it is appropriate [*schickliches*] such behavior becomes skillful [*geschickt*]. When we want to say that someone is particularly skilled at something we still employ such turns of speech as "he has a gift for that and is destined for it." In this fashion we hit upon the genuine meaning of σοφόν, which we translate as "fateful" ["*geschicklich*"]. But "fateful" from the start says something more than "skillful." When proper hearing, as ὁμολογεῖν, is, then the fateful comes to pass, and mortal Λέγειν is dispatched to the Λόγος. It becomes concerned with the Laying that gathers. Λέγειν is dispatched to what is appropriate, to whatever rests in the assemblage of the primordially gathering laying-before, i.e., in that which the Laying that gathers has sent. Thus it is indeed fateful when mortals accomplish proper hearing. But σοφόν is not τὸ Σοφόν, the "fateful" is not "Fate," so called because it gathers to itself all dispensation, and precisely that which is appropriate to the behavior of mortals. We have not yet made out what, according to the thinking of Heraclitus, ὁ Λόγος is; it remains still undecided whether the translation of Λόγος as "the Laying that gathers" captures even a small part of what the Λόγος is.

And already we face a new riddle: the word τὸ Σοφόν. If we are to think it in Heraclitus' way, we toil in vain so long as we do not pursue it in the saying in which it speaks, up to the very words that conclude it.

Ὁμολογεῖν occurs when the hearing of mortals has become proper hearing. When such a thing happens something fateful comes to pass. Where, and as what, does the fateful presence? Heraclitus says: ὁμολογεῖν σοφόν ἐστιν Ἐν Παντα, "the fateful comes to pass insofar as One All."

Notes

1   The word "Dasein" plays so important a role in this work and is already so familiar to the English-speaking reader who has read about Heidegger, that it seems simpler to leave it untranslated except in the relatively rare passages in which Heidegger himself breaks it up with a hyphen ("Da-sein") to show its etymological construction: literally "Being-there." Though in traditional German philosophy it may be used quite generally to stand for almost any kind of Being or "existence" which we can say that something *has* (the "existence" of God, for example), in everyday usage it tends to be used more narrowly to stand for the kind of Being that belongs to *persons*. Heidegger follows the everyday usage in this respect, but goes somewhat

further in that he often uses it to stand for any *person* who has such Being, and who is thus an "entity" himself.

2 "...das Ganze eines Begründungszusammenhanges wahrer Sätze ..."

3 "Zu dieser Seinsverfassung des Daseins gehört aber dann, dass es in seinem Sein zu diesem Sein ein Seinsverhältnis hat." This passage is ambiguous and might also be read as: "...and this implies that Dasein, in its Being towards this Being, has a relationship of Being."

4 "...dass es ontologisch *ist*." As "ontologisch" may be either an adjective or an adverb, we might also write: "...that it *is* ontologically." A similar ambiguity occurs in the two following sentences, where we read "Ontologisch-sein" and "ontisch-seiend" respectively.

5 "...dass es je sein Sein als seiniges zu sein hat ..."

6 We shall translate "existenziell" by "existentiell," and "existenzial" by "existential."

7 "...innerhalb der Welt ..." Heidegger uses at least three expressions which might be translated as "in the world": "innerhalb der Welt," "in der Welt," and the adjective (or adverb) "innerweltlich." We shall translate these respectively by "within the world," "in the world," and "within-the-world."

8 Italics only in earlier editions.

9 The word "Umsicht," which we translate by "circumspection," is here presented as standing for a special kind of "Sicht" ("sight"). Here, as elsewhere, Heidegger is taking advantage of the fact that the prefix "*um*" may mean either "around" or "in order to." "*Umsicht*" may accordingly be thought of as meaning "looking around" or "looking around for something" or "looking around for a way to get something done." In ordinary German usage, "Umsicht" seems to have much the same connotation as our "circumspection" – a kind of awareness in which one looks around before one decides just what one ought to do next. But Heidegger seems to be generalizing this notion as well as calling attention to the extent to which circumspection in the narrower sense occurs in our everyday living. (The distinction between "sight" (Sicht") and "seeing" ("Sehen") will be developed further below.)

10 "...im Sinne der Sichtlosigkeit ..." The point of this sentence will be clear to the reader who recalls that the Greek verb θεωρεῖν, from which the words "theoretical" and "atheoretical" are derived, originally meant "to see." Heidegger is pointing out that this is not what we have in mind in the traditional contrast between the "theoretical" and the "practical."

11 "Das Werk trägt die Verweisungsganzheit, innerhalb derer das Zeug begegnet." In this chapter the word "Werk" ("work") usually refers to the product achieved by working rather than to the process of working as such. We shall as a rule translate "Verweisungsganzheit" as "referential totality," though sometimes the clumsier "totality of assignments" may convey the idea more effectively. (The older editions read "deren" rather than "derer.")

12 "...ein zünächst an sich vorhandener Weltstoff ..." The earlier editions have "...zunächst ein an sich vorhandener Weltstoff ...."

13 *"Die am innerweltlich Seienden sich meldende Weltmässigkeit der Umwelt."*

14 In the earlier editions "Welt" appears with quotation marks. These are omitted in the later editions.

15 Heidegger's distinction between "conspicuousness" (Auffälligkeit'), "obtrusiveness" ("Aufdringlichkeit"), and "obstinacy" ("Aufsässigkeit") is hard to present unambiguously in translation. He seems to have in mind three rather similar situations. In each of these we are confronted by a number of articles which are ready-to-hand. In the first situation we wish to use one of these articles for some purpose, but we find that it cannot be used for that purpose. It then becomes "conspicuous" or "striking," and *in a way* "un-ready-to-hand" – in that we are not able to use it. In the second situation we may have precisely the same articles before us, but we want one which is not there. In this case the missing article too is "un-ready-to-hand," but in another way – in that it is not there to be used. This is annoying, and the articles which are still ready-to-hand before us, thrust themselves upon us in such a way that they become "obtrusive" or even "obnoxious." In the third situation, some of the articles which are ready-to-hand before us are experienced as *obstacles* to the achievement of some purpose; as obstacles they are "obstinate," "recalcitrant," "refractory," and we have to attend to them or dispose of them in some way before we can finish what we want to do. Here again the obstinate objects are un-ready-to-hand, but simply in the way of being obstinate.

In all three situations the articles which are ready-to-hand for us tend to lose their readiness-to-hand in one way or another and reveal their presence-at-hand; only in the second situation, however, do we encounter them as "just present-at-hand and no more" ("nur noch Vorhandenes").

16 Here "Zeug" is used in the pejorative sense of "stuff."

17 "... kann zwar selbst von diesem als Abstand vorfindlich werden ... "

18 "Befindlichkeit." More literally: "the state in which one may be found." (The common German expression "Wie befinden Sie sich?" means simply "How are you?" or "How are you feeling?") Our translation, "state-of-mind," comes fairly close to what is meant; but it should be made clear that the "of-mind" belongs to English idiom, has no literal counterpart in the structure of the German word, and fails to bring out the important connotation of finding oneself.

19 "... die Stimmung, das Gestimmtsein." The noun "Stimmung" originally means the tuning of a musical instrument, but it has taken on several other meanings and is the usual word for one's mood or humour. We shall usually translate it as "mood," and we shall generally translate both "Gestimmtsein" and "Gestimmtheit" as "having a mood," though sometimes, as in the present sentence, we prefer to call attention to the root metaphor of "Gestimmtsein" by writing "Being-attuned," etc.

20 In this sentence "equanimity" represents "Gleichmut," "ill-humour" represents "Missmut," and "bad moods" represents "Verstimmungen."

21 "... den phänomenalen Tatbestand der stimmungsmässigen Erschlossenheit des Seins des Da in seinem Dass ... " It would be more literal to write simply "in its 'that'"; but to avoid a very natural confusion between the conjunction "that" and pronoun "that," we shall translate "das Dass" as "the 'that-it-is'," even though we use the same expression *unhyphenated* for "das 'Dass es ist'" in this paragraph and in that which follows. (The striking contrast between the "Da" and the "Dass" is of course lost in translation.)

22 "*Geworfenheit.*"

23 In this sentence there is a contrast between "wahrnehmendes Sich-vorfinden" ("coming across itself by perceiving") and "gestimmtes Sichbefinden" ("finding itself in the mood that it has"). In the next sentence, on the other hand, "found" and "finding" represent "gefunden" and "Finden."

24 "...so verschlägt das alles nichts gegen den phänomenalen Tatbestand, dass die Stimmung das Dasein vor das Dass seines Da bringt, als welches es ihm in unerbitt-licher Rätselhaftigkeit entgegenstarrt." The pronoun "es" (the reference of which is not entirely unambiguous) appears only in the later editions.

25 "...weil diese selbst wesenhaft In-der-Welt-sein ist." It is not clear whether the antecedent of "diese" is "Existenz" ("existence") or *Erschlossenheit* ("*disclosedness*").

26 "Diese Angänglichkeit gründet in der Befindlichkeit, als welche sie die Welt zum Beispiel auf Bedrohbarkeit hin erschlossen hat." The pronoun "sie" appears only in the newer editions.

27 "befindlichen In-der-Welt-seins." In previous chapters we have usually translated "befindlich" by such expressions as "which is to be found," etc., where this adjective is applied to a number of things which are hardly of the character of Dasein. In the present chapter, however, the word is tied up with the special sense of "Befindlichkeit" as "state-of-mind," and will be translated by expressions such as "with a state-of-mind," "having a state-of-mind," etc.

28 In this sentence Heidegger has been calling attention to two ways of using the word "Sinn" which might well be expressed by the word "sense" but hardly by the word "meaning": (1) "die Sinne" as "the five senses" or the "senses" one has when one is "in one's senses"; (2) "der Sinn" as the "sense" one has "for" something – one's "sense for clothes," one's "sense of beauty," one's "sense of the numinous," etc.

29 "'Selbsterkenntnis'." This should be carefully distinguished from the "Sichkennen." Perhaps this distinction can be expressed – though rather crudely – by pointing out that we are here concerned with a full and sophisticated knowledge of the Self in all its implications, while in the earlier passage we were concerned with the kind of "self-knowledge" which one loses when one "forgets oneself" or does something so out of character that one "no longer knows oneself."

30 "*Auslegung.*"

31 "Auslegung." The older editions have "Auslegung."

32 "...gibt sich ...zu verstehen, welche Bewandtnis es je mit dem Begegnenden haben kann."

33 "auseinandergelegt." Heidegger is contrasting the verb "auslegen" (literally, "lay out") with the cognate "auseinanderlegen" ("lay asunder" or "take apart").

34 "Als verstehendes In-der-Welt-sein mit den Anderen ist es dem Mitdasein und ihm selbst 'hörig' und in dieser Hörigkeit zugehörig." In this sentence Heidegger uses some cognates of "hören" ("hearing") whose interrelations disappear in our version.

35 "...des Folgens ..." In the earlier editions there are quotation marks around "Folgens."

36 Here we follow the reading of the newer editions: "...nicht eine Mannigfaltigkeit von Tondaten." The older editions have "reine" instead of "eine."

37 The author is here alluding to the German proverb, "Wer nicht hören kann, muss fühlen." (I.e. he who cannot heed, must suffer.)

5

THE ONTOLOGICAL DIMENSION OF EMBODIMENT: HEIDEGGER'S THINKING OF BEING

David Michael Levin

The hint half guessed, the gift half understood, is Incarnation.
T. S. Eliot, The Dry Salvages

Dimensionality consists in a reaching out that opens up, in which futural approaching brings about what has been, what has been brings about futural approaching, and the reciprocal relation of both brings about the opening up of openness.
Heidegger, On Time and Being[1]

I

Metaphysics begins with the question of being. This question calls our experience into question. Since we are embodied beings, we must ask ourselves: How is the experience that the question of being calls forth embodied? Could it be embodied differently? And how might it be embodied differently?

The reading of Heidegger that will be proposed here is intended to make a small contribution to the emerging body of understanding that is inscribed, yet left in the dark, in Heidegger's work of thought: a body of understanding "emerging" both in the sense that it is being brought forth hermeneutically from out of its implicitness, its hiddenness in the weave of the philosopher's text, and in the sense that the attempt to articulate its presence in the text enables us to develop, as a way of being in the world, the potential granted us by grace of our embodiment. The potential in question, the potential at stake, is the gift of a body of ontological understanding: a body that manifests our ontological understanding – a body that is responsive to the demand for openness constitutive of the question of being; a body that is therefore, in effect, an organ of being, deeply engaged by the claim on its capacity for openness to the otherness of all that is other.

Metaphysical thinking is an "I think" that takes place in the theoretical "mind." But our comportment belies this, showing that we implicitly acknowledge a thinking which takes place in the life of our feet and hands and eyes. Our thinking will not find its way without first "losing itself" as a metaphysical "thinking" and going very deeply *into* the body. The body of understanding, standing and walking with the support of the earth, gesturing with a sense of the gravity of the earth and the receptive openness of a space cleared for it, is already a move beyond metaphysics, since traditional metaphysics can conceptualize only an objective body, not the body which we are and live. And as we question the body of mood, we move closer to that field in which our motility takes place: a field of many dimensions, upon which the capacity we call "motility" is dependent. What we need is a thinking that actually deepens our contact with the choreography of this motility-field, a thinking that can actually take us into the depths of our topological attunement, in our motility, in our gesturing, to the grace of the field through whose clearing we move and pass. We need to attend to the ways we "use" our hands and experience their "activity." We need to sense in a bodily way the "tone" of our gestures, and become more aware of how that "tone" is related to our technological modes of production. A more developed awareness of our gestures would contribute to an *ontological* critique of technology. New historical initiatives have *already* been placed in our hands, for our touching, handling, pointing, and writing *already* hold beings open to the *field* of their being. But until this endowment is understood, we must also qualify the "already" with a deferral, adding "and yet, not yet." Ontologically understood, our gestures appropriate the topological configuration of corporeal capacities as a local disclosedness inseparable from its situational field and functioning as an immediately meaningful disclosure. A body of ontological understanding may begin to emerge when our gestures relate to the various beings of our world in a way that maintains their contact, and our own, with the clearing of space that would let them, and us, first meet in the "enchantment" of presence. It is a question of rooting our gestures in the tact and contact of their proper field: a field that has already made a clearing for their movement and already given them an initial *sense* of meaning. The emotional depth of the field's reserve of ontological "enchantment" might thus be made sensible for our emerging body of felt understanding, setting in motion the grace of our gestures.

According to the conventional wisdom that has been circulating for many years among scholars of Heidegger's thought, there is virtually nothing on the body to be found in Heidegger's writings. To a certain extent – that is to say, when read in a certain light and from a certain angle – these writings unquestionably confirm such a judgment. For whenever the course of Heidegger's thinking compels him to broach the problematic of embodiment as such – especially, for example, when the question of human nature arises, or when the related question of our kinship and "elective affinity" with the nature of animals calls for thought, Heidegger finds himself entering a realm where he has no compass and loses his way. If he allows himself to give thought to these matters, he soon leaves them behind, without achieving any breakthrough or resolution. Often, he touches on them, only to interrupt himself and break off precipitously. Thus, for example, in *Being and Time*, he says: "This 'bodily nature' hides a whole problematic of its own, though we shall not treat it here."[2] But this declaration is extremely perplexing, (1) because it interrupts a discussion of Dasein's way of inhabiting space that he immediately continues and (2) because one might have thought that a phenomenological account of how Dasein ekstatically spatializes – how the world it inhabits gets to be organized, relative to the position and orientation of the body, in terms of "up" and "down," "height" and "depth," "right" and "left," "in front" and "in back," "near" and "far" – would be considered a crucial part of the "problematic." Could it be that, in spite of his efforts to decenter the subject through a phenomenological account of Dasein's ekstatic temporality, Heidegger could not liberate the human body from the traditional interpretation, which since ancient times has inscribed it in a metaphysics of substances?

Thirty-seven years later Heidegger will once again confront and then turn away from the body, taking refuge in the acknowledgment of a problem he is not able to think through ontologically. Echoing the words he wrote in *Being and Time*, he remarks, in a reply to Eugen Fink during their 1966–7 seminar on Heraclitus, that "The body phenomenon is the most difficult problem."[3] What is it about the body that makes it such a difficult problem? The beginning of an answer – but only a beginning – can perhaps be drawn from an observation that Heidegger makes in his work on Nietzsche:

> Most of what we know from the natural sciences about the body and the way it embodies are specifications based on the established misinterpretation of the body as a mere natural body.[4]

Taking up, in this text, the metaphysical doctrine that splits off the body from the "mind," or "soul," Heidegger contends that "Bodily being does not mean that the soul is burdened by a hulk we call the body.... We do not 'have' a body; rather, we 'are' bodily."[5] For Heidegger, these reflections draw him into thoughtful contact with bodily feeling, with sense and sensibility: "Every feeling," he says, "is an embodiment attuned in this or that way, a mood that embodies in this or that way."[6]

But in spite of the existence of textual passages where Heidegger seems to express his unwillingness, or inability, to engage in a sustained meditation on the body, an unprejudiced reading of Heidegger's writings would be obliged to conclude that the conventional wisdom of the scholars is actually far from the truth. The conventional wisdom is based on a false impression: a false impression into the confusion of which Heidegger himself – strange to say – might even himself have fallen. The false impression, the confusion, comes, I think, from a peculiarly restricted conception of the body – or, say, of that which constitutes a discourse on the body. We will be struck by a quite different impression, however, if we count, as a discourse of thought on the body, all of Heidegger's reflections on perception; his etymologically generated meditations on the relationship between the human and the earth; his reflections on philosophical interpretations of "human nature" and the definition "rational animal." On my reading, Heidegger's discourse on the body includes, for example, what he has to say about the *Befindlichkeit* of feeling and mood; the platonic separation of the sensuous and the supersensuous; hearing the call of conscience; the habitual patterns of listening (*Hören*) into which we fall and the arduous task of learning how to attune our ears in the spirit of hearkening (*Horchen*); the errancy in phenomenalism (e.g., its failure to understand the difference between hearing a sequence of detached sounds and hearing the sounds as those of a worldly thing); the ego-logical pathologies that dominate our "normal," everyday sight and the difficulties that separate us from the "moment of vision" (*Augenblick*); the way we normally, typically, and habitually relate to the lighting that makes vision possible; and, finally, the activities of the human hand (including the labor of the hands, their technological skills, and the hand's cultural significance in writing, gesturing, and calligraphy), the role of the hands in reducing the presencing of being to an ontology limited to being-ready-to-hand and being-present-at-hand, and the essential difference between the human hand and the paws, claws, and talons of other animal species – matters that he touches on or discusses in some depth in his 1927 *Basic Problems of Phenomenology*, the 1929 book *Being and Time*, his 1942–3 lecture course on Parmenides, his 1946 study "The Anaximander Fragment," his lectures on technology during the period from 1949 to 1955, and his 1951–2 course of lectures, *What Is Called Thinking?*[7]

In view of these extensive discussions, it is surely possible to think beyond the traditional wisdom – that Heidegger gave virtually no thought to the body. If, however, we remain within the old conception of the body, we will be compelled to marginalize or exclude the phenomenology of perception, the phenomenology of lived space, and the phenomenology of practical activities involving the body – activities of the hands such as touching, handling, grasping, holding, handing down, praying, greeting, and writing, even though the ontology (the forms of being) that predominates in our epoch and that Heidegger subjects to a critique – the forms of being, namely, whereby being presences as being-present-at-hand and being-present-to-hand – *cannot be made intelligible* without a recognition of the body, and not, indeed, without a recognition of what I am calling, and calling forth, here, with these very words, the *ontological* body. For us, then, the body must be a material, objective, physical, worldly substance, a living, animal nature that *somehow* is *also* human, ensouled, spiritual. And the so-called "problematic of the body" must then refer to the question of the *relationship* between our animal nature and our human nature, our animal being (as a physical body) and our human being (as a spiritual being endowed with reason and speech). But if this be the only question the discussion of which counts as "the problematic of the body," then it is indeed the case that, as conventional wisdom insists, Heidegger has very little to say about the body – and certainly never reached an elucidatory understanding with which he and his heirs could be satisfied.

In the Heraclitus Seminar with Eugen Fink, Heidegger's final words on this problematic are: "The bodily [element] in the human is not something animal-istic. The manner of understanding that accompanies it is something that metaphysics up till now has not touched on."[8] This is at one and the same time a sweeping repudiation of metaphysics and a frank admission that he is not able to think *beyond* the metaphysical interpretation of the body. And yet, I think he went in fact much farther than he believed – but his continuing entanglement in metaphysics made it impossible for him to see and measure the extent of this achievement. It has been equally difficult, if not more so, for the scholars who have attempted to follow nimbly in his footsteps to move beyond the culturally hegemonic metaphysical interpretation. Hence their inability to find in Heidegger's work a sustained meditation on embodiment.

Many scholars read as "metaphorical" all of Heidegger's references to percep-tion (to listening and seeing, for example); references to "dwelling on the earth" and "obedience to the earth";[9] references to being "gathered on the ground of existence";[10] references to the activities, gestures, and skills (*technai*) of the hands; references to the possibility of "poetic dwelling," "provided our hands, which express in a whole, complicated way how we are, how we are living, in a situation, do not abruptly grasp but are guided by gestures [*Gebärde*] befitting the measure";[11] references to "lending a hand" to the coming to presence of being;[12] references to "the full breadth of the space proper to [the human] essence";[13] references to the character of our relationship to the earth and the sky; references to our "standing upright," "walking," "falling down"; references to "steps" on the path (*Weg*) and "going astray." But Heidegger again and again tells us that his work comes out of the *experience* of thought, *aus der Erfahrung des Denkens*. Would it not be a tragic error, then, to read Heidegger's words as "mere" metaphors – metaphors in the sense of rhetorical embellishments, "figurative" designs to heighten the poetic beauty of the text? If this is what "metaphorical" is taken to mean, then Heidegger's words must be understood, on the contrary, as purporting "literal" truth. It would be better, however, to follow the etymological hints that are preserved in the word *metaphor* (Greek: *metapherein*) and think of metaphors as words that *carry forward* our experience. I take Heidegger's references – references such as those I have just named – to be metaphorical ways of thinking about our embodied experience, our experience as beings embodied. They are ways of articulating the body of our experience: ways that enable this experience to realize some of its *Seinskönnen*, the "dispositions" of its potentiality-for-being.

As I have already suggested, a major problem confronting a reading of Heidegger that takes him to be writing about the body of experience – the very same problem that both Heidegger and the scholars following in his footsteps never adequately thematized, and therefore never worked intensively on – is that "body" is thought in such a way that discussions about seeing and hearing, posture and gesture, bearing and handling, standing and falling are not regarded as discussions about the body. This, I submit, is a serious mistake. It means, among other things, that what Heidegger says about "thinking" is not connected with these "dispositions" of our being, not connected with our experience as embodied beings. And this means that the implications of his radical thinking about "thinking" cannot be taken to heart, cannot be "translated" into a process of experience that will carry this experience forward. But without this "translation," what Heidegger means by "thinking" – and what he would like to accomplish thereby – remains hostage to the very metaphysics beyond which it is attempting to carry us. Without this "translation," "thinking" remains imprisoned in the metaphysical dualisms of philosophy and life, mind and body, thought and action, theory and praxis, thinking and experiencing, reason and feeling, the intelligible and the sensuous. Whereas the entire thrust of Heidegger's work of thought is to deconstruct these dualisms, these reifications. In an attempt, in his later years, to break the spell cast by metaphysics, Heidegger spoke of thinking as "building" (*bauen*) and "dwelling" (*wohnen*). In the first lecture of the course published under the title *What Is Called Thinking?* Heidegger says: "We are trying to learn thinking. Perhaps thinking . . . is something like building a cabinet [*wie das Bauen an einem Schrein*]. At any rate, it is a craft, a handicraft" [*ein Hand-werk*].[14] "All the work of the hand," he adds, "is rooted in thinking."[15] And in the second of these lectures, after reminding us that, "We have called thinking the most excellent handicraft [*das ausgezeichnete Handwerk*]," he declares: "Thinking guides and sustains every gesture of the hand [*Das Denken leitet und trägt jede Gebärde der Hand*]."[16] Not to take what Heidegger says here as actually referring to our hands, our gestures, is not to take Heidegger's words seriously; it is to rob them of all meaning and all effect. They lose their radicality, their transformative power, their power to speak – though I hesitate to say this, even with fear and trembling – for the sake of redemption.

There is an alternative. It is useful to break out of our culture's substance metaphysics by thinking of the body, the body that, as Heidegger says, "I am," as an organically intricate system of dispositions and capacities. (The relevant word in Heidegger's texts would be *Vermögen*.) Now, to be sure, to think of the body in this way still involves thinking in terms of actuality and potentiality; but these terms can be released from their determination according to an Aristotelian teleology. And when they are thus released, they function quite differently: both in regard to their existence and in regard to their realization, our potentialities-for-being as embodied beings are radically contingent. But the point on which I want now to concentrate is that it is inherent in the very logic of such dispositions and capacities that they can be developed – that they can be taken up and nurtured, unfolded, carried forward, metaphored, through *Bildungsprozesse*, processes of learning. (In *The Fundamental Concepts of Metaphysics*,[17] Heidegger emphasizes that "what philosophy deals with only discloses itself at all within and from out of a transformation of human Dasein" and repeatedly indicates that the task of thinking is "to liberate the humanity in man.")

Even though Heidegger was a deeply concerned teacher, a teacher who gave thought to ways of teaching and learning and himself continued to learn and grow throughout his lifetime, he did not give thought in any sufficiently explicit way to the learning processes that our dispositions and capacities as embodied beings could undergo and be guided to undergo. What we are concerned with here, calling it "the body," is a system of ongoing processes. Thus it is more appropriate to think, not in terms of "the body," but much more dynamically, and less objectivatingly, in terms of "embodiment." This latter word carries us past the inveterate tendency to reify what we are trying to think and understand and engage. If I were tempted to express this point in Derridean terms, I might say that, for phenomenology, there *is* no body: no such thing.

In order to think our embodiment in the context of Heidegger's discourse of being and carry forward Heidegger's own thinking in the spirit of this discourse and with the resources it hands down, we need to begin thinking embodiment ontologically – thinking it, that is, in terms of its ontological dimensionality, its relationship to being. What does this involve?

Briefly stated, the ontological dimension of our embodiment is its (our) openness-to-being, its (our) ekstatic exposedness, its (our) receptive responsiveness and responsive receptivity to the presencing of being. As Heidegger points out, philosophical thinking began with an experience of enchantment and wonder. This experience brought forth perplexities and questions. The history of metaphysics is a history, a narrative of the question(ing) of being. Why are there beings? Why is there not nothing? What do we mean when we speak of the being of these beings? And what is being, being as such? But metaphysics broached these questions, only immediately to foreclose the process of questioning. Instead of allowing themselves to be claimed by the dimensions of the question; instead of letting the dimensions of the question open up a corresponding dimension of thoughtful experience, the metaphysical philosophers immediately reduced the problematic to a less threatening dimensionality. Heidegger accordingly implies that they betrayed their initial experience – the wonder and enchantment that drew them out of themselves and opened their eyes and ears to the very being of world. And they betrayed their initial question(ing), turning it into a question about the most original or highest or greatest or most universal being. In Heidegger's terminology, they turned an *ontological* question into an *ontical* question. We need instead, according to Heidegger, to let the question(ing) of being open up our experience. We need to let it draw us out of our ego-logically limited selves into the dimensionality toward which it projects us. We need to let it expose us to the unsettling, the uncanny claims that it makes on our capacity for responsiveness, our capacity to receive the "gift," the contingent, inexplicable, groundless "event" of being: the sheer "facticity" of being, the "fact" that there is anything at all, that there is what there is.

But the ontology of *Being and Time* is not intelligible, not possible, except for embodied beings, beings endowed with eyes, ears, arms and hands, throat and lips. The modes of being in and as which being presences itself only express themselves through, and *a fortiori* depend on, these organs of our embodiment. In relation to our embodiment, the question(ing) of being becomes a questioning of the *hermeneutical character* of our various dispositions and capacities: a questioning of their disclosive responsiveness to the presencing of being. As a "gift," an "event" or "fact" without reason, absolutely groundless, this presencing makes a claim on us: it calls for a disclosive response. The "question of being" thus becomes a questioning of our character: the hermeneutical character of our response. For example: A questioning of our capacity, as beings gifted with eyes for sight, to see in an open and opening way the presencing of being in and as visible beings.[18] A questioning of our capacity, as beings gifted with ears for hearing, to hearken in an open and opening way to the presencing of being in and as sonorous beings.[19] And a questioning of our capacity, as beings gifted with arms and hands, to engage our embodiment in gestures that are appropriately responsive to the presencing of being and serve to bring it forth, manifesting its hermeneutical dimensionality in the practical world.[20] The presencing of being (the ontological) makes difficult and unsettling claims on us that call for realization in the ontical world. From the very beginning, the presencing of being stakes out for us our ontological responsibility. As embodied beings, as beings endowed with a particular embodiment and the potentiality-for-being inherent in its (our) dispositions and capacities, we are rendered *beholden* (my translation of Heidegger's term, *schuldig*, usually translated, in my judgment wrongly, as "guilty") *and are therefore responsible*, simply because we exist, because we are, for the extent of our exposedness, and the quality and character of our responsiveness, to the presencing of being.[21]

This broaches the question of learning, the question of our willingness to strive for the realization of our ontological potentiality-for-being as embodied beings. It is to this question that we now return.

In the analytic of *Being and Time*, Heidegger still thinks in many ways like the philosophers of old: *Dasein*, accordingly, is treated as if it were a timeless transcendental structure, albeit a structure that situates the human being in a temporal and historical world that it has itself made temporal and historical. In spite of his affirmation of Dasein's "potentiality-for-being," in spite of his insistence on the importance of mortality, of being-toward-death (*Sein-zum-Tode*), there is no recognition, no discussion, of the seasons of a lifetime – the passage from birth to death by way of infancy, childhood, youth, adulthood, and old age – and the learning, the growth, that these different seasons call for. In brief, there is no attempt to draft a phenomenological portrait or narrative of Dasein's self-realization, self-development, and self-fulfillment: no attempt to articulate in ontological terms the learning processes implied by his vision of the "ontological destination" (later called the *Geschick*) to which he thinks we mortals are called.

And yet, it is possible to draw on the analytic in Heidegger's *Being and Time* to formulate, at least schematically, the profile of a developmental process, a learning process essentially involving our embodiment, our sensibility, our perceptivity, our experience as bodily beings in the world. To accomplish this, however, we must proceed on the course of a path that Heidegger himself seems not to have sought out or noticed. Nevertheless, it is on this path, I think, that we may carry forward his thinking in a greatly needed direction.

In "What is Metaphysics?" Heidegger relates the question of being to our ownmost, or most essential, way of being, saying that it depends on our capacity for revealing beings as a whole and being as such:

> being attuned, in which we "are" one way or another and which determines us through and through, lets us find ourselves among beings as a whole. The founding mode of attunement [*Befindlichkeit der Stimmung*] not only reveals beings as a whole in various ways, but this revealing – far from being merely incidental – is also the basic occurrence of our Da-sein.[22]

Our interpretation, here, will make new use of Heidegger's concepts, putting them to work in a phenomenology of embodiment. In particular: (1) *Befindlichkeit*, which is usually translated as "state-of-mind,"[23] but which I want to translate as our bodily felt sense of being in a situation in the world; (2) Dasein's pre-ontological understanding (or ontological pre-understanding) of being, which is usually thought of in intellectual terms, with no recognition of our embodiment; and (3) *Stimmung*, usually translated as "moodedness" and "attunement," but usually given an interpretation that is far removed from a phenomenology of embodiment and sensibility.[24] I want to argue (although I cannot lay out in full, here, the argumentation that needs to be made) for interpretations of these *Daseinsanalytik* concepts that contextualize them in a hermeneutical phenomenology of embodiment, a "narrative" of developmental learning-processes through which the hermeneutical dispositions and capacities inherent in this embodiment (I am referring, here, to our ontologically inscribed potentiality, as embodied beings, for responding hermeneutically to the interplay of concealment and unconcealment as which the being of beings presences) are brought out, articulated, and made more explicit than they are in Heidegger's own texts. (Heidegger speaks of the importance he attaches to the philosophical task of "awakening" our fundamental attunement to and by the presencing of beings as a whole and being as such.[25] But he does not explicitly recognize it is by grace of our embodiment that *Dasein* is disposed in accordance with this fundamental attunement.) In this way, we shall begin to discern and recognize, emerging from the weave of Heidegger's texts, an emerging body of ontological understanding.

In spite of the double meaning persistently carried by the word "sense" ("Sinn" in German), whereby it can refer, not only to conceptual meaning, not only to the cognitive, but also to bodily felt meaning and the realm of the sensuous, Heidegger restricted the reference of this word in *Being and Time* to the realm of the cognitive, the realm of the "understanding," likewise thought in a strictly cognitive sense. He does not allow his thinking to be guided by the doubleness of the word *Sinn*.[26] Were he to have followed the hints, the *Winke* suggested by this doubleness, perhaps he would have come to recognize two kinds, or rather levels, of meaningfulness, one that is engaged by our actions and interactions as embodied beings and one that is engaged through the intentionality of discourse, through *Rede*; and he would not have unwittingly perpetuated a tradition of intellectualism according to which meaning is denied to the realm of the sensuous, the realm of perception, sensibility, and gesture. Nor would he have treated language as if it were disembodied, split off from the sense-making constitutive of our bodily being-in-the-world. And perhaps he would not have been tempted to think of hermeneutics in the traditional way, restricting it to discourse, the realm of the cognitive, the intellectual, the ideal. *Befindlichkeit* is our always already hermeneutical embodiment.

I propose to think of hermeneutics as a process of disclosing, of unconcealment, that can take place not only in the reading or interpreting of texts, but rather in all our engagements with meaning – in perception and feeling, for example, as well as in our practical interactions, as embodied beings, with the world around us. I also propose to think our pre-ontological understanding (or ontological pre-understanding) of being in connection with our *Befindlichkeit*, and as a primordial level of hermeneutical intentionality and understanding that we are enjoined to experience simply by grace of the fact that we are "thrown" (like dice) into existence and "find ourselves" as embodied beings in the world. This level of understanding is initially pre-predicative, a deep, bodily felt sense of being in the world, an experience that may be faithfully described, perhaps, in terms of a deep sense of inherence, belonging, rootedness, and grounding, and that normally and for the most part *remains* deeply, darkly implicit, pre-reflective, unthematized, unquestioned. As a level of intentionality, this *Befindlichkeit* is primordially passive – more passive than passive, as Levinas would say. It is a bodily felt responsiveness that is called forth, solicited, in an immemorial time of origin *prior* to all reflective awareness, all forms of intentionality that express the ego-logical will. It is an attunement (*Stimmung*), an enjoinment (*Fuge, Fügung*) that reflection experiences as always already in effect, the *arkhé* of an immemorial "dispensation" (*Geschick*) ruling over our embodiment and laying down the existential coordinates of our ontological disposition as beings bodily related to, and called into question by, the presencing (unconcealment) of being. Thus, for example, the primordial level of our capacity for hearing is retrievable phenomenologically as the bodily felt sense of an auditory belongingness (*Zugehörigkeit*), a primordial claim on our ability to be responsive – and a first solicitation of our "responsibility" for the hermeneutical, ontologically disclosive character of our responsiveness as beings gifted with the capacity for listening and hearing. Infants enjoy without thought the existential condition bestowed by this primordial intentionality: it is, for them, what we might call the grace of a "pre-ontological understanding" (or "ontological pre-understanding") of being.[27]

But, of course, infants grow up. This developmental process is both a natural process, happening in accordance with the preprogramming dictated by nature, and also a cultural process, happening in response to the forces of socialization to which the child is exposed. Thus, unlike the natural process, the cultural is not predetermined in advance: the child's individuation all depends on the (hermeneutical) character of the socialization. Above all, it depends on whether this process *imposes* socially constructed, culturally hegemonic interpretations on the child's experience, in which case the violence of this violation will be repeated in the character of the adult, or whether, instead, it works with phenomenological respect for the child's own experience as it is lived, approaching the child's experience in a caring, preserving way to draw out, or elicit hermeneutically, the most excellent ontological potentialities-for-being.

However, regardless of the character of the socialization, the child's maturation involves a process of closure, a certain *Seinsvergessenheit*, a forgetting of the preontological understanding it once enjoyed. The natural and the cultural processes of development conspire to construct a system of ego-logical defenses. When the being of the child is reduced to the condition of subject and the being of the beings that the child encounters is reduced to the condition of object, these ego-logical defenses are firmly in place. This is the "fallen" condition of mortals, immersed in the everyday world, preoccupied with self-preservation, dreams and aspirations, worldly projects, obligations, responsibilities. It is the condition of ontical, average everydayness, unmindful of the ontological dimensionality – the presencing, the "taking place" and "clearing" of being – in which, and only by grace of which, we are able to live. Long before we are old enough to realize it, we have always already closed what Blake called the "doors of perception," shutting off the frightening solicitations, the unfathomable claims on our capacity for disclosive, unconcealing responsiveness, that come from the presencing of being.

This ontic condition of normality can somewhat, however, be altered. The ego-logical process of ontological forgetfulness can to some extent be reversed, even when this would go against the grain – against the *Gestell* – of our present epoch. Realizing that we are in a "fallen" condition, we can, as thoughtful, reflective adults, resolve to undertake and undergo a certain process of recollection: a recollection of being, an ingathering into memory of the immemorial presencing of being. Given our ontology, the ways that being has presenced, it should be clear that, and why, this recollection (*Erinnerung* as *Wiederholung*) can only take place in and through our embodiment.[28] As an infinite *task* for our embodiment. What this recollection attempts to retrieve and take up for ongoing realization and development is precisely that originary pre-ontological understanding of being with which we were "entrusted" at the very beginning of our lives, and traces of which the dispositions of our embodiment continue to carry in spite of our ego-logical forgetfulness. Through this recollection, the defenses that the ontically delimited ego has constructed can be to some extent breached, so that we are exposed to the solicitations of the presencing of being and opened up to the dimensionality of this presencing. As beings endowed with "ontological bodies," we mortals can build and dwell in the clearing opened up by the presencing of being, letting ourselves undergo the opening-up and carrying-forward of our experience that this presencing can solicit.

One of the German words for perception is *Wahrnehmung*, a word composed of the German words for "true" (*wahr*) and "taking" (*nehmen*). (The other word for perception, often used by Heidegger, is *das Vernehmen*.) The word *wahr* figures in a family of words: not only in the noun, *Wahrheit*, meaning truth, but also in *Wahrnis* (safekeeping), *wahren* (to watch over and keep safe), *währen* (to endure), *bewahren* (to preserve), and *gewähren* (to vouchsafe, to warrant). Listening deeply to these etymological connections, Heidegger takes the task of philosophy, which in Greek means "the love of wisdom," to be a question of caring for the truth. But what is truth? Challenging the tradition, which can think of truth only one-dimensionally, only ontically, as an adequation, or correspondence, between a state of the "mind" and a state of "reality" (or say between a proposition and a state of affairs), and which therefore locates the truth in an assertion made in language, Heidegger argues that what the tradition *calls* "truth," what it sees and hears of truth, is the phenomenon of "correctness," and that there is a dimension of truth to which the tradition has been totally deaf and blind. Drawing on the discourse of the earliest Greek philosophers, he calls this dimension *aletheia*, unconcealment, and maintains that "correctness," truth understood as "correctness," depends on and presupposes this dimension: the determination of "correctness" is not possible without unconcealment. This more primordial moment, event, or phenomenon is the opening up, the clearing, and the laying-down of a context, a field of meaningfulness; and it is within this contextual field opened up for our questioning that the determination of correctness can take place. Without the recognition of this open and opening dimension, the "truth" becomes nothing but an idol, a reified, fetishized abstraction detached from the process of questioning; and it can seem to become an eternal truth, an eternal possession of knowledge.

Heidegger's radical formulation of the phenomenological method in his Introduction to *Being and Time* represents an attempt to think what "caring for the truth" should mean as an attitude, a mode of comportment toward the presencing of being. Nothing could be more radical than the aletheic formulation that he settled on there: to let the phenomenon show itself from out of itself. (Though it is indebted to Edmund Husserl's formulation of the method in *Ideas* I, it is far more radical in its recognition of the giving and the receiving.) As Heidegger's 1994–5 dialogue on *Gelassenheit* (his *Feldweg-Gespräch über das Denken*) demonstrates, the implications of this method for his phenomenology of perception could not be more far-reaching, more radical. Thought by way of a recollection of the aletheic dimension of truth, perception gets to be rooted in the groundless interplay of concealment and unconcealment. Freed from the control of the ontical ego, from its totalizing enclosure within the structure of subject and object, perception is no longer merely a taking, seizing and possessing, no longer an act of muted violence; rather, it can become a way of *caring* for the truth, a way of watching over it, keeping it safe, preserving it.[29] As Heidegger makes clear in *Being and Time*, but also, for example, in *Plato's Doctrine of Truth*, his essay "On the Essence of Truth," and the *Parmenides* lectures, "preserving" the truth does not mean protecting it from questioning, from contestation; on the contrary, for Heidegger, the whole point of recollecting the ontological, aletheic dimension of truth is to make sure that what we *take* to be true, true in the sense of "correct," will always be kept exposed to new contestations from the always open context. The only way to respect and care for the truth, the only way to watch over it and preserve it, is to keep all claims to truth exposed to the interplay of concealment and unconcealment, and thus to the possibility that they will be judged as illusion or error. Conventional wisdom has made it virtually impossible for scholars to recognize, in what

Heidegger has to say about perception, about seeing and hearing, the gestures of the hands and the postures of the body, the profoundly transformative intervention of his radical critique of the correspondence theory of truth and his recollection of its aletheic dimensionality.

What I am calling the ontological dimension of our embodiment is thus our bodily felt experience of an ongoing breaching, opening and carrying-forward manifesting through appropriately disclosive hermeneutical gestures, movements, and organs of perception in relation to the ongoing (abyssal) questioning and measuring of our existence by the presencing of being. What we need to learn in order to live ekstatically as mortals from out of an experience with thinking – what we need to learn in order to live as mortals in accordance with the "measure" of the ontological, is an embodiment – a way of standing, walking, gesturing, seeing and hearing – that, by virtue of its (our) skillful (*geschicklich*), hermeneutically disclosive comportment, is appropriate to the immeasurable interplay of presence and absence, as which the being of beings presences. What we need to learn is how to dwell: how to stand on the earth and under the sky. Learning this, a task for our embodiment, we may perhaps begin to "redeem" the gift of a pre-ontological understanding through an emerging body of ontological understanding.

By grace of the bodily attunement (*Stimmung*) inherent in the pre-ontological understanding of being that is distinctive of our human way of being (our *Befindlichkeit* as human beings), we are woven into a field or clearing (Merleau-Ponty would speak, here, of "la chair," an elemental flesh) that we share with all other beings. Thus, it is through our bodies that a sense of moral responsibility first takes hold of us. To the extent that our gestures, our seeing, our listening, and our speaking are rooted in the ontological dimension of our embodiment, drawing their inspiration from this dimension and flowing from the measure of grace and tact that this dimension accords to them, they may enjoy a certain freedom from the dominant ontology, the prevailing ways that being presences. And they would therefore be more capable of practising care and compassion, because in the ontological dimension of embodiment, our being is not bound to the ego-logically constructed structure of subject and object, but is intertwined with other beings through the being of the field.

The ontological is entirely a question of dimensionality. In an embodiment that recollects and retrieves the gift of nature, a pre-ontological understanding of being, bringing this attunement into the thoughtful care of everyday living, the pre-ontological understanding is raised up by thought and redeemed in a genuinely ontological understanding. Were our gestures thereby rooted in the ontological dimension of our embodiment, flowing from it, they would become the elegant organs of being – gestures of an embodiment always in question with regard to its openness to the otherness of all that is other. It is this question of openness – openness to alterity – that constitutes the ontological dimension of our embodiment.

II

Hermeneutics as gesture: a reading of Heidegger's "Logos (Herakleitos B50)" study

ouk emou alla tou Logou akousantas. homologein sophon estin Hen Panta. [When you have listened not to me but to the Logos, it is wise correspondingly to say: One is All.] Heraclitus

Legein and *logos* are the words of Herakleitos: mere fragments of his thought.[30] They are words that refer, let us say, to articulation – gestures of articulation. *Logos*, a noun, may be translated as "meaning," "word," "speech," "discourse," "account," and "reason." *Legein*, the corresponding verb, may be translated as "to speak," "to give an account," and "to explain." But according to Heidegger, these ancient Greek words will be most fruitfully opened up at this time in history when they are understood, hermeneutically and more "primordially," to mean a *gathering* and *laying-down*. This is an "ontological" understanding of the articulatory gesture, because it retrieves, and opens up, a certain "primordial" experience of being.

Heidegger's thinking, in this essay on Heraclitus, has a two fold focus: first and foremost, an understanding of the *Legein* of the *Logos*, that toward which Herakleitos directs our listening; and secondarily, the *legein* of our own mortal *logos*. According to Heidegger, *homologein* describes the essential character of our own articulatory gestures, but only insofar as they are, or could become, more ontologically "appropriate," more responsive, to the claim primordially laid down for them by the *Legein* of the *Logos*. But Heidegger is mainly concerned to bring out the more "formal" ontological character of the mortal *homologein*. He does not take the time to specify it as an ontological question (a *Seinsfrage*) referring us directly, i.e., phenomenologically, to *our own experience* as gesturing beings, beings born with the potential for a unique grace in motility. What he has not thought through defines our present task. For we do need to ask ourselves: What *is* mortal *legein*, what is its "character," understood as articulatory gesture, when thinking places it, by virtue of the relationship called *homologein* in the ontological dimension of the *Legein* of the primordial *Logos*?

In Heidegger's essay, the "Question of Being" calls our gesturing, and our motility in general, into question. It motivates a shift in our attention, our awareness; it questions our motivation. It could also touch us in our innermost being, and move us to take the measure of our gestural being, recollecting the dimensionality of the ontological difference (i.e., the difference between being and beings) as the difference between our gesturing in its ontical everydayness and a gesturing opened by its awareness to the field of the being of beings as a whole. As we shall see, this question (*Seinsfrage*) summons us to consider the *character* of the ontologically hermeneutical gesture. It will be a question of "measuring" the character of our gestures, the ontic *legein* of our worldly gestures, against the dimensionality of the ontological *Legein*, against the openness that articulates being as such. What, then, is ontological hermeneutics, i.e., what is the hermeneutics of unconcealment, the hermeneutics through which the presencing of being shows itself as the interplay of concealment and unconcealment, when it takes the embodied form of a human gesture?

III

Thinking with our hands

According to our tradition of metaphysics, the human body is not capable of thinking. Thinking takes place only in the "mind." And this "mind" is contingently located in the region of the head – which, for that reason, is often not counted as part of the human "body." If we want ever to break out of this tradition, we must first of all acknowledge that we can think (for example) with our hands. Until we acknowledge this, it will not be possible for us to retrieve (*wiederholen*) for the future a different way for being to presence, although such a way must be already latent as an historical possibility in the primordial experience of the presencing of being that our technological sensibility tends to conceal behind *Zuhandensein* and *Vorhandensein*, i.e., behind the only two modes in (as) which the being of beings has presenced in the history of our Western world, namely, being-ready-to-hand and being-present-at-hand.[31] Yet this retrieval may be crucial for our capacity to realize (or rather, make ourselves ready for) new historical possibilities. What accordingly differentiates Heidegger's sense of "thinking" from the more familiar sense still dominant in our tradition is the fact that "thinking" in his sense – most certainly not a Cartesian "res cogitans" – allows us to understand *this* kind of experience. Our unwillingness to acknowledge a wonderful intelligence inwrought in the hands themselves makes us, in our daily living, profoundly *indifferent* to the "ontological difference," and to the ontological "potential-for-being" of which we are capable by grace and virtue of the gift of our hands.

Etymology tells us that "to gesture" means "to bear," "to bring forth," "to give birth," and "to make appear." The gesturing of our hands is a *techné*, a skill, an articulatory capacity; it can also be *poiesis*, poetizing, bringing what we touch and handle into the beauty of the unconcealment of truth (*Schein*, the play of appearances). But to speak of capacity, of skill, is to acknowledge the possibility of *development* and to assume some *responsibility* for this process. And if the capacity in question is a gift (an *Es gibt*, our embodied *Geschick*), then the bearing of this responsibility, transforming every gesture into a movement of rejoicing and thanksgiving, would be an appropriate (*schicklich*) response, an appropriate (*schicklich*) reception.[32] But what, then, do our gestures normally, typically and habitually bring forth? To what do they give birth? What kinds of beings do they make appear in the world of their normally, typically and habitually restless activity? What is the *character* of their everyday *legein*? The way our hands *are* does not touch, does not reach to, the way they *could* be: the way they *would* be, were we to realize their ingrained "destiny" of character (*vom Geschick her*) and develop and maintain their inherent gifts of skill.[33] Our skillful (*geschickt*) hands are a most precious gift.[34] We need to reciprocate this gift by giving them, in return, the gift of our thought, our awareness. (The etymology of our word, "awareness," connects it with the German words for truth, entrustment, preserve, protect, and vouchsafe.)

In a lecture published in *What is Called Thinking?* Heidegger recognizes this deeply repressed, unrecognized need to reciprocate and accordingly undertakes a sustained meditation on the hands and their craft. "All the work of the hand," he says, "is rooted in thinking."[35] Is there a way of understanding this rootedness so that we may also say that there is a thinking of being, a maintenance of thought, which is rooted in the work of the hands? There is a letter in which Heidegger himself seems to prepare for this very question, for he counsels the student to "Stay on the path, in genuine need, and learn the *craft* of thinking."[36] There is also a passage in "The Turning," where Heidegger calls on thinking "to lend a hand [*an die Hand gehen*] to the coming-to-presence of being."[37] Heidegger's words, always carefully chosen, suggest that it is possible for the gesturing of the hands to become in a hermeneutically disclosive way what in a concealed way (a sense forgotten since time immemorial) it already essentially is, namely, a way of giving thought to being; and his words suggest that when our hands are *moved* by an awareness of their ontological span, they begin to realize their inwrought potential, opening themselves as much as conditions permit to the open dimensionality of the presencing of being, and preparing thereby for other, different ways for being to presence, ways other than as practical readiness-to-hand and theoretical presence-to-hand.

Now, this guardian awareness, this maintaining of the element of being, is *not* a pure, disembodied thought. Therefore, it will not be "directly" concerned with being "as such." In the case of our hands, for example, it will be concerned, rather, with various touchable, manipulable things, things which are tangibly in being: things like the wood which the cabinet-maker works. For there is a *tactful* way of handling and manipulating things which is mindful of their dimensionality, the span of their presence, and which holds, keeps, and maintains beings *in the immeasurable dimension of their being*, i.e., in the tangibly open dimension of the ontological difference. The hands give to (the presencing of) being our gift of thought *whenever* they handle things with appropriate skill, with care for their being. Whenever this kind of skill is at work, and wherever this kind of sensibility, this kind of reverence, is still handed down as the gift of an ancient tradition, there I think we will find a *living* response to the nihilism of our technological epoch.[38]

Since the child's first concepts (*Begriffe*) are schemata of comprehension formed in the very process of reaching-out-for, grasping (*greifen*) and manipulating, it is only to be expected that our experience of tangible beings, and hence, more abstractly and reflectively, our experience of being itself, will tend to be determined in ways that *correspond* to the initial character of the inquiring, learning gesture. The circumstances of early life, and the gestures they elicit, set the predominant tone (*Stimmung*) and character of the child's first concept-formations. If we are concerned about pathologies in the character of comprehension, we should look to afflictions in the character of our conceptual prehensions. Since the "origin" of technology refers us back to the *techné* of our hands, a more developed awareness of the ontological character of our gestures – of their relation to the presencing tangibility of being – would contribute to the critique of technology; and it would also help us to retrieve otherwise concealed opportunities for an historical response to the technology-driven dangers that now threaten us.

It is with this consideration in mind, I believe, that Heidegger takes up the question of "proper use."[39] His analysis of use brings out the "essential nature" of our hands and helps us to define the gestures of which we, as thinking mortals, are most worthy. It is a question of defining and measuring the "appropriate" fulfillment of our hands and gestures in relation to the dimensionality of the presencing of being, and therefore in relation to the *claims* on us that derive from the openness and difference of this dimension. According to Heidegger, then, we are appropriately *caring* when we relate "to the thing in hand according to its nature," thus "letting that nature become manifest by the handling"[40] and letting ourselves – our hands, our gestures – be appropriated (*ereignet*) by the presencing of the thing. This, of course, would be the embodiment of *Gelassenheit*. The grasp characteristic of technology (*das Ge-stell*) cannot reach into the essential nature of things, for its operations reify: they are tactless transgressions. The tender, caring touch, which *feels* what it touches with a reverence that is also active "aesthetic" appreciation, gets in touch with a thing's essential nature more deeply and closely than the hand which wilfully grasps and clings, moved by desire (i.e., by attraction and aversion), or than the hand which is indifferent to the beauty of the thing in the disclosure of its truth, its ontological dimension of difference.

The rooting of gesture in thinking requires attention to the perceptive body of feeling. For bodily feeling, being the mode of our *original* understanding, i.e., our global pre-comprehension of things in a primordial "mood" (*Stimmung*) of openness, is our most tactful *way* into the opening depths of things. Touching with *Gelassenheit*, handling with care and tact, we leave things whole and intact.[41] And we let them yield the richness of their more intangible nature, their deeper and otherwise inaccessible nature.

What *is* our capacity to be touched, and moved, by that which we are given for our touching? What is the *character* of our touch? By what are we touched, by what moved? Touching *presupposes* our capacity to be touched,[42] and this reciprocity calls into question our inveterate tendency to polarize the tactile field into a subject and its object and lose touch with beings as a whole.

IV

The implicit legein of our motility

I want to argue that Heidegger's interpretation of *legein* as a gathering and laying-down is confirmed by our motility – that if we cultivate a phenomenologically vigilant awareness in our experience of motility itself, we will eventually encounter the implicit ontological *Legein* which has always and already defined the *deeper ontological character* of our ontical gestures and movements, normally, typically, and habitually confined to the ontologically forgetful dimensions of everyday ontic life. Merleau-Ponty will be extremely helpful in establishing the phenomenological evidence for this demonstration.

According to Merleau-Ponty, the human being enjoys "a global bodily knowledge which systematically embraces all its parts."[43] This body-knowledge is a "gathering." Furthermore, we are obliged to acknowledge that this innate "gesture" of physiognomic integration, a spontaneous functioning of the body which is concealed in the ontical understandings of both common sense and science, even touches and embraces the motility-field as a whole (PP, 317). It is, in fact, a "gathering" of the field. In his critique of empiricism, Merleau-Ponty observes that the gesturing of my hand "is not [intelligible as] a collection of points" (PP, 98). What this means is that a series of points along a linear trajectory cannot accurately graph the topology of even my simplest gesture. The truth of the matter is that, as he says, "Each instant of the movement embraces its whole span" (PP, 140). It is the concept of gathering, and not the concept of points, which graphs the human gesture. As he reflects on the observations which record the fate of Schneider, a patient suffering from serious motor disorder as a result of lesions damaging the brain, Merleau-Ponty begins to *see* what Schneider's gestures lack and what "normal" gestures enjoy, namely, a certain style of movement, a certain deeply implicit "melody" (PP, 105). And he calls this "melody" an "intentional arc": "It is this intentional arc which brings about the unity of the senses, of intelligence, of sensibility and motility" (PP, 136).

Now the point I wish to make is that this "melody," this "intentional arc" which Merleau-Ponty's eye of phenomenological reflection has unquestionably *seen* in the nature of human motility, is to be hermeneutically disclosed in its deeper *aletheic* truth as a gathering and laying-down. Concealed within every gesture and movement we make, there is an implicit ontical *legein* which is always and already engaged in (1) laying down an encompassing field of motility, (2) gathering up the compass of the field into a practical gestural trajectory, and (3) gathering the gesture itself into a unified, intelligible whole. This *legein* of the gesture (of the gesture as a *logos*) is not normally experienced with much awareness. For this reason, Merleau-Ponty wants to characterize the deeper experiencing of the melody as taking place, during the gesture, in a prepersonal or anonymous level of awareness.

Nevertheless, Heidegger's Question of Being pressures us to go still more deeply into the truth of our motility. For the Question of Being reminds us that we need to bring to light the *ontological relationship* between the character of the mortal *legein* and the primordial *Legein* of the *Logos*. It reminds us that we need to understand the *relationship* between the gathering and laying-down that is characteristic of the gestures of mortals and the gathering and laying-down of the *Logos* (being) itself. And it reminds us of the relationship *in order to challenge us* to continue deepening the reach and range of our experience of gestural motility as a guardian awareness of being.

V

Gestural motility and the primordial legein

Going still more deeply into the felt experience of gesturing and moving, we find ourselves "returning" to a still more "primordial stratum" of corporeal intentionalities that are always already functioning even without our reflective, thematizing recognition. Going beyond Merleau-Ponty, but still using his method of radical reflection, we eventually encounter a dimension of our motility-experience in which it is possible for us to realize the thorough-going, ongoing "interaction" – one might even say the "interpenetration" or "interweaving" – of the immeasurable *Legein* of the primordial *Logos* and the finitely measured *legein* of our mortal motility. Putting this in other words, I will argue that there is a dimension of our motility-being where, if we are sufficiently open to experiencing it, we can reach and retrieve an implicit awareness (our "pre-ontological understanding") of the primordial *Legein* as it touches our flesh, takes hold of our embodiment, outlines for us its measure, and lays claim to our gestural motivation. Merleau-Ponty writes that, "We must return to the *cogito* in search of a more fundamental *Logos* than that of objective thought" (PP, 365). We can, and I believe should, make the attempt to trace "objective being" to its rootedness, its inherence, in a "pre-objective" being: a "pre-logical" dimension of our experienced embodiment that I would call, using Heidegger's terminology, the *Befindlichkeit* of the "pre-ontological under-standing of being" which attunes and destines our gestural being, and that is to be found and retrieved by a reflection which parts company with the subjectiv-ity of the *ego-cogito* and its co-emergent object in order to recollect, "beneath the subject," a more primordial, anonymous structuration, a more original dynamism, a "prepersonal tradition" (PP, 254, 353, 336). This radicalized reflection is necessary because both common sense and its reflection in the objective sciences tend to lose touch with the more open experience that always underlies them. Thus, says Merleau-Ponty, when I "think," I *reduce* the field of my being, whereas, "when I perceive, I belong, through my point of view, to the world as a whole" (PP, 329). Recollecting this belongingness, this "gather-ing" inherence in the world as a whole, we regain for our gestures a lost dimension of significance.

Continuing our radical reflection, we discover that there is "a communica-tion with the world more ancient than thought" (PP, 254), a *legein* that has always and already "marked out" for us, as a general "project," the place and the field of our motility. The *Legein* of the *Logos* enters into a primordial commun-ication with us through the *legein* of our prepersonally organized motility; its primordial gathering of our temporally dispersed "consciousnesses" always *underlies* our personal life, that not only overlays this primordial contact, but also tends to conceal and restrict it (PP, 347). But all the "gatherings" of which *we* are capable essentially depend on the still more primordial layout and gathering of the *Logos* itself. Presencing in our world as the *clearing* by grace of which we may enjoy a space of freedom in which to move, the *Logos* serves, as Merleau-Ponty says of "space," "to embrace every being that one can imagine" (PP, 288). The *Legein* of the *Logos* is a "setting," granting our motility a basic (con)text and a "grammar."[44] It "lays down" an organized field of coordi-nates and trajectories; it orients our movements to the possibilities of our world; it anchors and aligns the body; finally, it offers itself as a "corporeal schema" to orchestrate and choreograph the *sense* of our motility (PP, 100). The *Legein* of the *Logos* is the "origin" of our world-space, in that it is that ekstatic topology, that elemental "inscription" of a "primordial field" (PP, 242), that "universal setting" (PP, 326), by grace of which alone it first becomes possible for us to find our bearings and move about in the space of our world (PP, 251). This, in sum, is how the gathering and laying-down of the primordial *Logos* presences – and works – within the motility-field of our experience.

VI

The homologein

The gift (the "Es gibt") of the *Logos* is the laying out (or "layout") of a clearing and the gathering of a continuous field. And the receiving of this gift takes place in the anonymous, prepersonal, pre-ontological dimension where our motility first makes contact with the topology of the *Logos*. But the giving of this gift *lays claim* to our motility – a claim we may well feel a need to redeem by recognition and guardian awareness. We can, as it were, redeem our beholdenness (*Schuldigsein*) insofar as we disclosively re-collect the original *Legein*, now overlaid by the paths of our forgetfulness, gathering up into the time of our own re-membering that by the grace of which our motility was first enabled to become, itself, a laying-down of coordinates and a coherent gathering of motivating energy. Through the grace in the re-membering, a turbulent and fragmented body is gathered up into its felt wholeness.

The primordial laying-down-and-gathering-of-a-field, i.e., the effective presencing of the *Logos* in our world, sets mortal beings in motion. But our thinking, deeply moved by the Question of Being, sets in motion a process of recollection (*anamnesis*) which *opens* us to the claim on our motility that has already been implicitly acknowledged by our guardian ontological awareness – by the *Befindlichkeit* of our pre-ontological understanding of being. The claim of the *Logos* calls for our articulation, for a *response* from our own mortal *legein*. With the concept of the *homologein*, our re-membering begins to respond to this claim, and it gathers our still undeveloped pre-ontological capacities for motility into the melodic wholeness of their most appropriate ontological fulfillment. Our everyday forms of motility – the characteristically ontic forms of human motility – take place, in truth, in a field or clearing of being with whose immeasurable dimensionality we naturally tend to lose touch, despite the reminders kept alive in our cultural myths. The being of this field, in which we may always recognize the workings of the primordial *Logos*, articulates through our bodily nature the very possibilities for movement that ground, and clear an open space for, all actual "passages" of human motility. The being of this field essentially outlines, and sets in motion, the schema of corporeal opportunities for deepening our natural capacity to "bring forth." Since reflection re-collects, in the *depth* of our motility, the primordial articulations of the *Logos*, the *deepening* of our capacity points to our skillfulness in bringing forth this primordial articulation – making it luminously manifest in the "elegance" of our gestures and movements. ("Elegance" refers here, by way of etymology, to the *perfection* of our *legein*.)

In regard to human motility, a natural capacity awaiting its most appropriate alignment and fulfillment, the Question of Being calls attention to the primordial claim on our grounding, our alignment, and our gestural grace; it calls attention to a claim that the clearing and grounding *Logos* has *already*, i.e., pre-ontologically, set in motion. The Question *gathers* our customary motility into a thoughtful recollection of (our relation, as beings who gesture, to) the openness of being, which is always already presencing *for us* as the *clearing* we need to move in and the *ground* we need to stand on – the ground we need, in fact, to stand being ourselves. When our ontical motility responds to this ontological claim, thoughtfully celebrating the inherence of the gift (the "Es gibt") in the very movements themselves, the *homologein* is a wondrous manifestation of being.

The *homologein*, binding mortal *legein* to the *Legein* of the *Logos*, is a relationship which takes place through the guardian awareness that lives in the very flesh of our motility. It is an ontic *mimesis* of the *Legein* of the *Logos*, taking place in and as the *legein* of our own gestures. It is an isomorphism between *our* gestures and the "gestures" of being, to the extent that our gestures, by virtue of recollection, become a *legein* (a gathering and laying down) that hermeneutically repeats and unconceals the topology of being, showing it as the primordial *Legein* upon which our gestures depend for the opening up of a meaningful world. As the *Legein* of the *Logos* is a setting-down and gathering that sets in motion the *ek-stasis* of our motility, the *homologein* that shines forth in mortal *legein* is a *corresponding* gesture, an articulation (*Wiederholung*) that "repeats" the primordial gesture in an appropriate way, i.e., with hermeneutical elegance. Our *homologein* consists, to begin with, in a motility moved by our understanding that our motility is isomorphically "the same" as the motility of the *Logos*, in the sense that *it itself* "clears a space," that *it itself* sets down, that *it itself* can gather and open. But we need to understand that the *homologein* will nevertheless *never* be fully appropriate, never authentically "finished," until the primordial *Legein* is, as such, articulately bodied forth in a human motility whose very gestures and movements, being "the same," "pay homage" to their unfathomable source. Our very motility, our own clearing of space, our own laying-out and setting-down, and our own ways of opening and gathering, are called upon to become the route of this radical recollection: a "truthing" (an *aletheia*), a disclosive event (*Ereignis*) within, and also of, the primordial articulation of the *Logos*. The *homologein* takes place *only* when the hermeneutical "character" of our motility, as a form of mortal *legein*, brings the primordial *Legein* into presence *as* the primordial, and brings it forth in the *truth* of its own primordiality, i.e., as that event of gathering and setting-out by grace of which our own mortal *legein*, in gestures and movements, first becomes feasible. Thus we may say that the *Logos* "needs" our motility to disclose its presencing in the very *giving* of that (clearing, grounding and gathering lay-out) by grace of which our own ontical *legein* is first set in motion, and on which our motility essentially depends. But there is no point in saying this unless it is understood, first, that we mortals are the ones in need, needing to commemorate the ontological clearing, the laying down, and the gathering of the *Logos*, without which our own ontical clearing and gathering would not at all be feasible. Second, it must also be understood that our own motility enjoys ontological fulfillment only insofar as it can appropriately "repeat" (*weiderholen*) the original *Legein* in the celebration of a hermeneutical disclosure.

VII

The skillful character of the hermeneutical gesture

If we now gather together the results of our foregoing analysis, it will be noted that we have described human gesture, human motility, at five distinct levels of being. (1) The ontic level of naive and unreflective everyday experience (the level of the "natural attitude," the level of conformable behavior belonging to "everyone-and-anyone"), where gestures of clearing, gathering, and laying-down are always already taking place, but without any awareness and understanding. (2) The deeper level of "objective thought," where motility, ontically understood (and ontologically concealed) in terms of Euclidean geometry, Newtonian physics, classical neurophysiology, mechanistic psychology, and traditional metaphysics, is mapped in linear time along a linear series of points simply added together in space. (3) and (4) The two deeper levels of radical reflection, where motility is encountered, first of all, in the experience of the "intentional arc," a melodic gathering and laying down, and then, second, in the more primitive, pre-ontological experience of an anonymous, prepersonal, non-egological clearing, laying-down and gathering which is not of my own doing, and on which, in fact, my own motility necessarily depends for its feasibility. And finally (5) the level of ontological thinking, where the ontical motility of mortals is disclosively articulated as (i) having been already pre-ontologically determined (*bestimmt*) by the *Legein* of the primordial *Logos*, and (ii) as continuing to call for a fulfillment which can only take place through the ongoing cultivation, or deepening, of an individual hermeneutic "appreciation" of being within the field of motility.

The first two understandings are levels which assume, and work entirely within, the traditional theory of truth as correspondence – a correspondence between an articulatory gesture and the reality it signifies, whereas the second two levels involve understandings which begin to recognize that the *traditional* theory of truth is essentially *derivative* from a more primordial *experience* of truth as unconcealment, hermeneutical disclosure. It is only in the even more radical ontological understanding of the fifth level, however, that the gesture is finally *appropriately understood* in the context of a hermeneutical theory and it is accordingly disclosed as an organ for the taking-place of a hermeneutical event of being (*Ereignis*). Thus, when the fifth and deepest level of awareness is bodied forth, the articulation of the ontological difference appears in all its beauty as the space-clearing "gesture" of the *Logos* and its primordial gathering of all beings. Thus what I have called, above, the cultivation of an "appreciation" of being means that we *develop* our capacity to gesture and move – or, more specifically, that we develop our *natural* gestures, which are *already* clearing an open space, laying-down, and gathering – in such a way that, by the character of these gestures *as such*, we gather into our collective memory, re-collect, and bring to living presence, the primordial clearing, laying-down, and gathering of being itself, giving thanks, in the very joy of this embodied recollection, to the primordial "gesture": thanks for the field it has laid down, and thanks for the motility its gathering has made possible and set in motion. Thanks by virtue of gestures that bring thoughtful disclosive *caring* into all our worldly interactions. (See Heidegger's very important discussion of "Care" in *Being and Time*, §§ 41–2, pp. 235–44.) Such caring depends on the extent of our openness to the otherness of that which is other. The extent of our openness to alterity is thus the measure of what I have called the ontological dimension of our embodiment.

Notes

1   Martin Heidegger, *On Time and Being* (New York: Harper & Row, 1972), pp. 14–15; *Zur Sache des Denkens* (Tübingen: Max Niemeyer Verlag, 1969), p. 15.

2   Heidegger, *Being and Time* (New York: Harper & Row, 1962), Pt I, ch. 3, §23, p. 143.

3   Eugen Fink and Martin Heidegger, *Heraclitus Seminar 1966–1967* (University, Alabama: University of Alabama Press, 1979), p. 146. For further discussion, see the first volume of my trilogy, *The Body's Recollection of Being* (London: Routledge & Kegan Paul, 1985), esp. pp. 38–89.

4   Heidegger, *Nietzsche*, vol. I, *The Will to Power as Art* (New York: Harper & Row, 1979), p. 209.

5   Ibid., pp. 98–9.

6   Ibid., p. 100.

7   Also see Heidegger's discussion of the vision of the "seer" in "The Anaximander Fragment," *Early Greek Thinking*, pp. 33–8; his extremely important discussion of light, lighting, and the relation of the gaze to brightness, concealment, and

unconcealment, our entrustment with presencing, and our responsibility for taking care of the lighting, in "Aletheia (Heraclitus, Fragment B16)," *Early Greek Thinking*, pp. 118–23; and his discussion, in "Moira (Parmenides VIII, 34–41)," pp. 96–100, of the forgetfulness of ordinary perception in relation to the light of what presences in the field of presencing.

8   Heidegger and Fink, *Heraclitus Seminar*, p. 146.

9   Heidegger, "Hölderlin und das Wesen der Dichtung," *Erläuterungen zu Hölderlins Dichtung* (Frankfurt: Vittorio Klostermann, 1971), p. 36: "Seine Zugehörigkeit zur Erde."

10   Ibid., p. 45: "gesammelt auf den Grund seines Daseins."

11   Heidegger, "Poetically Man Dwells . . . ." in A. Hofstader (ed.), *Poetry, Language, Thought* (New York: Harper & Row, 1971), p. 223. For the German, see "Dichterisch Wohnet der Mensch . . .," *Vorträge und Aufsätze* (Pfullingen: Gunther Neske, 1954), p. 198.

12   Heidegger, "The Turning" in *The Question of Technology and Other Essays* (New York: Harper & Row, 1977), p. 40. For the German, see "Die Kehre" in *Vorträge und Aufsätze*, p. 40: "Was sollen wir tun, dies bedenken: *Wie müssen wir denken?* Denn das Denken ist das eigentliche Handeln, wenn Handeln heißt, dem Wesen des Seins an die Hand gehen." For Heidegger, it is thinking that is the "genuine" activity. He also believes, as this quotation shows, that our *hands* can serve the presencing of being, perhaps learning to bring it forth in an historically different way.

13   Heidegger, "The Turning," p. 39.

14   Heidegger, *What is Called Thinking?* (New York: Harper & Row, 1968), p. 16. For the German, see *Was Heisst Denken?* (Tübingen: Niemeyer Verlag, 1954), pp. 50–1.

15   Ibid., p. 16. In the German text, p. 51.

16   Ibid., p. 23. In the German text, p. 53.

17   See Heidegger, *The Fundamental Concepts of Metaphysics: World, Finitude, Solitude* (Bloomington: Indiana University Press, 1995), §70 and §§38–9, pp. 292, 162, 172.

18   For a more elaborate treatment, see the second volume of my trilogy, *The Opening of Vision: Nihilism and the Postmodern Situation* (London: Routledge, 1988). See also my chapter on "Decline and Fall: Ocularcentrism in Heidegger's Reading of the History of Metaphysics" in David Michael Levin (ed.), *Modernity and the Hegemony of Vision* (Los Angeles: University of California Press, 1993), pp. 186–217 and "The Field of Vision: Intersections of the Visible and the Invisible in Heidegger's *Feldweg-Gespräch über das Denken* and Merleau-Ponty's *Working Notes*," forthcoming in Hugh Silverman and Wilhelm Wurzer (eds), *Visibility and Expressivity* (Evanston, Ill.: Northwestern University Press).

19   For a more elaborate treatment, see the third volume of my trilogy, *The Listening Self: Personal Growth, Social Change, and the Closure of Metaphysics* (New York: Routledge, 1989).

20   For more on hands, handling, practical activity, the work of the hands, handwriting, typewriting, and the hands' relation to signs and hermeneutical disclosure,

see Heidegger's *Parmenides* (Bloomington Indiana University Press, 1992), pp. 80–7. On "the proper use of the hands," see "The Anaximander Fragment," *Early Greek Thinking*, pp. 51–2, *What is Called Thinking?*, pp. 186–7, 191, 195–6.

21 This holds true even of our breath, in that breathing can occur either with or without an ontological awareness and rhythm, and we are correspondingly responsible for the extent to which it is permeated by such awareness, such a sense of measure. See my study, "Logos and Psyche: A Hermeneutics of Breathing," *Research in Phenomenology*, vol. XIV, 1984, pp. 121–47.

22 Heidegger, "What is Metaphysics?" in David Farrell Krell (ed.), *Basic Writings*, 2nd edn (New York: Harper & Row, 1993), p. 100; *Was Ist Metaphysik?* (Frankfurt am Main: Vittorio Klostermann, 1955), p. 31.

23 For Heidegger's discussion of "Befindlichkeit" see *Being and Time*, §29, pp. 172–7.

24 In particular, it is a question of a "fundamental attunement" (*Grundstimmung*). For a good discussion of this fundamental attunement, see *The Fundamental Concepts of Metaphysics*, §2 (p. 7), §§ 16–18 (pp. 59–71), §74 (p. 350).

25 On "awakening," see Heidegger, *The Fundamental Concepts of Metaphysics*, §§16–18 (pp. 59–71), §21 (p. 82), and §37 (p. 161).

26 I am indebted to Donn Welton for an e-mail communication (May 17, 1996) which reminded me to discuss Heidegger's neglect of the doubleness of the word *Sinn*.

27 See Maurice Merleau-Ponty, *Phenomenology of Perception* (London: Routledge & Kegan Paul, 1962), p. 168: "Metaphysics – the coming to light of something beyond nature – is not localized at the level of knowledge: it begins with the opening out upon another." He also says (ibid., p. 206) that it is a question of learning, or relearning, "to feel our body," to make contact with "that other knowledge" that is "underneath the objective and detached knowledge of the body." This "other knowledge," bodily felt, prepersonal, is "an opening upon a field of beings" in the world" (ibid., p. 216).

28 For further discussion of this process of recollection as a task for our embodiment, see the first volume of my trilogy, *The Body's Recollection of Being* (London: Routledge & Kegan Paul, 1985).

29 For Heidegger's discussion of "care" see "Dasein's Being as Care," *Being and Time*, §§ 41 and 42, pp. 235–44.

30 Heidegger, "Logos (Heraclitus B50)," *Early Greek Thinking*, pp. 59–78.

31 See Heidegger, *Being and Time*, Division I, ch. 3, pp. 98–9, 101–4.

32 See Heidegger, "Logos (Heraclitus B50)," pp. 68, 74.

33 Ibid., p. 74.

34 Ibid., p. 68.

35 Heidegger, *What is Called Thinking?* Part I, Lecture I, p. 16.

36 See Heidegger's letter to Mr Buchner, a "young student," dated June 18, 1950, in *Poetry, Language, Thought*, translated by Albert Hofstadter (New York: Harper & Row, 1971), p. 186.

37 Heidegger, "The Turning," p. 40. For the German, see *Die Technik und die Kehre* (Pfullingen: Günther Neske, 1962), p. 40. Also see "Poetically Man Dwells. . .," p. 223.

38   See my book, *The Body's Recollection of Being*. Also see Heidegger, *Parmenides* (Bloomington: Indiana University Press, 1993), pp. 80–7.

39   See Heidegger, *What is Called Thinking?*, pp. 14–15 and 186–96; *Parmenides*, pp. 80–7; and "The Anaximander Fragment," *Early Greek Thinking*, pp. 51–2.

40   Heidegger, *What is Called Thinking?*, p. 195. Also see *Being and Time*, Div. I, ch. 5, §36, p. 215, where Heidegger translates Aristotle's observation that "All men by nature desire to know" and gives it an explicitly *embodied* meaning, taking the Greek word for "know" in its root sense, "to see." Heidegger's translation is therefore: "The care for seeing is essential to man's being."

41   Heidegger, *Being and Time*, Div. I, ch. 6, §41, pp. 235–44.

42   Ibid., Div. I, ch. 3, pp. 30–1.

43   Maurice Merleau-Ponty, *Phenomenology of Perception* [hereafter PP], translated by Colin Smith (London: Routledge and Kegan Paul, 1962), p. 314.

44   See Heidegger, *Being and Time*, Div. I, ch. 3, p. 143 on the up – down, right – left, front – back axes that represent the spatialization of our embodiment.

Maurice Merleau-Ponty

Situating the Body

What has to be understood, then, is how the psychic determining factors and the physiological conditions gear into each other: it is not clear how the imaginary limb, if dependent on physiological conditions and therefore the result of a third person causality, can *in another context* arise out of the personal history of the patient, his memories, emotions and volitions. For in order that the two sets of conditions might together bring about the phenomenon, as two components bring about a resultant, they would need an identical point of application or a common ground, and it is difficult to see what ground could be common to "physiological facts" which are in space and "psychic facts" which are nowhere: or even to objective processes like nervous influxes which belong to the realm of the *in-itself*, and *cogitationes* such as acceptance and refusal, awareness of the past, and emotion, which are of the order of the *for-itself*. A hybrid theory of the phantom limb which found a place for both sets of conditions[1] may, then, be valid as a statement of the known facts; but it is fundamentally obscure. The phantom limb is not the mere outcome of objective causality; no more is it a *cogitatio*. It could be a mixture of the two only if we could find a means of linking the "psychic" and the "physiological", the "for-itself" and the "in-itself", to each other to form an articulate whole, and to contrive some meeting-point for them: if the third person processes and the personal acts could be integrated into a common middle term.

In order to describe the belief in the phantom limb and the unwillingness to accept mutilation, writers speak of a "driving into the unconscious" or "an organic repression".[2] These un-Cartesian terms force us to form the idea of an

From Maurice Merleau-Ponty, *Phenomenology of Perception*, trans. by Colin Smith (London : Routledge & Kegan Paul, 1962; Atlantic Highlands, NJ: Humanities Press, 1981), pp. 77–80, 87–9, 137-42, 146–7, 157–66, 317–27 organic thought through which the relation of the "psychic" to the "physiolog-ical" becomes conceivable. We have already met elsewhere, in the case of substitutions, phenomena which lie outside the alternatives of psychic and physiological, of final and mechanistic causes.[3] When the insect, in the per-formance of an instinctive act, substitutes a sound leg for one cut off, it is not, as we saw, that a stand-by device, set up in advance, is automatically put into operation and substituted for the circuit which is out of action. But neither is it the case that the creature is aware of an aim to be achieved, using its limbs as various means, for in that case the substitution ought to occur every time the act is prevented, and we know that it does not occur if the leg is merely tied. The insect simply continues to belong to the same world and moves in it with all its powers. The tied limb is not replaced by the free one, because it continues to count in the insect's scheme of things, and because the current of activity which flows towards the world still passes through it. There is in this instance no more choice than in the case of a drop of oil which uses all its strength to solve in practical terms the maximum and minimum problem which confronts it. The difference is simply that the drop of oil adapts itself to given external forces, while the insect itself projects the norms of its environment and itself lays down the terms of its vital problem;[4] but here it is a question of an *a priori* of the species and not a personal choice. Thus what is found behind the phenomenon of substitution is the impulse of being-in-the-world, and it is now time to put this notion into more precise terms. When we say that an animal *exists*, that it *has* a world, or that it *belongs* to a world, we do not mean that it has a perception or objective consciousness of that world. The situation which unleashes instinct-ive operations is not entirely articulate and determinate, its total meaning is not possessed, as is adequately shown by the mistakes and the blindness of instinct. It presents only a practical significance; it asks for only bodily recognition; it is experienced as an "open" situation, and "requires" the animal's movements, just as the first notes of a melody require a certain kind of resolution, without its being known in itself, and it is precisely what allows the limbs to be substituted for each other, and to be of equal value before the self-evident demands of the task. In so far as it anchors the subject to a certain "environment", is "being-in-the-world" something like "attention to life" in Bergson or "the function of the real" in P. Janet? Attention to life is the awareness we experience of "nascent movements" in our bodies. Now reflex movements, whether adumbrated or executed, are still only objective processes whose course and results conscious-ness can observe, but in which it is not involved.[5] In fact the reflexes themselves are never blind processes: they adjust themselves to a "direction" of the situa-tion, and express our orientation towards a "behavioural setting" just as much as the action of the "geographical setting" upon us. They trace out from a distance the structure of the object without waiting for its point by point stimulation. It is this global presence of the situation which gives a meaning to the partial stimuli and causes them to acquire importance, value or existence for the organism. The reflex does not arise from objective stimuli, but moves back towards them, and invests them with a meaning which they do not possess taken singly as psychological agents, but only when taken as a situation. It causes them to exist as a situation, it stands in a "cognitive" relation to them, which means that it shows them up as that which it is destined to confront. The reflex, in so far as it opens itself to the meaning of a situation, and perception; in so far as it does not first of all posit an object of knowledge and is an intention of our whole being, are modalities of a *pre-objective view* which is what we call being-in-the-world. Prior to stimuli and sensory contents, we must recognize a kind of inner diaphragm which determines, infinitely more than they do, what our reflexes and perceptions will be able to aim at in the world, the area of our possible operations, the scope of our life. Some subjects can come near to blindness without changing their "world": they can be seen colliding with objects everywhere, but they are not aware of no longer being open to visual qualities, and the structure of their conduct remains unmodified. Other patients, on the other hand, lose their world as soon as its contents are removed; they abandon their habitual way of life even before it has become impossible, making themselves into premature invalids and breaking their vital contact with the world before losing sensory contact with it. There is, then, a certain consistency in our "world", relatively independent of stimuli, which refuses to allow us to treat being-in-the-world as a collection of reflexes – a certain energy in the pulsation of existence, relatively independent of our voluntary thoughts, which prevents us from treating it as an *act* of consciousness. It is because it is a preobjective view that being-in-the-world can be distinguished from every third person process, from every modality of the *res extensa*, as from every *cogitatio*, from every first person form of knowledge – and that it can effect the union of the "psychic" and the "physiological." . . .

If man is not to be embedded in the matrix of that syncretic setting in which animals lead their lives in a sort of *ek-stase*, if he is to be aware of a world as the common reason for all settings and the theatre of all patterns of behaviour, then between himself and what elicits his action a distance must be set, and, as Malebranche put it, forms of stimulation from outside must henceforth impinge on him "respectfully"; each momentary situation must cease to be, for him, the totality of being, each particular response must no longer fill his whole field of action. Furthermore, the elaboration of these responses, instead of occurring at the centre of his existence, must take place on the periphery and finally the responses themselves must no longer demand that on each occasion some special position be taken up, but they must be outlined once and for all in their generality. Thus it is by giving up part of his spontaneity, by becoming involved in the world through stable organs and pre-established circuits that man can acquire the mental and practical space which will theoretically free him from his environment and allow him to *see* it. And provided that even the realization of an objective world is set in the realm of existence, we shall no longer find any contradiction between it and bodily conditioning: it is an inner necessity for the most integrated existence to provide itself with an habitual body. What allows us to link to each other the "physiological" and the "psychic," is the fact that, when reintegrated into existence, they are no longer distinguishable respectively as the order of the *in-itself*, and that of the *for-itself*, and that they are both directed towards an intentional pole or towards a world. Probably the two histories never quite coincide: one is commonplace and cyclic, the other may be open and unusual, and it would be necessary to keep the term "history" for the second order of phenomena if history were a succession of events which not only have a meaning, but furnish themselves with it. However, failing a true revolution which breaks up historical categories so far valid, the figure in history does not create his part completely: faced with typical situations he takes typical decisions and Nicholas II, repeating the very words of Louis XVI, plays the already written part of established power in face of a new power. His decisions translate the *a priori* of a threatened prince as our reflexes translate a specific *a priori*. These stereotypes, moreover, are not a destiny, and just as clothing, jewellery and love transfigure the biological needs from which they arise, in the same way within the cultural world the historical *a priori* is constant only for a given phase and provided that the balance of *forces* allows the same *forms* to remain. So history is neither a perpetual novelty, nor a perpetual repetition, but the *unique* movement which creates stable forms and breaks them up. The organism and its monotonous dialectical processes are therefore not alien to history and as it were inassimilable to it. Man taken as a concrete being is not a psyche joined to an organism, but the movement to and fro of existence which at one time allows itself to take corporeal form and at others moves towards personal acts. Psychological motives and bodily occasions may overlap because there is not a single impulse in a living body which is entirely fortuitous in relation to psychic intentions, not a single mental act which has not found at least its germ or its general outline in physiological tendencies. It is never a question of the incomprehensible meeting of two causalities, nor of a collision between the order of causes and that of ends. But by an imperceptible twist an organic process issues into human behaviour, an instinctive act changes direction and becomes a sentiment, or conversely a human act becomes torpid and is continued absent-mindedly in the form of a reflex. Between the psychic and the physiological there may take place exchanges which almost always stand in the way of defining a mental disturbance as psychic *or* somatic. The disturbance described as somatic produces, on the theme of the organic accident, tentative psychic commentaries, and the "psychic" trouble confines itself to elaborating the human significance of the bodily event. A patient feels a second person implanted in his body. He is a man in half his body, a woman in the other half.

How are we to distinguish in this symptom the physiological causes and psychological motives? How are we to associate the two explanations and how imagine any point at which the two determinants meet? "In symptoms of this kind, the psychic and the physical are so intimately linked that it is unthinkable to try to complete one of these functional domains by the other, and that both must be subsumed under a third ... (We must) ... move on from knowledge of psychological and physiological facts to a recognition of the animic event as a vital process inherent in our existence."[6] Thus, to the question which we were asking, modern physiology gives a very clear reply: the psycho-physical event can no longer be conceived after the model of Cartesian physiology and as the juxtaposition of a process in itself and a *cogitatio*. The union of soul and body is not an amalgamation between two mutually external terms, subject and object, brought about by arbitrary decree. It is enacted at every instant in the movement of existence. We found existence in the body when we approached it by the first way of access, namely through physiology. We may therefore at this stage examine this first result and make it more explicit, by questioning existence this time on its own nature, which means, by having recourse to psychology.

The Lived Body

These elucidations enable us clearly to understand motility as basic intentionality. Consciousness is in the first place not a matter of "I think that" but of "I can".[7] Schneider's motor trouble cannot, any more than his visual deficiency, be reduced to any failure of the general function of representation. Sight and movement are specific ways of entering into relationship with objects and if, through all these experiences, some unique function finds its expression, it is the momentum of existence, which does not cancel out the radical diversity of contents, because it links them to each other, not by placing them all under the control of an "I think", but by guiding them towards the intersensory unity of a "world". Movement is not thought about movement, and bodily space is not space thought of or represented. "Each voluntary movement takes place in a setting, against a background which is determined by the movement itself. ... We perform our movements in a space which is not "empty" or unrelated to them, but which on the contrary, bears a highly determinate relation to them: movement and background are, in fact, only artificially separated stages of a unique totality."[8] In the action of the hand which is raised towards an object is contained a reference to the object, not as an object represented, but as that highly specific thing towards which we project ourselves, near which we are, in anticipation, and which we haunt. Consciousness is being towards the thing through the intermediary of the body. A movement is learned when the body has understood it, that is, when it has incorporated it into its "world", and to move one's body is to aim at things through it; it is to allow oneself to respond to their call, which is made upon it independently of any representation. Motility, then, is not, as it were, a handmaid of consciousness, transporting the body to that point in space of which we have formed a representation beforehand. In order that we may be able to move our body towards an object, the object must first exist for it, our body must not belong to the realm of the "in-itself". Objects no longer exist for the arm of the apraxic, and this is what causes it to remain immobile. Cases of pure apraxia in which the perception of space remains unaffected, in which even the "intellectual notion of the gesture to be made" does not appear to be obscured, and yet in which the patient cannot copy a triangle;[9] cases of constructive apraxia, in which the subject shows no gnosic disturbance except as regards the localization of stimuli on his body, and yet is incapable of copying a cross, a *v* or an *o*,[10] all prove that the body has its world and that objects or space may be present to our knowledge but not to our body.

We must therefore avoid saying that our body is *in* space, or *in* time. It *inhabits* space and time. If my hand traces a complicated path through the air, I do not need, in order to know its final position, to add together all movements made in the same direction and subtract those made in the opposite direction. "Every identifiable change reaches consciousness already loaded with its relations to what has preceded it, as on a taxi meter the distance is given already converted into shillings and pence."[11] At every moment, previous attitudes and movements provide an ever ready standard of measurement. It is not a question of a visual or motor "memory" of the starting position of the hand: cerebral lesions may leave visual memory intact while destroying awareness of movement. As for the "motor memory," it is clear that it could hardly establish the present position of the hand, unless the perception which gave rise to it had not, stored up in it, an absolute awareness of "here," for without this we should be thrown back from memory to memory and never have a present perception. Just as it is necessarily "here," the body necessarily exists "now"; it can never become "past," and if we cannot retain in health the living memory of sickness, or, in adult life that of our body as a child, these "gaps in memory" merely express the temporal structure of our body. At each successive instant of a movement, the preceding instant is not lost sight of. It is, as it were, dovetailed into the present, and present perception generally speaking consists in drawing together, on the basis of one's present position, the succession of previous positions, which envelop each other. But the impending position is also covered by the present, and through it all those which will occur throughout the movement. Each instant of the movement embraces its whole span, and particularly the first which, being the active initiative, institutes the link between a here and a yonder, a now and a future which the remainder of the instants will merely develop. In so far as I have a body through which I act in the world, space and time are not, for me, a collection of adjacent points nor are they a limitless number of relations synthesized by my consciousness, and into which it draws my body. I am not in space and time, nor do I conceive space and time; I belong to them, my body combines with them and includes them. The scope of this inclusion is the measure of that of my existence; but in any case it can never be all-embracing. The space and time which I inhabit are always in their different ways indeterminate horizons which contain other points of view. The synthesis of both time and space is a task that always has to be performed afresh. Our bodily experience of movement is not a particular case of knowledge; it provides us with a way of access to the world and the object, with a "praktognosia,"[12] which has to be recognized as original and perhaps as primary. My body has its world, or understands its world, without having to make use of my "symbolic" or "objectifying function." Certain patients can imitate the doctor's movements and move their right hand to their right ear and their left to their nose, so long as they stand beside the doctor and follow his movements through a mirror, but not if they face him. Head explained the patient's failure in terms of the inadequacy of his "formulation:" according to him the imitation of the action is dependent upon a verbal translation. In fact, the formulation may be correct although the imitation is unsuccessful, or again the imitation may be successful without any formulation. Writers on the subject[13] then introduce, if not exactly verbal symbolism, at least a general symbolic function, an ability to "transpose," in which imitation, like perception or objective thought, is merely a particular case. But it is obvious that this general function does not explain adapted action. For patients are capable, not only of formulating the action to be performed, but of picturing it to themselves. They are quite aware of what they have to do, and yet, instead of moving the right hand to the right ear and the left hand to the nose, they touch one ear with both hands, or else their nose and one eye, or one ear and one eye.[14] What has become impossible is the application and adaptation to their own body of the objective particularity of the action. In other words, the right and left hand, the eye and ear are still presented to them as absolute locations, and not inserted into any system of correlations which links them up with the corresponding parts of the doctor's body, and which makes them usable for imitation, even when the doctor is face to face with the patient. In order to imitate the actions of someone facing me, it is not necessary that I should know expressly that "the hand which appears on the right side of my visual field is for my partner the left one." Now it is precisely the victim of disturbances who has recourse to these explanations. In normal imitation, the subject's left hand is immediately identified with his partner's, his action immediately models itself on the other's, and the subject projects himself or loses his separate reality in the other, becomes identified with him, and the change of co-ordinates is pre-eminently embodied in this existential process. This is because the normal subject has his body not only as a system of present positions, but besides, and thereby, as an open system of an infinite number of equivalent positions directed to other ends. What we have called the body image is precisely this system of equivalents, this immediately given invariant whereby the different motor tasks are instantaneously transferable. It follows that it is not only an experience of my body, but an experience of my body in the world, and that this is what gives a motor meaning to verbal orders. The function destroyed in apraxic disturbances is therefore a motor one. "It is not the symbolic or sense-giving function in general which is affected in cases of this kind: it is a much more primary function, in its nature motor, in other words, the capacity for motor differentiation within the dynamic body image."[15] The space in which normal imitation operates is not, as opposed to concrete space with its absolute locations, an "objective space" or a "representative space" based on an act of thought. It is already built into my bodily structure, and is its inseparable correlative. "Already motility, in its pure state, possesses the basic power of giving a meaning (*Sinngebung*)."[16] Even if subsequently, thought and the perception of space are freed from motility and spatial being, for us to be able to conceive space, it is in the first place necessary that we should have been thrust into it by our body, and that it should have provided us with the first model of those transpositions, equivalents and identifications which make space into an objective system and allow our experience to be one of objects, opening out on an "in itself." "Motility is the primary sphere in which initially the meaning of all significances (*der Sinn aller Signifikationen*) is engendered in the domain of represented space."[17] . . .

To sum up, what we have discovered through the study of motility, is a new meaning of the word "meaning." The great strength of intellectualist psychology and idealist philosophy comes from their having no difficulty in showing that perception and thought have an intrinsic significance and cannot be explained in terms of the external association of fortuitously agglomerated contents. The *Cogito* was the coming to self-awareness of this inner core. But all meaning was *ipso facto* conceived as an act of thought, as the work of a pure *I*, and although rationalism easily refuted empiricism, it was itself unable to account for the variety of experience, for the element of senselessness in it, for the contingency of contents. Bodily experience forces us to acknowledge an imposition of meaning which is not the work of a universal constituting consciousness, a meaning which clings to certain contents. My body is that meaningful core which behaves like a general function, and which nevertheless exists, and is susceptible to disease. In it we learn to know that union of essence and existence which we shall find again in perception generally, and which we shall then have to describe more fully. . . .

The Body In Its Sexual Being

Erotic perception is not a *cogitatio* which aims at a *cogitatum*; through one body it aims at another body, and takes place in the world, not in a consciousness. A sight has a sexual significance for me, not when I consider, even confusedly, its possible relationship to the sexual organs or to pleasurable states, but when it exists for my body, for that power always available for bringing together into an erotic situation the stimuli applied, and adapting sexual conduct to it. There is an erotic "comprehension" not of the order of understanding, since understanding subsumes an experience, once perceived, under some idea, while desire comprehends blindly by linking body to body. Even in the case of sexuality, which has nevertheless long been regarded as pre-eminently the type of bodily function, we are concerned, not with a peripheral involuntary action, but with an intentionality which follows the general flow of existence and yields to its movements. Schneider can no longer put himself into a sexual situation any more than generally he occupies an affective or an ideological one. Faces are for him neither attractive nor repulsive, and people appear to him in one light or another only in so far as he has direct dealings with them, and according to the attitude they adopt towards him, and the attention and solicitude which they bestow upon him. Sun and rain are neither gay nor sad; his humour is determined by elementary organic functions only, and the world is emotionally neutral. Schneider hardly extends his sphere of human relationships at all, and when he makes new friendships they sometimes come to an unfortunate end: this is because they never result, as can be seen on analysis, from a spontaneous impulse, but from a decision made in the abstract. He would like to be able to think about politics and religion, but he does not even try, knowing that these realms are closed to him, and we have seen that generally speaking he never performs an act of authentic thought and substitutes for the intuitive understanding of number or the grasp of meanings the manipulation of signs and a technique depending on "points of support."[18] We discover both that sexual life is one more form of original intentionality, and also bring to view the vital origins of perception, motility and representation by basing all these "processes" on an "intentional arc" which gives way in the patient, and which, in the normal subject, endows experience with its degree of vitality and fruitfulness.

Thus sexuality is not an autonomous cycle. It has internal links with the whole active and cognitive being, these three sectors of behaviour displaying one typical structure, and standing in a relationship to each other of reciprocal expression. Here we concur with the most lasting discoveries of psychoanalysis. Whatever the theoretical declarations of Freud may have been, psychoanalytical research is in fact led to an explanation of man, not in terms of his sexual substructure, but to a discovery in sexuality of relations and attitudes which had previously been held to reside *in consciousness*. Thus the significance of psycho-analysis is less to make psychology biological than to discover a dialectical process in functions thought of as "purely bodily," and to reintegrate sexuality into the human being. A breakaway disciple of Freud[19] shows, for example, that frigidity is scarcely ever bound up with anatomical or physiological conditions, but that it expresses in most cases a refusal of orgasm, of femininity or of sexuality, and this in turn expresses the rejection of the sexual partner and of the destiny which he represents. It would be a mistake to imagine that even with Freud psychoanalysis rules out the description of psychological motives, and is opposed to the phenomenological method: psychoanalysis has, on the contrary, albeit unwittingly, helped to develop it by declaring, as Freud puts it, that every human action "has a meaning,"[20] and by making every effort to understand the event, short of relating it to mechanical circumstances.

For Freud himself the sexual is not the genital, sexual life is not a mere effect of the processes having their seat in the genital organs, the libido is not an instinct, that is, an activity naturally directed towards definite ends, it is the general power, which the psychosomatic subject enjoys, of taking root in different settings, of establishing himself through different experiences, of gaining structures of conduct. It is what causes a man to have a history. In so far as a man's sexual history provides a key to his life, it is because in his sexuality is projected his manner of being towards the world, that is, towards time and other men. There are sexual symptoms at the root of all neuroses, but these symptoms, correctly interpreted, symbolize a whole attitude, whether, for example, one of conquest or of flight. Into the sexual history, conceived as the elaboration of a general form of life, all psychological constituents can enter, because there is no longer an interaction of two causalities and because the genital life is geared to the whole life of the subject. So the question is not so much whether human life does or does not rest on sexuality, as of knowing what is to be understood by sexuality. Psychoanalysis represents a double trend of thought: on the one hand it stresses the sexual substructure of life, on the other it "expands" the notion of sexuality to the extent of absorbing into it the whole of existence. But precisely for that reason, its conclusions, like those of our last paragraph but one, remain ambiguous. When we generalize the notion of sexuality, making it a manner of being in the physical and inter-human world, do we mean, in the last analysis, that all existence has a sexual significance or that every sexual phenomenon has an existential significance? In the first hypothesis, existence would be an abstraction, another name for the sexual life. But since sexual life can no longer be circumscribed, since it is no longer a separate function definable in terms of the causality proper to a set of organs, there is now no sense in saying that all existence is understood through the sexual life, or rather this statement becomes a tautology. Must we then say, conversely, that the sexual phenomenon is merely an expression of our general manner of projecting our setting? But the sexual life is not a mere reflection of existence: an effective life, in the political and ideological field, for example, can be associated with impaired sexuality, and may even benefit from such impairment. On the other hand, the sexual life may, as in Casanova's case for example, possess a kind of technical perfection corresponding to no particularly vigorous version of being in the world. Even though the sexual apparatus has, running through it, the general current of life, it may monopolize it to its own advantage. Life is particularized into separate currents. If words are to have any meaning, the sexual life is a sector of our life bearing a special relation to the existence of sex. There can be no question of allowing sexuality to become lost in existence, as if it were no more then an epiphenomenon. For if we admit that the sexual troubles of neurotics are an expression of their basic drama in magnified form, it still remains to be seen why the sexual expression of the drama is more immature, more frequent and more striking than the rest; and why sexuality is not only a symptom, but a highly important one. Here we meet once more a problem which we have already encountered several times. We showed with Gestalt theory that no layer of sensory data can be identified as immediately dependent on sense-organs: the smallest sensory datum is never presented in any other way than integrated into a configuration and already "patterned." This, as we have said, does not prevent the words "see" and "hear" from having a meaning. We have drawn attention elsewhere[21] to the fact that the specialized regions of the brain, the "optical zone," for example, never function in isolation. The fact remains, as we pointed out, that the visual or auditory side predominates in the picture of the illness, according to the region in which the lesions are situated. Finally, as we have indicated above, biological existence is synchronized with human existence and is never indifferent to its distinctive rhythm. Nevertheless, we shall now add, "living" (leben) is a primary process from which, as a starting point, it becomes possible to "live" (erleben) this or that world, and we must eat and breathe before perceiving and awakening to relational living, belonging to colours and lights through sight, to sounds through hearing, to the body of another through sexuality, before arriving at the life of human relations. Thus sight, hearing, sexuality, the body are not only the routes, instruments or manifestations of personal existence: the latter takes up and absorbs into itself their existence as it is anonymously given. When we say that the life of the body, or the flesh, and the life of the psyche are involved in a relationship of reciprocal expression, or that the bodily event always has a psychic meaning, these formulations need to be explained. Valid as they are for excluding causal thought, they do not mean that the body is the transparent integument of Spirit. The return to existence, as to the setting in which the communication between body and mind can be understood, is not a return to Consciousness or Spirit, and existential psychoanalysis must not serve as a pretext for a revival of mentalistic philosophy (spiritualisme). This will be better understood if we clarify the notions of "expression" and "meaning" which belong to the world of language and thought as already constituted, which we have just applied uncritically to the body-mind relationship, and which bodily experience must in fact lead us to correct.

A girl[22] whose mother has forbidden her to see again the young man with whom she is in love, cannot sleep, loses her appetite and finally the use of speech. An initial manifestation of this loss of speech is found to have occurred during her childhood, after an earthquake, and subsequently again following a severe fright. A strictly Freudian interpretation of this would introduce a reference to the oral phase of sexual development. But what is "fixated" on the mouth is not merely sexual existence, but, more generally, those relations with others having the spoken word as their vehicle. In so far as the emotion elects to find its expression in loss of speech, this is because of all bodily functions speech is the most intimately linked with communal existence, or, as we shall put it, with co-existence. Loss of speech, then, stands for the refusal of co-existence, just as, in other subjects, a fit of hysterics is the means of escaping from the situation. The patient breaks with relational life within the family circle. More generally, she tends to break with life itself: her inability to swallow food arises from the fact that swallowing symbolizes the movement of existence which carries events and assimilates them; the patient is unable, literally, to "swallow" the prohibition which has been imposed upon her.[23] In the subject's childhood, fear was translated by loss of speech because the imminence of death violently interrupted co-existence, and threw her back upon her own personal fate. The symptom of aphonia reappears because the mother's prohibition restores the situation metaphorically, and because, more-over, by shutting off the future from the subject, it leads her back to her favourite forms of behaviour. These motivations may be supposed to take advantage of a particular sensitivity of the throat and the mouth in the case of our subject, a sensitivity which may be related to the history of her libido and to the oral phase of sexuality. Thus through the sexual significance of symptoms can be discerned, in faint outline, their more general significance in relation to past and future, to the self and others, that is to say, to the fundamental dimensions of existence. But as we shall see, the body does not constantly express the modalities of existence in the way that stripes indicate rank, or a house-number a house: the sign here does not only convey its significance, it is filled with it; it is, in a way, what it signifies, as a portrait is the quasi-presence of the absent Peter,[24] or as wax figures in magic are what they stand for. The sick girl does not mime with her body a drama played out "in her consciousness." By losing her voice she does not present a public version of an "inner state," she does not make a "gesture" like that of the head of a state shaking hands with the engine driver and embracing a peasant, or that of a friend who takes offence and stops speaking to me. To have lost one's voice is not to keep silence: one keeps silence only when one can speak. It is true that loss of voice is not paralysis, and this is proved by the fact that, treated by psychological means and left free by her family to see the man she loves, the girl recovers her power of speech. Yet neither is aphonia a deliberate or voluntary silence. It is generally known how, by the notion of pithiatism,[25] the theory of hysteria has been carried beyond the dilemma of paralysis (or of anasthesia) and simulation. If the hysterical patient is a deceiver, it is first and foremost himself that he deceives, so that it is impossible to separate what he *really* feels or thinks and what he overtly expresses: pithiatism is a disease of the *Cogito*, consciousness which has become ambivalent and not a deliberate refusal to declare what one knows. Here, in the same way, the girl does not *cease* to speak, she "loses" her voice as one loses a memory. It is true again that, as psychoanalysis shows, the lost memory is not accidentally lost, it is lost rather in so far as it belongs to an area of my life which I reject, in so far as it has a certain significance and, like all significances, this one exists only for someone. Forgetfulness is therefore an act; I keep the memory at arm's length, as I look past a person whom I do not wish to see. Yet, as psychoanalysis too shows to perfection, though the resistance certainly presupposes an intentional relationship with the memory resisted, it does not set it before us as an object; it does not specifically reject the memory. It is directed against a region of our experience, a certain category, a certain class of memories. The subject who has left a book, which was a present from his wife, in a drawer, and forgotten all about it, and who rediscovers it when they have become reconciled once more,[26] had not really lost the book, but neither did he *know* where it was. Everything connected with his wife had ceased to exist for him, he had shut it out from his life, and at one stroke, broken the circuit of all actions relating to her, and thus placed himself on the hither side of all knowledge and ignorance, assertion and negation, in so far as these were voluntary. Thus, in hysteria and repression, we may well overlook something although we know of it, because our memories and our body, instead of presenting themselves to us in singular and determinate conscious acts, are enveloped in generality. Through this generality we still "have them," but just enough to hold them at a distance from us. We discover in this way that sensory messages or memories are expressly grasped and recognized by us only in so far as they adhere generally to that area of our body and our life to which they are relevant. Such adherence or rejection places the subject in a definite situation and sets bounds, as far as he is concerned, to the immediately available mental field, as the acquisition or loss of a sense organ presents to or removes from his direct grasp an object in the physical field. It cannot be said that the factual situation thus created is the mere consciousness of a situation, for that would amount to saying that the "forgotten" memory, arm or leg are arrayed before my consciousness, present and near to me in the same sense as are the "preserved" regions of my past or of my body. No more can it be said that the loss of voice is voluntary. Will presupposes a field of possibilities among which I choose: here is Peter, I can speak to him or not. But if I lose my power of speech, Peter no longer exists for me as an interlocutor, sought after or rejected; what collapses is the whole field of possibilities. I cut myself off even from that mode of communication and significance which silence provides. Of course we may go on to speak of hypocrisy or bad faith. But then it will be necessary to draw a distinction between psychological and metaphysical hypocrisy. The former deceives others by concealing from them thoughts expressly in the mind of the subject. It is fortuitous and easily avoided. The latter is self-deceiving through the medium of generality, thus leading finally to a state or a situation which is not an inevitability, but which is not posited or voluntary. It is even to be found in the "sincere" or "authentic" man whenever he undertakes to be something or other unqualifiedly. It is part of the human lot. When the hysterical fit has reached its climax, even if the subject has sought it as the means of escaping from an intolerable situation and plunges into it as into a place of refuge, he *scarcely* hears anything more, he can *scarcely* see, he has *almost* become the spasmodic and panting existence which struggles on the bed. The intensity of resentment is such that it becomes resentment against X, against life, an absolute resentment. With every minute that passes, freedom is depreciated and becomes less probable. Even if freedom is never impossible and even if it may always derail the dialectics of bad faith, the fact remains that a night's sleep has the same power: what can be surmounted by this anonymous force must indeed be of the same nature as it, and so it must at least be admitted that resentment or loss of voice, as they persist, become consistent like things, that they assume a structure, and that any decision that interrupted them would come from a *lower* level than that of "will." The patient cuts himself off from his voice as certain insects sever one of their own legs. He is literally without a voice. In treating this condition, psychological medicine does not act on the patient by making him *know* the origin of his illness: sometimes a touch of the hand puts a stop to the spasms and restores to the patient his speech[27] and the same procedure, having acquired a ritual significance, will subsequently be enough to deal with fresh attacks. In any case, in psychological treatment of any kind, the coming to awareness would remain purely cognitive, the patient would not accept the meaning of his disturbances as revealed to him without the personal relationship formed with the doctor, or without the confidence and friendship felt towards him, and the change of existence resulting from this friendship. Neither symptom nor cure is worked out at the level of objective or positing consciousness, but below that level. Loss of voice as a situation may be compared to sleep: I lie down in bed, on my left side, with my knees drawn up; I close my eyes and breathe slowly, putting my plans out of my mind. But the power of my will or consciousness stops there. As the faithful, in the Dionysian mysteries, invoke the god by miming scenes from his life, I call up the visitation of sleep by imitating the breathing and posture of the sleeper. The god is actually there when the faithful can no longer distinguish themselves from the part they are playing, when their body and their consciousness cease to bring in, as an obstacle, their particular opacity, and when they are totally fused in the myth. There is a moment when sleep "comes," settling on this imitation of itself which I have been offering to it, and I succeed in becoming what I was trying to be: an unseeing and almost unthinking mass, riveted to a point in space and in the world henceforth only through the anonymous alertness of the senses. It is true that this last link makes waking up a possibility: through these half-open doors things will return or the sleeper will come back into the world. In the same way the patient who has broken with co-existence can still perceive the sensible integument of other people, and abstractly conceive the future by means, for instance, of a calendar. In this sense the sleeper is never completely isolated within himself, never totally a sleeper, and the patient is never totally cut off from the intersubjective world, never totally ill. But what, in the sleeper and the patient, makes possible a return to the real world, are still only impersonal functions, sense organs and language. We remain free in relation to sleep and sickness to the exact extent to which we remain always involved in the waking and healthy state, our freedom rests on our being in a situation, and is itself a situation. Sleep and waking, illness and health are not modalities of consciousness or will, but presuppose an "existential step."[28] Loss of voice does not merely represent a refusal of speech, or anorexia a refusal of life; they are that refusal of others or refusal of the future, torn from the transitive nature of "inner phenomena," generalized, consummated, trans-formed into *de facto* situations.

The body's role is to ensure this metamorphosis. It transforms ideas into things, and my mimicry of sleep into real sleep. The body can symbolize existence because it brings it into being and actualizes it. It sustains its dual existential action of systole and diastole. On the one hand, indeed, it is the possibility enjoyed by my existence of discarding itself, of making itself anon-ymous and passive, and of bogging itself down in a scholastic. In the case of the girl just discussed, the move towards the future, towards the living present or towards the past, the power of learning, of maturing, of entering into commun-ication with others, have become, as it were, arrested in a bodily symptom, existence is tied up and the body has become "the place where life hides away."[29] For the patient, nothing further happens, nothing assumes meaning and form in life, or more precisely there occurs only a recurrent and always identical "now," life flows back on itself and history is dissolved in natural time. Even when normal and even when involved in situations with other people, the subject, in so far as he has a body, retains every moment the power to withdraw from it. At the very moment when I live in the world, when I am given over to my plans, my occupations, my friends, my memories, I can close my eyes, lie down, listen to the blood pulsating in my ears, lose myself in some pleasure or pain, and shut myself up in this anonymous life which subtends my personal one. But precisely because my body can shut itself off from the world, it is also what opens me out upon the world and places me in a situation there. The momentum of existence towards others, towards the future, towards the world can be restored as a river unfreezes. The girl will recover her voice, not by an intellectual effort or by an abstract decree of the will, but through a conversion in which the whole of her body makes a concentrated effort in the form of a genuine gesture, as we seek and recover a name forgotten not "in our mind," but "in our head" or "on the tip of our tongue." The memory or the voice is recovered when the body once more opens itself to others or to the past, when it opens the way to co-existence and once more (in the active sense) acquires significance beyond itself. Moreover, even when cut off from the circuit of existence, the body never quite falls back on to itself. Even if I become absorbed in the experience of my body and in the solitude of sensations, I do not succeed in abolishing all reference of my life to a world. At every moment some intention springs afresh from me, if it is only towards the things round about me which catch my eye, or towards the instants, which are thrown up, and which thrust back into the past what I have just lived through. I never become quite a thing in the world; the density of existence as a thing always evades me, my own substance slips away from me internally, and some intention is always foreshadowed. In so far as it carries within it "sense organs," bodily existence is never self-sufficient, it is always a prey to an active nothingness, it continually sets the prospect of living before me, and natural time at every successive moment adumbrates the empty form of the true event. This prospect may indeed fail to elicit any response. The instant of natural time does not establish anything, it has to be immediately renewed, and indeed is renewed in another instant, and the sensory functions by themselves do not cause me to be in the world: when I become absorbed in my body, my eyes present me with no more than the perceptible outer covering of things and of other people, things themselves take on unreality, behaviour degenerates into the absurd, and the present itself, as in cases of false recognition, loses its consistency and takes on an air of eternity. Bodily existence which runs through me, yet does so independently of me, is only the barest raw material of a genuine presence in the world. Yet at least it provides the possibility of such presence, and establishes our first consonance with the world. I may very well take myself away from the human world and set aside personal existence, but only to rediscover in my body the same power, this time unnamed, by which I am condemned to being. It may be said that the body is "the hidden form of being ourself,"[30] or on the other hand, that personal existence is the taking up and manifestation of a being in a given situation. If we therefore say that the body expresses existence at every moment, this is in the sense in which a word expresses thought. Anterior to conventional means of expression, which reveal my thoughts to others only because already, for both myself and them, meanings are provided for each sign, and which in this sense do not give rise to genuine communication at all; we must, as we shall see, recognize a primary process of signification in which the thing expressed does not exist apart from the expression, and in which the signs themselves induce their significance externally. In this way the body expresses total existence, not because it is an external accompaniment to that existence, but because existence comes into its own in the body. This incarnate significance is the central phenomenon of which body and mind, sign and significance are abstract moments.

The Natural World and the Body

We are now in a position to approach the analysis of the thing as an intersensory entity. The thing as presented to sight (the moon's pale disc) or to touch (my skull as I can feel it when I touch it), and which stays the same for us through a series of experiences, is neither a *quale* genuinely subsisting, nor the notion or consciousness of such an objective property, but what is discovered or taken up by our gaze or our movement, a question to which these things provide a fully appropriate reply. The object which presents itself to the gaze or the touch arouses a certain motor intention which aims not at the movements of one's own body, but at the thing itself from which they are, as it were, suspended. And in so far as my hand knows hardness and softness, and my gaze knows the moon's light, it is as a certain way of linking up with the phenomenon and communicating with it. Hardness and softness, roughness and smoothness, moonlight and sunlight, present themselves in our recollection, not preeminently as sensory contents, but as certain kinds of symbiosis, certain ways the outside has of invading us and certain ways we have of meeting this invasion, and memory here merely frees the framework of the perception from the place where it originates. If the constants of each sense are thus understood, the question of defining the inter-sensory thing into which they unite as a collection of stable attributes or as the notion of this collection, will not arise. The sensory "properties" of a thing together constitute one and the same thing, just as my gaze, my touch and all my other senses are together the powers of one and the same body integrated into one and the same action. The surface which I am about to recognize as the surface of the table, when vaguely looked at, already summons me to focus upon it, and demands those movements of convergence which will endow it with its "true" aspect. Similarly any object presented to one sense calls upon itself the concordant operation of all the others. I see a surface colour because I have a visual field, and because the arrangement of the field leads my gaze to that surface – I perceive a thing because I have a field of existence and because each phenomenon, on its appearance, attracts towards that field the whole of my body as a system of perceptual powers. I run through appearances and reach the real colour or the real shape when my experience is at its maximum of clarity, in spite of the fact that Berkeley may retort that a fly would see the same object differently or that a stronger microscope would transform it: these different appearances are for me appearances of a certain true spectacle, that in which the perceived configuration, for a sufficient degree of clarity, reaches its maximum richness.[31] I have visual objects because I have a visual field in which richness and clarity are in inverse proportion to each other, and because these two demands, either of which taken separately might be carried to infinity, when brought together, produce a certain culmination and optimum balance in the perceptual process. In the same way, what I call experience of the thing or of reality – not merely of a reality-for-sight or for-touch, but of an absolute reality – is my full co-existence with the phenomenon, at the moment when it is in every way at its maximum articulation, and the "data of the different senses" are directed towards this one pole, as my "aims" as I look through a microscope vacillate about one predominant "target." I do not propose to bestow the term "visual thing" upon a phenomenon which, like areas of colour, presents no maximum visibility through the various experiences which I have of it, or which, like the sky, remote and thin on the horizon, unlocalized and diffuse at the zenith, allows itself to be contaminated by the structures closest to it without setting over against them any configuration of its own. If a phenomenon – for example, a reflection or a light gust of wind – strikes only one of my senses, it is a mere phantom, and it will come near to real existence only if, by some chance, it becomes capable of speaking to my other senses, as does the wind when, for example, it blows strongly and can be seen in the tumult it causes in the surrounding countryside. Cézanne declared that a picture contains within itself even the smell of the landscape.[32] He meant that the arrangement of colour on the thing (and in the work of art, if it catches the thing in its entirety) signifies by itself all the responses which would be elicited through an examination by the remaining senses; that a thing would not have this colour had it not also this shape, these tactile properties, this resonance, this odour, and that the thing is the absolute fullness which my undivided existence projects before itself. The unity of the thing beyond all its fixed properties is not a substratum, a vacant X, an inherent subject, but that unique accent which is to be found in each one of them, that unique manner of existing of which they are a second order expression. For example, the brittleness, hardness, transparency and crystal ring of a glass all translate a single manner of being. If a sick man sees the devil, he sees at the same time his smell, his flames and smoke, because the significant unity "devil" is precisely that acrid, fire-and-brimstone essence. There is a symbolism in the thing which links each sensible quality to the rest. Heat enters experience as a kind of vibration of the thing; with colour on the other hand it is as if the thing is thrust outside itself, and it is *a priori* necessary that an extremely hot object should redden, for it is its excess of vibration which causes it to blaze forth.[33] The passing of sensory givens before our eyes or under our hands is, as it were, a language which teaches itself, and in which the meaning is secreted by the very structure of the signs, and this is why it can literally be said that our senses question things and that things reply to them. "The sensible appearance is what reveals (*kundgibt*), and expresses as such what it is not itself."[34] We understand the thing as we understand a new kind of behaviour, not, that is, through any intellectual operation of subsumption, but by taking up on our own account the mode of existence which the observable signs adumbrate before us. A form of behaviour outlines a certain manner of treating the world. In the same way, in the interaction of things, each one is characterized by a kind of *a priori* to which it remains faithful in all its encounters with the outside world. The significance of a thing inhabits that thing as the soul inhabits the body: it is not behind appearances. The significance of the ash-tray (at least its total and individual significance, as this is given in perception) is not a certain idea of the ash-tray which co-ordinates its sensory aspects and is accessible to the understanding alone, it animates the ash-tray, and is self-evidently embodied in it. That is why we say that in perception the thing is given to us "in person," or "in the flesh." Prior to and independently of other people, the thing achieves that miracle of expression: an inner reality which reveals itself externally, a significance which descends into the world and begins its existence there, and which can be fully understood only when the eyes seek it in its own location. Thus the thing is correlative to my body and, in more general terms, to my existence, of which my body is merely the stabilized structure. It is constituted in the hold which my body takes upon it; it is not first of all a meaning for the understanding, but a structure accessible to inspection by the body, and if we try to describe the real as it appears to us in perceptual experience, we find it overlaid with anthropological predicates.

The relations between things or aspects of things having always our body as their vehicle, the whole of nature is the setting of our own life, or our interlocutor in a sort of dialogue. That is why in the last analysis we cannot conceive anything which is not perceived or perceptible. As Berkeley says, even an unexplored desert has at least one person to observe it, namely myself when I think of it, that is, when I perceive it in purely mental experience. The thing is inseparable from a person perceiving it, and can never be actually *in itself* because its articulations are those of our very existence, and because it stands at the other end of our gaze or at the terminus of a sensory exploration which invests it with humanity. To this extent, every perception is a communication or a communion, the taking up or completion by us of some extraneous intention or, on the other hand, the complete expression outside ourselves of our perceptual powers and a coition, so to speak, of our body with things. The fact that this may not have been realized earlier is explained by the fact that any coming to awareness of the perceptual world was hampered by the prejudices arising from objective thinking. The function of the latter is to reduce all phenomena which bear witness to the union of subject and world, putting in their place the clear idea of the object as *in itself* and of the subject as pure consciousness. It therefore severs the links which unite the thing and the embodied subject, leaving only sensible qualities to make up our world (to the exclusion of the modes of appearance which we have described), and preferably visual qualities, because these give the impression of being autonomous, and because they are less directly linked to our body and present us with an object rather than introducing us into an atmosphere. But in reality all things are concretions of a setting, and any explicit perception of a thing survives in virtue of a previous communication with a certain atmosphere. We are not "a collection of eyes, ears and organs of touch with their cerebral projections. . . . Just as all literary works . . . are only particular cases of the possible permutations of the sounds which make up language and of their literal signs, so qualities or sensations represent the elements from which the great poetry of our world (*Umwelt*) is made up. But just as surely as someone knowing only sounds and letters would have no understanding of literature, and would miss not only its ultimate nature but everything about it, so the world is not given and things are not accessible to those for whom "sensations" are the given."[35] The perceived is not necessarily an object present before me as a piece of knowledge to be acquired, it may be a "unity of value" which is present to me only practically. If a picture has been removed from a living room, we may perceive that a change has taken place without being able to say what. I perceive everything that is part of my environment, and my environment includes "everything of which the existence or nonexistence, the nature or modification counts in practice for me":[36] the storm which has not yet broken, whose signs I could not even list and which I cannot even forecast, but for which I am "worked up" and prepared – the periphery of the visual field which the hysterical subject does not expressly grasp, but which nevertheless co-determines his movements and orientation – the respect of other men, or that loyal friendship which I take for granted, but which are none the less there for me, since they leave me morally speaking in mid-air when I am deprived of them.[37] Love *is* in the flowers prepared by Félix de Vandenesse for Madame de Mortsauf, just as unmistakeably as in a caress: "I thought that the colours and the foliage had a harmony and a poetry which emerges into the understanding by delighting the gaze, just as musical phrases awaken countless memories in hearts that love and are loved. If colour is organized light, must it not have a meaning, as different combinations of air have theirs. . . Love has its heraldry and the countess secretly deciphered it. She gave me one of those sharp looks that seem like the cry of a sick man touched on his wound: she was both embarrassed and delighted." The flowers are self-evidently a love bouquet, and yet it is impossible to say what in them signifies love, and that is even the reason why Mme de Mortsauf can accept them without breaking her vows. There is no way of understanding them other than by looking at them, but to the beholder they say what they mean. Their significance is the track of an existence, legible and comprehensible for another existence. Natural perception is not a science, it does not posit the things with which science deals, it does not hold them at arm's length in order to observe them, but lives with them; it is the "opinion" or the "primary faith" which binds us to a world as to our native land, and the being of what is perceived is the antepredicative being towards which our whole existence is polarized.

However, we have not exhausted the meaning of "the thing" by defining it as the correlative of our body and our life. After all, we grasp the unity of our body only in that of the thing, and it is by taking things as our starting point that our hands, eyes and all our sense-organs appear to us as so many interchangeable instruments. The body by itself, the body at rest is merely an obscure mass, and we perceive it as a precise and identifiable being when it moves towards a thing, and in so far as it is intentionally projected outwards, and even then this perception is never more than incidental and marginal to consciousness, the centre of which is occupied with things and the world. One cannot, as we have said, conceive any perceived thing without someone to perceive it. But the fact remains that the thing presents itself to the person who perceives it as a thing in itself, and thus poses the problem of a genuine *in-itself-for-us*. Ordinarily we do not notice this because our perception, in the context of our everyday concerns, alights on things sufficiently attentively to discover in them their familiar presence, but not sufficiently so to disclose the non–human element which lies hidden in them. But the thing holds itself aloof from us and remains self-sufficient. This will become clear if we suspend our ordinary preoccupations and pay a metaphysical and disinterested attention to it. It is then hostile and alien, no longer an interlocutor, but a resolutely silent Other, a Self which evades us no less than does intimacy with an outside consciousness. The thing and the world, we have already said, are offered to perceptual communication as is a familiar face with an expression which is immediately understood. But then a face expresses something only through the arrangements of the colours and lights which make it up, the meaning of the gaze being not behind the eyes, but in them, and a touch of colour more or less is all the painter needs in order to transform the facial expression of a portrait. In the work of his earlier years, Cézanne tried to paint the expression first and foremost, and that is why he never caught it. He gradually learned that expression is the language of the thing itself and springs from its configuration. His painting is an attempt to recapture the physiognomy of things and faces by the integral reproduction of their sensible configuration. This is what nature constantly and effortlessly achieves, and it is why the paintings of Cézanne are "those of a pre-world in which as yet no men existed."[38] The thing appeared to us above as the goal of a bodily teleology, the norm of our psycho-physiological setting. But that was merely a psychological definition which does not make the full meaning of the thing defined explicit, and which reduces the thing to those experiences in which we encounter it. We now discover the core of reality: a thing is a thing because, whatever it imparts to us, is imparted through the very organization of its sensible aspects. The "real" is that environment in which each moment is not only inseparable from the rest, but in some way synonymous with them, in which the "aspects" are mutually significatory and absolutely equivalent. This is perfect fulness: it is impossible completely to describe the colour of the carpet without saying that it *is* a carpet, made of wool, and without implying in this colour a certain tactile value, a certain weight and a certain resistance to sound. The thing is an entity of a kind such that the complete definition of one of its attributes demands that of the subject in its entirety: an entity, consequently, the significance of which is indistinguishable from its total appearance. Cézanne again said: "The outline and the colour are no longer distinct; in proportion as one paints, one outlines, and the more the colour is harmonized, the more definite the outline becomes ... when the colour is at its richest, the form is at its most complete."[39] With the structure lighting-lighted, background and foreground are possible. With the appearance of the thing, there can at last be univocal forms and positions. The system of appearances, the prespatial fields acquire an anchorage and ultimately become a space. But it is not the case that geometrical features alone are merged with colour. The very significance of the thing is built up before our eyes, a significance which no verbal analysis can exhaust, and which merges with the exhibiting of the thing in its self-evidence. Every touch of colour applied by Cézanne must, as E. Bernard says, "contain the atmosphere, the light, the object, the relief, the character, the outline and the style."[40] Each fragment of a visible spectacle satisfies an infinite number of conditions, and it is of the nature of the real to compress into each of its instants an infinity of relations. Like the thing, the picture has to be seen and not defined, nevertheless, though it is a small world which reveals itself within the larger one, it cannot lay claim to the same substantiality. We feel that it is put together by design, that in it significance precedes existence and clothes itself in only the minimum of matter necessary for its communication. The miracle of the real world, on the other hand, is that in it significance and existence are one, and that we see the latter lodge itself in no uncertain fashion in the former. In the realm of imagination, I have no sooner formed the intention of seeing than I already believe that I have seen. The imaginary has no depth, and does not respond to our efforts to vary our points of view; it does not lend itself to our observation.[41] We never have a hold upon it. In every perception, on the other hand, it is the material itself which assumes significance and form. If I wait for someone at a door in a poorly lit street, each person who comes out has an indistinct appearance. *Someone* is coming out, and I do not yet know whether I can recognize him as the person I am waiting for. The familiar figure will emerge from this nebulous background as the earth does from a ground mist. The real is distinguishable from our fictions because in reality the significance encircles and permeates matter. Once a picture is torn up, we have in our hands nothing but pieces of daubed canvas. But if we break up a stone and then further break up the fragments, the pieces remaining are still pieces of stone. The real lends itself to unending exploration; it is inexhaustible. This is why objects belonging to man, tools, seem to be placed on the world, whereas things are rooted in a background of nature which is alien to man. For our human existence, the thing is much less a pole which attracts than one which repels. We do not begin by knowing the perspective aspects of the thing; it is not mediated by our senses, our sensations or our perspectives; we go straight to it, and it is only in a secondary way that we become aware of the limits of our knowledge and of ourselves as knowing. Here is a die; let us consider it as it is presented, in the natural attitude, to a subject who has never wondered about perception, and who lives among things. The die is there, lying in the world. When the subject moves round it, there appear, not *signs*, but sides of the die. He does not perceive projections or even profiles of the die, but he sees the die itself at one time from this side, at another from that, and those appearances which are not yet firmly fixed intercommunicate, run into each other, and all radiate from a central *Würfelhaftigkeit*[42] which is the mystical link between them.

A set of reductions makes its appearance from the moment we take the perceiving subject into account. In the first place I notice that this die is for me only. Perhaps after all people nearby do not see it, and this alone deprives it of some element of its reality; it ceases to be *in itself* in order to become the pole of a personal history. Then I observe that the die is, strictly speaking, presented to me only through sight, and immediately I am left with nothing but the outer surface of the whole die; it loses its materiality, empties itself, and is reduced to a visual structure of form, colour, light and shade. But the form, colour, light and shade are not in a void, for they still retain a point of support, namely the visual thing. Furthermore the visual thing has still a spatial structure which endows its qualitative properties with a particular value: if I learn that the die is merely an illusory one, its colour changes straight away, and it no longer has the same manner of modulating space. All the spatial relations to be found in the die and which are capable of being made explicit, for example the distance from its nearer to its farther face, the "real" size of the angles, the "real" direction of its sides, are indivisible in its being as a visible die. It is by way of a third reduction that we pass from the visual thing to the perspective aspect: I observe that the faces of the die cannot all fall beneath my gaze, and that certain of them undergo distortions. Through a final reduction, I arrive ultimately at the sensation which is no longer a property of the thing, or even of the perspective aspect, but a modification of my body.[43] The experience of the thing does not go through all these mediations, and consequently the thing is not presented to a mind which seizes each constituent layer as representative of a higher layer, building it up from start to finish. It exists primarily in its self-evidence, and any attempt to define the thing either as a pole of my bodily life, or as a permanent possibility of sensations, or as a synthesis of appearances, puts in place of the thing itself in its primordial being an imperfect reconstruction of the thing with the aid of bits and pieces of subjective provenance. How are we to understand both that the thing is the correlative of my knowing body, and that it rejects that body?

What is given is not the thing on its own, but the experience of the thing, or something transcendent standing in the wake of one's subjectivity, some kind of natural entity of which a glimpse is afforded through a personal history. If one tried, according to the realistic approach, to make perception into some coincidence with the thing, it would no longer be possible to understand what the perceptual event was, how the subject managed to assimilate the thing, how after coinciding with the thing he was able to consign it to his own history, since *ex hypothesi* he would have nothing of it in his possession. In order to perceive things, we need to live them. Yet we reject the idealism involved in the synthetic view, because it too distorts our lived-through relationship to things. In so far as the perceiving subject synthesizes the percept, he has to dominate and grasp in thought a material of perception, to organize and himself link together, from the inside, all the aspects of the thing, which means that perception ceases to be inherent in an individual subject and a point of view, and that the thing loses its transcendence and opacity. To "live" a thing is not to coincide with it, nor fully to embrace it in thought. Our problem, therefore, becomes clear. The perceiving subject must, without relinquishing his place and his point of view, and in the opacity of sensation, reach out towards things to which he has, in advance, no key, and for which he nevertheless carries within himself the project, and open himself to an absolute Other which he is making ready in the depths of his being. The thing is not all of a piece, for though the perspective aspects, and the ever-changing flow of appearances, are not explicitly posited, all are at least ready to be perceived and given in non-positing consciousness, to precisely the extent necessary for me to be able to escape from them into the thing. When I perceive a pebble, I am not expressly conscious of knowing it only through my eyes, of enjoying only certain perspective aspects of it, and yet an analysis in these terms, if I undertake it, does not surprise me. Beforehand I knew obscurely that my gaze was the medium and instrument of comprehensive perception, and the pebble appeared to me in the full light of day in opposition to the concentrated darkness of my bodily organs. I can imagine possible fissures in the solid mass of the thing if I take it into my head to close one eye or to think of the perspective. It is in this way that it is true to say that the thing is the outcome of a flow of subjective appearances.

And yet I did not actually constitute it, in the sense that I did not actively and through a process of mental inspection posit the interrelations of the many aspects presented to the senses, and the relations of all of them to my different kinds of sensory apparatus. We have expressed this by saying that I perceive with my body. The visual thing appears when my gaze, following the indications offered by the spectacle, and drawing together the light and shade spread over it, ultimately settles on the lighted surface as upon that which the light reveals. My gaze "knows" the significance of a certain patch of light in a certain context; it understands the logic of lighting. Expressed in more general terms, there is a logic of the world to which my body in its entirety conforms, and through which things of intersensory significance become possible for us. In so far as it is capable of synergy, my body knows the significance, for the totality of my experience, of this or that colour added or subtracted, and the occurrence of any such change is immediately picked out from the object's presentation and general significance. To have senses, sight for example, is to possess that general apparatus, that cast of possible, visual relations with the help of which we are able to take up any given visual grouping. To have a body is to possess a universal setting, a schema of all types of perceptual unfolding and of all those inter-sensory correspondences which lie beyond the segment of the world which we are actually perceiving. A thing is, therefore, not actually *given* in perception, it is internally taken up by us, reconstituted and experienced by us in so far as it is bound up with a world, the basic structures of which we carry with us, and of which it is merely one of many possible concrete forms. Although a part of our living experience, it is nevertheless transcendent in relation to our life because the human body, with its habits which weave round it a human environment, has running through it a movement towards the world itself. Animal behaviour aims at an animal setting (*Umwelt*) and centres of resistance (*Widerstand*). If we try to subject it to natural stimuli devoid of concrete significance, we produce neuroses.[44] Human behaviour opens upon a world (*Welt*) and upon an object (*Gegenstand*) beyond the tools which it makes for itself, and one may even treat one's own body as an object. Human life is defined in terms of this power which it has of denying itself in objective thought, a power which stems from its primordial attachment to the world itself. Human life "understands" not only a certain definite environment, but an infinite number of possible environments, and it understands itself because it is thrown into a natural world.

Notes

1   The phantom limb lends itself neither to a purely physiological explanation, nor to a purely psychological one. Such is the conclusion of J. Lhermitte, *L'Image de notre Corps*, p. 126.

2   Schilder, *Das Körperschema*; Menninger-Lerchenthal, *Das Truggebilde der eigenen Gestalt*, p. 174; Lhermitte, *L'Image de notre Corps*, p. 143.

3   Cf. *La Structure du Comportement*, pp. 47 and ff.

4   Cf. *La Structure du Comportement*, pp. 196 and ff.

5   When Bergson stresses the unity of perception and action and invents, for its expression, the term "sensory-motor process," he is clearly seeking to involve consciousness in the world. But if feeling is representing a quality to oneself, and if movement is changing one's position in the objective world, then between sensation and movement, even taken in their nascent state, no *compromise* is possible, and they are distinct from each other as are the *for-itself* and the *in-itself*. Generally speaking, Bergson saw that the body and the mind communicate with each other through the medium of time, that to be a mind is to stand above time's flow and that to have a body is to have a present. The body, he says, is an instantaneous section made in the becoming of consciousness (*Matière et Mémoire*, p. 150). But the body remains for him what we have called the objective body; consciousness remains knowledge; time remains a successive "now," whether it "snowballs upon itself" or is spread in spatialized time. Bergson can therefore only compress or expand the series of "present moments"; he never reaches the unique movement whereby the three dimensions of time are constituted, and one cannot see why duration is squeezed into a present, or why consciousness becomes involved in a body and a world....

6   E. Menninger-Lerchenthal, *Das Truggebilde der eigenen Gestalt*.

7   This term is the usual one in Husserl's unpublished writings.

8   Goldstein, *Über die Abhängigkeit*, p. 163.

9   Lhermitte, G. Lévy and Kyriako, *Les Perturbations de la représentation spatiale chez les apraxiques*, p. 597.

10   Lhermitte and Trelles, *Sur l'apraxie constructive, les troubles de la pensée spatiale et de la somatognosie dans l'apraxie*, p. 428. Cf. Lhermitte, de Massary and Kyriako, *Le Rôle de la pensée spatiale dans l'apraxie*.

11   Head and Holmes, *Sensory disturbances from cerebral lesions*, p. 187.

12   Grünbaum, *Aphasie und Motorik*.

13   Goldstein, Van Woerkom, Bouman and Grünbaum.

14   Grünbaum, op. cit., pp. 386–92.

15   Grünbaum, op. cit., pp. 397–8.

16   *Ibid.*, p. 394.

17   *Ibid.*, p. 396.

18   Cf. supra, p. 133.

19   W. Stekel, *La Femme frigide*.

20   Freud, *Introductory Lectures*, p. 31. Freud himself, in his concrete analyses, abandons causal thought, when he demonstrates that symptoms always have several meanings, or, as he puts it, are "overdetermined." For this amounts to admitting that a symptom, at the time of its onset, always finds *raisons d'être* in the subject, so that no event in a life is, strictly speaking, externally determined. Freud compares the accident occurring from outside to the foreign body which, for the oyster, is

merely the occasion for secreting a pearl. See for example *Cinq psychanalyses*, Ch. I, p. 91, note 1.

21   *La Structure du Comportement*, pp. 80 and ff.

22   Binswanger, *Über Psychotherapie*, pp. 113 and ff.

23   Binswanger (*Über Psychotherapie*, p. 188), points out that one patient, as he recollects a traumatic memory, and tells it to the doctor, relaxes the sphincter.

24   J.-P. Sartre, *L'Imaginaire*, p. 38.

25   *Pithiatism*: the class of hysterical symptoms which can be made to disappear or be reproduced by means of suggestion (Translator's note).

26   Freud, *Introductory Lectures*, p. 43.

27   Binswanger, *Über Psychotherapie*, pp. 113 and ff.

28   Binswanger, *Über Psychotherapie*, p. 188.

29   *Ibid.*, p. 182

30   Binswanger, *Über Psychotherapie*, "eine verdeckte Form unseres Selbstseins" p. 188.

31   Schapp, *Beiträge zur Phänomenologie der Wahrnehmung*, pp. 59 and ff.

32   J. Gasquet, *Cézanne*, p. 81.

33   This unity of the sensory experiences rests on their integration in a single life of which they thus become the visible witness and emblem. The perceived world is not only a system of symbols of each sense in terms of the other senses, but also a set of symbols of human life, as is proved by the "flames" of passion, the "light" of the spirit and so many other metaphors and myths. H. Conrad-Martius, *Realontologie*, p. 302.

34   H. Conrad-Martius, ibid., p. 196. The same author (*Zur Ontologie und Erscheinungslehre der realen Aussenwelt*) speaks of a *Selbstkundgabe* of the object (p. 371).

35   Scheler, *Der Formalismus in der Ethik und die materiale Wertethik*, pp. 149–51.

36   *Ibid.*, p. 140.

37   *Ibid.*

38   F. Novotny, *Das Problem des Menschen Cézanne im Verhältnis zu seiner Kunst*, p. 275.

39   Gasquet, *Cézanne*, p. 123.

40   E. Bernard, *La Méthode de Cézanne*, p. 298.

41   J.-P. Sartre, *L'Imaginaire*, p. 19.

42   Scheler, *Der Formalismus in der Ethik*, p. 52.

43   Scheler, *Der Formalismus in der Ethik*, pp. 51–4.

44   See *La Structure du Comportement*, pp. 72 and ff.

References

Bergson, *Matiere et mémoire*, Paris, Alcan, 1919.

Bernard, *La Méthode de Cézanne*, Mercure de France, 1920.

Binswanger, *Traum und Existenz*, Neue Schweizer Rundschau, 1930.

Binswanger, *Über Psychotherapie*, Nervenarzt, 1935.

Conrad-Martius, *Zur Ontologie und Erscheinungslehre der realen Aussenwelt*, Jahrbuch für Philosophie und Phänomenologische Forschung, III.

Conrad-Martius, *Realontologie*, Jahrbuch für Philosophie und Phänomenologische Forschung, VI.

Freud, *Introductory Lectures on Psycho-Analysis*, London, Allen and Unwin, 1922.

—— *Cinq Psychanalyses*, Paris, Denoël et Steele, 1935.

Gasquet, *Cézanne*, Paris, Bernheim Jeune, 1926.

Goldstein, *Über die Abhängigkeit der Bewegungen von optischen Vorgängen*, Monatschrift für
Psychiatrie und Neurologie, Festschrift Liepmann, 1923.

Grünbaum, *Aphasie und Motorik*, Zeitschrift f. d. ges. Neurologie und Psychiatrie, 1930.

Head and Holmes, "Sensory Disturbances From Cerebral Lesions," *Brain*, 1911–12.

Janet, *De l'Angoisse à l'Extase*, II, Paris, Alcan, 1928.

Katz, *Der Aufbau der Tastwelt*, Zeitschrift für Psychologie, Ergbd. 11, Leipzig, 1925.

Lhermitte, "L'Image de notre corps," *Nouvelle Revue critique*, 1939.

Lhermitte, Lévy and Kyriako, "Les Perturbations de la pensée spatiale chez les apraxiques, à propos de deux cas clinique d'apraxie," *Revue Neurologique*, 1925.

Lhermitte, De Massary and Kyriako, "Le Röle de la pensée spatiale dans l'apraxie,"
Revue Neurologique, 1928.

Lhermitte and Trelles, "Sur L'apraxie pure constructive, les troubles de la pensée spatiale
et de la somatognosie dans l'apraxie," *Encéphale*, 1933.

Liepmann, *Über Störungen des Handelns bei Gehirnkranken*, Berlin, 1905.

Menninger-Lerchenthal, *Das Truggebilde der eigenen Gestalt*, Berlin, Karger, 1923.

Merleau-Ponty, *La Structure du Comportement*, Paris, Presses Universitaires de France,
1942.

—— *Phenomenology of Perception*, trans. Colin Smith, New York, Humanities Press,
1974.

Novotny, *Das Problem des Menschen Cézanne im Verhältnis zu seiner Kunst*, Zeitschrift für
Aesthetik und allgemeine Kunstwissenschaft, No. 26, 1932.

Piaget, *La Représentation du monde chez l'enfant*, Paris, Alcan, 1926.

Sartre, *Esquisse d'une théorie de l'émotion*, Paris, Hermann, 1939.

—— *L'Imaginaire*, Paris, Gallimard, 1940.

Schapp, *Beiträge zur Phänomenologie der Wahrnehmung*, Inaugural Dissertation, Göttingen,
Kaestner, 1910, and Erlangen, 1925.

Scheler, *Der Formalismus in der Ethik und die materiale Wertethik*, Jahrbuch für Philosophie
und Phänomenologische Forschung, I–II, Halle, Niemeyer, 1927.

Schilder, *Das Körperschema*, Berlin, Springer, 1923.

Sittig, *Über Apraxie, eine klinische Studie*, Berlin, Karger, 1931.

Stein, *Beiträge zur phislosophischen Begründung der Psychologie und der Geisteswissenschaften*,
I, *Psychische Kausalität*, Jahrbuch für Philosophie und Phänomenologische Forschung,
V.

Stekel, *La Femme frigide*, Paris, Gallimard, 1937.

Valéry, *Introduction à la Méthode de Léonard de Vinci, Variété*.

7

SATURATED INTENTIONALITY

Anthony J. Steinbock[1]

The first breakthrough of this universal a priori of correlation between the experienced object and manners of givenness (which occurred during my Logical Investigations around 1898) affected me so deeply that my whole subsequent life- work has been dominated by the task of systematically elaborating on this a priori of correlation.

Edmund Husserl[2]

To our mind Husserl's originality goes beyond the notion of intentionality; it is found in the elaboration of this notion and in the discovery, beneath the intentionality of representations, of a deeper intentionality that others have called existence.

Maurice Merleau-Ponty[3]

Introduction

Phenomenologically, intentionality is saturated; intentionality is characterized not by lack, but surplus, not by absence, but too much presence. Saturation is not the mere present, nor is it the non-present, but a type of *presence,* generative presence. Saturated presence is not co-original with experienced absence, for absence points irreversibly to saturated presence.

Such statements certainly go against the grain of much work today that wants either to challenge a "metaphysics of presence," to emphasize negativity, or to maintain that phenomenology – perhaps in spite of itself – was really about the task of harkening to absence. I suggest that the understanding of absence, lack, and negativity pursued and developed in so-called "postmodern" discourses can be misleading, not because they criticize a kind of punctual present, etc., but because they miss "the thing itself" as saturated presence.

If consciousness is desiring consciousness, it is not because it is missing something merely, but because it is satiated and wants more on the basis of plenitude. If we are inclined to take in more of an object, it is not merely because we want to see more, but because *it* affectively sketches the course of its givenness, because it has already been given fully. If we turn away from something in repulsion or disgust, it is not because we lack interest, but more primordially, because we have already "had *too much*" of it. If we are disappointed, it is not because something did not arise, but more deeply because something else took its place too fully, or because what appears "falls short" of its optimal givenness. If "Others" are accessible only in the mode of inaccessibility – to employ a phenomenological and Levinasian formulation – it is not because they are irretrievably absent, removed from the perceptual present; it is their *personal presence* that makes them inaccessible. When we do experience absence or lack, it is not because the latter are ontologically or phenomenologically primary; rather, lack implicitly refers to a *uniquely* saturated, "specific" presence. In short, if we prefer, value, hesitate, love, lack, are disappointed, denounce, reject, judge, etc., it is because our comportment to the world and to others is saturated.

The task of this essay is to elaborate what I am calling here "saturated intentionality." On the one hand, my analysis will have the advantage of saying nothing new, since saturated intentionality was already implied in the phenomenological descriptions by Edmund Husserl and Maurice Merleau-Ponty. On the other hand, intentionality has often been misunderstood, and it is to this extent that the notion of saturated intentionality will appear unique or distinctive.

Let me add that intentionality is not a thing, but a relation. More actively stated, it is a process of relating that lends itself to an internal discrimination in terms of correlates. Nevertheless, describing intentionality in terms of "subjective" and "objective" correlates can be misleading if they are taken as independent entities. To keep the focus on saturation as a whole, I speak instead of intertwining subjective and objective "vectors." I discuss the "subjective" vector of saturation by examining the way in which saturation is expressed in the process of "intending." When I discuss this vector of saturated intentionality, I will only be emphasizing a particular nuance of saturation, and I will not – and indeed cannot – isolate it from the objective vector of saturation. Thus, in my second section I examine the forces that exceed subjective intending and dynamically elicit the becoming of sense. For intentionality is saturated because both subjective and objective vectors are "active" forces, as it were, "overdetermining" the intentional relation. Finally, I suggest implications of saturation that draw one in the direction beyond saturation.

1 The Subjective Vector of Saturation

In this section I take up the subjective vector of saturation in three modalities: conscious intending, operative intending, and what I call global intentionality.

In the first instance I point to saturation by presenting some basic formulations of intentionality on the level of consciousness. Here saturation is grasped through sense-giving, and in particular, through the interplay of simple and categorial perception. Operative intending will take up saturation more specifically on the level of embodied intentionality and the habitual body. Finally, we will see a transition from the subjective to the objective vector of saturation by examining briefly the phenomenological role of the earth as earth-ground which itself saturates the lived-body.

Conscious intending

One of Husserl's primary contributions to the early phenomenological concept of intentionality can be seen in the Fifth Logical Investigation where he regards the intentional object not merely as a mundane thing, an ontological "What," but in terms of its *modes* or *ways* of givenness, or as he writes, its "How." The question relevant to phenomenology (as constitutive philosophy) is not *what* objects are, real or possible, asserted or doubted (i.e., taken for granted), but *how* objects, *as* appearing, appear to consciousness.[4] I will explain the significance of Husserl's distinctions within a phenomenology of conscious intending by drawing initially on the perceptual sphere.

1 *Sense-giving as mystery and the surplus of sense*   In perception I am conscious, say, of the boulder. To perceive the boulder means that I posit or presuppose its being in some way. It has sense for me (as being a boulder to climb on, to sit upon, etc.) because I "mean" it, "posit" it, or "take" it in such a way. This thetic or doxic quality of the intending act determines the way in which the act is in relation to the object. So, for example, I believe the presence of the object in perceiving it, doubting it, wishing for it, judging it, etc.

This manner of formulating the subjective contribution to the intentional structure can be summarized in a word: sense-giving [*Sinngebung*]. Consciousness is a process of giving-sense or meaning. This process of sense-giving is one of the first clues to saturation. In one respect, there is "no reason" for the world to take on the sense it has. The fact that it has this sense rather than that, the fact that a boulder has the sense *as* boulder is a mystery. This sense-giving as mystery means simply that out of the fullness of the intentional act there is sense, or again, that we presuppose or posit in advance [*voraus-setzen*] objects such that they have sense prior to justifying this sense; the justification is intrinsic to the self-giving.[5] The reduction to the dimensions of constituting sense serves, then, to disclose mystery *qua* mystery, i.e., that there is sense at all by pointing to "fundamental strangeness" and the "miracle of appearing." Some names Merleau-Ponty gives to this emergence of sense include "transcendence" and "ontological contingency."[6] This movement lies at the heart of his oft-cited phrase that we are "condemned to sense."

The expression "modes of givenness" is fundamentally ambiguous and has at least two meanings. First, it can depict the process of subjective sense-giving. Second, it can refer to the way in which the objective vector gives itself. Let me interpret saturated intentionality further by examining two sense-giving and sense-fulfilling levels: simple and categorial perception.

2 *Simple and categorial saturation*   Simple perceptions are those of a single "act level" and are not founded on other acts. Accordingly, simple objects are brought to givenness in a simple manner [*in schlichter Weise*], which is to say, the object comes to self-givenness directly just as it is meant without recourse to more basic acts; objects of simple perception do not presuppose acts that have already constituted objects.

With regard to simple perception, categorial perception stands in a relation of surplus [*Überschuß*].[7] In this case, the simple is saturated by the categorial. For example, I touch the gritty sandstone: This "gritty sandstone" is given in simple perception. But I cannot touch "simply" "that-the-sandstone-*is*-gritty."[8] While I cannot perceive categorial forms in simple perception, categorial objects in general are given in their ideality in a correlative intuition proper to these types of objects, namely, in the categorial perception of affair-complexes, or essences and idealities.[9] With this distinction between simple and categorial levels, we can be more specific about saturation on both these levels.

(i) In simple perception, the unity of the object is not an accumulation of partial intentions. I intend the whole object by co-intending its "internal horizons" belonging to the object itself, and "external horizons" as in a field of things.[10] Since every perspective points to an unending series of different perspectives, since the latter are implicit in the prominent perspective, I intend or "mean" more than what is given, even in intuitive, anticipatory intentions.[11] In simple perception the same object is given *fully*, but *not exhaustively*, since its fullness generates other modes of full presentation.

Fulfillment, accordingly, is not an instantaneous accomplishment, but a generative movement of being given more fully. As intending beings, we mean or intend more through this fullness, not primordially through emptiness or absence. The experienced lack is indicative of a specific presence, even if we are not able to identify cognitively what that presence is. We would not miss someone, for example, if his or her presence had not already imbued the surroundings, saturated the conversations, colored the music we listen to, etc. Likewise, we can already miss someone who is going to leave even though he or she is present now, because a delineated futural presence and the possibilities it holds saturates the full intentional reality. It is not absence that generates this felt experience, for we miss something, someone, some specific presence that shows up in our experience as lacking, missing. Intentionality is saturated on the simple level because what is given is always given fully and because I always intend more than what is given fully.

(ii) Even though the simple act is said to found the categorial one, there is another sense in which the simple perception is founded in a categorial perception: Simple perception is saturated by the categorial. The reason I can see *a* boulder *as* boulder (which is to say implicitly the being of the boulder) is due to the fact that I perceive the boulder as it is meant in its ideality through categorial perception; that is, in and through the simple presence of this boulder, I grasp *the* boulder concretely. Accordingly, the categorial is said to be founded in the simple because it is only through the simple concrete reality that the categorial can be given. But a peculiar inversion of the order of foundation is in play that embellishes further the relation of saturation. In order to see this particular boulder, I must also see it as an instance of *the* boulder such that the categorial essence "boulder" guides the simple perception of this boulder *as* this boulder.[12] Here the simple is saturated by and in this sense founded in the categorial. Accordingly, I am not just drawn to the back side of the boulder because I suspect that something is missing. Rather, it is already sketched out for simple perception through the categorial full givenness that guides my perceiving.

Finally, not only is there a surplus of the categorial over the simple, but we find a surplus of the simple over the categorial. This happens when the simple perception not only ruptures or breaks with the categorial object, i.e., when it does not follow the anticipated essence as an aberration or abnormality; rather it occurs when the latter, the abnormal [*anomale*] perception actually institutes a new normality, a new telos, which is to say, a new categorial object. This relation enables us to say that the categorial is also saturated by the simple.[13]

Perception is always ahead of itself and the experience of the boulder is saturated from the start because more is given than what I can simply intend. What I simply perceive is guided by what I categorially perceive. Without this relation of saturation between simple and categorial perception, perception would be flat.

Far from these relations of saturation obviating the phenomena of surprise or disappointment, the latter are expressive of saturated presence. Surprise, like the experience of strangeness or relief in something not having taken place, is founded in a unique presence that ruptures or exceeds anticipation. Similarly, disappointment arises when some other presence falls short or disrupts a pattern of expectation. In both cases the initial presence anticipated remains efficacious as a possibility.

Operative intending

The surplus of sense-giving explicated on the level of consciousness is not as full as it could be. An exposition of saturated intentionality from the perspective of the subjective vector requires a movement to the embodied dimension of experience, to the level of kinaesthetic motivations or bodily movement.

Operative intentionality [*fungierende Intentionalität*] designates prereflective experience that is functional without having to be thematic or engaged in an explicit epistemic acquisition. It constitutes the prepredicative unity of objects, of the world, and of our life.[14] This dimension of experience is described by Husserl under the aegis of "aesthetic experience," and more particularly with the expressions "passive synthesis" and "instinct" or "drive-intentionality" [*Triebintentionalität*]. For Merleau-Ponty operative intentionality includes the intentionality of movement, erotic intentionality, the habitual body, etc. Phenomenological analyses of these modes of intentionality take place on the level of the lived-body [*Leib, le corps propre*].

Lived-body intentionality functions on the order of an "I can" [*Ich kann, je peux*] and not as an "I think." For bodily space may be given to me in an intention to grasp without being given in an intention to know.[15] The "I can" is the embodied ability to instigate a flow of appearances, to pursue richer fulfillment and to move towards an anticipated situation that is given (teleologically) from the start.[16] It becomes even more clear on the level of operative intentionality that fulfillment is not a sudden acquisition, accomplished without further ado. Rather, the full givenness of the object draws us to fulfill more: "and in this [system of indicating implications, the object] *beckons to us*, as it were: 'there is still more to see here; turn me so you can see all my sides, let your gaze run through me, draw closer to me, open me up, divide me; keep on looking over me anew, turning me to see all sides.'"[17]

As I come across a boulder in my path, a field of possibilities open up that sketch it either as obstacle or as opportunity to climb. When I put my foot on the lower ridge and push up, pockets, ridges, rifts present themselves as points of stability to ascend or as too small to grip. My stepping up motivates new appearances that are highlighted, drawing out new gestures on my part. In each movement, this rock is constituted, confirmed, or rejected as either passable or obstacle. In Merleau-Ponty's words, the "I can" or "intentional arc" is the "general power of putting ourselves in a situation."[18]

The phenomenological reduction to the "I can" discloses the lived-body as a privileged, absolute, thick presence. Merleau-Ponty writes: "The permanence and absence of external objects are only variations within a field of primordial presence, a perceptual domain over which my body has power." If this presence is permanent, it is an absolute permanence that serves as ground for the relative permanence and absence of objects.[19] A dancer on stage makes her presence be felt absolutely. She creates space by modulating the near and the far with her body, she molds with an arabesque a dissimulating pattern of lines, and weaves an inextricable matrix of movements in one sweep of the arm, articulating in the ease of a gracious smile what could only be accomplished by a mute strain of seemingly incongruous gestures. All this is brought to bear in an over-full presence that seems to occupy the entire stage. Put differently, the absolute presence of the body saturates its situation; it not only orients itself, but in doing so orients objects in the world, giving them significance in relation to the body.

The lived-body as an absolute presence functions in certain respects as a "zero point of orientation."[20] Spatial and temporal determinations like up and down, before and after, left and right, under and over – directionality in general – have sense by virtue of the lived-body. To take fairly simple examples, when a vertical line is projected on the wall of a dark room, tilting my head will institute a tilting of the "objective" vertical line as well; the transformation of a hastily drawn curved line will be given perceptually as a complete circle simply by the expectation of the sense circle; something becomes a tool only with the intention or possibility of it being grasped as such.[21] If we consider more complex structures like the World Trade Center in Manhattan, we notice a similar efficacy on the part of the lived-body: despite its size and prominence on the horizon, the World Trade Center stands to the left or right *of my body*, it lies "before" me or it lies in front of me; in fact, it can only be said to be "over-whelming" in relation to my stature. These examples support Merleau-Ponty's claim that "it is *as* my body, always present for me, and yet engaged in the midst of [objects] by so many objective relationships, that their [the objects'] coex-istence with it is maintained and shares with them all the pulse of its duration."[22]

The expression "zero-point" of orientation for this absolute presence can be misleading, however, because the body is spatially and temporally filled out, beyond itself, and not like a mathematical point. The so-called zero-point is too full to be punctual. Through experiences that are retained and unfolded con-cordantly, actions and functions are sedimented such that the past becomes efficacious for the present. The lived-bodily "I can" is a *habitus*; the body is a habitual body.[23]

Moving down the street, I exhibit a style of walking, a gait that is recogniz-able to others as "my style," "my gait." Each step recuperates the sedimented past; my intention towards the future (e.g., making it to the ice cream stand) reawakens the past ability to move along with its gestures and enables the present gesture to have precisely this sense. I carve out a world through this habitual body, and this world remains familiar as long as I have in my legs and in my hands the main distance and directions involved.[24] Furthermore, I can retain this bodily style even if I am not conscious of it. Writing a letter I display the same poor penmanship that I have when writing on the blackboard, even though entirely different muscles are in play. We can speak of a bodily style not because there is a mere accumulation of acts, but because each movement shares or expresses the same significance.

Moreover, the lived-body is not parcelled out in independent realms of sense-experience. As a saturated body, the lived-body functions as a synaesthetic whole, as an intertwining of the senses such that each sense is overdetermined by the others: "One sees the elasticity of steel, the ductility of red-hot steel, the hardness of a blade in a wood plane, the softness of the shavings. . . . In the same way, I hear the hardness and unevenness of cobble stones in the clattering of a car, and we rightly speak of a 'soft,' 'dull' or 'sharp' [sec] sound."[25]

Rather than a zero-point, the lived-body is an anchorage in a world as a momentum towards an open situation.[26] This momentum peculiar to the lived-body as a habitual body is expressive of the more fundamental momentum of existence which is transformative power.[27] Existence as transformative or expressive in its surplus gives itself, for example, as the lived-body, enabling it to have this momentum of transformation.

The dispositional tendencies of the habitual "I can" enable the body itself to become typified. A saturated body will exhibit a type that is optimal for it under certain circumstances making the saturated body a body type.[28] Thus, for example, a classical dancer will develop powerful thigh muscles and quite literally restructure his stance; he will turn out (i.e., walk like a duck) such that one could say, "oh, he is a dancer." Since it is already too much for itself, the lived-body carves out a setting that is optimal for it; it prefers the skip in the step over the shuffle, it favors the curved lip rather than the frown. The habitual comportment for this body and the patterned movement that propels the body in this direction as if with ease, in turn, hones the "I can" so that it is not a mere neutral power. Because its very freedom to move its "I can" has become predisposed to certain movements, it "cannot" help itself moving in this way rather than that. The lived-body has generated its own density, its duration that coaxes the world to be grasped in this way rather than that. So, for instance, it is entirely conceivable that the reason one cannot move well as a modern dancer results from being able to move too well as a classical dancer. Put more generally, the phenomenon of saturation suggests that we live less by restriction, and more profoundly by fullness.

The saturated comportment of the lived-habitual body means that I typify the world and its objects, and that I integrate new projects into a unique bodily pattern. In the same way that "I can" perceive this four-legged animal across the street *as* a dog, even though I have never seen this one before, "I can" climb a rock I have never climbed before.[29] It is not a matter of learning objective spatial positions or of letting go involuntary rote movement; rather, I incorporate in my movement the relevant directions and dimensions. The rock is a possibility of achieving certain motor or aesthetic values, and the new ridges, cracks, ledges, etc., are the opportunities for fulfilling these values. Writing of an organist, Merleau-Ponty observes: "In reality his gestures during rehearsal are gestures of consecration: they draw affective vectors, they discover emotional sources, they create an expressive space like the gestures of the augur delimit the *templum*."[30]

The momentum of existence brought to expression in the habitual body enables habit not to be static, but open to new situations: "Habit expresses the power we have of dilating our being in the world, or of changing our existence by annexing new instruments."[31] Habit is the power to respond to new situations of a general form; it is normalizing in the sense not only of adapting to, but of creating new norms.

To show the saturation of the subjective vector of intentionality, we have gone from conscious intending to operative intending in the form of the lived-body as an "I can," an absolute presence, a zero-point of orientation, and the habitual body as a body type. But the subjective vector of saturation is not exhausted by conscious intending or by the operative lived-body in all these facets. For the lived-body is not only saturated through its past and future directionality, but by the fact that it is an earth-body.

Global intentionality

It goes to Husserl's credit to have extended the aesthetic or perceptual domain of experience beyond the individual lived-body to the aesthetic dimension of the earth.[32] Not only is the lived-body an absolute presence, but in relation to the lived-body there is still a ground of orientation that is "more" absolute. The lived-body is not self-grounding, but grounded in the earth as earth-ground [*Erdboden*].[33] Let me highlight the salient points that contribute to the phenomenological concept of saturation.

A consideration of the earth is significant because it both fulfills the subjective vector, and because it flows over to the objective vector of saturation. The earth, according to Husserl, is not merely an intentional object for consciousness but the unique ground [*Urboden*] that itself constitutes the lived-body as constituting. The constitution of intentional sense is literally global; the subjective vector is sense-giving by virtue of what is more than itself, namely, the earth-ground.

Just as the lived-body is so close to us that we tend to forget it as a constituting force, so too is the earth-ground forgotten, even though its presence is pervasive in the constitution of sense. This earth-ground forgetfulness reached new proportions in the Modern world-view instigated by the Copernican Revolution. Only in an abstract theoretical view of the earth is the latter just another stellar body relative to all other bodies, and a mere object for a subject. Reminiscent of the way in which the lived-body is not one object among others, phenomenologically, that is, where the genesis of sense is concerned, the earth is not merely one planet among others.[34] Rather, all bodies, planetary, lived, and physical are phenomenologically relative to the earth-body.

As experienced, we live the earth both as a primordial ground of orientation and of movement. The earth as an absolute presence is a primordial presence for directional sense givenness, "grounding" the lived-body as an absolute presence and as a source of directional sense. I have an upright posture, I am right side up or upside down, I experience weightiness or lightness in relation to the earth as ground. Similarly, the lived-body is not the sole basis for movement, for I experience my movement or rest and the motion or stillness of other things by being grounded in the earth.[35] Even the sense of possible worlds, like geometrical idealities, are variations of the earth and hence are grounded in the earth-ground.

The earth saturates the lived-body. Where the constitution of sense is concerned, it is never possible to leave the earth, just as it is not possible for us to leave our lived-body. What Merleau-Ponty writes of anonymous sensible "flesh," we can say of the earth, namely, that it stops up [il bouche] our view, it extends beyond the visible present in depth; it occupies us only because we who see it do not see it from the depths of nothingness, but from the midst of itself.[36] As an absolute presence, as the ground of rest and motion, it is too much with us, so much so that we would carry the earth with us in our earthly constitution even if we were to voyage for generations on another "flying ark."[37] The earth, contends Husserl, remains phenomenologically our "primordial homeland" [Urheimat].[38]

The subjective vector of saturated intentionality is expressed in the mystery of sense-giving, the overabundance of sense in the giving, the full and inexhaustible presence of what is given on simple and categorial levels, the surplus of sense by the categorial in the simple, in the lived-body as an absolute presence, as the temporally overdetermined habitual body, and the aesthetic dimension of the earth-ground. Insofar as the earth is a presence more primordial than the lived-body, it can be regarded as an enrichment of the subjective vector of saturated intentionality. But insofar as it transcends subjective constitution and is constitutive of the subject, it goes beyond itself in the direction of the objective vector of saturation.

Intentionality would not be saturated if it were limited only to the subjective vector, for there would only be a surplus by the subjective vector, and not a saturation of the subjective vector. The subjective vector is so full that it is unable to contain itself; in saturating presence, it becomes saturated. Implied all the while in the subjective vector of saturation is the vector of force I have called the objective vector of saturated intentionality. I will now turn to the objective vector of saturation.

2 The Objective Vector of Saturation

"What then will intentionality be," asks Merleau-Ponty, "if it is no longer the mind's grasping of a sensible matter as exemplary of an essence, [or] the recognition in things of what we have put there?"[39] The response to Merleau-Ponty's inquiry lies in saturated intentionality from the perspective of the objective vector.

An initial clue to the notion of saturation by the objective vector can be taken from Merleau-Ponty's insight into the thing itself. The thing, he writes, "ignores us, it rests in itself"... "hostile and alien."[40] A thing is a thing because it holds itself at a distance, and because it gives itself to us by virtue of its very internal organization. "It is insuperable plenitude," Merleau-Ponty continues (or as we would say, "saturation"): "[it is] impossible to describe completely the color of the carpet without saying that it is a carpet, made of wool, and without implying in this color a certain tactile value, a certain weight, a certain resistance to sound."[41] In other words, the meaning of the thing itself is indistinguishable from its total appearance as a synaesthetic whole.[42]

But what exactly makes up its so-called total appearance? What is responsible for the thing's internal organization that allows it to give itself as it is? How does the meaning guide this appearance in all its facets such that it is precisely this thing? In order to understand phenomenologically the objective vector of saturated intentionality, let me begin with an initial discussion of the objective sense. Through a series of elaborations in this analysis, I will touch on the notion of optimality, and then develop the objective vector of saturation in terms of the affective force of sense. This in turn will culminate in a phenomenological notion of "terrain."

Objective sense

I begin my description of the objective vector of saturated intentionality with the noematic objective sense because it serves as a preliminary way of showing how the objective vector is active, how it saturates subjective intending, and how fullness in the object points to other modes of full presentation such that this movement organizes internally the saturated appearance of the object. In short, it will suggest how the saturated presence of the objective vector provokes the becoming of sense.

Correlative to the thetic character of the intending act (noesis) is the noema. There are two phenomenologically distinct components that are important to note for this analysis. Within what Husserl calls the full noema (the boulder as perceived correlative to perceiving; the boulder *as* remembered correlative to remembering, etc.), we can distinguish between (a) the objective sense [*gegen-ständlicher Sinn, Gegenstandsinn*] or the core of sense, and (b) sense as modes of givenness.[43] In a static register (that is, without attention to temporal development) the objective sense is characterized as a point of unity, as that which remains identical throughout the variations of sense.[44]

For example, I perceive the boulder as tall, as gray, as gritty; I remember the boulder, I perceive it, imagine it, etc. Throughout these modifications and their diverse ways of appearing, the boulder keeps a sense that remains identical; it is the same object appearing now in this way, now in that way.

The objective sense is intially described by Husserl as a core of sense that functions as a rule-governing schema; it guides how the object is to be fulfilled. Prescribing an infinite process of continual appearances that determine the objective more clearly, this schema sketches out or prescribes possible ways in which the object must be fulfilled in order to remain, for example, precisely this boulder.[45] Thus, the objective vector is essentially active in the formation of sense.

The difficulty with such a static treatment is that it regards the objective sense as a kind of "indigenous abstract form" obtaining in the noema. The notion of objective sense, however, implies much more.

In Husserl's *genetic* analysis, where the "universal dimension of temporality" comes into play, the notion of objective sense begins to fill out. The identical objective sense is specified as temporal, as an identical sense built up over time through repetition; it is duration itself. The different noematic modes of givenness are qualified in terms of modes of orientation in time, as temporal adumbrations or temporal perspectives through which duration itself appears.[46] Acquiring a temporal density, a weightiness of being, the genetic objective sense functions as a "self," as a telos, and no longer an abstract form.[47]

It is at this juncture of a genetic analysis that the function of objective sense dovetails with that of horizon, although Husserl never explicitly states this as such. Within a genetic register, a horizon has an active function as an open system or a framework [*Zusammenhang*] of indicating implications [*Verweisungen*]. It is a kind of temporal presence through which the givenness of one aspect that has come into relief can point to another. This pointing is not arbitrary, but follows a pattern or style of unfolding for the present sketched out by a concordant past. Likewise, horizons function concretely as orienting the subjective vector. Given such an understanding of horizon, would we not have to challenge its simple equation with absence? By elucidating more concretely the futural dimension in play, the genetic concept of the objective sense is described as soliciting particular motivational tendencies in the direction of the richer presence to be achieved.

Being itself never self-contained, the objective sense does not command a fixed sequence of appearances. The fact that it is open, inexhaustible, maintains

Husserl, "excludes a perception that would furnish absolute knowledge of the object in which the tension would collapse between the object in the How of determinacy (which is relative and changing, remaining incomplete), and the object itself. For evidently, the possibility of a *plus ultra* is in principle never excluded."[48] The objective vector is so thick and irreducible to the power and vagaries of subjective intending that Husserl writes even God must perceive objects through perspectival adumbrations.[49]

While the notion of objective sense provides a preliminary understanding of the saturated objective vector, there still remains too much that is implicit. In particular, this concept of the objective sense does not yet specify the relation of the objective vector to the subjective. The objective sense should not be considered neutral, and the modes through which the object gives itself are not equivalent. Rather, the sense that an object has is also elicited by its context, and it can only function as a telos guiding perception insofar as it is normative. In short, the objective sense is contextually and normatively optimal.

Briefly, the optimal is what counts as the best in experience, as the maximum of richness and differentiation in the unitary givenness of the object. What is given optimally counts practically as the "thing itself." The optimal is a kind of ideality that is instituted concretely in experience and simultaneously functions as a norm in relation to which other perspectives are experientially evaluated as better or worse, normal or abnormal for the very experience of the thing.[50] In a vein quite similar to Husserl, Merleau-Ponty explains:

> I have visual objects because I have a visual field, where *richness and distinctness* are in inverse proportion to one another, and because these two demands – which taken separately would go to infinity – once reunited determine a certain *point of maturity* and *maximum* in the perceptual process. In the same manner, I call experience of the thing or of reality. . . my *full* coexistence with the phenomenon, at the moment when it would be at its *maximum articulation* in all its relations, and when the "givens [*données*] of different senses" are oriented towards this unique pole like my intentions [*visées*] in the microscope oscillate around a *privileged object* [*visée privilégiée*].[51]

Such a privileged object serves as the dynamic objective sense and summons me to perceive the object in such a way that it can be fulfilled more completely.[52] Accordingly, I am not always the instigator of orientation or sense. For example, when I do not comprehend something or when something is not clear, my body, wanting to orient itself, responds: I tilt my head. The fact that I yield to the objective vector does not point up a lack on my part, but testifies to the surplus of the object exerting its pull on me, "beckoning" me to it.[53]

The optimal is a futural presence (and not merely a present in the future) that guides the present fullness, structuring the course of appearances. It implicitly regulates or evaluates my intendings to be optimal. The optimal announces itself ahead of the present perception and saturates that perception (and hence subjective intending) from the future. When the optimal is ratified again and again in experience, the optimal acquires a genetic density. This genetic density of the optimal is stylized and stylizing such that it predisposes comportment for the thing itself, for the normal *qua* optimal. This is yet another way in which the objective vector saturates the subjective.

If the objective vector can draw me and resituate me, the subject, if it can solicit my explorations, it is due to the fact that what comes into relief exercises an affective force. It is active, rendering subjective sense-giving as much responsive as it is initiating. I explore this dimension of saturation by discussing the phenomenon of affective force.

Affective force

I suggested at the outset of this section that the sensible order according to Merleau-Ponty is "being at a distance." And while he understands this dynamically to mean transcendence, gestalt, or the figure-ground structure, such formulations of the objective vector tend to be too vague.[54]

The relationship of the thing to us cannot be described merely as at a distance, or as "ignoring" the subject. For this only suggests the thing resisting the subject. Other favored expressions like "reversibility" or "non-coincidence" – while wanting to convey an equi-primordiality and insuperable tension – remain on the other hand too anonymous, too neutral. There is saturation because sense is active, imposing, exerting a force on us in order to come into relief, in order to be at a distance. This solicitation from the objective vector is described with pioneering and trenchant insight in Husserl's lectures on "passive synthesis."

Husserl's primary contribution to the theory of relief [*Relief*] or prominence [*Abgehobenheit*] is not that there is always a figure that stands out from a background; rather, it lies in his contention that what comes into relief is always charged with significance, effective in the sense of exerting an affective force [*affektiver Kraft*] on an intending subject, and further, that this affective force of something prominent is linked to the discriminating experience of optima.

Husserl asserts, for example, that a unity of sense is only constituted as such by being affective! He writes: "Affective unities must be constituted *in order for a world of objects to be constituted* in subjectivity at all."[55] Affective unities are constituted by simultaneously affecting us. In short, the type of constitution Husserl is concerned with here is not the constitution by an ego, but a primordial constitution which is called (misleadingly) "passive" and (more favorably) "aesthetic" in relation to the activity of the ego.

Moreover, what we learn from genetic phenomenology and throughout these lectures is that primordial constitution [*Ur-konstitution*] must presuppose a past temporal dimension in order for sense to be constituted in the present. As Jean-Luc Marion writes in a different context, as opposed to the metaphysical concept of time, the present does not order the analysis of temporality, but results from it.[56] What I have been calling "saturated presence" or saturation would suggest something quite different than a metaphysics of presence.

Within the field of primordial constitution, we can say that sense is not simply the result of the intentional directedness on the part of the subject, but coevally the affective force on the part of the object or object phase that solicits the subject. It is a proposal, a proposition, or as Whitehead would also say, a lure. There are no sense-unities, to say nothing of objects, that are merely indifferent or simply for themselves. They are at the same time for the subject, affecting the subject, as propulsive or repulsive. Where the affective force is strongest, it provides "favorable conditions" and summons privileged comportment in relation to which it can become prominent and optimal.[57]

Since there is no neutral constitution, and in fact, no constitution of objectivities at all without affection, the elemental living present as primordially constituted is essentially an "affective unity." The fact that something comes into relief or prominence is not separate from the affective force that it exerts on the subject in order to incorporate it into its perceptual process. If something is there for me at all, it is because it is charged with significance. Hence, claims Husserl, "the perspective is an affective perspective," and a relief is always already an "affective relief."[58]

If there are horizons, if there are hidden dimensions, latency, opacity, they are not due to a lack. Rather, the affective reliefs that solicit our perception become prominent by "actively hiding the others, by denouncing them in the act of masking them."[59] Merleau-Ponty writes: "I cannot conceive the world as a sum of things, nor time as a sum of punctual 'nows' ['maintenant' ponctuels], since each thing can offer itself with its *full determinations* only if other things withdraw into the vagueness of the distance; each present can offer itself in its reality only by excluding the *simultaneous presence* [la présence simultanée] of preceding and successive presents [présents]."[60] Objectivities are too much, vying for ratification, exerting varying gradations of force; in order to appear some must become invisible, as the depth of the visible, allowing each thing to be elsewhere and otherwise.[61]

There is a conflict or rivalry [Widerstreit] between affective prominences for their emergence as normative optima, some of which will be qualified as "better" or "worse" in and through the experience itself. Affective phenomena move us, decenter the subject, as it were. I take my bearings from them and they can locate me. A bright star at night can orient me; a large building in a new town can serve as my point of orientation. I can also be oriented by the presence of another person. For example, I can stand before a judge or before a moral authority such as a rabbi without them first standing before me.[62] Since the affective force of the objective vector precedes the constitution by the ego, and since it is not dominated by its contexts, but in privileged instances can determine them, saturating the contexts, the phenomenological notion of affective force evokes new possibilities for phenomenology.

The concept of affective relief or affective perspective suggests that if something is prominent in our field of comportment, it is prominent because it says something to us in a way that makes a difference, and does not achieve prominence in an indiscriminate manner. That is, while there may be many affective forces soliciting our response and affirmation we can never turn to them all at once or indifferently. So, contends Husserl: "Our interest is thereby not indifferently parcelled out to all the characteristics that become prominent; rather, our gaze is directed towards especially impressive properties, through which the object of precisely this type or of this individual object distinguishes itself from other objects of an equal or similar type."[63] The compresence of affective forces for the constitution of sense implies that we cannot be neutral in the face of saturated phenomena. As a result, something becomes precisely optimal and normative by taking it up as such.

Saturated phenomena are compelling as particularly relevant or advantageous for an optimal mode of comportment. Thus if we can say that the object "gives itself," self-giving [*Selbstgebung*] must include a *demand* on the part of the self-giving in order to become precisely this sense. As affective, as soliciting comportment, optima are privileged by the style of the life being lived and the mode of disclosure of the norm itself, exerting more or less force. They are binding for experience to this extent.

More precisely, the way optima are binding for experience is related to the function of a "terrain." While I do not have space to develop the phenomenological notion of terrain here, let me sketch some of its main features.[64]

A terrain is not a neutral environing-world that we subjectively create or to which we must adapt unilaterally. Rather, a terrain is a typically familiar milieu that is affectively oriented and orientating; it is affective in experience and constituted as privileged in and through optimal modes of comportment and correlatively, optimal meanings and physiognomies. In other words, since a terrain is constituted through the affective stylization of interaction between the subjective and objective vectors, the environing-world becomes a habitat of types or temporally dense optima. Hence, a terrain is an affectively optimal, orientated environing-world.

As a specific context for a certain action, group or species, as constantly there throughout various divergences and discordances, a terrain becomes the milieu we especially count on. By repeating what is optimal, a structure of normal comportment emerges that becomes typically familiar of the experience. It is precisely in this sense that one is justified in speaking of the terrain as "familiar" [*vertraut*] or as what one is accustomed to [*gewöhnt*]. The everyday [*das Alltä-*

gliche] is what is familiar to us through types, and upon which we rely for the efficacy of action; it is usual, pregiven with more or less specific familiarity, and not average. In the first instance, it is optimal or typical. Only insofar as the average is typically constant and hence familiar can one claim that the everyday is average.

Our familiarity with our terrain is the prereflective and pregiven familiarity of types that is constituted intercorporeally, intersubjectively. Since the terrain is pregiven in experience as familiar through its typical affective force, a terrain is always a privileged terrain, and not simply one among others. The familiar terrain is privileged not merely because we prefer it for some reason or by chance; rather, we actually carry with us the structure of our terrain in the structure of our lived-bodies, in our typical comportment and in our practices; it saturates us.

3 Conclusion: From Saturation to Verticality

Intentionality is saturated. This is implicit in the earliest formulations of the phenomenological concept of intentionality; it is what I have attempted to show through a series of elaborations within the subjective and objective vectors. Concerning the subjective vector I have worked through the process of sense-giving, its embellishment in simple givenness, the saturation of the simple by categorial givenness, the elaboration of perception in operative intending expressed as an absolute presence of the lived-body, the saturation of this presence in the habitual body, and in global intentionality in the mode of the earth-ground as encompassing the lived-body.

Saturation in the objective vector was explicated correlatively through the notion of objective sense and its elaboration as the optimal. The optimal was more fully developed in terms of the affective forces that the objective vector exerts on the subjective forces of sense constitution. This notion of affective force received a still richer elaboration through a phenomenological description of terrain.

These vectors I have described here, moreover, are to be understood as phenomenological discriminations within a process I have called saturated intentionality. That is, the "intertwining" of all these dimensions simultaneously within and between the vectors enables intentionality to be clarified as saturated.

I have used the expression "saturation" as a leading clue to this elaboration of intentionality. In addition to the reasons just delineated, I believe this term is appropriate because it suggests a full but inexhaustible presence, surplus, over-determination, or what Merleau-Ponty might call *sur-* or hyper-presence. Even though experienced absence can function in pointing up a unique presence, absence neither dissolves into presence, nor is essential for the experience of saturated presence.

Is the expression "saturation," however, self-sufficient? Does it fall short of the phenomenon that has been guiding the analyses of saturation from the start? While saturation does convey a kind of hyper-presence, it might also be conceived misleadingly as too flat, suggesting that some plenitude were reached, or that there is a mere overflowing. What I have meant by saturated presence is not merely the surplus of sense, but in this surplus, an ongoing process of generating sense. As generative, saturated intentionality cannot be a mere "structure" of existence; from the start it is itself generative of sense, generative of existence. Moreover, saturated presence is forcefully affective, enticing, luring, making appeal, demanding response, inviting evaluation, eliciting discriminating experience. Accordingly, saturation requires that we take a position and presupposes that we have taken one through preferring, desiring, selecting, etc., while we are living it. There is no neutrality or indifference.

Saturated presence, then, may be said to be wild or brute, if we mean with Merleau-Ponty that it cannot be controlled or dominated by reflection, that it cannot be exhausted in experience. On the other hand, it should not suggest arbitrariness, randomness or a mere play. Saturated presence means generative presence. For the affective forces of sense etch out a directedness [*sens*] that is taken up one way or another, making a historical difference.

In making a difference, saturated presence is disclosed in the field of experience as an open hierarchy of sense that elicits the historical movement of meaning. Put differently, the experience of verticality is implied in saturated or generative presence. Since this movement of meaning concerns who we generatively are and who we can optimally become, the transformative movement of existence takes on a vertical significance. Guiding the very notion of saturation – in the perceptual dimension, the moral (as practical, personal), the political, the religious, the aesthetic dimensions, etc. – is verticality.[65] While implicit in and beyond the scope of this essay, a more fully elaborated study of saturation would have to be taken up in the direction of movement and verticality.

Notes

1   This is an expanded version of a paper first presented at the 21st annual meeting of the Merleau-Ponty Circle, Rome, Georgia, and published as "Merleau-Ponty, Husserl, and Saturated Intentionality" in *Re-Reading Merleau-Ponty: Essays Across the Continental–Analytic Divide*, edited by Lawrence Hass and Dorothea Olkowski (New Jersey: Humanities Press, 1996), and was dedicated to Professor Bernhard Waldenfels on the occasion of his 60th birthday. I borrow the expression "satu-

rated" both from Husserl's lectures on passive synthesis and from Jean-Luc Marion's lecture given at the Society for Phenomenology and Existential Philosophy, October, 1993, New Orleans, dealing with Kant and his (Marion's) interpretation of a "saturated phenomenon."

To maintain consistency of style, all translations from the German and the French are my own.

2   *Die Krisis der europäischen Wissenschaften und die transzendentale Phänomenologie. Eine Einleitung in die phänomenologische Philosophie*, ed. Walter Biemel, *Husserliana* vol. 6, p. 169, n. 1. Hereafter cited as Hua vol. 6. English translation by David Carr, *The Crisis of European Sciences and Transcendental Phenomenology: An Introduction to Phenomenological Philosophy* (Evanston, ILL.: Northwestern University Press, 1970), p. 166, n. (my emphasis). Hereafter cited as *Crisis*.

All translations from the French and German are my own. I will indicate exceptions to this by citing the English translation.

3   Maurice Merleau-Ponty, *Phénoménologie de la perception* (Paris: Gallimard, 1945), p. 141, n. 4 (my emphasis); hereafter cited as *Phénoménologie*.

4   Edmund Husserl, *Logische Untersuchungen. Vol. II: Untersuchungen zur Phänomenologie und Theorie der Erkenntnis, Part I* (Tübingen: Niemeyer, 1968), 400: "In Beziehung auf den als Gegenstand des Aktes verstanden intentionalen Inhalt ist folgendes zu unterscheiden: der *Gegenstand, so wie er intendiert ist*, und schlechthin der *Gegenstand, welcher* intendiert ist." Hereafter cited as *Logische Untersuchungen*, II/1. See also *Husserl, Logische Untersuchungen*, II/1, pp. 415ff. This import of this distinction is also emphasized by Husserl during the *Crisis* years. See Edmund Husserl, *Die Krisis der europäischen Wissenschaften und die transzendentale Phänomenologie. Eine Einleitung in die phänomenologische Philosophie*, ed. Walter Biemel, *Husserliana* vol 6. (The Hague: Martinus Nijhoff, 1962), §§46 and 48. Hereafter cited as *Krisis 1*.

5   Or as Husserl would say, the justification is intrinsic to the givenness itself. See Edmund Husserl, *Ideen zu einer reinen Phänomenologie und phänomenologischen Philosophie. Erstes Buch: Allgemeine Einführung in die reine Phänomenologie*, ed. Walter Biemel, *Husserliana* vol. 3 (The Hague: Martinus Nijhoff, 1950), §§21, 141; hereafter cited as *Ideen I*.

6   *Phénoménologie*, pp. 456, 384, 197. Maurice Merleau-Ponty, *Sens et non-sens* (Paris: Nagel, 1966), pp. 165–72. See also Merleau-Ponty, *Phénoménologie*, p. xvi: "The world and reason. . . are *mysterious*, but this mystery defines them; it would not be a question of dispelling the mystery by some 'solution'; it is this side of all solutions." And see p. xiv.

7   *Logische Untersuchungen*, II/2, pp. 129, 135–6.

8   Husserl, *Logische Untersuchungen*, II/2, §47.

9   Husserl, *Logische Untersuchungen*, II/2, §52.

10   Edmund Husserl, *Erfahrung und Urteil*, ed. Ludwig Landgrebe (Hamburg: Meiner, 1985), pp. 28ff. And Husserl, *Krisis 1*, p. 165.

11   Husserl, *Krisis 1*, p. 161.

12   See Jean-Luc Marion, *Recherches sur Husserl, Heidegger et la phénoménologie* (Paris: PUF, 1989), pp. 23–6.

13   I cannot go into detail here regarding the relation between the normal and the abnormal from a phenomenological perspective. See Anthony J. Steinbock, "Phenomenological Concepts of Normality and Abnormality" in *Man and World*, vol. 28 (1995), pp. 241–60 and for a more detailed analysis, Anthony J. Steinbock, *Home and Beyond: Generative Phenomenology after Husserl* (Evanston, ILL.: Northwestern University Press, 1995), Sections 3 and 4. Hereafter cited as *Home and Beyond*.

14   Merleau-Ponty, *Phénoménologie*, p. xiii.

15   Merleau-Ponty, *Phénoménologie*, p. 121. And "we say that the body has understood and habit is acquired when it is impregnated by a new significance, when it has assimilated a new expressive core" (p. 171).

16   Merleau-Ponty, *Phénoménologie*, pp. 110, 128, 169.

17   Husserl, Hua vol. 11, p. 7; ". . . *ertönt ja der Ruf*. . .," my emphasis.

18   Merleau-Ponty, *Phénoménologie*, pp. 158–63.

19   Merleau-Ponty, *Phénoménologie*, p. 108.

20   See Edmund Husserl, *Ideen zu einer reinen Phänomenologie und phänomenologischen Philosophie: Zweites Buch*, ed. Marly Biemel, *Husserliana* vol. 4 (The Hague: Martinus Nijhoff, 1952), pp. 158–9; hereafter cited as *Ideen II*. And see Edmund Husserl, "Notizen zur Raumkonstitution," published posthumously in *Philosophy and Phenomenological Research* vol. 1, no. 1 (1940/41), pp. 27, 34; hereafter cited as "Notizen." See also Martin Heidegger, *Sein und Zeit* (Tübingen: Niemeyer, 1979), pp. 101ff.

21   See Elmar Holenstein, *Menschliches Selbstverständnis* (Frankfurt am Main: Suhrkamp, 1985), pp. 19, 21.

22   Merleau-Ponty, *Phénoménologie*, pp. 108–9.

23   Husserl, *Ideen II*, pp. 270, 277.

24   Merleau-Ponty, *Phénoménologie*, p. 151.

25   Merleau-Ponty, *Phénoménologie*, pp. 264–6.

26   Merleau-Ponty, *Phénoménologie*, pp. 166ff., 169.

27   Merleau-Ponty, *Phénoménologie*, pp. 128ff., 171, 180, and especially 197: "We will call transcendence this movement by which existence takes up again and transforms a *de facto* situation for its own advantage."

28   In Husserl's words, there is "a certain *typical* constancy in the comportment of lived-corporeality." Edmund Husserl, *Zur Phänomenologie der Intersubjektivität*, ed. Iso Kern, *Husserliana* vol. 14 (The Hague: Martinus Nijhoff, 1973), p. 121, my emphasis.

29   See Schutz's lucid clarification of typification in Alfred Schutz, *Collected Papers III: Studies in Phenomenological Philosophy* (The Hague: Martinus Nijhoff, 1966), esp. pp. 92–116; 124–30.

30   Merleau-Ponty, *Phénoménologie*, p. 170.

31   Merleau-Ponty, *Phénoménologie*, p. 168.

32   See Edmund Husserl, "Grundlegende Untersuchungen zum phänomenologischen Ursprung der Räumlichkeit der Natur" in *Philosophical Essays in Memory of Edmund Husserl* (Cambridge, Mass.: Harvard University Press, 1940). Hereafter the article will be cited as "Ursprung."

33   Because I have already developed the concept of earth as earth-ground in another essay, I will not engage in a detailed analysis of this important and original notion for phenomenology. See my "Reflections on Earth and World: Merleau-Ponty's Transcendental Geology and Transcendental History," in *Merleau-Ponty: Differences, Materiality, Painting*, ed. Véronique Fóti (New Jersey: Humanities Press, 1995).

34   See Husserl, "Ursprung," pp. 312, 317, 320, 323.

35   Husserl, "Ursprung," pp. 324, 313; "Notizen," pp. 27, 32.

36   Maurice Merleau-Ponty, *Le Visible et l'invisible* (Paris: Gallimard, 1964), pp. 152–3; hereafter cited as *Le Visible*. English translation by Alphonso Lingis, *The Visible and the Invisible* (Evanston, Ill.: Northwestern University Press, 1964), pp. 113–14; hereafter this work will be cited as *The Visible*.

37   Husserl, "Ursprung," pp. 315, 319, 324.

38   A still more fully elaborated dimension of intentional saturation would have to take into account the role of generative "*homeworld*" in relation to "alienworld." This would depict saturation as *intersubjective*. Such an exposition, however, is beyond the scope of this essay. See my "Homeworld/Alienworld: Towards Husserl's Generative Phenomenology of Intersubjectivity," in *Selected Studies in Phenomenology and Existential Philosophy*, vol. 19, ed. Lenore Langsdorf and Stephen H. Watson (New York: SUNY Press, 1994).

39   Merleau-Ponty, *Signes* (Paris: Gallimard, 1960), p. 211

40   Merleau-Ponty, *Phénoménologie*, p. 372.

41   Merleau-Ponty, *Phénoménologie*, p. 373; my emphasis.

42   Merleau-Ponty, *Phénoménologie*, p. 373; my emphasis.

43   Husserl, Hua vol. 3, pp. 318–25.

44   Husserl, Hua vol. 3, p. 323.

45   Husserl, *Ideen I*, p. 351.

46   In a manuscript entitled "Consciousness – Sense – Noema," published in Edmund Husserl, *Analysen zur passiven Synthesis. Aus Vorlesungs- und Forschungsmanuskripten 1918–1926*, ed. M. Fleischer, *Husserliana* vol. 11 (The Hague: Martinus Nijhoff, 1966), pp. 304–35; cf. especially, pp. 323, 328, 330, 332. Hereafter cited as *Analysen*.

47   Husserl, *Analysen*, especially Lecture 4.

48   Husserl, Hua vol. 11, p. 21. "It is thus the idea of the absolute Self of the object and of its absolute and complete determinacy, or as we can also put it, of its absolute individual essence." And as Merleau-Ponty reminds us, "In a philosophy that takes into consideration the operative world, functioning, present and coherent, as it is, the essence is not at all a stumbling block: it has its place there as an operative, functioning, essence." *Le Visible*, p. 158; *The Visible*, p. 118.

49   Husserl, Hua vol. 3, p. 351.

50   Husserl discusses the optimal in a plethora of manuscripts from 1917–21. It is a notion upon which Merleau-Ponty draws for his analysis of the "thing." See Steinbock, *Home and Beyond*, Section 3.

51   Merleau-Ponty, *Phénoménologie*, pp. 367–8; my emphases.

52   See Husserl, *Ideen II*, pp. 55–90; Husserl, *Analysen*, p. 24. And see Merleau-Ponty, *Phénoménologie*, pp. 348–9, 367–8.

53   See Husserl, *Analysen*, p. 7; Husserl, *Ideen II*, 4, p. 98.

54   Merleau-Ponty, *Le Visible*, pp. 248, 250, 262.

55   Husserl, *Analysen*, p. 162; my emphasis.

56   Jean-Luc Marion, *Dieu sans l'être* (Paris: PUF, 1991), p. 242.

57   See Husserl, *Analysen*, pp. 163ff.

58   See Husserl, *Analysen*, pp. 168 and 172; my emphasis.

59   Maurice Merleau-Ponty, *Signes*, p. 29.

60   Merleau-Ponty, *Phénoménologie*, p. 384; my emphasis.

61   Merleau-Ponty, *Signes*, pp. 29–30.

62   Elmar Holenstein, *Menschliches Selbstverständnis*, pp. 18, 28.

63   Husserl, *Erfahrung und Urteil*, p. 139; my emphasis.

64   I develop the phenomenological notion of terrain in my *Home and Beyond*, Section 3.

65   This is what Merleau-Ponty means when he writes provocatively that Being is vertical. See Merleau-Ponty, *Le Visible*, pp. 229, 231–2, 257, 287–8, 296.

8

FLESH AND BLOOD: A PROPOSED SUPPLEMENT TO MERLEAU-PONTY

Drew Leder

In the *Phenomenology of Perception* Merleau-Ponty identifies the *corps propre* or lived body, not a purified consciousness, as the seat of all human relation to the world. Prior to the reflective turn, we grasp the world via a bodily sensorimotor intentionality, pragmatic, ambiguous and pre-thetic in nature. The primacy of embodiment and the primacy of perception that Merleau-Ponty advances are usually understood as one and the same thesis. Yet, I would contend that this identification of the body primarily with its perceptual faculty signals a limitation in Merleau-Ponty's project. Admittedly, perception is understood by him in the widest possible fashion; it is inextricably linked with the "I can" of voluntary movement, the pervasive atmosphere of sexuality, the expressiveness of language. Yet such functions hardly exhaust the breadth and depths of the human body. Beneath the surface body, perceiving and perceived, acting and acted upon, lies an anonymous visceral dimension which this essay will address.

My sensorimotor being-in-the-world rests upon a set of vegetative functions hidden from myself no less than others. Within me proceed circulatory, digestive, and respiratory pathways which resist the apprehension and control of the conscious "I" and yet, like Descartes' God, sustain the "I" at every moment. Moreover, I discover this viscerality not only within my spatiofunctional depths but in the depths of my past. The perceptual subject is a later thing, arising out of a fetal state of impersonal circulatory and metabolic exchanges. Nightly, in deep sleep, I slip back into this existence, abandoning my sensorimotor sheath. By referring only in passing to the visceral functions, pre-natality, sleep, Merleau-Ponty, in the *Phenomenology of Perception*, never fully articulates the impersonal horizons that in all directions outrun the body-as-perceiver.

In the working notes collected in *The Visible and the Invisible* he criticizes this earlier work, "due. to the fact that in part I retained the philosophy of

Drew Leder, "Flesh and Blood: A Proposed Supplement to Merleau-Ponty," *Human Studies*, 13 (1990), 209–19.

'consciousness'" (1968: 183).[1] He is now seeking to escape more thoroughly the limits of an analysis based on intentionality and subjective awareness. Commentators, such as Gary Madison (1981), have emphasized the crucial shift this effects in his project. If space is to be made for the largely unconscious corporeal depths, we might then search for it in Merleau-Ponty's culminating, though unfinished work. It is to this work that the remainder of this essay will be devoted.

Flesh: The Chiasmatic Structure

In *The Visible and the Invisible*, Merleau-Ponty seeks to bring to "ontological explicitation" (p. 183) his previous phenomenological study. He thus supplants his terminology of the lived body with the ontological notion of "flesh" (*la chair*). Flesh belongs neither to the subject nor world exclusively. It is a primal "element" (p. 139) out of which both are born in mutual relation. It cannot then be conceived of as mind or as material substance. Rather, the "flesh" is a kind of circuit, a "coiling over of the visible upon the visible" (p. 140) which traverses me, but of which I am not the origin.

Merleau-Ponty gives specificity to this notion by articulating a series of "chiasmatic" relations, "intertwinings" (*entrelacs*) which characterize the flesh. Just as the three-dimensionality of visual space depends upon the optic chiasm blending fibers from both eyes, so the world leaps out of a "chiasm" between subject and object, my vision and that of others, perception and language. I will briefly explore these chiasmatic links, arguing their ultimate insufficiency and need for supplementation if the visceral is to be expressed.

Because the human body is an "*exemplar sensible*" (p. 135) – a structure in which is captured and exhibited the general structure of the world – Merleau-Ponty begins his analysis of flesh by examining the lived body. Utilizing the example of one hand touching another, he shows that the body can play the role both of perceiver and perceived, subject and object. It is as if the body had "two outlines," "two sides," "two leaves" (pp. 136–7). As he discusses, these never quite coincide. Insofar as I touch my right hand, I capture it as material object, but no longer experience through it as the toucher. There is a "divergence" (*écart*), a "fission," that stops the phenomenal and objective body from quite merging. Yet this is an identity-in-difference.[2] The two sides of the body are not ontologically separate categories as Sartre might have it, the subject's absolute nothingness, the object's plenitude of Being. My hand could not touch unless it itself were tangible, installed in the same world as its objects. The lived body is necessarily chiasmatic, a perceiver/perceived.

This intertwining characterizes not only the nature of the isolated body but its relation to world. As perceiver, I am necessarily made of the same flesh as the world I confront. Conversely, for Merleau-Ponty, the world is always a world-as-perceived, clothed with the flesh of my gaze (p. 131). "The flesh of the world is of the Being-seen, i.e., is a Being that is *eminently percipi...*" (p. 250).

The full reality of this sensible world arises not simply from the power of sight, or any single such mode, but from the mutual reference and intertwining of all forms of perception. "There is double and crossed situating of the visible in the tangible and of the tangible in the visible; the two maps are complete, and yet they do not merge into one" (p. 134). This chiasm of sensory worlds can occur only because my body is an intertwining, not just of perceiver and perceived, but of different *ways* of perceiving woven together by a prereflective link. "My synergic body... assembles into a cluster the 'consciousnesses' adherent to its hands, to its eyes, by an operation that is in relation to them lateral, transversal..." (p. 141).

World and self still lack their full depth, however, until reference is made to another chiasmatic relation: that which connects me to other perceivers. My perspective and that of the other intertwine in mutual validation, while never quite coinciding. The reality of the world is secured via its presence to other eyes, other hands, than my own. Even my own body is brought to fruition only through this gaze of another; "For the first time, the seeing that I am is for me really visible; for the first time I appear to myself completely turned inside out under my own eyes" (p. 143).

One final chiasmatic relation remains to be explored: that between the "visible" and the "invisible." Being is fleshed out by virtue of invisible dimensions which are *not* "non-visibles" opposed to perception, but installed within the visible world (pp. 149, 215, 227–8, 236). There is an invisibility that lines the perceiving subject, whose perceptual powers never fully coincide with the object body. The seer is always "*a little behind,*" "*a little further*" than the body I see (p. 261). Correlatively, there is an invisible ideality that adheres to all sensible objects. The experienced world is not a collection of sense data, but organized into meaningful gestalts. The visible profile of an object suggests its other hidden sides without which it would have no depth or solidity. In a sequence of musical notes I grasp a structure, an idea which resides in these sounds while never quite being reducible to them: once again there is identity-in-difference. This ideality of perception can emigrate "into another less heavy, more transparent body" (p. 153), that of language. Yet even this "purified" ideality remains of the flesh. Language is itself embodied through the signifier. And while supplementing the sense of the perceptual world, words are always dependent upon it, drawing their meaning from an ideality which "already streams forth along the articulations of the aesthesiological body, along the contours of the sensible things..." (p. 152).

This is but a brief description of Merleau-Ponty's richly textured notion of flesh, left uncompleted at his death. Yet it will suffice for the point I wish to make. All of the chiasmatic relations to which Merleau-Ponty refers are those involving the sensorimotor, expressive body. The philosopher's language has changed dramatically from his earlier phenomenology of perception. Yet the flesh remains, in the broadest sense, an ontology of perception. It includes the intertwining of perceiver and perceived; the synergic crossing of different perceptual modalities; the reversibility of my perception with that of another; the fleshing out of perception with ideality and language. Another name Merleau-Ponty offers for the flesh is "Visibility" (p. 139). It is ultimately the body surface, visioning and visible, that is taken as the *exemplar sensible* of flesh.

Viscerality

Yet this sensible/sentient surface cannot be equated with the body as a whole. It rests upon a deeper and visceral foundation. My inner organs are, for the most part, neither the agents nor objects of sensibility. I do not perceive through my liver or kidneys; their intricate processes of filtration and excretion proceed mainly beneath the reach of conscious apprehension. They are not the conduit by which I immediately know the world, or by which the world knows me. They constitute their own circuitry of vibrant, pulsing life which precedes the perceptual in fetal life, outruns it in sleep, sustains it from beneath at all moments. Rather than "Visibility," one might call this the dimension of "Viscerality." Like the Visible, the Visceral cannot be properly said to belong to the subject: it is a power that traverses me, granting me life in ways I have never fully willed nor understood.

These two corporeal levels remain phenomenologically distinct, manifesting very different sensorimotor and existential structures. In place of the rich synesthetic presence of the surface body, our corporeal depths are perceptually elusive, a pattern of vague and shifting calls. Visceral interoceptions tend to be qualitatively restricted, temporally intermittent, spatially indefinite and causally ambiguous compared to the world exteroception reveals. In terms of motility, the "I can" of the surface body gives way, on the visceral level, to something like an "it can." For I cannot simply choose to contract my stomach as I could my hand. Merleau-Ponty (1962: 94) refers to the immediate and magical relation between my decisions and my bodily movement, but this is operative primarily in the case of surface, voluntary musculature. A deeper magic takes hold of the viscera; digestion simply is accomplished within me, without my intervention, guidance, or skill.

Yet while phenomenologically distinct, the visceral circuit is intertwined, an identity-in-difference, with that of the body-as-visibility. I know that my vegetative organs, my sleeping and fetal body, though ordinarily out of sight, are ultimately installed within the visible. I can imagine the red, textured spectacle that awaits the surgeon who opens me up. Conversely, my powers of vision are installed in viscerality, shaped and sustained by anonymous life. The eye is fed by the labor of the stomach. A hunger or digestive problem soon spreads throughout vision, altering the appearance and significances of the experienced world.

This does not undermine, but adds further dimension to Merleau-Ponty's chiasmatic analysis. The body is not just a chiasm of perceiver and perceived. Nor is it just an intertwining of perceptual powers, a "lateral, transversal" synergy of hands and eyes. There is also what one might call a "vertical" synergy: my surface powers rest upon deeper vegetative processes, and the unconscious depths of pre-natality and sleep. More than just a "cluster of 'consciousnesses,'" my body is a chiasm of conscious and unconscious levels, a viscero-aesthesiological being.

Flesh and Blood

While not fully captured in Merleau-Ponty's articulation of "flesh," this term could be expanded to include our findings. No quarrel is raised with Merleau-Ponty's emphasis on corporeality or his characterization of this as a chiasmatic series. But in order to emphasize the important supplementation the visceral chiasm effects, I will supplement Merleau-Ponty's language; rather than the term "flesh," I will speak of the "flesh and blood."[3]

The very word "flesh" commonly refers to the body surface. (While true as well of the French equivalent, la chair, this is even more pronounced in the English translation.) Most typically, the flesh of an animal is equated with its superficial muscle and fatty tissue. One dictionary definition of "flesh" (Urdang, 1968: 504) is simply "the surface of the human body, esp. with respect to its color or outward appearance." This term thus already suggests Merleau-Ponty's tendency to focus on the sensorimotor surface of the body. Admittedly, "flesh," as in the biblical sense, can also have a much broader significance, referring to the entirety of the body or physical nature in general. Merleau-Ponty is clearly playing upon such associations. Yet this ambiguous equation of the body-entire with the body-surface, which is embodied in the very word "flesh," is precisely what I would wish to avoid.

The term "flesh and blood" suggests a dimension of depth hitherto unspoken. (Its nearest French equivalent is "en chair et en os" – "in flesh and bone".) Beneath the surface flesh, visible and tangible, lies a hidden vitality that courses within me. "Blood" is our metaphor for this viscerality. "Flesh and blood" expresses well the chiasmatic identity-in-difference of perceptual and visceral life. The expression itself appears in the dictionary as if one word. To be "flesh and blood" is clearly to be one thing, a life entire unto itself. Yet the "and" is never expunged. There is always an *écart*, a divergence of two existential levels.

Body and World

If the body is an *exemplar sensible*, this notion of flesh and blood must characterize not only the body in isolation but the relation between body and world. In the perceptual chiasm, body and world reach out to each other from across an ineradicable space. Merleau-Ponty writes of a "thickness of flesh between the seer and the thing," a distance that is consonant with proximity (p. 135). Perception is only possible via the mutual exteriority of perceiver and perceived.

Yet, in addition to this perceptual communion of the flesh, I am sustained through a deeper "blood" relation with the world. It is installed within me, not just encountered from without. The inanimate, calcified world supports my flesh from within in the form of bones. A world of organic, autonomous powers circulate within my visceral depths. Their otherness haunts the "I," surfacing at times of illness or approaching death. My own blood belongs as much to the world as to me: enfolded into my body, it is never quite mine.

This encroachment from within is renewed at every moment by visceral exchanges with the environment. In sleep I give myself over to anonymous breathing, relinquishing the separative stance of distance perception.[4] Even waking perception is ultimately in service to the visceral. In the most basic sense, the animal looks around to find things to eat and avoid being eaten (Jonas 1966; Sherrington 1947). (Merleau-Ponty's own term already suggests this significance: "*la chair*" in French, like the English word "flesh," commonly refers to meat, that which I devour.)[5] As I eat, the thickness of the flesh which separates self from world melts away. No longer perceived across a distance, the world dissolves into my own blood, sustaining me from within via its nutritive powers.

It is through visceral, not just perceptual, exchange that the total interpenetration of body and world is realized. When seeking to dissolve the fiction of the separated ego, the zen meditator quiets exteroception to focus upon the visceral process of the breath. Shunryu Suzuki (1970: 29) addresses his students:

> When we practice zazen our mind always follows our breathing. When we inhale, the air comes into the inner world. When we exhale, the air goes out to the outer world... We say "inner world" or "outer world," but actually there is just one whole world... What we call "I" is just a swinging door which moves when we inhale and when we exhale.

I am not just a gazing upon the world, but one who breathes, feeds, and drinks of it, such that inner and outer corporeality intertwine.

Neo-Confucian philosophers, such as Wang Yang-ming, claim that we "form one body" with the universe.[6] While reminiscent of Merleau-Ponty's notion of flesh, the Chinese formulation recognizes explicitly the visceral dimension. All things in the cosmos are said to be made of "*ch'i*," an element translated variously and inadequately as "vital force," "material force," or even "matter-energy." One might say of *ch'i*, as Merleau-Ponty does of flesh, that "there is no name in traditional philosophy to designate it" (p. 139), at least none in the Western tradition. Neither disembodied spirit nor pure matter, *ch'i* is a psycho-physiological power associated particularly with the blood and the breath. As Tu Wei-ming (1985: 45) comments:

> The idea of forming one body with the universe is predicated on the assumption that since all modalities of being are made of *ch'i*, all things cosmologically share the same consanguinity with us and are thus our companions.

I can perceive and commune with all things because, first and foremost, we are of the same blood.

Self and Other

My relation to other subjects is, as well, a relation of flesh *and blood*. In Merleau-Ponty's description, I discover my own visibility and that of the world only fully through the gaze of another. Yet, prior to this intertwining from without by two perceivers, was an intertwining from within. My lived body is literally formed from within that of another. I arise out of viscerality, not visibility. In my gestation, I was hidden from the gaze of my mother, and had yet to develop the birth of my own vision.[7] My very conception had originated from a visceral, not a perceptual, chiasm. In the sexual act, my parents' bodies and cells inter-twined, an identity-in-difference, giving rise to me. My fetal and embryonic development then proceeded through a series of visceral *écarts*: the mitosis of my cells, differentiating one from another; the progressive divergence of my body from that of my mother's, culminating in birth. The maternal/fetal relation is an exemplar of chiasmatic identity-in-difference. While separate, the two bodies are enfolded together, sharing one pulsing bloodstream. Even after birth, through the act of breast-feeding, one body is nourished directly by another.[8]

Thus, there is an intercorporeity of the blood, of which the fleshly, perceptual encounter is a sublimated reflection. Though my own gestation is hidden, lost in my pre-history, this bodily intertwining is never fully effaced from adult life. It is recapitulated in a limited way via the sexual act. It is experienced by women during pregnancy.[9] It is sensed in the similarity of features my body shares with those of my parents. I am "of their flesh and blood," their genes residing within me. The visible image of our interpenetration is etched right on my face.

Visibility and Invisibility

The final chiasm to which Merleau-Ponty refers is that of the visible and the invisible. This too demands re-vision. The invisibilities which Merleau-Ponty describes all belong to the aesthesiological and expressive body: that of the perceiver, never quite coinciding with his/her visible surface, and of the perceived, lined by an ideality which migrates into language. Merleau-Ponty refers to these as "depths," giving dimension to the visible world (pp. 136, 149, 219, 236). Yet in this essay we have encountered another sort of depth, another sort of invisibility. This is an invisible not just of the flesh, the perceptual circuit, but of the blood. The visceral organs, the fetal body from which I emerge, the sleeping body into which I lapse, are regions ineluctably hidden from my perception. Yet my lived world is textured by this unconscious vitality, as much as by the sublimations of language and thought. My days are horizoned by a nightly disappearance into a shrouded body I can never see. I know that I am not the author of my own existence; remembering back through my past I reach the nullpoint of a gestation I neither willed nor experienced. I know that the entirety of my perceptual world rests upon the unperceived coursing of my blood – if it were to cease, all else would cease as well. Merleau-Ponty's own premature death stands as bitter reminder. The visible world rests upon a visceral invisibility that is never fully written within Merleau-Ponty's text.

Nor can this be thought of as a mere extension of the invisibility that adheres to the sentient surface. My eyes constitute a "nullpoint" in my visual field because they lie at its very origin. I see with and through these eyes; hence they are the one thing I cannot see except through indirect mirrorings. They resist my perceptual objectification, for they are the transparent medium through which perception comes to be. There are nullpoints of the *visceral* field as well: for example, one seems to have no interoceptive awareness of the parenchyma of one's liver. Yet here the operative principle is of a different sort. The liver experientially disappears precisely because it is *not* the origin of any sensory field. It does not disappear in the act of perceiving, as does the eye, but by virtue of its withdrawal from the perceptual circuit. The liver secretes its bile, processes its toxins, performs a myriad of metabolic functions. Yet I am neither the observer nor the director of such occurrences. They unfold according to an anonymous logic, concealed from the egoic self.

Elsewhere, I characterize these two forms of invisibility as, respectively, the "ecstatic" and "recessive" modes (Leder 1990). My surface body disappears by virtue of an ec-stasis outward; sensorimotor intentionality is primarily directed away from the self, toward an outer world. Conversely, my visceral organs recede, fall back, beneath the reach of this intentional arc. What perception I do have of my visceral processes is limited, discontinuous, ambiguous. While sustaining the life of the conscious "I," the visceral perpetually eludes its grasp.

A recognition of viscerality has thus led to the revision of all chiasmatic relations contained in the notion of flesh. The relations holding within my own body, between body and world, self and other, visibility and the invisible, attain their *full* depths only when this vital dimension is recalled. In each case a perceptual chiasm is supplemented by a chiasm with, or of, the visceral. I am not merely consciousness – this Merleau-Ponty argues – but neither am I merely flesh. I am flesh and blood.

Notes

1   Hereafter, all references to *The Visible and the Invisible* will be cited in the text only by page number within parentheses.

2   On the concept of "identity-within-difference," and for an admirably clear treatment of the notion of "flesh" upon which this essay draws, see Dillon (1983).

3   The notion of "flesh and blood" is here meant to serve as a description of lived experience and our relation to the life-world. Unlike Merleau-Ponty, I am not proposing it as an ontological framework, though I believe it has ontological ramifications. To work these out would require addressing questions of the following sort: Does the inanimate and the purely vegetative world partake of both flesh and blood? In what sense? Could one or the other term of this relation be more primary? If not, does this threaten us with a new dualism? Such explorations would, however, take us beyond the bounds of the current project.

4   As Straus (1963: 284) writes: "(The sleeper) has, in fact, not withdrawn his interest from the world; rather, in lying down and sleeping he gives himself completely to the world. He gives up his stance which 'opposes' and confronts the world. Thus, he can no longer freely relate to the world and therefore no longer delimit and claim that which is his own."

5   The threatening nature of the "look" which Sartre describes can be understood in this biological context. For Sartre (1966: 340–400), insofar as I am a perceiving subject I turn the Other into an object, and hence a wrestling for power ensues. The root of the threat involved is clear on an animal level: encountering another living thing, I may be the eater, but I am also vulnerable to being eaten. Whether the body assumes subject or object role can literally be a matter of life and death.

It is, however, worth noting that life preserves itself not only through the destruction of, but through a mutuality with other life. My exhaled carbon dioxide is food to the plants while their oxygen sustains me. As ecologists are detailing, the biosphere maintains itself through such complementary exchanges.

6   See Wang Yang-ming (1963: 659, 685). Also see the entries by Chang Tsai and Wang Fu-chih.

7   In "Eye and Mind," the last work published in his lifetime, Merleau-Ponty (1964: 167–8) writes, "It can be said that a human is born at the instant when something that was only virtually visible, inside the mother's body, becomes at one and the same time visible for itself and for us." However, this is but a brief reference designed to explicate the birth of *perception* in the painter. Indeed, Merleau-Ponty often uses sexual and birth imagery in his discussions of perception. It is characterized as a mutual interpenetration of subject and object, or a "natal bond with the world" (1968: 32). Perceptual intersubjectivity comes to be when "the other is born in the body (of the other)" and there is a "coupling of the bodies" (1968: 233). Merleau-Ponty's language always bears a suggestion of the visceral chiasm that perception mirrors and sublimates. Yet he rarely engages the visceral as a phenomenon in its own right. When, for example, he writes in *The Visible and the Invisible* of the embryo, it is merely as a preliminary stage for the perceiving subject, a set of unemployed circuits preparing for the advent of vision (1968: 147, 233–4).

8   For a discussion of the embodied maternal–infant relation as an originary semiotic structure, see O'Neill (1985).

9   Because of their bodily involvement in the reproductive cycle through hormonal shifts, menstruation, and the possibility of pregnancy, women may tend to have a greater awareness of this visceral dimension of embodiment and of human interrelatedness than do men. It is probably no coincidence that this dimension has been neglected by *male* philosophers. For a discussion of the lived body in pregnancy, see Young (1984).

References

Dillon, M. (1983) "Merleau-Ponty and the Reversibility Thesis." *Man and World* 16: 365–88.

Jonas, H. (1966) *The Phenomenon of Life*. Chicago: University of Chicago Press.

Leder, D. (1990) *The Absent Body*. Chicago: University of Chicago Press.

Madison, G. B. (1981) *The Phenomenology of Merleau-Ponty*. Athens, OH: Ohio University Press.

Merleau-Ponty, M. (1962) *Phenomenology of Perception*, trans. Colin Smith. London: Routledge and Kegan Paul.

—— (1964) "Eye and Mind." In J. M. Edie (ed.), *The Primacy of Perception*. Evanston, Ill.: Northwestern University Press.

—— (1968) *The Visible and the Invisible*, ed. Claude Lefort, trans. Alphonso Lingis. Evanston, Ill.: Northwestern University Press.

O'Neill, J. (1985) "The Mother-tongue: The Infant Search for Meaning." *The University of Ottawa Quarterly* 55: 59–71.

Sartre, J.-P. (1966) *Being and Nothingness*, trans. Hazal Barnes. New York: Washington Square Press.

Sherrington, C. (1947) *The Integrative Action of the Nervous System*. New Haven: Yale University Press.

Straus, E. (1963) *The Primary World of Senses*, trans. Jacob Neddleman. Glencoe, NY: Free Press of Glencoe.

Suzuki, S. (1970) *Zen Mind, Beginner's Mind*. New York: Weatherhill.

Tu Wei-ming (1985) *Confucian Thought: Selfhood as Creative Transformation*. Albany: State University of New York Press.

Urdang, L. (ed.) (1968) *The Random House Dictionary of the English Language: College Edition*. New York: Random House.

Wang Yang-ming (1963) "Inquiry on the Great Learning." In Wing-tsit Chan (ed.), *A Sourcebook in Chinese Philosophy*. Princeton: Princeton University Press.

Young, I. (1984) "Pregnant Embodiment: Subjectivity and Alienation." *The Journal of Medicine and Philosophy* 9: 45–62.

PART II

PSYCHO- AND SOCIOTROPIC
GENEALOGICAL ANALYSES

JACQUES LACAN

Towards a Genetic Theory of the Ego

The theory we have in mind is a genetic theory of the ego. Such a theory can be considered psycho-analytic in so far as it treats the relation of the subject to his own body in terms of his identification with an *imago*, which is the psychic relationship *par excellence*; in fact, the concept we have formed of this relationship from our analytic work is the starting point for all genuine and scientific psychology.

It is with the body-image that we propose to deal now. If the hysterical symptom is a symbolic way of expressing a conflict between different forces, what strikes us is the extraordinary effect that this "symbolic expression" has when it produces segmental anaesthesia or muscular paralysis unaccountable for by any known grouping of sensory nerves or muscles. To call these symptoms functional is but to confess our ignorance, for they follow the pattern of a certain imaginary Anatomy which has typical forms of its own. In other words, the astonishing somatic compliance which is the outward sign of this imaginary anatomy is only shown within certain definite limits. I would emphasize that the imaginary anatomy referred to here varies with the ideas (clear or confused) about bodily functions which are prevalent in a given culture. It all happens as if the body-image had an autonomous existence of its own, and by autonomous I mean here independent of objective structure. All the phenomena we are discussing seem to exhibit the laws of *gestalt*; the fact that the penis is dominant in the shaping of the body-image is evidence of this. Though this may shock the sworn champions of the autonomy of female sexuality, such dominance is a fact and one moreover which cannot be put down to cultural influences alone.

From Jacques Lacan, "Some Reflections on the Ego," *The International Journal of Psycho-Analysis*, Vol. 34 (1953), 12–15

Furthermore, this image is selectively vulnerable along its lines of cleavage. The fantasies which reveal this cleavage to us seem to deserve to be grouped together under some such term as the "image of the body in bits and pieces" (*imago du corps morcelé*) which is in current use among French analysts. Such typical images appear in dreams, as well as in fantasies. They may show, for example, the body of the mother as having a mosaic structure like that of a stained-glass window. More often, the resemblance is to a jigsaw puzzle, with the separate parts of the body of a man or an animal in disorderly array. Even more significant for our purpose are the incongruous images in which disjointed limbs are rearranged as strange trophies; trunks cut up in slices and stuffed with the most unlikely fillings, strange appendages in eccentric positions, reduplications of the penis, images of the cloaca represented as a surgical excision, often accompanied in male patients by fantasies of pregnancy. This kind of image seems to have a special affinity with congenital abnormalities of all sorts. An illustration of this was provided by the dream of one of my patients, whose ego development had been impaired by an obstetrical brachial plexus palsy of the left arm, in which the rectum appeared in the thorax, taking the place of the left sub-clavicular vessels. (His analysis had decided him to undertake the study of medicine.)

What struck me in the first place was the phase of the analysis in which these images came to light: they were always bound up with the elucidation of the earliest problems of the patient's ego and with the revelation of latent hypochondriacal preoccupations. These are often completely covered over by the neurotic formations which have compensated for them in the course of development. Their appearance heralds a particular and very archaic phase of the transference, and the value we attributed to them in identifying this phase has always been confirmed by the accompanying marked decrease in the patient's deepest resistances.

We have laid some stress on this phenomenological detail, but we are not unaware of the importance of Schilder's work on the function of the body-image, and the remarkable accounts he gives of the extent to which it determines the perception of space.

The meaning of the phenomenon called "phantom limb" is still far from being exhausted. The aspect which seems to me especially worthy of notice is that such experiences are essentially related to the continuation of a pain which can no longer be explained by local irritation; it is as if one caught a glimpse here of the existential relation of a man with his body-image in this relationship with such a narcissistic object as the lack of a limb.

The effects of frontal leucotomy on the hitherto intractable pain of some forms of cancer, the strange fact of the persistence of the pain with the removal of the subjective element of distress in such conditions, leads us to suspect that the cerebral cortex functions like a mirror, and that it is the site where the images are integrated in the libidinal relationship which is hinted at in the theory of narcissism.

So far so good. We have, however, left untouched the question of the nature of the imago itself. The facts do, however, involve the positing of a certain formative power in the organism. We psycho-analysts are here reintroducing an idea discarded by experimental science, i.e. Aristotle's idea of *Morphe*. In the sphere of relationships in so far as it concerns the history of the individual we only apprehend the exteriorized images, and now it is the Platonic problem of recognizing their meaning that demands a solution.

In due course, biologists will have to follow us into this domain, and the concept of identification which we have worked out empirically is the only key to the meaning of the facts they have so far encountered.

It is amusing, in this connexion, to note their difficulty when asked to explain such data as those collected by Harrison in the *Proceedings of the Royal Society*, 1939. These data showed that the sexual maturation of the female pigeon depends entirely on its seeing a member of its own species, male or female, to such an extent that while the maturation of the bird can be indefinitely postponed by the lack of such perception, conversely the mere sight of its own reflection in a mirror is enough to cause it to mature almost as quickly as if it had seen a real pigeon.

We have likewise emphasized the significance of the facts described in 1941 by Chauvin in the *Bulletin de la Société entomologique de France* about the migratory locust, *Schistocerca*, commonly known as a grasshopper. Two types of development are open to the grasshopper, whose behaviour and subsequent history are entirely different. There are solitary and gregarious types, the latter tending to congregate in what is called the "cloud." The question as to whether it will develop into one of these types or the other is left open until the second or third so-called larval periods (the intervals between sloughs). The one necessary and sufficient condition is that it perceives something whose shape and movements are sufficiently like one of its own species, since the mere sight of a member of the closely similar *Locusta* species (itself non-gregarious) is sufficient, whereas even association with a *Gryllus* (cricket) is of no avail. (This, of course, could not be established without a series of control experiments, both positive and negative, to exclude the influence of the insect's auditory and olfactory apparatus, etc., including, of course, the mysterious organ discovered in the hind legs by Brunner von Wattenwyll.)

The development of two types utterly different as regards size, colour and shape, in phenotype, that is to say, and differing even in such instinctual characteristics as voraciousness is thus completely determined by this phenomenon of Recognition. M. Chauvin, who is obliged to admit its authenticity, nevertheless does so with great reluctance and shows the sort of intellectual timidity which among experimentalists is regarded as a guarantee of objectivity.

This timidity is exemplified in medicine by the prevalence of the belief that a fact, a bare fact, is worth more than any theory, and is strengthened by the inferiority feelings doctors have when they compare their own methods with those of the more exact sciences.

In our view, however, it is novel theories which prepare the ground for new discoveries in science, since such theories not only enable one to understand the facts better, but even make it possible for them to be observed in the first place. The facts are then less likely to be made to fit, in a more or less arbitrary way, into accepted doctrine and there pigeon-holed.

Numerous facts of this kind have now come to the attention of biologists, but the intellectual revolution necessary for their full understanding is still to come. These biological data were still unknown when in 1936 at the Marienbad Congress I introduced the concept of the "Mirror Stage" as one of the stages in the development of the child.

I returned to the subject two years ago at the Zürich Congress. Only an abstract (in English translation) of my paper was published in the Proceedings of the Congress. The complete text appeared in the *Revue française de Psychanalyse*.

The theory I there advanced, which I submitted long ago to French psychologists for discussion, deals with a phenomenon to which I assign a twofold value. In the first place, it has historical value as it marks a decisive turning-point in the mental development of the child. In the second place, it typifies an essential libidinal relationship with the body-image. For these two reasons the phenomenon demonstrates clearly the passing of the individual to a stage where the earliest formation of the ego can be observed.

The observation consists simply in the jubilant interest shown by the infant over eight months at the sight of his own image in a mirror. This interest is shown in games in which the child seems to be in endless ecstasy when it sees that movements in the mirror correspond to its own movements. The game is rounded off by attempts to explore the things seen in the mirror and the nearby objects they reflect.

The purely imaginal play evidenced in such deliberate play with an illusion is fraught with significance for the philosopher, and all the more so because the child's attitude is just the reverse of that of animals. The chimpanzee, in particular, is certainly quite capable at the same age of detecting the illusion, for one finds him testing its reality by devious methods which shows an intelligence on the performance level at least equal to, if not better than, that of the child at the same age. But when he has been disappointed several times in trying to get hold of something that is not there, the animal loses all interest in it. It would, of course, be paradoxical to draw the conclusion that the animal is the better adjusted to reality of the two!

We note that the image in the mirror is reversed, and we may see in this at least a metaphorical representation of the structural reversal we have demonstrated in the ego as the individual's psychical reality. But, metaphor apart, actual mirror reversals have often been pointed out in Phantom Doubles. (The importance of this phenomenon in suicide was shown by Otto Rank.) Furthermore, we always find the same sort of reversal, if we are on the look-out for it, in those dream images which represent the patient's ego in its characteristic role; that is, as dominated by the narcissistic conflict. So much is this so that we may regard this mirror-reversal as a prerequisite for such an interpretation.

But other characteristics will give us a deeper understanding of the connexion between this image and the formation of the ego. To grasp them we must place the reversed image in the context of the evolution of the successive forms of the body image itself on the one hand, and on the other we must try to correlate with the development of the organism and the establishment of its relations with the Socius those images whose dialectical connexions are brought home to us in our experience in treatment.

The heart of the matter is this. The behaviour of the child before the mirror seems to us to be more immediately comprehensible than are his reactions in games in which he seems to wean himself from the object, whose meaning Freud, in a flash of intuitive genius, described for us in *Beyond the Pleasure Principle*. Now the child's behaviour before the mirror is so striking that it is quite unforgettable, even by the least enlightened observer, and one is all the more impressed when one realizes that this behaviour occurs either in a babe in arms or in a child who is holding himself upright by one of those contrivances to help one to learn to walk without serious falls. His joy is due to his imaginary triumph in anticipating a degree of muscular coordination which he has not yet actually achieved.

We cannot fail to appreciate the affective value which the gestalt of the vision of the whole body-image may assume when we consider the fact that it appears against a background of organic disturbance and discord, in which all the indications are that we should seek the origins of the image of the "body in bits and pieces" (*corps morcelé*).

Here physiology gives us a clue. The human animal can be regarded as one which is prematurely born. The fact that the pyramidal tracts are not myelinated at birth is proof enough of this for the histologist, while a number of postural reactions and reflexes satisfy the neurologist. The embryologist too sees in the "foetalization," to use Bolk's term, of the human nervous system, the mechanism responsible for Man's superiority to other animals – viz. the cephalic flexures and the expansion of the fore-brain.

His lack of sensory and motor coordination does not prevent the newborn baby from being fascinated by the human face, almost as soon as he opens his eyes to the light of day, nor from showing in the clearest possible way that from all the people around him he singles out his mother.

It is the stability of the standing posture, the prestige of stature, the impressiveness of statues, which set the style for the identification in which the ego finds its starting-point and leave their imprint in it for ever.

Miss Anna Freud has enumerated, analysed and defined once and for all the mechanisms in which the functions of the ego take form in the psyche. It is noteworthy that it is these same mechanisms which determine the economy of obsessional symptoms. They have in common an element of isolation and an emphasis on achievement; in consequence of this one often comes across dreams in which the dreamer's ego is represented as a stadium or other enclosed space given over to competition for prestige.

Here we see the ego, in its essential resistance to the elusive process of Becoming, to the variations of Desire. This illusion of unity, in which a human being is always looking forward to self-mastery, entails a constant danger of sliding back again into the chaos from which he started; it hangs over the abyss of a dizzy Assent in which one can perhaps see the very essence of Anxiety....

The See-saw of Desire

You know that the attitude of the infant between six and eighteen months in front of a mirror informs us about the fundamental relation to the image of the human individual. Last year, I was able to show you the infant's jubilation in front of the mirror throughout the whole of this period in a film made by M. Gesell, who, however, had never so much as heard of my mirror stage, and has never asked himself any question of an analytical nature, believe you me. This makes the fact that he has so well isolated the significant moment even more impressive. Certainly, *he* does not himself underline its fundamental feature, which is its exalting character. Because it isn't the appearance of this behaviour at six months which is the most important thing, but rather its dissolution at eighteen months. All of a sudden, the behaviour changes completely, as I showed last year, so as to be nothing more than an appearance, *Erscheinung*, one experience amongst others upon which is exerted the action of control and of instrumental play. All the signs so clearly accentuated in the previous period disappear.

To explain what happens, I will make use of a term which some of your reading must at least have made familiar to you, one of those terms which we use in a confused manner, but which all the same corresponds in us to a mental schema. You know that at the moment of the dissolution of the Oedipus complex, something happens which we call *introjection*.

From Jacques Lacan, *The Seminar of Jacques Lacan*, ed. by Jacques-Alain Miller (New York: W. W. Norton, 1988), *Book I*, trans. by John Forrester, pp. 168–71; *Book II*, trans. by Sylvana Tomaselli, pp. 166–7, 169–70

I beg you not to be hasty in giving this term too definite a meaning. Let us say that it is used when something like a reversal takes place – what was the outside becomes the inside, what was the father becomes the super-ego. Something takes place at the level of this invisible, unthinkable subject, which is never named as such. Is it at the level of the ego, of the id? Somewhere between the two. That's why we call it the super-ego. . . .

Let us pick up the thread again. The point at which the mirror stage vanishes is analogous to the moment of see-sawing which occurs at certain points in psychic development. We can observe it in these phenomena of transitivism in which one finds the infant taking as equivalent his own action and that of the other. He says – *François hit me*, whereas it was him who hit François. There's an unstable mirror between the child and his fellow being. How are we to explain these phenomena?

There's a moment when the infant in jubilation assumes a mastery which he has not yet attained, through the mediation of the image of the other. Now, the subject shows himself entirely capable of assuming this mastery within himself. See-saw.

To be sure, he can only do it in a state of empty form. This form, this envelope of mastery, is something so certain that Freud, who came to it along paths quite different from mine, along the paths of the dynamic of libidinal investment, could find no other way of putting it – read *The Ego and the Id*. When Freud speaks of the *ego*, it is not at all a question of something so incisive, so determining, so imperative, that it gets confused with what in academic psychology are called the *higher agencies*. Freud underlines that it must have an intimate connection with the surface of the body. Not the sensitive, sensory, impressionistic surface, but this surface in so far as it is reflected in a form.[1] There is no form which lacks a surface, a form is defined by the surface – by difference in the identical, that is to say the surface.

The image of the other's form is assumed by the subject. Thanks to this surface, situated within the subject, what is introduced into human psychology is this relation between the outside and the inside whereby the subject knows himself, gets acquainted with himself as body.

Besides, it is the sole truly fundamental difference between human and animal psychology. Man knows himself as body, whereas there is, after all, no reason why he should know himself, since he is inside it. The animal is also inside it, but we have no reason for thinking that he represents it to himself.

It is within the see-saw movement, the movement of exchange with the other, that man becomes aware of himself as body, as the empty form of the body. In the same way, everything which is then within him in a pure state of desire, original desire, unconstituted and confused, which finds expression in the wailing of the child – he will learn to recognise it through its inversion in the other. He will learn, because he has not yet learned, in as much as we have not brought communication into play.

This anteriority is not chronological, but logical, and here we are only performing a deduction. It is no less fundamental for all that, since it allows us to distinguish the planes of the symbolic, of the imaginary and of the real, without which one can only make progress in the analytic experience by using expressions bordering on the mystical.

Before desire learns to recognise itself – let us now say the word – through the symbol, it is seen solely in the other.

At first, before language, desire exists solely in the single plane of the imaginary relation of the specular stage, projected, alienated in the other. The tension it provokes is then deprived of an outcome. That is to say that it has no other outcome – Hegel teaches us this – than the destruction of the other.

The subject's desire can only be confirmed in this relation through a competition, through an absolute rivalry with the other, in view of the object towards which it is directed. And each time we get close, in a given subject, to this primitive alienation, the most radical aggression arises – the desire for the disappearance of the other in so far as he supports the subject's desire.

Here we meet up again with what the simple psychologist can observe in the behaviour of subjects. Saint Augustine, for example, notes, in a phrase I've often repeated, this all-consuming, uncontrollable jealousy which the small child feels for his fellow being, usually when the latter is clinging to his mother's breast, that is to say to the object of desire which is for him essential.

This is a key function. The relation of the subject to his *Urbild*, his *Idealich*, through which he enters into the imaginary function and learns to recognise himself as a form, can always see-saw. Each time the subject apprehends himself as form and as ego, each time that he constitutes himself in his status, in his stature, in his static, his desire is projected outside. From whence arises the impossibility of all human coexistence.

But, thank God, the subject inhabits the world of the symbol, that is to say a world of others who speak. That is why his desire is susceptible to the mediation of recognition. Without which every human function would simply exhaust itself in the unspecified wish for the destruction of the other as such.

Inversely, each time that, in the phenomenon of the other, something appears which once again allows the subject to reproject, to recomplete, to *feed*, as Freud says somewhere, the image of the *Idealich*, each time that the jubilant assumption of the mirror stage is retrieved along similar lines, each time that the subject is captivated by one of his fellow beings, well, then the desire revives in the subject. But it is revived verbally. . . .

The Imaginary, the Symbolic, and the Body

What did I try to get across with the mirror stage? That whatever in man is loosened up, fragmented, anarchic, establishes its relation to his perceptions on a plane with a completely original tension. The image of his body is the principle of every unity he perceives in objects. Now, he only perceives the unity of this specific image from the outside, and in an anticipated manner. Because of this double relation which he has with himself, all the objects of his world are always structured around the wandering shadow of his own ego. They will all have a fundamentally anthropomorphic character, even egomorphic we could say. Man's ideal unity, which is never attained as such and escapes him at every moment, is evoked at every moment in this perception. The object is never for him definitively the final object, except in exceptional experiences. But it thus appears in the guise of an object from which man is irremediably separated, and which shows him the very figure of his dehiscence within the world – object which by essence destroys him, anxiety, which he cannot recapture, in which he will never truly be able to find reconciliation, his adhesion to the world, his perfect complementarity on the level of desire. It is in the nature of desire to be radically torn. The very image of man brings in here a mediation which is always imaginary, always problematic, and which is therefore never completely fulfilled. It is maintained by a succession of momentary experiences, and this experience either alienates man from himself, or else ends in a destruction, a negation of the object.

If the object perceived from without has its own identity, the latter places the man who sees it in a state of tension, because he perceives himself as desire, and as unsatisfied desire. Inversely, when he grasps his unity, on the contrary it is the world which for him becomes decomposed, loses its meaning, and takes on an alienated and discordant aspect. It is this imaginary oscillation which gives to all human perception the dramatic subjacency experienced by a subject, in so far as his interest is truly aroused.

So we do not have to look to regression for the reason why it is imaginary apparitions [surgissements] which are characteristic of the dream. To the extent that a dream may get to the point of entering the order of anxiety, and that a drawing nigh of the ultimate real is experienced, we find ourselves present at this imaginary decomposition which is only the revelation of the normal component parts of perception. For perception is a total relation to a given picture, in which man always recognises himself somewhere, and sometimes even sees himself in several places. If the picture of the relation to the world is not made unreal by the subject, it is because it contains elements representing the diversified images of his ego, and these are so many points of anchorage, of stabilisation, of inertia. That is exactly how I teach you to interpret dreams in supervisions – the main thing is to recognise where the ego of the subject is.

That's what we find already in the *Traumdeutung*, where Freud recognises on so many occasions that it is he, Freud, who is represented by this or that person. For instance, when he analyses the dream of the castle, of the Spanish-American war, in the chapter which we have begun to study, Freud says – *I'm not in the dream where one might think. The character who just died, this commandant who is with me, it is he who is I.*[2] At the moment when something of the real, something at its most unfathomable, is attained, the second part of the dream of Irma's injection highlights these fundamental components of the perceptual world constituting the narcissistic relation. The object is always more or less structured as the image of the body of the subject. The reflection of the subject, its mirror image, is always found somewhere in every perceptual picture, and that is what gives it a quality, a special inertia. This image is masked, sometimes even entirely so. But in the dream, because of an alleviation of the imaginary relations, it is easily revealed at every moment, all the more so to the extent that the point of anxiety where the subject encounters the experience of his being torn apart, of his isolation in relation to the world has been attained. There is something originally, inaugurally, profoundly wounded in the human relation to the world. . . .

Well, approaching from a different angle, we come upon the same thing again – every imaginary relation comes about via a kind of *you or me* between the subject and the object. That is to say – *If it's you, I'm not. If it's me, it's you who isn't.* That's where the symbolic element comes into play. On the imaginary level, the objects only ever appear to man within relations which fade. He recognises his unity in them, but uniquely from without. And in as much he recognises his unity in an object, he feels himself to be in disarray in relation to the latter.

This disarray, this fragmentedness, this fundamental discordance, this essential lack of adaptation, this anarchy, which opens up every possibility of displacement, that is of error, is characteristic of the instinctual life of man – the very experience of analysis shows us that. What is more, if the object is only ever graspable as a mirage, the mirage of a unity which can never be grasped again on the imaginary level, every object relation can only be infected with a fundamental uncertainty by it. That is in fact what so many different experiences show one, and calling them psychopathological conveys nothing since they lie on a continuum with many experiences which themselves are regarded as normal.

That is where the symbolic relation comes in. The power of naming objects structures the perception itself. The *percipi* of man can only be sustained within a zone of nomination. It is through nomination that man makes objects subsist with a certain consistence. If objects had only a narcissistic relationship with the subject, they would only ever be perceived in a momentary fashion. The word, the word which names, is the identical. The word doesn't answer to the spatial distinctiveness of the object, which is always ready to be dissolved in an identification with the subject, but to its temporal dimension. The object, at one instant constituted as a semblance[3] of the human subject, a double of himself, nonetheless has a certain permanence of appearance over time, which however does not endure indefinitely, since all objects are perishable. This appearance which lasts a certain length of time is strictly only recognisable through the intermediary of the name. The name is the time of the object. Naming constitutes a pact, by which two subjects simultaneously come to an agreement to recognise the same object. If the human subject didn't name – as Genesis says it was done in earthly Paradise – the major species first, if the subjects do not come to an agreement over this recognition, no world, not even a perception, could be sustained for more than one instant. That is the joint, the emergence of the dimension of the symbolic in relation to the imaginary.

Anamorphosis

1

I saw myself seeing myself, young Parque says somewhere. Certainly, this statement has rich and complex implications in relation to the theme developed in *La Jeune Parque*, that of femininity – but we haven't got there yet. We are dealing with the philosopher, who apprehends something that is one of the essential correlates of consciousness in its relation to representation, and which is designated as *I see myself seeing myself*. What evidence can we really attach to this formula? How is it that it remains, in fact, correlative with that fundamental mode to which we referred in the Cartesian *cogito*, by which the subject apprehends himself as thought?

What isolates this apprehension of thought by itself is a sort of doubt, which has been called methodological doubt, which concerns whatever might give support to thought in representation. How is it, then, that the *I see myself seeing myself* remains its envelope and base, and, perhaps more than one thinks, grounds its certainty? For, *I warm myself by warming myself* is a reference to the body as body – I feel that sensation of warmth which, from some point inside me, is diffused and locates me as body. Whereas in the *I see myself seeing myself*, there is no such sensation of being absorbed by vision.

Furthermore, the phenomenologists have succeeded in articulating with precision, and in the most disconcerting way, that it is quite clear that I see *outside*,

From Jacques Lacan, *The Four Fundamental Concepts of Psycho-Analysis*, ed. by Jacques-Alain Miller, trans. by Alan Sheridan (London: The Hogarth Press, 1977), pp. 80–90 that perception is not in me, that it is on the objects that it apprehends. And yet I apprehend the world in a perception that seems to concern the immanence of the *I see myself seeing myself*. The privilege of the subject seems to be established here from that bipolar reflexive relation by which, as soon as I perceive, my representations belong to me.

This is how the world is struck with a presumption of idealization, of the suspicion of yielding me only my representations. Serious practice does not really weigh very heavy, but, on the other hand, the philosopher, the idealist, is placed there, as much in confrontation with himself as in confrontation with those who are listening to him, in an embarrassing position. How can one deny that nothing of the world appears to me except in my representations? This is the irreducible method of Bishop Berkeley, about whose subjective position much might be said – including something that may have eluded you in passing, namely, this *belong to me* aspect of representations, so reminiscent of property. When carried to the limit, the process of this meditation, of this reflecting reflection, goes so far as to reduce the subject apprehended by the Cartesian meditation to a power of annihilation.

The mode of my presence in the world is the subject in so far as by reducing itself solely to this certainty of being a subject, it becomes active annihilation. In fact, the process of the philosophical meditation throws the subject towards the transforming historical action, and, around this point, orders the configured modes of active self-consciousness through its metamorphoses in history. As for the meditation on being that reaches its culmination in the thought of Heidegger, it restores to being itself that power of annihilation – or at least poses the question of how it may be related to it.

This is also the point to which Maurice Merleau-Ponty leads us. But, if you refer to his text, you will see that it is at this point that he chooses to withdraw, in order to propose a return to the sources of intuition concerning the visible and the invisible, to come back to that which is prior to all reflection, thetic or non-thetic, in order to locate the emergence of vision itself. For him, it is a question of restoring – for, he tells us, it can only be a question of a reconstruction or a restoration, not of a path traversed in the opposite direction – of reconstituting the way by which, not from the body, but from something that he calls the flesh of the world, the original point of vision was able to emerge. It would seem that in this way one sees, in this unfinished work, the emergence of something like the search for an unnamed substance from which I, the seer, extract myself. From the toils (*rets*), or rays (*rais*), if you prefer, of an iridescence of which I am at first a part, I emerge as eye, assuming, in a way, emergence from what I would like to call the function of *seeingness* (*voyure*).

A wild odour emanates from it, providing a glimpse on the horizon of the hunt of Artemis – whose touch seems to be associated at this moment of tragic failure in which we lost him who speaks.

Yet is this really the way he wished to take? The traces that remain of the part to come from his meditation permits us to doubt it. The reference-points that are provided in it, more particularly for the strictly psycho-analytic unconscious, allow us to perceive that he may have been directed towards some search, original in relation to the philosophical tradition, towards that new dimension of meditation on the subject that analysis enables us to trace.

Personally, I cannot but be struck by certain of these notes, which are for me less enigmatic than they may seem to other readers, because they correspond very exactly to the schemata – with one of them, in particular – that I shall be dealing with here. Read, for example, the note concerning what he calls the turning inside-out of the finger of a glove, in as much as it seems to appear there – note the way in which the leather envelops the fur in a winter glove – that consciousness, in its illusion of *seeing itself seeing itself*, finds its basis in the inside-out structure of the gaze.

2

But what is the gaze?

I shall set out from this first point of annihilation in which is marked, in the field of the reduction of the subject, a break – which warns us of the need to introduce another reference, that which analysis assumes in reducing the privileges of the consciousness.

Psycho-analysis regards the consciousness as irremediably limited, and institutes it as a principle, not only of idealization, but of *méconnaissance*, as – using a term that takes on new value by being referred to a visible domain – *scotoma*. The term was introduced into the psycho-analytic vocabulary by the French School. Is it simply a metaphor? We find here once again the ambiguity that affects anything that is inscribed in the register of the scopic drive.

For us, consciousness matters only in its relation to what, for propaedeutic reasons, I have tried to show you in the fiction of the incomplete text – on the basis of which it is a question of recentring the subject as speaking in the very lacunae of that in which, at first sight, it presents itself as speaking. But I am stating here only the relation of the pre-conscious to the unconscious. The dynamic that is attached to the consciousness as such, the attention the subject brings to his own text, remains up to this point, as Freud has stressed, outside theory and, strictly speaking, not yet articulated.

It is here that I propose that the interest the subject takes in his own split is bound up with that which determines it – namely, a privileged object, which has emerged from some primal separation, from some self-mutilation induced by the very approach of the real, whose name, in our algebra, is the *objet a*.

In the scopic relation, the object on which depends the phantasy from which the subject is suspended in an essential vacillation is the gaze. Its privilege – and also that by which the subject for so long has been misunderstood as being in its dependence – derives from its very structure.

Let us schematize at once what we mean. From the moment that this gaze appears, the subject tries to adapt himself to it, he becomes that punctiform object, that point of vanishing being with which the subject confuses his own failure. Furthermore, of all the objects in which the subject may recognize his dependence in the register of desire, the gaze is specified as unapprehensible. That is why it is, more than any other object, misunderstood (*méconnu*), and it is perhaps for this reason, too, that the subject manages, fortunately, to symbolize his own vanishing and punctiform bar (*trait*) in the illusion of the consciousness of *seeing oneself see oneself*, in which the gaze is elided.

If, then, the gaze is that underside of consciousness, how shall we try to imagine it?

The expression is not inapt, for we can give body to the gaze. Sartre, in one of the most brilliant passages of *L'Être et le Néant*, brings it into function in the dimension of the existence of others. Others would remain suspended in the same, partially de-realizing, conditions that are, in Sartre's definition, those of objectivity, were it not for the gaze. The gaze, as conceived by Sartre, is the gaze by which I am surprised – surprised in so far as it changes all the perspectives, the lines of force, of my world, orders it, from the point of nothingness where I am, in a sort of radiated reticulation of the organisms. As the locus of the relation between me, the annihilating subject, and that which surrounds me, the gaze seems to possess such a privilege that it goes so far as to have me scotomized, I who look, the eye of him who sees me as object. In so far as I am under the gaze, Sartre writes, I no longer see the eye that looks at me and, if I see the eye, the gaze disappears.

Is this a correct phenomenological analysis? No. It is not true that, when I am under the gaze, when I solicit a gaze, when I obtain it, I do not see it as a gaze. Painters, above all, have grasped this gaze as such in the mask and I have only to remind you of Goya, for example, for you to realize this.

The gaze sees itself – to be precise, the gaze of which Sartre speaks, the gaze that surprises me and reduces me to shame, since this is the feeling he regards as the most dominant. The gaze I encounter – you can find this in Sartre's own writing – is, not a seen gaze, but a gaze imagined by me in the field of the Other.

If you turn to Sartre's own text, you will see that, far from speaking of the emergence of this gaze as of something that concerns the organ of sight, he refers to the sound of rustling leaves, suddenly heard while out hunting, to a footstep heard in a corridor. And when are these sounds heard? At the moment when he has presented himself in the action of looking through a keyhole. A gaze surprises him in the function of voyeur, disturbs him, overwhelms him and reduces him to a feeling of shame. The gaze in question is certainly the presence of others as such. But does this mean that originally it is in the relation of subject to subject, in the function of the existence of others as looking at me, that we apprehend what the gaze really is? Is it not clear that the gaze intervenes here only in as much as it is not the annihilating subject, correlative of the world of objectivity, who feels himself surprised, but the subject sustaining himself in a function of desire?

Is it not precisely because desire is established here in the domain of seeing that we can make it vanish?

3

We can apprehend this privilege of the gaze in the function of desire, by pouring ourselves, as it were, along the veins through which the domain of vision has been integrated into the field of desire.

It is not for nothing that it was at the very period when the Cartesian meditation inaugurated in all its purity the function of the subject that the dimension of optics that I shall distinguish here by calling "geometral" or "flat" (as opposed to perspective) optics was developed.

I shall illustrate for you, by one object among others, what seems to me exemplary in a function that so curiously attracted so much reflection at the time.

One reference, for those who would like to carry further what I tried to convey to you today, is Baltrušaitis' book, *Anamorphoses*.

In my seminar, I have made great use of the function of anamorphosis, in so far as it is an exemplary structure. What does a simple, non-cylindrical anamorphosis consist of? Suppose there is a portrait on this flat piece of paper that I am holding. By chance, you see the blackboard, in an oblique position in relation to the piece of paper. Suppose that, by means of a series of ideal threads or lines, I reproduce on the oblique surface each point of the image drawn on my sheet of paper. You can easily imagine what the result would be – you would obtain a figure enlarged and distorted according to the lines of what may be called a perspective. One supposes that – if I take away that which has helped in the construction, namely, the image placed in my own visual field – the impression I will retain, while remaining in that place, will be more or less the same. At least, I will recognize the general outlines of the image – at best, I will have an identical impression.

I will now pass around something that dates from a hundred years earlier, from 1533, a reproduction of a painting that, I think, you all know – Hans Holbein's *The Ambassadors*. It will serve to refresh the memories of those who know the picture well. Those who do not should examine it attentively. I shall come back to it shortly.

Vision is ordered according to a mode that may generally be called the function of images. This function is defined by a point-by-point correspondence of two unities in space. Whatever optical intermediaries may be used to establish their relation, whether their image is virtual, or real, the point-by-point correspondence is essential. That which is of the mode of the image in the field of vision is therefore reducible to the simple schema that enables us to establish anamorphosis, that is to say, to the relation of an image, in so far as it is linked to a surface, with a certain point that we shall call the "geometral" point. Anything that is determined by this method, in which the straight line plays its role of being the path of light, can be called an image.

Art is mingled with science here. Leonardo da Vinci is both a scientist, on account of his dioptric constructions, and an artist. Vitruvius's treatise on architecture is not far away. It is in Vignola and in Alberti that we find the progressive interrogation of the geometral laws of perspective, and it is around research on perspective that is centred a privileged interest for the domain of vision — whose relation with the institution of the Cartesian subject, which is itself a sort of geometral point, a point of perspective, we cannot fail to see. And, around the geometral perspective, the picture — this is a very important function to which we shall return — is organized in a way that is quite new in the history of painting.

I should now like to refer you to Diderot. The *Lettre sur les aveugles à l'usage de ceux qui voient* (Letter on the Blind for the use of those who see) will show you that this construction allows that which concerns vision to escape totally. For the geometral space of vision — even if we include those imaginary parts in the virtual space of the mirror, of which, as you know, I have spoken at length — is perfectly reconstructible, imaginable, by a blind man.

What is at issue in geometral perspective is simply the mapping of space, not sight. The blind man may perfectly well conceive that the field of space that he knows, and which he knows as real, may be perceived at a distance, and as a simultaneous act. For him, it is a question of apprehending a temporal function, instantaneity. In Descartes, dioptrics, the action of the eyes, is represented as the conjugated action of two sticks. The geometral dimension of vision does not exhaust, therefore, far from it, what the field of vision as such offers us as the original subjectifying relation.

This is why it is so important to acknowledge the inverted use of perspective in the structure of anamorphosis.

It was Dürer himself who invented the apparatus to establish perspective. Dürer's "lucinda" is comparable to what, a little while ago, I placed between that blackboard and myself, namely, a certain image, or more exactly a canvas, a treliss that will be traversed by straight lines — which are not necessarily rays, but also threads — which will link each point that I have to see in the world to a point at which the canvas will, by this line, be traversed.

It was to establish a correct perspective image, therefore, that the *lucinda* was introduced. If I reverse its use, I will have the pleasure of obtaining not the restoration of the world that lies at the end, but the distortion, on another surface, of the image that I would have obtained on the first, and I will dwell, as on some delicious game, on this method that makes anything appear at will in a particular stretching.

I would ask you to believe that such an enchantment took place in its time. Baltrusaïtis' book will tell you of the furious polemics that these practices gave rise to, and which culminated in works of considerable length. The convent of the Minims, now destroyed, which once stood near the rue des Tournelles, carried on the very long wall of one of its galleries and representing as if by chance St John at Patmos a picture that had to be looked at through a hole, so that its distorting value could be appreciated to its full extent.

Distortion may lend itself – this was not the case for this particular fresco – to all the paranoiac ambiguities, and every possible use has been made of it, from Arcimboldi to Salvador Dali. I will go so far as to say that this fascination complements what geometral researches into perspective allow to escape from vision.

How is it that nobody has ever thought of connecting this with . . . the effect of an erection? Imagine a tattoo traced on the sexual organ *ad hoc* in the state of repose and assuming its, if I may say so, developed form in another state.

How can we not see here, immanent in the geometral dimension – a partial dimension in the field of the gaze, a dimension that has nothing to do with vision as such – something symbolic of the function of the lack, of the appearance of the phallic ghost?

Now, in *The Ambassadors* – I hope everyone has had time now to look at the reproduction – what do you see? What is this strange, suspended, oblique object in the foreground in front of these two figures?

The two figures are frozen, stiffened in their showy adornments. Between them is a series of objects that represent in the painting of the period the symbols of *vanitas*. At the same period, Cornelius Agrippa wrote his *De Vanitate scientiarum*, aimed as much at the arts as the sciences, and these objects are all symbolic of the sciences and arts as they were grouped at the time in the *trivium* and *quadrivium*. What, then, before this display of the domain of appearance in all its most fascinating forms, is this object, which from some angles appears to be flying through the air, at others to be tilted? You cannot know – for you turn away, thus escaping the fascination of the picture.

Begin by walking out of the room in which no doubt it has long held your attention. It is then that, turning round as you leave – as the author of the *Anamorphoses* describes it – you apprehend in this form . . . What? A skull.

This is not how it is presented at first – that figure, which the author compares to a cuttlebone and which for me suggests rather that loaf composed of two books which Dali was once pleased to place on the head of an old woman, chosen deliberately for her wretched, filthy appearance and, indeed, because she seems to be unaware of the fact, or, again, Dali's soft watches, whose signification is obviously less phallic than that of the object depicted in a flying position in the foreground of this picture.

All this shows that at the very heart of the period in which the subject emerged and geometral optics was an object of research, Holbein makes visible for us here something that is simply the subject as annihilated — annihilated in the form that is, strictly speaking, the imaged embodiment of the *minus-phi* $[-\phi]$ of castration, which for us, centres the whole organization of the desires through the framework of the fundamental drives.

But it is further still that we must seek the function of vision. We shall then see emerging on the basis of vision, not the phallic symbol, the anamorphic ghost, but the gaze as such, in its pulsatile, dazzling and spread out function, as it is in this picture.

This picture is simply what any picture is, a trap for the gaze. In any picture, it is precisely in seeking the gaze in each of its points that you will see it disappear. I shall try to develop this further next time.

Questions and Answers

F. WAHL: *You have explained that the original apprehension of the gaze in the gaze of others, as described by Sartre, was not the fundamental experience of the gaze. I would like you to explain in greater detail what you have already sketched for us, the apprehension of the gaze in the direction of desire.*

LACAN: If one does not stress the dialectic of desire one does not understand why the gaze of others should disorganize the field of perception. It is because the subject in question is not that of the reflexive consciousness, but that of desire. One thinks it is a question of the geometral eye-point, whereas it is a question of a quite different eye — that which flies in the foreground of *The Ambassadors*.

WAHL: *But I don't understand how others will reappear in your discourse . . .*

LACAN: Look, the main thing is that I don't come a cropper!

WAHL: *I would also like to say that, when you speak of the subject and of the real, one is tempted, on first hearing, to consider the terms in themselves. But gradually one realizes that they are to be understood in their relation to one another, and that they have a topological definition — subject and real are to be situated on either side of the split, in the resistance of the phantasy. The real is, in a way, an experience of resistance.*

LACAN: My discourse proceeds, in the following way: each term is sustained only in its topological relation with the others, and the subject of the *cogito* is treated in exactly the same way.

WAHL: *Is topology for you a method of discovery or of exposition?*

LACAN It is the mapping of the topology proper to our experience as analysts, which may later be taken in a metaphysical perspective. I think Merleau-Ponty was moving in this direction – see the second part of the book, his reference to the *Wolf Man* and to the finger of a glove.

P. KAUFMAN: *You have provided us with a typical structure of the gaze, but you have said nothing of the dilation of light.*

LACAN: I said that the gaze was not the eye, except in that flying form in which Holbein has the cheek to show me my own soft watch ... Next time, I will talk about embodied light.

26 February 1964

Notes

1   See (1923b) GW XIII 253; Stud III 294; SE XIX 26.
2   GW II/III 466–70; Stud II 447–50; SE V 463–7. It is referred to again in chapter VII. GW II/III 553; Stud II 523; SE V 547, but the passage Lacan is paraphrasing is on p. 467/448/464.
3   "*un semblant.*"

References

Freud, Sigmund (1940–68) *Gesammelte Werke*, 18 volumes, (London: Hogarth Press).

Lacan, Jacques (1988) *The Seminar of Jacques Lacan, Book II*, trans. Sylvana Tomaselli, ed. Jacques-Alain Miller (New York: W. W. Norton).

10

THE STATUS AND SIGNIFICANCE OF THE BODY IN LACAN'S IMAGINARY AND SYMBOLIC ORDERS

Charles W. Bonner

The subject of the unconscious is only in touch with the soul via the body, by introducing thought into it. . . . Man does not think with his soul . . . He thinks as a consequence of the fact that a structure, that of language . . . carves up his body, a structure that has nothing to do with anatomy.

Lacan, *Television*

For the phenomenologically minded reader, the name of the renowned French psychoanalyst Jacques Lacan evokes reactions ranging from accusations of irrelevance to testimonials bordering on reverence. The present essay will steer clear of these two ultimately unproductive positions. My concern is instead to explicate an aspect of Lacanian theory which I believe to be particularly pertinent to a phenomenologically conceived psychology – the status and significance of the body. The body has been a relatively neglected area for interpreters of Lacan's corpus, with far greater heed being given to his more plentiful references to the role of language in constituting human subjectivity. Yet, as the above quote suggests, Lacan proposes a profound relationship between language and the body in the coming-to-be of the subject.[1]

It was in his earlier work that Lacan (1938/1988, 1949/1977, 1953) most explicitly explored the place of the body. Not coincidentally, these earlier papers have also been regarded as best reflecting the influence of phenomenology – an influence which Lacan and his interpreters have at times sought to dismiss in favor of his later emphasis on structural linguistics. For example, Lee (1990) claims that "despite their theoretical sophistication, these early papers nevertheless betray Lacan's own inability to escape fully the presumptions of phenomenology" (p. 30). In contrast to this type of claim, Thompson (1985) has contended that phenomenological concepts continued to serve Lacan even in his later preoccupation with structural linguistics. Indeed, Thompson declares that "Lacan's indebtedness to phenomenology is so vast that one must conclude that he divorced himself from it for political reasons" (ibid.: p. 177).

More recently, Boothby (1993) and Samuels (1993) have maintained that phenomenological categories are virtually synonymous with the concepts required to explicate the perceptual functions that are such an essential aspect of Lacan's imaginary order. This point will be illustrated in the opening section, which presents a detailed developmental description of the relation between bodiliness and ego formation in the mirror phase. Lacan's convergence with Merleau-Ponty (1964) is also underscored in this first section. The two subsequent sections will retain a developmental focus in tracing the pivotal role played by the body in facilitating the subject's accession to symbolic modes of functioning, which come to supplement the previously established imaginary modes.

1 Body Image Formation and the Phenomenology of the Imaginary in the Mirror Phase

Furthering Freud's (1923: 26) contention that "the ego is first and foremost a bodily ego," Lacan is particularly innovative in accounting for the relation between the infant's bodiliness and ego formation. In setting up his discussion of the ego's genesis, Lacan (1938/1988, 1949/1977, 1953, 1988a, 1988b) punctuates the "specific prematurity" of the human infant's birth compared to other species. Focusing upon the infant's anatomical incompleteness, Lacan accentuates

> the ontological status of *beance*, an abyss, gap, lack, or dehiscence marking the human being from birth, which ... dispels any talk of a preformed, preadapted, or harmonious relationship of man to his environment. (Muller 1982a: 234)

Lacan emphasizes how the infant's intra-uterine body organization is deficient relative to the demands of extra-uterine life, with there being insufficient coordination among its sensory systems and motor movements. In Lacan's view, the infant's birth irrevocably disrupts the homeostasis that – at least retroactively – is experienced by the infant as having characterized intra-uterine existence. Therefore, contrary to what has been posited and presupposed in countless developmental theories, Lacan conceives extra-uterine life as introducing a "fundamental discord" that cannot be understood to include any inherent sense of unity or self.

In specifying the ways in which the infant's bodily and perceptual experience is chaotic and fragmentary, Lacan first highlights the host of bodily discomforts related to being fed and being weaned. During approximately the first six months of life, through the "oral fusion" established with the mother during feeding, Lacan sees the infant as retroactively experiencing a fantasy of intra-uterine fusion (Muller 1988). However, this fusional fantasy is frustrated by the disruptive discontinuities associated with feeding, weaning, and other somatic experiences. In an attempt to minimize or refuse this frustration of desire for wholeness, the infant incorporates what Lacan (1938/1988) called the "imago of the maternal breast" – which he took to be an essential aspect of the "weaning complex," within which a dialectical tension is set in motion between the soothing qualities of the maternal imago and the chaotic bodily experience created by the cleavage of premature birth. Lacan (1938/1988) alludes to this dialectic when he notes that "the maternal imago cannot be separated from the chaos of interoceptive sensations from which it emerges" (p. 15).

In addition to the discomforts related to feeding and weaning, Lacan also describes the infant's lack of motor coordination – giving particular attention to how the infant experiences its body as consisting of discrete parts without a sense of their interrelation. That is to say, the infant experiences itself at one moment as a hand, at another as a foot, a leg, or an arm. With this motor incoordination, the infant is of course profoundly helpless and dependent. The infant's sensory life likewise lacks coherence, with the world consisting of the predominantly dissociated experiences provided by the following three categories of sensory receptors:

1   The interoceptive receptors, which are related to such visceral sensations as breathing, eating, and digestion.
2   The proprioceptive receptors, which are related to sensations produced by the body's movement, including sucking and gripping.
3   The exteroceptive receptors, which are related to external stimuli as they impact upon the senses of sight, sound, and smell.

Particularly during the first six months of life, Lacan notes how the infant's "extero- proprio- and interoceptive sensations are not . . . sufficiently coordinated to allow recognition of one's own body to occur, nor, correlatively, to allow any idea of what is outside the body" (Lacan 1938/1988: 14). Indeed, in viewing others, the infant before six months tends to focus upon and scrutinize discrete body parts rather than being oriented to the other's bodily totality (Merleau-Ponty 1964).

In the midst of the infant's sensory-motor incoordination, Lacan (1938/1988) is impressed by the precocious ability the infant demonstrates in recognizing its mother figure's face, an ability which is evident within the first ten days of life (Merleau-Ponty 1964). Lacan (1938/1988) further observes how "the reaction of interest that a child shows in the presence of the human face . . . cannot be separated from the development by which the human face will assume its value as a mirror of psychic expression" (p. 14). Lacan here anticipates the superiority that the sense of sight will gradually gain relative to the infant's other, less developed sensory-motor modalities. With the advent of what he called the "mirror phase" between six to eight months, Lacan will attribute profound developmental consequences to the precocity of the infant's visual perception.

That is to say, Lacan (1953, 1949/1977) seizes upon the fact that by the age of six to eight months the infant's visual perception is sufficiently superior to its motor coordination that it becomes fascinated by the sight of its image in a mirror. Not yet able to stand up, and supported by a caregiver or a prosthetic device, the infant enthusiastically responds to the upright posture presented by its mirror image *as if* it has already achieved the motor mastery depicted by the image. For Lacan and his followers, the infant's behavior in front of the mirror provides a profound metaphor of how the infant comes to experience its mother's more coordinated movements as bestowing upon it a unity that it otherwise lacks (Ragland-Sullivan 1986).[2] Through its reflection in actual mirrors and the metaphorical mirror of its mother's image and reactions, the infant is for the first time able to imagine itself as a corporeal unity or gestalt (Muller and Richardson 1982; Jalbert 1983), henceforth allowing it to experience its body parts and movements as integrated and coordinated in a way not yet physically possible.

With its placidity and stability, the infant's mirror image offers a seductive alternative to the infant's own motoric insufficiency and incoordination. As Benvennuto and Kennedy (1986) have described, "the mirror image is held together, it can come and go with a slight change of the infant's position, and the mastery of the image fills him with triumph and joy" (p. 54). The mirror image thus provides the promise of a bodily mastery of which the infant is not yet capable. As Lacan (1949/1977) puts it, through its mirror image the infant "anticipates in a mirage the maturation of his power" (p. 2). In jubilantly identifying with the unified body-image of the other, the infant borrows an "envelope of mastery" (Lacan 1988a: 170–1) which serves to contain and coordinate the anarchy of its otherwise chaotic bodily experience (Boothby 1991; Jalbert 1983; Lacan 1988a; Ver Eecke 1989).

Lacan thus clearly posits a primacy of the visual in the construction of the body-image. Such senses as hearing, touching, and smelling make a less dramatic contribution to this construction since they only permit partial experiences of the body. In contrast, the sense of sight alone allows the child access to a totalized body-image (Grosz 1990; Merleau-Ponty 1964; Ver Eecke 1975, 1989). Research on the development of children born blind reveals that it takes them significantly longer to appropriate a unified body-image and to subsequently learn the stable use of the pronoun "I" (Fraiberg and Adelson 1973; cited in Ver Eecke 1989). Further, even once this appropriation is achieved, blind children's "postural schema... [and] image and experience of ... [their bodies] ... vary considerably from that of sighted subjects" (Grosz 1990).

To substantiate his theory of the mirror phase, Lacan integrated empirical research from numerous fields – including ethology, anthropology, and physiology (Ver Eecke 1983). The empirical support for Lacan's theory of the mirror phase has continued to accumulate, as Muller (1982b, 1986) has documented in his reviews of numerous contemporary studies from experimental and developmental psychology. These studies have confirmed that the mirror phase typically unfolds between 6–18 months – a period which coincides with the consolidation of object permanence and with the developing capacity for long-term memory of visual forms (Muller 1986).

Among the most significant references for Lacan was the work of French psychiatrist Henri Wallon (1984). Wallon's work included extensive observations and descriptions of infants' and young children's behavior before mirrors. From Wallon's work, a developmental delineation of the mirror phase is possible (Jalbert 1983; also reviewed in Merleau-Ponty 1964), with three movements of the mirror phase being summarized as follows:

1   The infant perceives the mirror image *as if* it were real, attempting to grasp it as though it were an object. During this part of the mirror phase, which lasts until about age one, the child has not yet learned to "discriminate between the proprioceptive sensations of its body and the exteroceptive experience of its body image" (Jalbert 1983: 138), in this way making possible the identification of the one with the other. It is during the early months of the mirror phase that the child forms an identification with the mirror image and exhibits reactions that Lacan characterizes as jubilant.

2   Through experimenting with the mirror image and the mirror surface, especially by noting the absence of anything behind the mirror surface, the child recognizes the non-reality of the mirror image. The child is thus confronted with the difference between "the proprio-interoceptive [i.e., felt] experience of the body and the exteroceptive [i.e., seen] experience of the body image" (Jalbert 1983: 139).

3   By age 18 months the child has usually determined – at least cognitively – that the exteroceptively perceived body-image is an effect or consequence of the body as "located in the space of proprioceptive sensations" (Jalbert 1983: 136), in this way subordinating the two-dimensional body-image to the body as experienced in three-dimensional space. Within this "rapport of subordination," then, the child maintains *both* a differentiation between the experienced body and the body-image *and* the previously established identification between these two domains.

This developmental sketch of the mirror phase, though, is already somewhat of an idealized account insofar as it posits a primacy of cognition in the infant's coming to comprehend the "non-reality" of the specular image. Merleau-Ponty (1964) warns against this understanding when he states that "if the comprehension of the specular image were solely a matter of cognition, then once the phenomenon were understood its past would be completely reassimilated" (p. 138). To substantiate this point, Merleau-Ponty (1964) cites observations of a five-year-old boy touching, licking, and striking his mirror image. The cognitive perspective – exemplified for Merleau-Ponty by the work of Wallon (1984) – assumes that the influence of the specular image disappears once the child understands that it is "simply" a material reflection of its introceptively experienced body. However, Merleau-Ponty maintains that "the operations that constitute the ... [specular image] involve not only the intelligence proper but, rather, all the individual's relations with others" (p. 138), with the specular image therefore becoming generalized as the child grows increasingly aware of itself as seen by others.

Merleau-Ponty (1964) credits Lacan with surpassing Wallon's limited interpretation of the specular image, particularly insofar as Lacan's account recognizes the affective and intersubjective implications of the child's specular identification. The mirror phase inducts the infant into what Lacan (1988a, 1988b) called the "imaginary order," from which only varying degrees of escape will ever be possible. It is therefore Lacan's (1949/1977) contention that the mirror phase culminates in "the assumption of an alienating identity, which will mark with its rigid structure the subject's entire mental development" (p. 4). The infant's identification with the specular image provides the foundation for the formation of the ego as well as for subsequent identifications, introducing a "formal stagnation ... which constitutes the ego and its objects with the attributes of permanence, identity, and substantiality" (ibid.: 17). That is, Lacan's imaginary order is relevant not only to the ego's relations with others, but to the perceptual relation of the ego to objects – wherein the perceived unity of the ego comes to be correlative with the perceived unity of objects in the perceptual field. Along these lines, Boothby (1993) has accentuated how "a key aspect of the imaginary function, perhaps its very essence, consists in its capacity to adumbrate the unitary contour of perceptual objects" (p. 11).

Here Lacan converges with the Husserlian phenomenology of consciousness insofar as there is an intentional relation between the ego and the perceptual unities constituted by the ego (Husserl 1982). However, in Lacan's phenomenology of the imaginary, the unity of the ego and consciousness is equally dependent upon the perceived unity of the perceptual field. Samuels (1993) makes this point by noting that "the unity of the self is dependent upon the establishment of unities in the outside world and vice versa" (p. 63). Lacan's account of the mirror phase therefore speaks to how the constituting ego is itself constituted by the perceived unity of others and objects – a perceptual gestalt which Lacan (1949/ 1977) notes is "certainly more constituent than constituted" (p. 2). With this radical dependency of the ego *qua* consciousness on others and objects, the ego's status is potentially reducible to nothingness. Samuels (1993) has noted how "consciousness is always consciousness of the other .... without the reflected image of the other, the ego is nothing" (pp. 73–4). The ego's potential nothingness is one of several alienating effects Lacan attributes to the infant's specular identification. The next section will focus on the body's fate within the intrasubjective and intersubjective dimensions of imaginary alienation.

2 The Body's Fate Within the Intrasubjective and Intersubjective Dimensions of Imaginary Alienation

In Lacan's view, the mirror image is a *mirage* in that it has no depth, it is not real, it is imaginary. Still, the infant is convinced that his image is *really him*, and longs to incarnate its unity, completeness, and tranquility. Lacan maintains that in being so captivated by its image the infant effects an alienation of itself from itself – not primarily because the image represents the infant as *other*, but due to the way in which the assumption of the imaginary gestalt entails the exclusion and restriction of the heterogeneity of bodily experience and desire. Boothby (1991: 57) has most eloquently explicated this aspect of Lacanian theory:

> the unity of the imago remains forever inadequate to the fullness of desire. There is always a remainder, always something left out. Desire is split against itself insofar as only a portion of the forces animating the living body find their way into the motivating imaginary *Gestalt*.

Lacan introduced the category of "the real" to designate the undifferentiated and unsymbolized dimensions of bodily existence, those that Boothby specifies as initially alienated by the formation of the ego in the mirror phase. In phenomenological terms, the identification with the specular image effects an at least partial alienation from the lived body.

As already noted, the infant's experience and expressions of jubilation are particularly notable during the early months of the mirror phase, when the infant has identified itself with its mirror image without yet differentiating it from its body as experienced in space. The jubilant aspect of the infant's initial identification with the mirror image is emphasized by Lacan (1953: 15) when he declares that

> We cannot fail to appreciate the affective value which the gestalt of the vision of the whole body-image may assume when we consider the fact that it appears

against a background of organic disturbance and discord, in which all indications are that we should seek the origins of the image of the "body in bits and pieces."

By the phrase "body in bits and pieces," Lacan is referring to what in other places he has described as the "imagos of bodily fragmentation" to be found in dreams, fantasies, and paintings, i.e., "the images of castration, mutilation, dismemberment, dislocation, evisceration, devouring, [and] bursting open of the body" (Lacan 1949/1977: 11). However, Lacan does not appear to take these fragmented body images to actually be present in the experience of the pre-mirror phase infant. In temporal terms, it is important to accentuate how the infant's jubilant, albeit illusory, anticipation of bodily unity *retroactively* determines the images of pre-mirror phase experience to be those of bodily fragmentation (Gallop 1985; Jalbert 1983; Laplanche and Pontalis 1967). Lacan (1949/1977) alludes to this important point when he states that

> The *mirror stage* is a drama whose internal thrust is precipitated from insufficiency to anticipation and which *manufactures for the subject*, caught up in the lure of spatial identification, the succession of phantasies that extends from a fragmented body-image to a form of its totality that I shall call orthopaedic. (p. 4, my emphasis)

By "orthopaedic," we can understand Lacan to be referring to the corrective function played by the totalized body-image relative to the fragmented body-images that it retroactively manufactures. Gallop (1985) articulates this subtle and complex point with particular clarity when she states that "the image of the body in bits and pieces is fabricated retroactively from the mirror stage. It is only the anticipated 'orthopedic' form of its totality that can define – retroactively – the body as insufficient [and fragmented]" (p. 86).[3]

Along with this retroactively defined sense of bodily insufficiency, the infant's body image also assumes a defensive function. That is, contained within the infant's anticipation of bodily unity, there is a defense against the anxiety of bodily fragmentation. A dialectical tension is constituted between the unified body-image presented by the mirroring other and the images of bodily fragmentation retroactively engendered by the infant's identification with this unified image (Bonner 1991, 1993; Grosz 1990; Lacan 1988b). The mirror phase infant's unified body-image promises an imaginary immunization against the anxiety of bodily fragmentation but, like any inoculation, it harbors traces of the very ailment against which it is intended to provide protection. Lacan (1949/1977) speaks to this point when he notes how the mirror image "is invested with all the original distress resulting from the child's intra-organic and relational discordance during the first six months [of life]" (p. 19).[4]

The infant's initially jubilant experience of its mirror image is thus relatively fleeting, since this image is so soon also invested with the ongoing and retroactively revitalized distress of his discordant bodily experience (Gallop 1985). Within a few months, a significant supplementary experience of distress develops. Having recognized that it possesses an external appearance, the infant next becomes aware that this external appearance is actually much more readily available to be viewed by others than viewed by itself. That is, as the infant begins to distinguish between its proprio-interoceptively experienced body and its unified body-image as revealed in the mirror, it becomes apparent that only the infant can directly experience the first corporeal dimension, while its outer appearance must always be mediated by the gaze of an other. A split is therefore introduced into the child's experience of its body, a split which will eclipse the previous sense of jubilation with one of anxiety.

The infant's jubilation in identifying with its mirror image had indicated that it initially experienced "his exteriority as an enrichment" (Ver Eecke 1984: 75). However, following this initial experience of enrichment, the infant gradually discovers the alienating and threatening dimension of depending upon others for the appropriation of its body as a unity. This discovery is usually made by age eight months and is exemplified by the phenomenon of "stranger anxiety," which was first described by developmental theorist Rene Spitz and has also been referred to as "stranger wariness" (Kaplan 1978). Spitz (1965) observed how at eight months many infants for the first time engaged in various anxious behaviors upon the approach of strangers, such as covering their eyes or hiding their heads under pillows – the purpose of these behaviors being to erase the visual image of the approaching stranger and, correlatively, to stage their own imagined disappearance.

It has been philosopher Wilfried Ver Eecke (1975, 1984, 1989) who, based upon a systematic study of Lacan, has seized upon the relation of stranger anxiety to the mirror phase. Ver Eecke has in essence revised Spitz's original observations within Lacan's theoretical framework. Ver Eecke speculates that the look of the stranger serves to alert and remind the infant of the alienating experiential split engendered by the fact that its external appearance is accessible predominantly through the eyes of others. As the child comes to see itself as being seen by others, the drama of the mirror phase therefore enters a significant new scene.

Ver Eecke (1984, 1989) makes the important observation that during the "stranger anxiety" phase the child does not usually experience the gaze of its mother with anxiety. Further, when in the presence of its mother, the child does not typically experience anxiety in the face of a stranger's gaze. Ver Eecke speculates that this is so since it is the mother who, it is hoped, has already recognized and responded to the infant's inner experience, in this way reassuring the child that it will not be reduced by her to its exteriority – which is precisely the anxiety-inducing threat posed by the gaze of a stranger (Ver Eecke 1975, 1984, 1989).

The infant thus depends on its mother to affirm and support the appropriation of its body both as a unified body-image and as a body-subject with experiences and desires distinct from her. In addition to the infant's radical dependence on the mirroring mother for facilitating the exteroceptive appropriation of its body as a unity, the infant is therefore also profoundly dependent on her for recognizing its inner bodily experience as valued in its own right – in this way allaying the experiences of anxiety, shame, and paranoia that can come to characterize a more problematic relation to bodiliness (Lacan 1953; Sartre 1953).

The phenomenon of stranger anxiety thus exemplifies the intersubjective dimension of the alienation that Lacan considered to be an essential dimension of the mirror phase's transformative effects. In initially identifying with the specular image, the infant had already to some extent become alienated from its interoceptive bodily experience and captured by the "imaginary me" offered by the image. Merleau-Ponty (1964) has described this dynamic as a "derealizing" function of the specular image, within which there is a "confiscation" of the "immediate me" by the "imaginary me" – that is to say, in intersubjective terms, there is a "'confiscation' of the subject by the others who look at him" (Merleau-Ponty 1964: 137). Particularly insofar as the infant's desire becomes invested in – if not fused with – the specular image, there exists the danger of its desire becoming alienated in and rigidified by the desire of the other who most incarnates this image (who, at least initially, is typically the mother figure).

Lacan (1978, 1988a) acknowledges the significance of Sartre's (1953) phenomenology of "the look" for his ideas on the intersubjectivity of the mirror phase – particularly the sense in which the other's gaze objectifies and alienates the subject. Ver Eecke (1975, 1985), though, deems Lacan's account to be more developmentally accurate than that of Sartre, since Lacan allows the look of the other to be more than the site of alienation. Insofar as there is the possibility for desire to be recognized, Ver Eecke affirms that the Lacanian look can facilitate the child's appropriation of its body as both a unity and a subjectivity.

Lacan (1978) further critiques Sartre for limiting his conception of "the look" to an intersubjective field in which the positions of observed and observer are potentially reversible. Lacan exceeds Sartre's understanding by granting a primacy to the position of "being seen," maintaining there is a radical "dependence of the visible on that which places us under the eye of the seer" (p. 72).[5] There can be no reciprocity between the other's gaze and the subject's perceptual experience, since the latter permits vision from a single perspective while the former submits the subject to being simultaneously seen from all sides. It is partly for this reason that Lacan (1978) speaks of "the split between the eye and the gaze" (p. 67). This split has an ontological status for Lacan that is irreducible to an intersubjective relationship, with the structure of the gaze by no means limited to the visual field. Explicating Sartre's famous phenomenology of the look, Lacan (1978) observes how "the gaze I encounter . . . . is, not a seen gaze, but a gaze imagined by me in the field of the Other" (p. 84). Lacan notes how Sartre's (1953) description of the look includes such auditory cues as hearing "a rustling of branches, or the sound of a footstep followed by silence" (p. 346). Beyond the sensory and intersubjective dimensions of the imaginary order, Lacan (1978) ultimately defines the gaze as a function of desire – a definition which will be fleshed out through the next section's discussion of the symbolic order and the Oedipalization of the subject.

3 The Acquisition of Language, Gender Identity Formation, and the Deconstruction of the Body-Image

During the course of the mirror phase the child gradually recognizes that others are not completely responsive to his or her primarily inarticulate demands for love and compliant mirroring. It is at this time, usually between 15–18 months, that the child begins to appropriate language as the means to make demands. The mother's ability to affirm her child's claim to autonomy will become especially significant as the child begins to appropriate speech as the main means of claiming a distinct point of view.

Ver Eecke (1984, 1989) has cogently described how the period of "no-saying" initiated between 15–18 months is the most significant linguistic index of the child's effort to ameliorate the alienation of the mirror phase. Initially in the form of shaking the head from side to side, and soon with the vigorous use of the word "no," "no-saying" by the child conveys the attempt to claim an autonomous viewpoint and to rupture the symbiotic bond with the mother. As Ver Eecke (1984) asserts, "to say *no* to a demand of the mother .... means that the child is no longer in need of his mother in overcoming the alienating dimension of appropriating his body" (p. 77). In saying "no" to the mother, the child is affirming ownership of his body as a source of desire separate from the image his mother and others may have of him. That is, "the child refuses to automatically be [or want] what his mother thinks him to be [or want]" (Ver Eecke 1984: 80).

The crucial question during the child's period of negativism is therefore whether and to what extent the mother can tolerate the aggressive refusal of her desire contained within her child's no-saying.[6] The aggressive intention of no-saying is clearly described by Ver Eecke (1984) when he states that "to say *no* is precisely to make use of a linguistic expression whose first function is to destroy the point of view taken by another" (p. 80). Here we see an intersubjective instantiation of Lacan's famous dictum that the word is "the murder of the thing" (1977: 104), with the specification that the word can also execute the symbolic murder of the other.

Ver Eecke (1984) emphasizes how the child's ability to productively employ "no-saying" depends upon his already having experienced his desires as frustrated by the prohibitions and no-saying of his parents. That is, the child identifies with the parents' prohibiting position and imitates their no-saying as a way to frustrate them as he has been frustrated – in more traditional psychoanalytic terms, there is an "identification with the aggressor." Although the no-saying of the mother is initially of greatest consequence for the child's ability to begin separating from her, the mother's capacity for no-saying is in turn dependent upon her recognition of the law of the father – a law which dictates that her child is not the exclusive focus for the fulfillment of her desire, which is instead delimited by a "third term" often but not necessarily occupied by the child's actual father.[7] Ver Eecke (1984) summarizes this cluster of Lacanian concepts when he states that "the mother's *no* is possible only through her recognition of the phallus of the father" (p. 81), a recognition which acknowledges her finitude and permits the child through his own no-saying to affirm the phallic attributes of the father.[8]

In referring to the father figure, I am of course alluding to the imminent Oedipalization of the child's desire. For Lacan, the Oedipal and castration complexes are intrinsically related to the child's acquisition of language. It is with the beginning of speech and the gradual entry into the Oedipal drama that the mirror phase subsides and the child passes from specular to the social forms of identification (Lacan 1949/1977 1988a). In becoming a "speaking subject," the child no longer lives exclusively in the "imaginary order," but accedes to what Lacan (1988b) called the "symbolic order" – that system of signifiers that constitute the subject's native language.

Lacan places particular importance on the influence of the signifier in the symbolic order insofar as the signifier is defined by the "interplay of opposition between sameness and differentness" (Jalbert 1983: 65), an interplay which assists the child in differentiating himself from others in a way that is problematic during the mirror phase. Where the imaginary order had previously been characterized by sameness, unity, continuity, and immediacy, the child's entry into the symbolic order therefore introduces difference, multiplicity, discontinuity, and mediation. This shift has significant consequences for the Oedipal child's identity formation insofar as he can no longer exclusively define himself as the sole object of his mother's desire. In this connection, Ver Eecke (1988) describes how the Oedipal child gradually

> accepts deprivation of an original but illusory identity and conquers a new identity. Even though this is a new identity, the child must create a kind of continuity for itself and must therefore feel that it is both the same and not the same as before. (p. 113)

Particularly important for this period of transition and transformation is the child's assumption of a sexual identity, a process which is initiated during the waning months of the mirror phase when – concurrent with the period of "no-saying" – there is an incipient awareness of sexual difference (i.e., of having or not having a penis). Contemporary psychoanalytic research on the infantile origins of sexual identity agrees that the second half of the second year is an especially critical period for the establishment of a core gender identity (Roiphe and Galenson 1981). Between the ages of 15–19 months, the genital zone "emerges as a distinct and differentiated source of endogenous pleasure" (ibid.: 284). There follows a burgeoning awareness of genital difference, with clear divergences becoming apparent between the way the male and female infant symbolize this nascent knowledge.

The significant fact for Lacan is that the discovery of genital difference itself engenders symbolization insofar as this discovery fragments the previously established unified body-image and calls upon the child to name through speech the discrete body parts that subsequently become apparent – with the penis or lack of penis of course being of particular concern. Indeed, the child's Oedipal-ization and concomitant castration complex entail the reappearance of the fragmented body images that had previously been contained by the imaginary bodily unity constituted in the mirror phase. Boothby (1990) has documented how during the Oedipal period there is a preoccupation with fragmented body images and fantasies of dismemberment. This preoccupation, rather than being a regressive event, plays an essential role in the child's transition to symbolic modes of functioning insofar as this transition entails a shift from the homo-geneity of desire defined by the imaginary unity of the ego to the heterogeneity of desire engendered by the diversity of signifying elements available through the linguistic system – a system "in which meaning [and desire] is free to circulate among associated elements without necessarily referring to a particular object or signified" (ibid.: 219). This shift from the homogeneity to the heterogeneity of desire "finds a perceptual analog in ... [the] contrast between the integrity of the body gestalt and its dismemberment into fragments" (ibid.: 222). Boothby is particularly articulate and suggestive in summarizing this aspect of Lacanian theory, describing how

> Lacan's theory locates the birth of the symbolic function in relation to a certain deconstruction of the Imaginary [order]. The fantasmatic violation of the body imago effected by castration furnishes a precondition for the unfolding of the capacity for signification. It is upon the site of the body image, or better, upon the *sight* of its dismemberment that the insertion of the subject into the symbolic order begins. The first movements of signification find their material support in the parts of the fragmented body.... (p. 227)

The imaginary body-gestalt provides an initial organization of unitary form upon which the differentiating function of linguistic signification can go to work. The body imago functions as an originary frame or matrix against which difference within identity can first be registered. (p. 224)

Thus, whereas the formation of the unified body image and ego identity had functioned to quell the anxiety of fragmented body images in the mirror phase, these fragmented body images in turn function to incite both the castration anxiety in and the symbolic transformation of the Oedipal child.

To illustrate these points, Boothby (1990) cites the behavior and drawings of children three- to six-years-old, who he initially notes "relish tearing off doll's heads. . . gleefully threaten to pluck out the eyes and bite off the fingers of caretakers and peers . . . [and] squirm with giddy but delighted fascination at fairy-tale scenes of violence" (p. 221).[9] In the drawings of a boy aged three and a half, though, Boothby notes how much attentiveness there is to including all bodily appendages and preserving the body's wholeness. Boothby wonders whether this attentiveness reflects "a dawning anxiety about the body's integrity" (ibid.: 228), a suspicion which seems supported by the dramatic differences in the drawings of the same boy beginning at age five. These later drawings consist of dismembered body parts which have been personified with faces and names, such as "Fingerman" and "Footman." Boothby observes how "when compared to the earlier drawings, which so conscientiously rendered the body's wholeness, this [later] series seems to suggest a sort of deliberate experimentation with the body's fragmentation, as if the challenge were to see how far the body could be cut up and still retain a sense of self" (p. 229). Clearly, the child's symbolic ability to name each body part is an essential aspect of pushing the boundaries of bodily fragmentation without undue anxiety about the body's actual integrity. Boothby (1992) further describes how the child's collection of body part drawings, "each with a face and a name, comprises a sort of compendium of experimental identities, a playbill of provisional subjectivities" (p. 26).

The child's Oedipalization therefore entails the anxiety-evoking edict that the previously constructed "unified body-image" must fragment and be reassembled in a less rigid form – a form which of course must now also include the recognition of being either a male or a female. Ver Eecke (1984) frames the child's discovery of sexual difference as a confrontation with the fundamental bodily dimension of his finitude – that of either being a boy or a girl, but not both. Fantasies of bisexuality or the denial of sexual difference represent the child's ambivalence about accepting bodily finitude and renouncing the desire for absolute fulfillment.

In a sense, Lacan develops an existential definition of castration. Boothby (1990) suggests this meaning in noting how for Lacan "castration involves coming to terms with what one is not, with what one does not have, with what one cannot be" (p. 217). As we have seen, the identity transformation entailed by the castrating assumption of the symbolic order is intrinsically related to a fundamental shift in how the child experiences his or her bodily integrity – an integrity originally constituted through the identification with the specular image during the mirror phase. For Lacan, then, the body by no means disappears with the accession to the symbolic order. Indeed, Samuels (1993) has highlighted how "a constant theme in Lacan's handling of the castration complex is its relation to a threat of bodily harm or fragmentation" (p. 153). Thus, at both the developmental and metapsychological levels, the body retains different yet significant roles in Lacan's imaginary and symbolic orders.

This point can be further illustrated by returning to and completing the discussion which concluded the previous section – that regarding the split between the eye and the gaze. On the one hand, the perceptual functions of the eye are but a species of Lacan's imaginary order – where the illusion of unity, dominance, and presence reigns. On the other hand, seen from all sides by an invisible gaze, the subject submits to the symbolic order's multiplicity of often hidden significations. Indeed, it has been noted how for Lacan "seeing involves an already being-seen within the circuit of signification" (Kochhar-Lingren 1992: 472). The circuit of signification includes much to which the subject cannot be perceptually present. Further, in contrast to the image, the function of the signifier requires continual reference to that which exceeds the perceptual presence of the signifier itself. In this connection, Boothby (1993) has noted how

> linguistic signification is characterized by a special kind of continuously shifting play of presence and absence. The functioning of the signifier, the very heartbeat of signification, is bound up with a constant oscillation of appearance and disappearance, a continuous formation and breakdown of perceptual gestalts. (p. 30)
> For the symbolic, by contrast [to the imaginary], the unity and phenomenal presence of the image are instantaneously evacuated or metastasized in favor of reverberation in an immensely complex network of associations. . . . The symbolic breaks the enthrallment with the presence of the object that characterizes the imaginary. (p. 34)

Despite the subject's accession to the symbolic order, the imaginary order as constituted in the mirror phase will nonetheless continue to structure the subject's desire and identity. Boothby (1990) has commented that "even after the Oedipal transition, the Imaginary [order] and its reverberations continue to orient the Symbolic process as Lacan conceives it" (p. 225), and he concludes by raising the question of whether "even on the far side of the Oedipus complex, the play of fantasy that lures desire . . . [retains] the stamp of the body image that originally structured imaginary identity" (p. 226). Here, Boothby accentuates the significant role the body image and its concomitant perceptual functions continue to play in the constitution, and possible pathology, of human subjectivity.

Insofar as the imaginary order remains an inescapable and indispensable dimension of psychological functioning, the insights afforded by phenomenology cannot be dismissed as irrelevant to the Lacanian enterprise. At the same time, as I believe this essay has demonstrated, Lacan's work reveals the limits of an exclusively phenomenological perspective on psychological functioning. Since the symbolic function operates according to a different set of rules than does the imaginary function, the categories of phenomenology must be supplemented by those developed in other disciplines – including psychoanalysis and structural linguistics.[10]

Returning to Freud's (1923: 26) formula that "the ego is first and foremost a bodily ego," we can conclude with Lacan that the bodily ego is fated to be carved up by language and inscribed within a symbolic order which exceeds somatic and intersubjective boundaries. The status of the bodily ego in Lacan's imaginary order is supplemented by the significance it assumes in permitting passage to the world of language. It is in this connection that Lacan's early ideas on ego formation during the mirror phase remain relevant to his later focus on the subject's accession to the symbolic order. Correlatively, the phenomenological foundations of Lacan's imaginary order did not disappear with the structural linguistic formulations required to explicate the symbolic function. Rather, having been among his first intellectual loves, phenomenology is not to be forgotten for the mark it made on the Lacanian corpus.

Notes

1   The introductory quotation is from Lacan's 1973 television interview, which was translated into English as *Television* (Lacan 1990). J.-A. Miller (1990) has noted how "the central problem of *Television*, which is not resolved this text, is this: how come the signifier, language ... has an effect on the body?" (p. 23). The present essay will of course offer only partial replies to this question, in addition to addressing the way in which the body offers itself to be carved up by language.

2   Jalbert (1983: 125) nicely articulates the metaphorical character of Lacan's conception of the mirror phase, an essential corrective to the incredibly common misunderstanding that Lacan was only concerned with literal mirrors. Jalbert states that

> the mirror phase is *not* merely an empirical, concrete event which consists of the child observing his or her self-image as it is reflected in the mirror surface. The mirror phase is also a *metaphor* which describes the child's psychological relationship with a primary caretaker who "reflects" the child's "image" to the child.... The main point Lacan seeks to make

concerning the mirror phase is that the child or the subject comes to see himself or herself *as being seen*, as an object who knows that he or she is being seen (Lacan, 1975, p. 240). This reflecting process is first of all *interpersonal* or intersubjective in that it occurs as the child relates to his or her primary caretakers. *The reflective process essentially takes place by means of the parents' response to the child's presence and uniqueness.*

3   In focusing here upon such concepts as "anticipation" and "retroaction," it must be acknowledged that Lacan employed a distinctly existential – phenomenological understanding of human temporality in his explication of the mirror phase, as well as in several other major theoretical contributions. Lacan was especially influenced by Heidegger's (1927/1962) emphasis on the primacy of the future in structuring human temporal experience and constituting human history. With this understanding of temporality, Lacan often criticized psychological theories which posited a chronological or natural progression of human development and maturation – theories frequently built on biological concepts alien to the human order.

4   Lacan (1953) speaks at more length to this point when he declares how the ego's "illusion of unity, in which a human being is always looking forward to self-mastery, entails a constant danger of sliding back again into the chaos from which he started; it hangs over the abyss of a dizzy Assent in which one can perhaps see the very essence of Anxiety" (p. 15).

5   Similarly, Lingis (1984) has spoken to the limits of Husserlian phenomenology for comprehending the Lacanian look, noting how "the eye is not moved by an intentionality of need, but of desire .... it is not on the lookout for things, for sense-data, for hyletic material, but on the lookout for a look, a look forever outside, exterior, the look of the other" (p. 157).

6   An example from the work of Ver Eecke illustrates this point. Ver Eecke (1975: 234) recalls an incident he observed in which

> a mother had before her a cake that was to be divided among her family and guests. She started by asking her youngest son, between 2 and 3 years old, if he wanted a piece. After saying "no" to the surprised mother, the mother repeated the question two more times, with the same result. When the child said "no" for the third time, he took the mother's hand and kissed it. The mother then divided up the cake and some was left over. After most had finished their piece, the mother asked if anybody wanted another. Before anybody could answer, the child said: "I want a piece."

Ver Eecke (1975, 1984, 1989) goes on to note how the child's no-saying in this situation signified an effort to differentiate his desire from that of his mother and declare a point of view independent of her without yet clarifying how his perspective is different from hers. Saying "no" to his mother's request did not mean that he didn't want a piece of cake. Rather, his "no" meant that he did not want his mother assuming that she knows what he wants or when he wants it. Further, his kiss on her hand following his third "no" expressed mild guilt about the aggressiveness expressed in his refusal of her offer.

7   Smith (1991: 96) speaks to this point when he writes that

> in general, a third term can be taken as any factor that unsettles the oneness and self-sameness presumably experienced in moments of symbiotic tranquility. Any primarily given or secondarily established trait, function, or structure that serves to maintain nondefensive differentiation is a third term. By nondefensive differentiation I mean differentiation in which loss, lack and limit are owned.

8   The no-saying child thus initially encounters his father through his mother as a phallic attribute (Ver Eecke 1984) and in so doing begins to differentiate between himself and his mother. The child next turns to the father with the hope that the father's sole task will be to fulfill the child's desires. However, this hope is dashed by the child's discovery that the father is a figure distinct from his mother and that he has an affective relation with her. The father is no longer experienced by the child as merely a phallic attribute of the mother but as a person who possesses the phallic attribute. In now being confronted with not just the attribution but the existence of the father, the child of course enters the Oedipal complex wherein the father is seen as an intruder who must be eliminated (Ver Eecke 1984).

9   Lacan (1949/1977) makes direct reference to this phenomenon when he observes how "one only has to listen to children aged between two and five playing, alone or together, to know that the pulling off of the head and the ripping open of the belly are themes that occur spontaneously to their imagination, and that this is corroborated by the experience of the doll torn to pieces" (p. 11).

10 This position has of course been previously advocated by numerous philosophical heavyweights, with Ricouer (1970) probably being the most compelling proponent.

References

Benvennuto, B. and Kennedy, R. (1986) *The Works of Jacques Lacan: An Introduction* (New York: St Martin's Press).

Bonner, C. (1991) "*The Significance of Lacan's Mirror Phase for the Formation and Function of Body-image.*" Paper presented at the 11th Annual Spring Meeting, the Division of Psychoanalysis, American Psychological Association, Chicago, Ill. (April 1991).

—— (1993) "*An Existential–Phenomenological Investigation of Identity Confusion as Exemplified by Adolescent Suicide Attempts.*" Doctoral dissertation, Duquesne University. Ann Arbor, Mich.: Dissertation Microfilms International.

Boothby, R. P. (1990) "Lacanian Castration: Body-Image and Signification in Psychoanalysis." In A. B. Dallery and C. E. Scott (eds) *Crises in Continental Philosophy* (New York: State University of New York Press).

—— (1991) *Death and Desire: Psychoanalytic Theory in Lacan's Return to Freud* (New York: Routledge).

—— (1992) "The Psychical Meaning of Life and Death: Reflections on the Lacanian Imaginary, Symbolic, and Real." Unpublished manuscript.

—— (1993) "'Now you see it . . .': The Dynamics of Presence and Absence in Psychoanalysis." Unpublished manuscript.

Fraiberg, S. and Adelson, E. (1973) "Self-representation in Language and Play: Observations of Blind Children," *Psychoanalyic Quarterly*, *42*: 539–62.

Freud, S. (1923) "The Ego and the Id." In J. Strachey (ed. and trans.) *The Standard Edition of the Complete Psychological Works of Sigmund Freud* (1961, vol. 19) (London: Hogarth Press).

Gallop, J. (1985) *Reading Lacan* (Ithaca, NY: Cornell University Press).

Grosz, E. (1990) *Jacques Lacan: A Feminist Introduction* (London: Routledge).

Heidegger, M. (1927/1962) *Being and Time*, trans. J. Macquarrie and E. Robinson (New York: Harper & Row).

Husserl, E. (1982) *Ideas Pertaining to a Pure Phenomenology and to a Phenomenological Philosophy: First Book*, trans. F. Kersten (The Hague: Martinus Nijhoff).

Jalbert, R. J. (1983) "*Lacan's Concept of Desire in the Mirror Phase and its Implications for Psychoanalytically-oriented Psychotherapy.*" Ph.D. dissertation, University of Pittsburgh.

Kaplan, L. J. (1978) *Oneness and Separateness: From Infant to Individual* (New York: Simon & Schuster).

Kochhar-Lingren, G. (1992) "The Cocked Eye: Robbe-Grillet, Lacan, and the Desire to See it All," *American Imago*, *49*: 467–79.

Lacan, J. (1938) "The Family Complexes," *Critical Texts*, 5 (1988), no. 3: 12–29. (Partial translation of original French text; Carolyn Asp, trans.)

—— (1949) "The Mirror Stage as Formative of the 'I' as Revealed in the Psychoanalytic Experience." In *Écrits: A Selection*, trans. Alan Sheridan (New York: W. W. Norton, 1977).

—— (1953) "Some Reflections on the Ego," *International Journal of Psychoanalysis*, 32: 11–17.

—— (1978) *The Four Fundamental Concepts of Psychoanalysis*, trans. Alan Sheridan (New York: W. W. Norton).

—— (1988a) *The Seminar of Jacques Lacan. Book I: Freud's Papers on Technique, 1953–1954*, ed. J.-A. Miller, trans. J. Forrester (New York: W. W. Norton).

—— (1988b) *The Seminar of Jacques Lacan. Book II: The Ego in Freud's Theory and in the Technique of Psychoanalysis, 1954–55*, ed. J.-A. Miller, trans. S. Tomaselli (New York: W. W. Norton).

—— (1990) *Television*, trans. D. Hollier, R. Krauss, and A. Michelson (New York: W. W. Norton).

Laplanche, J. and Pontalis, J.-B. (1967) *The Language of Psychoanalysis*, trans. D. Nicholson-Smith (New York: W. W. Norton).

Lee, J. S. (1990) *Jacques Lacan* (Amherst: University of Massachusetts Press).

Lingis, A. (1984) "The Visible and the Vision," *Journal of the British Society for Phenomenology*, 15: 155–63.

Merleau-Ponty, M. (1964) "The Child's Relations with Others," trans. W. Cobb. In *The Primacy of Perception* (Evanston, Ill.: Northwestern University Press).

Miller, J.-A. (1990) "A Reading of Some Details in *Television* in Dialogue with the Audience," *Newsletter of the Freudian Field*, 4: 4–30.

Muller, J. (1982a) "Ego and Subject in Lacan," *Psychoanalytic Review*, 69: 234–40.

—— (1982b) "Cognitive Psychology and the Ego: Lacanian Theory and Empirical Research," *Psychoanalysis and Contemporary Thought*, 5: 257–91.

—— (1986) "The Psychoanalytic Ego in Lacan: Its Origins and Self-serving Functions." In J. Suls and A. G. Greenwald (eds) *Psychological Perspectives on the Self*, vol. 3 (Hillsdale, NJ: Lawrence Erlbaum Associates).

—— (1988) "Lacan's Transmission," *Psychoanalysis and Contemporary Thought*, 11: 483–533.

Muller, J. and Richardson, W. (1982) *Lacan and Language: A Reader's Guide to the Écrits* (New York: International Universities Press).

Ragland-Sullivan, Ellie (1986) *Jacques Lacan and the Philosophy of Psychoanalysis* (Chicago: University of Illinois Press).

Ricouer, P. (1970) *Freud and Philosophy*, trans. D. Savage (New Haven: Yale University Press).

Roiphe and Galenson (1981) *Infantile Origins of Sexual Identity* (New York: International Universities Press).

Samuels, R. (1993) *Between Philosophy and Psychoanalysis: Lacan's Reconstruction of Freud* (New York: Routledge).

Sartre. J.-P. (1953) *Being and Nothingness*, trans. Hazel Barnes (New York: Washington Square Press).

Smith, J. (1991) *Arguing with Lacan: Ego Psychology and Language* (New Haven: Yale University Press).

Spitz, R. A. (1965) *The First Year of Life* (New York: International Universities Press).

Thompson, M. G. (1985) *The Death of Desire: A Study in Psychopathology* (New York: New York University Press).

Ver Eecke, W. (1975) "The Look, the Body, and the Other." In D. Ihde and R. M. Zaner (eds) *Dialogues in Phenomenology* (The Hague: Matinus Nijoff).

—— (1983) "Hegel as Lacan's Source for Necessity in Psychoanalytic Theory." In J. Smith and W. Kerrigan (eds) *Interpreting Lacan: Psychiatry and the Humanities*, vol. 6 (New Haven: Yale University Press).

—— (1984) *Saying "No": Its Meaning in Child Development, Psychoanalysis, Linguistics, and Hegel* (Pittsburgh: Duquesne University Press).

—— (1989) "Seeing and Saying Within the Theories of Spitz and Lacan," *Psychoanalysis and Contemporary Thought*, 12, (3): 383–431.

Wallon, H. (1984) "Kinesthesia and the Visual Body-image in the Child," trans. D. Nicholson-Smith. In G. Voyat (ed.) *The World of Henri Wallon* (original essay published 1954).

MICHEL FOUCAULT

Discipline and Punish

The body of the condemned

On 2 March 1757 Damiens the regicide was condemned "to make the *amende honorable* before the main door of the Church of Paris," where he was to be "taken and conveyed in a cart, wearing nothing but a shirt, holding a torch of burning wax weighing two pounds"; then, "in the said cart, to the Place de Grève, where, on a scaffold that will be erected there, the flesh will be torn from his breasts, arms, thighs and calves with red-hot pincers, his right hand, holding the knife with which he committed the said parricide, burnt with sulphur, and, on those places where the flesh will be torn away, poured molten lead, boiling oil, burning resin, wax and sulphur melted together and then his body drawn and quartered by four horses and his limbs and body consumed by fire, reduced to ashes and his ashes thrown to the winds" (*Pièces originales . . .*, 372–4).

"Finally, he was quartered," recounts the *Gazette d'Amsterdam* of 1 April 1757. "This last operation was very long, because the horses used were not accustomed to drawing; consequently, instead of four, six were needed; and when that did not suffice, they were forced, in order to cut off the wretch's thighs, to sever the sinews and hack at the joints . . .

"It is said that, though he was always a great swearer, no blasphemy escaped his lips; but the excessive pain made him utter horrible cries, and he often repeated: 'My God, have pity on me! Jesus, help me!' The spectators were all edified by the solicitude of the parish priest of St Paul's who despite his great age did not spare himself in offering consolation to the patient."

Bouton, an officer of the watch, left us his account: "The sulphur was lit, but the flame was so poor that only the top skin of the hand was burnt, and that

From Michel Foucault, *Discipline and Punish*, trans. by Alan Sheridan (New York: Vintage Books, 1979), pp. 3–11, 25–30, 136–8, 149–55 only slightly. Then the executioner, his sleeves rolled up, took the steel pincers, which had been especially made for the occasion, and which were about a foot and a half long, and pulled first at the calf of the right leg, then at the thigh, and from there at the two fleshy parts of the right arm; then at the breasts. Though a strong, sturdy fellow, this executioner found it so difficult to tear away the pieces of flesh that he set about the same spot two or three times, twisting the pincers as he did so, and what he took away formed at each part a wound about the size of a six-pound crown piece.

"After these tearings with the pincers, Damiens, who cried out profusely, though without swearing, raised his head and looked at himself; the same executioner dipped an iron spoon in the pot containing the boiling potion, which he poured liberally over each wound. Then the ropes that were to be harnessed to the horses were attached with cords to the patient's body; the horses were then harnessed and placed alongside the arms and legs, one at each limb.

"Monsieur Le Breton, the clerk of the court, went up to the patient several times and asked him if he had anything to say. He said he had not; at each torment, he cried out, as the damned in hell are supposed to cry out, "Pardon, my God! Pardon, Lord." Despite all this pain, he raised his head from time to time and looked at himself boldly. The cords had been tied so tightly by the men who pulled the ends that they caused him indescribable pain. Monsieur Le Breton went up to him again and asked him if he had anything to say; he said no. Several confessors went up to him and spoke to him at length; he willingly kissed the crucifix that was held out to him; he opened his lips and repeated: "Pardon, Lord."

"The horses tugged hard, each pulling straight on a limb, each horse held by an executioner. After a quarter of an hour, the same ceremony was repeated and finally, after several attempts, the direction of the horses had to be changed, thus: those at the arms were made to pull towards the head, those at the thighs towards the arms, which broke the arms at the joints. This was repeated several times without success. He raised his head and looked at himself. Two more horses had to be added to those harnessed to the thighs, which made six horses in all. Without success.

"Finally, the executioner, Samson, said to Monsieur Le Breton that there was no way or hope of succeeding, and told him to ask their Lordships if they wished him to have the prisoner cut into pieces. Monsieur Le Breton, who had come down from the town, ordered that renewed efforts be made, and this was done; but the horses gave up and one of those harnessed to the thighs fell to the ground. The confessors returned and spoke to him again. He said to them (I heard him): "Kiss me, gentlemen." The parish priest of St Paul's did not dare to, so Monsieur de Marsilly slipped under the rope holding the left arm and kissed him on the forehead. The executioners gathered round and Damiens told them not to swear, to carry out their task and that he did not think ill of them; he begged them to pray to God for him, and asked the parish priest of St Paul's to pray for him at the first mass.

"After two or three attempts, the executioner Samson and he who had used the pincers each drew out a knife from his pocket and cut the body at the thighs instead of severing the legs at the joints; the four horses gave a tug and carried off the two thighs after them, namely, that of the right side first, the other following; then the same was done to the arms, the shoulders, the arm-pits and the four limbs; the flesh had to be cut almost to the bone, the horses pulling hard carried off the right arm first and the other afterwards.

"When the four limbs had been pulled away, the confessors came to speak to him; but his executioner told them that he was dead, though the truth was that I saw the man move, his lower jaw moving from side to side as if he were talking. One of the executioners even said shortly afterwards that when they had lifted the trunk to throw it on the stake, he was still alive. The four limbs were untied from the ropes and thrown on the stake set up in the enclosure in line with the scaffold, then the trunk and the rest were covered with logs and faggots, and fire was put to the straw mixed with this wood.

". . . In accordance with the decree, the whole was reduced to ashes. The last piece to be found in the embers was still burning at half-past ten in the evening. The pieces of flesh and the trunk had taken about four hours to burn. The officers of whom I was one, as also was my son, and a detachment of archers remained in the square until nearly eleven o'clock.

"There were those who made something of the fact that a dog had lain the day before on the grass where the fire had been, had been chased away several times, and had always returned. But it is not difficult to understand that an animal found this place warmer than elsewhere" (quoted in Zevaes, 201–14).

Eighty years later, Léon Faucher drew up his rules "for the House of young prisoners in Paris":

"Art. 17. The prisoners' day will begin at six in the morning in winter and at five in summer. They will work for nine hours a day throughout the year. Two hours a day will be devoted to instruction. Work and the day will end at nine o'clock in winter and at eight in summer.

Art. 18. *Rising*. At the first drum-roll, the prisoners must rise and dress in silence, as the supervisor opens the cell doors. At the second drum-roll, they must be dressed and make their beds. At the third, they must line up and proceed to the chapel for morning prayer. There is a five-minute interval between each drum-roll.

Art. 19. The prayers are conducted by the chaplain and followed by a moral or religious reading. This exercise must not last more than half an hour.

Art. 20. *Work*. At a quarter to six in the summer, a quarter to seven in winter, the prisoners go down into the courtyard where they must wash their hands and faces, and receive their first ration of bread. Immediately afterwards, they form into work-teams and go off to work, which must begin at six in summer and seven in winter.

Art. 21. *Meal*. At ten o'clock the prisoners leave their work and go to the refectory; they wash their hands in their courtyards and assemble in divisions. After the dinner, there is recreation until twenty minutes to eleven.

Art. 22. *School*. At twenty minutes to eleven, at the drum-roll, the prisoners form into ranks, and proceed in divisions to the school. The class lasts two hours and consists alternately of reading, writing, drawing and arithmetic.

Art. 23. At twenty minutes to one, the prisoners leave the school, in divisions, and return to their courtyards for recreation. At five minutes to one, at the drum-roll, they form into work-teams.

Art. 24. At one o'clock they must be back in the workshops: they work until four o'clock.

Art. 25. At four o'clock the prisoners leave their workshops and go into the courtyards where they wash their hands and form into divisions for the refectory.

Art. 26. Supper and the recreation that follows it last until five o'clock: the prisoners then return to the workshops.

Art. 27. At seven o'clock in the summer, at eight in winter, work stops; bread is distributed for the last time in the workshops. For a quarter of an hour one of the prisoners or supervisors reads a passage from some instructive or uplifting work. This is followed by evening prayer.

Art. 28. At half-past seven in summer, half-past eight in winter, the prisoners must be back in their cells after the washing of hands and the inspection of clothes in the courtyard; at the first drum-roll, they must undress, and at the second get into bed. The cell doors are closed and the supervisors go the rounds in the corridors, to ensure order and silence' (Faucher, 274–82).

We have, then, a public execution and a time-table. They do not punish the same crimes or the same type of delinquent. But they each define a certain penal style. Less than a century separates them. It was a time when, in Europe and in the United States, the entire economy of punishment was redistributed. It was a time of great "scandals" for traditional justice, a time of innumerable projects for reform. It saw a new theory of law and crime, a new moral or political justification of the right to punish; old laws were abolished, old customs died out. "Modern" codes were planned or drawn up: Russia, 1769; Prussia, 1780; Pennsylvania and Tuscany, 1786; Austria, 1788; France, 1791, Year IV, 1808 and 1810. It was a new age for penal justice.

Among so many changes, I shall consider one: the disappearance of torture as a public spectacle. Today we are rather inclined to ignore it; perhaps, in its time, it gave rise to too much inflated rhetoric; perhaps it has been attributed too readily and too emphatically to a process of "humanization," thus dispensing with the need for further analysis. And, in any case, how important is such a change, when compared with the great institutional transformations, the formulation of explicit, general codes and unified rules of procedure; with the almost universal adoption of the jury system, the definition of the essentially corrective character of the penalty and the tendency, which has become increasingly marked since the nineteenth century, to adapt punishment to the individual offender? Punishment of a less immediately physical kind, a certain discretion in the art of inflicting pain, a combination of more subtle, more subdued sufferings, deprived of their visible display, should not all this be treated as a special case, an incidental effect of deeper changes? And yet the fact remains that a few decades saw the disappearance of the tortured, dismembered, amputated body, symbolically branded on face or shoulder, exposed alive or dead to public view. The body as the major target of penal repression disappeared.

By the end of the eighteenth and the beginning of the nineteenth century, the gloomy festival of punishment was dying out, though here and there it flickered momentarily into life. In this transformation, two processes were at work. They did not have quite the same chronology or the same *raison d'être*. The first was the disappearance of punishment as a spectacle. The ceremonial of punishment tended to decline; it survived only as a new legal or administrative practice. The *amende honorable* was first abolished in France in 1791, then again in 1830 after a brief revival; the pillory was abolished in France in 1789 and in England in 1837. The use of prisoners in public works, cleaning city streets or repairing the highways, was practised in Austria, Switzerland and certain of the United States, such as Pennsylvania. These convicts, distinguished by their "infamous dress" and shaven heads, "were brought before the public. The sport of the idle and the vicious, they often become incensed, and naturally took violent revenge upon the aggressors. To prevent them from returning injuries which might be inflicted on them, they were encumbered with iron collars and chains to which bomb-shells were attached, to be dragged along while they performed their degrading service, under the eyes of keepers armed with swords, blunderbusses and other weapons of destruction" (Roberts Vaux, *Notices*, 21, quoted in Teeters, 1937, 24). This practice was abolished practically everywhere at the end of the eighteenth or the beginning of the nineteenth century. The public exhibition of prisoners was maintained in France in 1831, despite violent criticism – "a disgusting scene," said Réal (cf. Bibliography); it was finally abolished in April 1848. While the chain-gang, which had dragged convicts across the whole of France, as far as Brest and Toulon, was replaced in 1837 by inconspicuous black-painted cell-carts. Punishment had gradually ceased to be a spectacle. And whatever theatrical elements it still retained were now downgraded, as if the functions of the penal ceremony were gradually ceasing to be understood, as if this rite that "concluded the crime" was suspected of being in some undesirable way linked with it. It was as if the punishment was thought to equal, if not to exceed, in savagery the crime itself, to accustom the spectators to a ferocity from which one wished to divert them, to show them the frequency of crime, to make the executioner resemble a criminal, judges murderers, to reverse roles at the last moment, to make the tortured criminal an object of pity or admiration. As early as 1764, Beccaria remarked: "The murder that is depicted as a horrible crime is repeated in cold blood, remorselessly" (Beccaria, 101). The public execution is now seen as a hearth in which violence bursts again into flame.

Punishment, then, will tend to become the most hidden part of the penal process. This has several consequences: it leaves the domain of more or less everyday perception and enters that of abstract consciousness; its effectiveness is seen as resulting from its inevitability, not from its visible intensity; it is the certainty of being punished and not the horrifying spectacle of public punishment that must discourage crime; the exemplary mechanics of punishment changes its mechanisms. As a result, justice no longer takes public responsibility for the violence that is bound up with its practice. If it too strikes, if it too kills, it is not as a glorification of its strength, but as an element of itself that it is obliged to tolerate, that it finds difficult to account for. The apportioning of blame is redistributed: in punishment-as-spectacle a confused horror spread from the scaffold; it enveloped both executioner and condemned; and, although it was always ready to invert the shame inflicted on the victim into pity or glory, it often turned the legal violence of the executioner into shame. Now the scandal and the light are to be distributed differently; it is the conviction itself that marks the offender with the unequivocally negative sign: the publicity has shifted to the trial, and to the sentence; the execution itself is like an additional shame that justice is ashamed to impose on the condemned man; so it keeps its distance from the act, tending always to entrust it to others, under the seal of secrecy. It is ugly to be punishable, but there is no glory in punishing. Hence that double system of protection that justice has set up between itself and the punishment it imposes. Those who carry out the penalty tend to become an autonomous sector; justice is relieved of responsibility for it by a bureaucratic concealment of the penalty itself. It is typical that in France the administration of the prisons should for so long have been the responsibility of the Ministry of the Interior, while responsibility for the *bagnes*, for penal servitude in the convict ships and penal settlements, lay with the Ministry of the Navy or the Ministry of the Colonies. And beyond this distribution of roles operates a theoretical disavowal: do not imagine that the sentences that we judges pass are activated by a desire to punish; they are intended to correct, reclaim, "cure"; a technique of improvement represses, in the penalty, the strict expiation of evil-doing, and relieves the magistrates of the demeaning task of punishing. In modern justice and on the part of those who dispense it there is a shame in punishing, which does not always preclude zeal. This sense of shame is constantly growing: the psychologists and the minor civil servants of moral orthopaedics proliferate on the wound it leaves.

The disappearance of public executions marks therefore the decline of the spectacle; but it also marks a slackening of the hold on the body. In 1787, in an address to the Society for Promoting Political Enquiries, Benjamin Rush remarked: "I can only hope that the time is not far away when gallows, pillory, scaffold, flogging and wheel will, in the history of punishment, be regarded as the marks of the barbarity of centuries and of countries and as proofs of the feeble influence of reason and religion over the human mind" (Teeters, 1935, 30). Indeed, sixty years later, Van Meenen, opening the second penitentiary congress, in Brussels, recalled the time of his childhood as of a past age: "I have seen the ground strewn with wheels, gibbets, gallows, pillories; I have seen hideously stretched skeletons on wheels" (*Annales de la Charité*, 529–30). Branding had been abolished in England (1834) and in France (1832); in 1820, England no longer dared to apply the full punishment reserved for traitors (Thistlewood was not quartered). Only flogging still remained in a number of penal systems (Russia, England, Prussia). But, generally speaking, punitive practices had become more reticent. One no longer touched the body, or at least as little as possible, and then only to reach something other than the body itself. It might be objected that imprisonment, confinement, forced labour, penal servitude, prohibition from entering certain areas, deportation – which have occupied so important a place in modern penal systems – are "physical" penalties: unlike fines, for example, they directly affect the body. But the punishment–body relation is not the same as it was in the torture during public executions. The body now serves as an instrument or intermediary: if one intervenes upon it to imprison it, or to make it work, it is in order to deprive the individual of a liberty that is regarded both as a right and as property. The body, according to this penality, is caught up in a system of constraints and privations, obligations and prohibitions. Physical pain, the pain of the body itself, is no longer the constituent element of the penalty. From being an art of unbearable sensations punishment has become an economy of suspended rights. If it is still necessary for the law to reach and manipulate the body of the convict, it will be at a distance, in the proper way, according to strict rules, and with a much "higher" aim. As a result of this new restraint, a whole army of technicians took over from the executioner, the immediate anatomist of pain: warders, doctors, chaplains, psychiatrists, psychologists, educationalists; by their very presence near the prisoner, they sing the praises that the law needs: they reassure it that the body and pain are not the ultimate objects of its punitive action. Today a doctor must watch over those condemned to death, right up to the last moment – thus juxtaposing himself as the agent of welfare, as the alleviator of pain, with the official whose task it is to end life. This is worth thinking about.

When the moment of execution approaches, the patients are injected with tranquillizers. A utopia of judicial reticence: take away life, but prevent the patient from feeling it; deprive the prisoner of all rights, but do not inflict pain; impose penalties free of all pain. Recourse to psycho-pharmacology and to various physiological "disconnectors," even if it is temporary, is a logical consequence of this "non-corporal" penality. . . .

We can surely accept the general proposition that, in our societies, the systems of punishment are to be situated in a certain "political economy" of the body: even if they do not make use of violent or bloody punishment, even when they use "lenient" methods involving confinement or correction, it is always the body that is at issue — the body and its forces, their utility and their docility, their distribution and their submission. It is certainly legitimate to write a history of punishment against the background of moral ideas or legal structures. But can one write such a history against the background of a history of bodies, when such systems of punishment claim to have only the secret souls of criminals as their objective?

Historians long ago began to write the history of the body. They have studied the body in the field of historical demography or pathology; they have considered it as the seat of needs and appetites, as the locus of physiological processes and metabolisms, as a target for the attacks of germs or viruses; they have shown to what extent historical processes were involved in what might seem to be the purely biological base of existence; and what place should be given in the history of society to biological "events" such as the circulation of bacilli, or the extension of the life-span (cf. Le Roy-Ladurie). But the body is also directly involved in a political field; power relations have an immediate hold upon it; they invest it, mark it, train it, torture it, force it to carry out tasks, to perform ceremonies, to emit signs. This political investment of the body is bound up, in accordance with complex reciprocal relations, with its economic use; it is largely as a force of production that the body is invested with relations of power and domination; but, on the other hand, its constitution as labour power is possible only if it is caught up in a system of subjection (in which need is also a political instrument meticulously prepared, calculated and used); the body becomes a useful force only if it is both a productive body and a subjected body. This subjection is not only obtained by the instruments of violence or ideology; it can also be direct, physical, pitting force against force, bearing on material elements, and yet without involving violence; it may be calculated, organized, technically thought out; it may be subtle, make use neither of weapons nor of terror and yet remain of a physical order. That is to say, there may be a "knowledge" of the body that is not exactly the science of its functioning, and a mastery of its forces that is more than the ability to conquer them: this knowledge and this mastery constitute what might be called the political technology of the body. Of course, this technology is diffuse, rarely formulated in continuous, systematic discourse; it is often made up of bits and pieces; it implements a disparate set of tools or methods. In spite of the coherence of its results, it is generally no more than a multiform instrumentation. Moreover, it cannot be localized in a particular type of institution or state apparatus. For they have recourse to it; they use, select or impose certain of its methods. But, in its mechanisms and its effects, it is situated at a quite different level. What the apparatuses and institutions operate is, in a sense, a micro-physics of power, whose field of validity is situated in a sense between these great functionings and the bodies themselves with their materiality and their forces.

Now, the study of this micro-physics presupposes that the power exercised on the body is conceived not as a property, but as a strategy, that its effects of domination are attributed not to "appropriation," but to dispositions, man-oeuvres, tactics, techniques, functionings; that one should decipher in it a network of relations, constantly in tension, in activity, rather than a privilege that one might possess; that one should take as its model a perpetual battle rather than a contract regulating a transaction or the conquest of a territory. In short this power is exercised rather than possessed; it is not the "privilege," acquired or preserved, of the dominant class, but the overall effect of its strategic positions – an effect that is manifested and sometimes extended by the position of those who are dominated. Furthermore, this power is not exercised simply as an obligation or a prohibition on those who "do not have it"; it invests them, is transmitted by them and through them; it exerts pressure upon them, just as they themselves, in their struggle against it, resist the grip it has on them. This means that these relations go right down into the depths of society, that they are not localized in the relations between the state and its citizens or on the frontier between classes and that they do not merely reproduce, at the level of indivi-duals, bodies, gestures and behaviour, the general form of the law or govern-ment; that, although there is continuity (they are indeed articulated on this form through a whole series of complex mechanisms), there is neither analogy nor homology, but a specificity of mechanism and modality. Lastly, they are not univocal; they define innumerable points of confrontation, focuses of instability, each of which has its own risks of conflict, of struggles, and of an at least temporary inversion of the power relations. The overthrow of these "micro-powers" does not, then, obey the law of all or nothing; it is not acquired once and for all by a new control of the apparatuses nor by a new functioning or a destruction of the institutions; on the other hand, none of its localized episodes may be inscribed in history except by the effects that it induces on the entire network in which it is caught up.

Perhaps, too, we should abandon a whole tradition that allows us to imagine that knowledge can exist only where the power relations are suspended and that knowledge can develop only outside its injunctions, its demands and its interests. Perhaps we should abandon the belief that power makes mad and that, by the same token, the renunciation of power is one of the conditions of knowledge. We should admit rather that power produces knowledge (and not simply by encouraging it because it serves power or by applying it because it is useful); that power and knowledge directly imply one another; that there is no power relation without the correlative constitution of a field of knowledge, nor any knowledge that does not presuppose and constitute at the same time power relations. These "power-knowledge relations" are to be analysed, therefore, not on the basis of a subject of knowledge who is or is not free in relation to the power system, but, on the contrary, the subject who knows, the objects to be known and the modalities of knowledge must be regarded as so many effects of these fundamental implications of power-knowledge and their historical transformations. In short, it is not the activity of the subject of knowledge that produces a corpus of knowledge, useful or resistant to power, but power-knowledge, the processes and struggles that traverse it and of which it is made up, that determines the forms and possible domains of knowledge.

To analyse the political investment of the body and the micro-physics of power presupposes, therefore, that one abandons – where power is concerned – the violence–ideology opposition, the metaphor of property, the model of the contract or of conquest; that – where knowledge is concerned – one abandons the opposition between what is "interested" and what is "disinterested," the model of knowledge and the primacy of the subject. Borrowing a word from Petty and his contemporaries, but giving it a different meaning from the one current in the seventeenth century, one might imagine a political "anatomy." This would not be the study of a state in terms of a "body" (with its elements, its resources and its forces), nor would it be the study of the body and its surroundings in terms of a small state. One would be concerned with the "body politic," as a set of material elements and techniques that serve as weapons, relays, communication routes and supports for the power and knowledge relations that invest human bodies and subjugate them by turning them into objects of knowledge.

It is a question of situating the techniques of punishment – whether they seize the body in the ritual of public torture and execution or whether they are addressed to the soul – in the history of this body politic; of considering penal practices less as a consequence of legal theories than as a chapter of political anatomy.

Kantorowitz gives a remarkable analysis of "The King's Body": a double body according to the juridical theology of the Middle Ages, since it involves not only the transitory element that is born and dies, but another that remains unchanged by time and is maintained as the physical yet intangible support of the kingdom; around this duality, which was originally close to the Christological model, are organized an iconography, a political theory of monarchy, legal mechanisms that distinguish between as well as link the person of the king and the demands of the Crown, and a whole ritual that reaches its height in the coronation, the funeral and the ceremonies of submission. At the opposite pole one might imagine placing the body of the condemned man; he, too, has his legal status; he gives rise to his own ceremonial and he calls forth a whole theoretical discourse, not in order to ground the "surplus power" possessed by the person of the sovereign, but in order to code the "lack of power" with which those subjected to punishment are marked. In the darkest region of the political field the condemned man represents the symmetrical, inverted figure of the king. We should analyse what might be called, in homage to Kantorowitz, "the least body of the condemned man."

If the surplus power possessed by the king gives rise to the duplication of his body, has not the surplus power exercised on the subjected body of the condemned man given rise to another type of duplication? That of a "non-corporal," a "soul," as Mably called it. The history of this "micro-physics" of the punitive power would then be a genealogy or an element in a genealogy of the modern "soul." Rather than seeing this soul as the reactivated remnants of an ideology, one would see it as the present correlative of a certain technology of power over the body. It would be wrong to say that the soul is an illusion, or an ideological effect. On the contrary, it exists, it has a reality, it is produced permanently around, on, within the body by the functioning of a power that is exercised on those punished – and, in a more general way, on those one supervises, trains and corrects, over madmen, children at home and at school, the colonized, over those who are stuck at a machine and supervised for the rest of their lives. This is the historical reality of this soul, which, unlike the soul represented by Christian theology, is not born in sin and subject to punishment, but is born rather out of methods of punishment, supervision and constraint. This real, non-corporal soul is not a substance; it is the element in which are articulated the effects of a certain type of power and the reference of a certain type of knowledge, the machinery by which the power relations give rise to a possible corpus of knowledge, and knowledge extends and reinforces the effects of this power. On this reality-reference, various concepts have been constructed and domains of analysis carved out: psyche, subjectivity, personality, conscious-ness, etc.; on it have been built scientific techniques and discourses, and the moral claims of humanism. But let there be no misunderstanding: it is not that a real man, the object of knowledge, philosophical reflection or technical inter-vention, has been substituted for the soul, the illusion of the theologians. The man described for us, whom we are invited to free, is already in himself the effect of a subjection much more profound than himself. A "soul" inhabits him and brings him to existence, which is itself a factor in the mastery that power exercises over the body. The soul is the effect and instrument of a political anatomy; the soul is the prison of the body. . . .

The classical age discovered the body as object and target of power. It is easy enough to find signs of the attention then paid to the body – to the body that is manipulated, shaped, trained, which obeys, responds, becomes skilful and increases its forces. The great book of Man-the-Machine was written simultaneously on two registers: the anatomico-metaphysical register, of which Descartes wrote the first pages and which the physicians and philosophers continued, and the technico-political register, which was constituted by a whole set of regulations and by empirical and calculated methods relating to the army, the school and the hospital, for controlling or correcting the operations of the body. These two registers are quite distinct, since it was a question, on the one hand, of submission and use and, on the other, of functioning and explanation: there was a useful body and an intelligible body. And yet there are points of overlap from one to the other. La Mettrie's *L'Homme-machine* is both a materialist reduction of the soul and a general theory of *dressage*, at the centre of which reigns the notion of "docility," which joins the analysable body to the manipulable body. A body is docile that may be subjected, used, transformed and improved. The celebrated automata, on the other hand, were not only a way of illustrating an organism, they were also political puppets, small-scale models of power: Frederick II, the meticulous king of small machines, well-trained regiments and long exercises, was obsessed with them.

What was so new in these projects of docility that interested the eighteenth century so much? It was certainly not the first time that the body had become the object of such imperious and pressing investments; in every society, the body was in the grip of very strict powers, which imposed on it constraints, prohibitions or obligations. However, there were several new things in these techniques. To begin with, there was the scale of the control: it was a question not of treating the body, *en masse*, "wholesale," as if it were an indissociable unity, but of working it "retail," individually; of exercising upon it a subtle coercion, of obtaining holds upon it at the level of the mechanism itself – movements, gestures, attitudes, rapidity: an infinitesimal power over the active body. Then there was the object of the control: it was not or was no longer the signifying elements of behaviour or the language of the body, but the economy, the efficiency of movements, their internal organization; constraint bears upon the forces rather than upon the signs; the only truly important ceremony is that of exercise. Lastly, there is the modality: it implies an uninterrupted, constant coercion, supervising the processes of the activity rather than its result and it is exercised according to a codification that partitions as closely as possible time, space, movement. These methods, which made possible the meticulous control of the operations of the body, which assured the constant subjection of its forces and imposed upon them a relation of docility-utility, might be called "disciplines." Many disciplinary methods had long been in existence – in monasteries, armies, workshops. But in the course of the seventeenth and eighteenth centuries the disciplines became general formulas of domination. They were different from slavery because they were not based on a relation of appropriation of bodies; indeed, the elegance of the discipline lay in the fact that it could dispense with this costly and violent relation by obtaining effects of utility at least as great. They were different, too, from "service," which was a constant, total, massive, non-analytical, unlimited relation of domination, established in the form of the individual will of the master, his "caprice." They were different from vassalage, which was a highly coded, but distant relation of submission, which bore less on the operations of the body than on the products of labour and the ritual marks of allegiance. Again, they were different from asceticism and from "disciplines" of a monastic type, whose function was to obtain renunciations rather than increases of utility and which, although they involved obedience to others, had as their principal aim an increase of the mastery of each individual over his own body. The historical moment of the disciplines was the moment when an art of the human body was born, which was directed not only at the growth of its skills, nor at the intensification of its subjection, but at the formation of a relation that in the mechanism itself makes it more obedient as it becomes more useful, and conversely. What was then being formed was a policy of coercions that act upon the body, a calculated manipulation of its elements, its gestures, its behaviour. The human body was entering a machinery of power that explores it, breaks it down and rearranges it. A "political anatomy," which was also a "mechanics of power," was being born; it defined how one may have a hold over others' bodies, not only so that they may do what one wishes, but so that they may operate as one wishes, with the techniques, the speed and the efficiency that one determines. Thus discipline produces subjected and practised bodies, "docile" bodies. Discipline increases the forces of the body (in economic terms of utility) and diminishes these same forces (in political terms of obedience). In short, it dissociates power from the body; on the one hand, it turns it into an "aptitude," a "capacity," which it seeks to increase; on the other hand, it reverses the course of the energy, the power that might result from it, and turns it into a relation of strict subjection. If economic exploitation separates the force and the product of labour, let us say that disciplinary coercion establishes in the body the constricting link between an increased aptitude and an increased domination. . . .

The control of activity

1. The *time-table* is an old inheritance. The strict model was no doubt suggested by the monastic communities. It soon spread. Its three great methods – establish rhythms, impose particular occupations, regulate the cycles of repetition – were soon to be found in schools, workshops and hospitals. The new disciplines had

no difficulty in taking up their place in the old forms; the schools and poor-houses extended the life and the regularity of the monastic communities to which they were often attached. The rigours of the industrial period long retained a religious air; in the seventeenth century, the regulations of the great manufactories laid down the exercises that would divide up the working day: "On arrival in the morning, before beginning their work, all persons shall wash their hands, offer up their work to God and make the sign of the cross" (Saint-Maur, article 1); but even in the nineteenth century, when the rural populations were needed in industry, they were sometimes formed into "congregations," in an attempt to inure them to work in the workshops; the framework of the "factory–monastery" was imposed upon the workers. In the Protestant armies of Maurice of Orange and Gustavus Adolphus, military discipline was achieved through a rhythmics of time punctuated by pious exercises; army life, Boussa-nelle was later to say, should have some of the "perfections of the cloister itself" (Boussanelle, 2; on the religious character of discipline in the Swedish army, cf. *The Swedish Discipline*, London, 1632). For centuries, the religious orders had been masters of discipline: they were the specialists of time, the great technicians of rhythm and regular activities. But the disciplines altered these methods of temporal regulation from which they derived. They altered them first by refining them. One began to count in quarter hours, in minutes, in seconds. This happened in the army, of course: Guibert systematically implemented the chronometric measurement of shooting that had been suggested earlier by Vauban. In the elementary schools, the division of time became increasingly minute; activities were governed in detail by orders that had to be obeyed immediately: "At the last stroke of the hour, a pupil will ring the bell, and at the first sound of the bell all the pupils will kneel, with their arms crossed and their eyes lowered. When the prayer has been said, the teacher will strike the signal once to indicate that the pupils should get up, a second time as a sign that they should salute Christ, and a third that they should sit down" (La Salle, *Con-duite*..., 27–8). In the early nineteenth century, the following time-table was suggested for the *Écoles mutuelles*, or "mutual improvement schools": 8.45 entrance of the monitor, 8.52 the monitor's summons, 8.56 entrance of the children and prayer, 9.00 the children go to their benches, 9.04 first slate, 9.08 end of dictation, 9.12 second slate, etc. (Tronchot, 221). The gradual extension of the wage-earning class brought with it a more detailed partitioning of time: "If workers arrive later than a quarter of an hour after the ringing of the bell..." (Amboise, article 2); "if any one of the companions is asked for during work and loses more than five minutes...", "anyone who is not at his work at the correct time..." (Oppenheim, article 7–8). But an attempt is also made to assure the quality of the time used: constant supervision, the pressure of supervisors, the elimination of anything that might disturb or distract; it is a question of con-stituting a totally useful time: "It is expressly forbidden during work to amuse one's companions by gestures or in any other way, to play at any game whatsoever, to eat, to sleep, to tell stories and comedies" (Oppenheim, article 16); and even during the meal-break, "there will be no telling of stories, adventures or other such talk that distracts the workers from their work"; "it is expressly forbidden for any worker, under any pretext, to bring wine into the manufactory and to drink in the workshops" (*Amboise*, article 4). Time measured and paid must also be a time without impurities or defects; a time of good quality, throughout which the body is constantly applied to its exercise. Precision and application are, with regularity, the fundamental virtues of disciplinary time. But this is not the newest thing about it. Other methods are more characteristic of the disciplines.

2. *The temporal elaboration of the act.* There are, for example, two ways of controlling marching troops. In the early seventeenth century, we have: "Accustomed soldiers marching in file or in battalion to march to the rhythm of the drum. And to do this, one must begin with the right foot so that the whole troop raises the same foot at the same time" (Montgommery, 86). In the mid-eighteenth century, there are four sorts of steps: "The length of the the short step will be a foot, that of the ordinary step, the double step and the marching step will be two feet, the whole measured from one heel to the next; as for the duration, that of the small step and the ordinary step will last one second, during which two double steps would be performed; the duration of the marching step will be a little longer than one second. The oblique step will take one second; it will be at most eighteen inches from one heel to the next.... The ordinary step will be executed forwards, holding the head up high and the body erect, holding oneself in balance successively on a single leg, and bringing the other forwards, the ham taut, the point of the foot a little turned outwards and low, so that one may without affectation brush the ground on which one must walk and place one's foot, in such a way that each part may come to rest there at the same time without striking the ground" ("Ordonnance du Ier janvier 1766, pour régler l'exercice de l'infanterie"). Between these two instructions, a new set of restraints had been brought into play, another degree of precision in the breakdown of gestures and movements, another way of adjusting the body to temporal imperatives.

What the ordinance of 1766 defines is not a time-table – the general framework for an activity; it is rather a collective and obligatory rhythm, imposed from the outside; it is a "programme"; it assures the elaboration of the act itself; it controls its development and its stages from the inside. We have passed from a form of injunction that measured or punctuated gestures to a web that constrains them or sustains them throughout their entire succession. A sort of anatomo-chronological schema of behaviour is defined. The act is broken down into its elements; the position of the body, limbs, articulations is defined; to each movement are assigned a direction, an aptitude, a duration; their order of succession is prescribed. Time penetrates the body and with it all the meticulous controls of power.

3. Hence *the correlation of the body and the gesture*. Disciplinary control does not consist simply in teaching or imposing a series of particular gestures; it imposes the best relation between a gesture and the overall position of the body, which is its condition of efficiency and speed. In the correct use of the body, which makes possible a correct use of time, nothing must remain idle or useless: everything must be called upon to form the support of the act required. A well-disciplined body forms the operational context of the slightest gesture. Good handwriting, for example, presupposes a gymnastics – a whole routine whose rigorous code invests the body in its entirety, from the points of the feet to the tip of the index finger. The pupils must always "hold their bodies erect, somewhat turned and free on the left side, slightly inclined, so that, with the elbow placed on the table, the chin can be rested upon the hand, unless this were to interfere with the view; the left leg must be somewhat more forward under the table than the right. A distance of two fingers must be left between the body and the table; for not only does one write with more alertness, but nothing is more harmful to the health than to acquire the habit of pressing one's stomach against the table; the part of the left arm from the elbow to the hand must be placed on the table. The right arm must be at a distance from the body of about three fingers and be about five fingers from the table, on which it must rest lightly. The teacher will place the pupils in the posture that they should maintain when writing, and will correct it either by sign or otherwise, when they change this position" (La Salle, *Conduite.* . . , 63–4). A disciplined body is the prerequisite of an efficient gesture.

4. *The body–object articulation*. Discipline defines each of the relations that the body must have with the object that it manipulates. Between them, it outlines a meticulous meshing. "Bring the weapon forward. In three stages. Raise the rifle with the right hand, bringing it close to the body so as to hold it perpendicular with the right knee, the end of the barrel at eye level, grasping it by striking it with the right hand, the arm held close to the body at waist height. At the second stage, bring the rifle in front of you with the left hand, the barrel in the middle between the two eyes, vertical, the right hand grasping it at the small of the butt, the arm outstretched, the trigger-guard resting on the first finger, the left hand at the height of the notch, the thumb lying along the barrel against the moulding. At the third stage, let go of the rifle with the left hand, which falls along the thigh, raising the rifle with the right hand, the lock outwards and opposite the chest, the right arm half flexed, the elbow close to the body, the thumb lying against the lock, resting against the first screw, the hammer resting on the first finger, the barrel perpendicular" ("Ordonnance du Ier janvier 1766. . . , titre XI, article 2"). This is an example of what might be called the instrumental coding of the body. It consists of a breakdown of the

total gesture into two parallel series: that of the parts of the body to be used (right hand, left hand, different fingers of the hand, knee, eye, elbow, etc.) and that of the parts of the object manipulated (barrel, notch, hammer, screw, etc.); then the two sets of parts are correlated together according to a number of simple gestures (rest, bend); lastly, it fixes the canonical succession in which each of these correlations occupies a particular place. This obligatory syntax is what the military theoreticians of the eighteenth century called "*manoeuvre.*" The traditional recipe gives place to explicit and obligatory prescriptions. Over the whole surface of contact between the body and the object it handles, power is introduced, fastening them to one another. It constitutes a body-weapon, body-tool, body-machine complex. One is as far as possible from those forms of subjection that demanded of the body only signs or products, forms of expression or the result of labour. The regulation imposed by power is at the same time the law of construction of the operation. Thus disciplinary power appears to have the function not so much of deduction as of synthesis, not so much of exploitation of the product as of coercive link with the apparatus of production.

5. *Exhaustive use.* The principle that underlay the time-table in its traditional form was essentially negative; it was the principle of non-idleness: it was forbidden to waste time, which was counted by God and paid for by men; the time-table was to eliminate the danger of wasting it – a moral offence and economic dishonesty. Discipline, on the other hand, arranges a positive economy; it poses the principle of a theoretically ever-growing use of time: exhaustion rather than use; it is a question of extracting, from time, ever more available moments and, from each moment, ever more useful forces. This means that one must seek to intensify the use of the slightest moment, as if time, in its very fragmentation, were inexhaustible or as if, at least by an ever more detailed internal arrangement, one could tend towards an ideal point at which one maintained maximum speed and maximum efficiency. It was precisely this that was implemented in the celebrated regulations of the Prussian infantry that the whole of Europe imitated after the victories of Frederick II:[1] the more time is broken down, the more its subdivisions multiply, the better one disarticulates it by deploying its internal elements under a gaze that supervises them, the more one can accelerate an operation, or at least regulate it according to an optimum speed; hence this regulation of the time of an action that was so important in the army and which was to be so throughout the entire technology of human activity: the Prussian regulations of 1743 laid down six stages to bring the weapon to one's foot, four to extend it, thirteen to raise it to the shoulder, etc. By other means, the "mutual improvement school" was also arranged as a machine to intensify the use of time; its organization made it possible to obviate the linear, successive character of the master's teaching: it regulated the counterpoint of operations performed, at the same moment, by different groups of pupils under the direction of monitors and assistants, so that

each passing moment was filled with many different, but ordered activities; and, on the other hand, the rhythm imposed by signals, whistles, orders imposed on everyone temporal norms that were intended both to accelerate the process of learning and to teach speed as a virtue;[2] "the sole aim of these commands ... is to accustom the children to executing well and quickly the same operations, to diminish as far as possible by speed the loss of time caused by moving from one operation to another" (Bernard).

Through this technique of subjection a new object was being formed; slowly, it superseded the mechanical body – the body composed of solids and assigned movements, the image of which had for so long haunted those who dreamt of disciplinary perfection. This new object is the natural body, the bearer of forces and the seat of duration; it is the body susceptible to specified operations, which have their order, their stages, their internal conditions, their constituent elements. In becoming the target for new mechanisms of power, the body is offered up to new forms of knowledge. It is the body of exercise, rather than of speculative physics; a body manipulated by authority, rather than imbued with animal spirits; a body of useful training and not of rational mechanics, but one in which, by virtue of that very fact, a number of natural requirements and functional constraints are beginning to emerge.

The History of Sexuality

It would be less than exact to say that the pedagogical institution has imposed a ponderous silence on the sex of children and adolescents. On the contrary, since the eighteenth century it has multiplied the forms of discourse on the subject; it has established various points of implantation for sex; it has coded contents and qualified speakers. Speaking about children's sex, inducing educators, physicians, administrators, and parents to speak of it, or speaking to them about it, causing children themselves to talk about it, and enclosing them in a web of discourses which sometimes address them, sometimes speak about them, or impose canonical bits of knowledge on them, or use them as a basis for constructing a science that is beyond their grasp – all this together enables us to link an intensification of the interventions of power to a multiplication of discourse. The sex of children and adolescents has become, since the eighteenth century, an important area of contention around which innumerable institutional devices and discursive strategies have been deployed. It may well be true that adults and children themselves were deprived of a certain way of speaking about sex, a mode that was disallowed as being too direct, crude, or coarse. But this was only the counterpart of other discourses, and perhaps the condition necessary in order for

From Michel Foucault, *The History of Sexuality*, Vol. 1 *An Introduction*, trans. by Robert Hurley (New York: Vintage Books, 1980), pp. 29–35, 92–108 them to function, discourses that were interlocking, hierarchized, and all highly articulated around a cluster of power relations.

One could mention many other centers which in the eighteenth or nineteenth century began to produce discourses on sex. First there was medicine, via the "nervous disorders"; next psychiatry, when it set out to discover the etiology of mental illnesses, focusing its gaze first on "excess," then onanism, then frustration, then "frauds against procreation," but especially when it annexed the whole of the sexual perversions as its own province; criminal justice, too, which had long been concerned with sexuality, particularly in the form of "heinous" crimes and crimes against nature, but which, toward the middle of the nineteenth century, broadened its jurisdiction to include petty offenses, minor indecencies, insignificant perversions; and lastly, all those social controls, cropping up at the end of the last century, which screened the sexuality of couples, parents and children, dangerous and endangered adolescents – undertaking to protect, separate, and forewarn, signaling perils everywhere, awakening people's attention, calling for diagnoses, piling up reports, organizing therapies. These sites radiated discourses aimed at sex, intensifying people's awareness of it as a constant danger, and this in turn created a further incentive to talk about it.

One day in 1867, a farm hand from the village of Lapcourt, who was somewhat simple-minded, employed here then there, depending on the season, living hand-to-mouth from a little charity or in exchange for the worst sort of labor, sleeping in barns and stables, was turned in to the authorities. At the border of a field, he had obtained a few caresses from a little girl, just as he had done before and seen done by the village urchins round about him; for, at the edge of the wood, or in the ditch by the road leading to Saint-Nicolas, they would play the familiar game called "curdled milk." So he was pointed out by the girl's parents to the mayor of the village, reported by the mayor to the gendarmes, led by the gendarmes to the judge, who indicted him and turned him over first to a doctor, then to two other experts who not only wrote their report but also had it published.[3] What is the significant thing about this story? The pettiness of it all; the fact that this everyday occurrence in the life of village sexuality, these inconsequential bucolic pleasures, could become, from a certain time, the object not only of a collective intolerance but of a judicial action, a medical intervention, a careful clinical examination, and an entire theoretical elaboration. The thing to note is that they went so far as to measure the brainpan, study the facial bone structure, and inspect for possible signs of degenerescence the anatomy of this personage who up to that moment had been an integral part of village life; that they made him talk; that they questioned him concerning his thoughts, inclinations, habits, sensations, and opinions. And then, acquitting him of any crime, they decided finally to make him into a pure object of medicine and knowledge – an object to be shut away till the end of his life in the hospital at Maréville, but also one to be made known to the world of learning through a detailed analysis. One can be fairly certain that during this same period the Lapcourt schoolmaster was instructing the little villagers to mind their language and not talk about all these things aloud. But this was undoubtedly one of the conditions enabling the institutions of knowledge and power to overlay this everyday bit of theater with their solemn discourse. So it was that our society – and it was doubtless the first in history to take such measures – assembled around these timeless gestures, these barely furtive pleasures between simple-minded adults and alert children, a whole machinery for speechifying, analyzing, and investigating.

Between the licentious Englishman, who earnestly recorded for his own purposes the singular episodes of his secret life, and his contemporary, this village halfwit who would give a few pennies to the little girls for favors the older ones refused him, there was without doubt a profound connection: in any case, from one extreme to the other, sex became something to say, and to say exhaustively in accordance with deployments that were varied, but all, in their own way, compelling. Whether in the form of a subtle confession in confidence or an authoritarian interrogation, sex – be it refined or rustic – had to be put into words. A great polymorphous injunction bound the Englishman and the poor Lorrainese peasant alike. As history would have it, the latter was named Jouy.[4]

Since the eighteenth century, sex has not ceased to provoke a kind of generalized discursive erethism. And these discourses on sex did not multiply apart from or against power, but in the very space and as the means of its exercise. Incitements to speak were orchestrated from all quarters, apparatuses everywhere for listening and recording, procedures for observing, questioning, and formulating. Sex was driven out of hiding and constrained to lead a discursive existence. From the singular imperialism that compels everyone to transform their sexuality into a perpetual discourse, to the manifold mechanisms which, in the areas of economy, pedagogy, medicine, and justice, incite, extract, distribute, and institutionalize the sexual discourse, an immense verbosity is what our civilization has required and organized. Surely no other type of society has ever accumulated – and in such a relatively short span of time – a similar quantity of discourses concerned with sex. It may well be that we talk about sex more than anything else; we set our minds to the task; we convince ourselves that we have never said enough on the subject, that, through inertia or submissiveness, we conceal from ourselves the blinding evidence, and that what is essential always eludes us, so that we must always start out once again in search of it. It is possible that where sex is concerned, the most long-winded, the most impatient of societies is our own.

But as this first overview shows, we are dealing less with *a* discourse on sex than with a multiplicity of discourses produced by a whole series of mechanisms operating in different institutions. The Middle Ages had organized around the theme of the flesh and the practice of penance a discourse that was markedly unitary. In the course of recent centuries, this relative uniformity was broken apart, scattered, and multiplied in an explosion of distinct discursivities which took form in demography, biology, medicine, psychiatry, psychology, ethics, pedagogy, and political criticism. More precisely, the secure bond that held together the moral theology of concupiscence and the obligation of confession (equivalent to the theoretical discourse on sex and its first-person formulation) was, if not broken, at least loosened and diversified: between the objectification of sex in rational discourses, and the movement by which each individual was set to the task of recounting his own sex, there has occurred, since the eighteenth century, a whole series of tensions, conflicts, efforts at adjustment, and attempts at retranscription. So it is not simply in terms of a continual extension that we must speak of this discursive growth; it should be seen rather as a dispersion of centers from which discourses emanated, a diversification of their forms, and the complex deployment of the network connecting them. Rather than the uniform concern to hide sex, rather than a general prudishness of language, what distinguishes these last three centuries is the variety, the wide dispersion of devices that were invented for speaking about it, for having it be spoken about, for inducing it to speak of itself, for listening, recording, transcribing, and redistributing what is said about it: around sex, a whole network of varying, specific, and coercive transpositions into discourse. Rather than a massive censorship, beginning with the verbal proprieties imposed by the Age of Reason, what was involved was a regulated and polymorphous incitement to discourse.

The objection will doubtless be raised that if so many stimulations and constraining mechanisms were necessary in order to speak of sex, this was because there reigned over everyone a certain fundamental prohibition; only definite necessities – economic pressures, political requirements – were able to lift this prohibition and open a few approaches to the discourse on sex, but these were limited and carefully coded; so much talk about sex, so many insistent devices contrived for causing it to be talked about – but under strict conditions: does this not prove that it was an object of secrecy, and more important, that there is still an attempt to keep it that way? But this often-stated theme, that sex is outside of discourse and that only the removing of an obstacle, the breaking of a secret, can clear the way leading to it, is precisely what needs to be examined. Does it not partake of the injunction by which discourse is provoked? Is it not with the aim of inciting people to speak of sex that it is made to mirror, at the outer limit of every actual discourse, something akin to a secret whose discovery is imperative, a thing abusively reduced to silence, and at the same time difficult and necessary, dangerous and precious to divulge? We must not forget that by making sex into that which, above all else, had to be confessed, the Christian pastoral always presented it as the disquieting enigma: not a thing which stubbornly shows itself, but one which always hides, the insidious presence that speaks in a voice so muted and often disguised that one risks remaining deaf to it. Doubtless the secret does not reside in that basic reality in relation to which all the incitements to speak of sex are situated – whether they try to force the secret, or whether in some obscure way they reinforce it by the manner in which they speak of it. It is a question rather of a theme that forms part of the very mechanics of these incitements: a way of giving shape to the requirement to speak about the matter, a fable that is indispensable to the endlessly proliferating economy of the discourse on sex. What is peculiar to modern societies, in fact, is not that they consigned sex to a shadow existence, but that they dedicated themselves to speaking of it *ad infinitum*, while exploiting it as *the* secret. . . .

Hence the objective is to analyze a certain form of knowledge regarding sex, not in terms of repression or law, but in terms of power. But the word *power* is apt to lead to a number of misunderstandings – misunderstandings with respect to its nature, its form, and its unity. By power, I do not mean "Power" as a group of institutions and mechanisms that ensure the subservience of the citizens of a given state. By power, I do not mean, either, a mode of subjugation which, in contrast to violence, has the form of the rule. Finally, I do not have in mind a general system of domination exerted by one group over another, a system whose effects, through successive derivations, pervade the entire social body. The analysis, made in terms of power, must not assume that the sovereignty of the state, the form of the law, or the overall unity of a domination are given at the outset; rather, these are only the terminal forms power takes. It seems to me that power must be understood in the first instance as the multiplicity of force relations immanent in the sphere in which they operate and which constitute their own organization; as the process which, through ceaseless struggles and confrontations, transforms, strengthens, or reverses them; as the support which these force relations find in one another, thus forming a chain or a system, or on the contrary, the disjunctions and contradictions which isolate them from one another; and lastly, as the strategies in which they take effect, whose general design or institutional crystallization is embodied in the state apparatus, in the formulation of the law, in the various social hegemonies. Power's condition of possibility, or in any case the viewpoint which permits one to understand its exercise, even in its more "peripheral" effects, and which also makes it possible to use its mechanisms as a grid of intelligibility of the social order, must not be sought in the primary existence of a central point, in a unique source of sovereignty from which secondary and descendent forms would emanate; it is the moving substrate of force relations which, by virtue of their inequality, constantly engender states of power, but the latter are always local and unstable. The omnipresence of power: not because it has the privilege of consolidating everything under its invincible unity, but because it is produced from one moment to the next, at every point, or rather in every relation from one point to another. Power is everywhere; not because it embraces everything, but because it comes from everywhere. And "Power," insofar as it is permanent, repetitious, inert, and self-reproducing, is simply the overall effect that emerges from all these mobilities, the concatenation that rests on each of them and seeks in turn to arrest their movement. One needs to be nominalistic, no doubt: power is not an institution, and not a structure; neither is it a certain strength we are endowed with; it is the name that one attributes to a complex strategical situation in a particular society.

Should we turn the expression around, then, and say that politics is war pursued by other means? If we still wish to maintain a separation between war and politics, perhaps we should postulate rather that this multiplicity of force relations can be coded – in part but never totally – either in the form of "war," or in the form of "politics"; this would imply two different strategies (but the one always liable to switch into the other) for integrating these unbalanced, heterogeneous, unstable, and tense force relations.

Continuing this line of discussion, we can advance a certain number of propositions:

——Power is not something that is acquired, seized, or shared, something that one holds on to or allows to slip away; power is exercised from innumerable points, in the interplay of nonegalitarian and mobile relations.

——Relations of power are not in a position of exteriority with respect to other types of relationships (economic processes, knowledge relationships, sexual relations), but are immanent in the latter; they are the immediate effects of the divisions, inequalities, and disequilibriums which occur in the latter, and conversely they are the internal conditions of these differentiations; relations of power are not in superstructural positions, with merely a role of prohibition or accompaniment; they have a directly productive role, wherever they come into play.

——Power comes from below; that is, there is no binary and all-encompassing opposition between rulers and ruled at the root of power relations, and serving as a general matrix – no such duality extending from the top down and reacting on more and more limited groups to the very depths of the social body. One must suppose rather that the manifold relationships of force that take shape and come into play in the machinery of production, in families, limited groups, and institutions, are the basis for wide-ranging effects of cleavage that run through the social body as a whole. These then form a general line of force that traverses the local oppositions and links them together; to be sure, they also bring about redistributions, realignments, homogenizations, serial arrangements, and convergences of the force relations. Major dominations are the hegemonic effects that are sustained by all these confrontations.

——Power relations are both intentional and nonsubjective. If in fact they are intelligible, this is not because they are the effect of another instance that "explains" them, but rather because they are imbued, through and through, with calculation: there is no power that is exercised without a series of aims and objectives. But this does not mean that it results from the choice or decision of an individual subject; let us not look for the headquarters that presides over its rationality; neither the caste which governs, nor the groups which control the state apparatus, nor those who make the most important economic decisions direct the entire network of power that functions in a society (and makes *it* function); the rationality of power is characterized by tactics that are often quite explicit at the restricted level where they are inscribed (the local cynicism of power), tactics which, becoming connected to one another, attracting and propagating one another, but finding their base of support and their condition elsewhere, end by forming comprehensive systems: the logic is perfectly clear, the aims decipherable, and yet it is often the case that no one is there to have invented them, and few who can be said to have formulated them: an implicit characteristic of the great anonymous, almost unspoken strategies which coordinate the loquacious tactics whose "inventors" or decisionmakers are often without hypocrisy.

——Where there is power, there is resistance, and yet, or rather consequently, this resistance is never in a position of exteriority in relation to power. Should it be said that one is always "inside" power, there is no "escaping" it, there is no absolute outside where it is concerned, because one is subject to the law in any case? Or that, history being the ruse of reason, power is the ruse of history, always emerging the winner? This would be to misunderstand the strictly relational character of power relationships. Their existence depends on a multiplicity of points of resistance: these play the role of adversary, target, support, or handle in power relations. These points of resistance are present everywhere in the power network. Hence there is no single locus of great Refusal, no soul of revolt, source of all rebellions, or pure law of the revolutionary. Instead there is a plurality of resistances, each of them a special case: resistances that are possible, necessary, improbable; others that are spontaneous, savage, solitary, concerted, rampant, or violent; still others that are quick to compromise, interested, or sacrificial; by definition, they can only exist in the strategic field of power relations. But this does not mean that they are only a reaction or rebound, forming with respect to the basic domination an underside that is in the end always passive, doomed to perpetual defeat. Resistances do not derive from a few heterogeneous principles; but neither are they a lure or a promise that is of necessity betrayed. They are the odd term in relations of power; they are inscribed in the latter as an irreducible opposite. Hence they too are distributed in irregular fashion: the points, knots, or focuses of resistance are spread over time and space at varying densities, at times mobilizing groups or individuals in a definitive way, inflaming certain points of the body, certain moments in life, certain types of behavior. Are there no great radical ruptures, massive binary divisions, then? Occasionally, yes. But more often one is dealing with mobile and transitory points of resistance, producing cleavages in a society that shift about, fracturing unities and effecting regroupings, furrowing across individuals themselves, cutting them up and remolding them, marking off irreducible regions in them, in their bodies and minds. Just as the network of power relations ends by forming a dense web that passes through apparatuses and institutions, without being exactly localized in them, so too the swarm of points of resistance traverses social stratifications and individual unities. And it is doubtless the strategic codification of these points of resistance that makes a revolution possible, somewhat similar to the way in which the state relies on the institutional integration of power relationships.

It is in this sphere of force relations that we must try to analyze the mechanisms of power. In this way we will escape from the system of Law-and-Sovereign which has captivated political thought for such a long time. And if it is true that Machiavelli was among the few – and this no doubt was the scandal of his "cynicism" – who conceived the power of the Prince in terms of force relationships, perhaps we need to go one step further, do without the persona of the Prince, and decipher power mechanisms on the basis of a strategy that is immanent in force relationships.

To return to sex and the discourses of truth that have taken charge of it, the question that we must address, then, is not: Given a specific state structure, how and why is it that power needs to establish a knowledge of sex? Neither is the question: What overall domination was served by the concern, evidenced since the eighteenth century, to produce true discourses on sex? Nor is it: What law presided over both the regularity of sexual behavior and the conformity of what was said about it? It is rather: In a specific type of discourse on sex, in a specific form of extortion of truth, appearing historically and in specific places (around the child's body, apropos of women's sex, in connection with practices restricting births, and so on), what were the most immediate, the most local power relations at work? How did they make possible these kinds of discourses, and conversely, how were these discourses used to support power relations? How was the action of these power relations modified by their very exercise, entailing a strengthening of some terms and a weakening of others, with effects of resistance and counterinvestments, so that there has never existed one type of stable subjugation, given once and for all? How were these power relations linked to one another according to the logic of a great strategy, which in retrospect takes on the aspect of a unitary and voluntarist politics of sex? In general terms: rather than referring all the infinitesimal violences that are exerted on sex, all the anxious gazes that are directed at it, and all the hiding places whose discovery is made into an impossible task, to the unique form of a great Power, we must immerse the expanding production of discourses on sex in the field of multiple and mobile power relations.

Which leads us to advance, in a preliminary way, four rules to follow. But these are not intended as methodological imperatives; at most they are cautionary prescriptions.

1 Rule of immanence

One must not suppose that there exists a certain sphere of sexuality that would be the legitimate concern of a free and disinterested scientific inquiry were it not the object of mechanisms of prohibition brought to bear by the economic or ideological requirements of power. If sexuality was constituted as an area of investigation, this was only because relations of power had established it as a possible object; and conversely, if power was able to take it as a target, this was because techniques of knowledge and procedures of discourse were capable of investing it. Between techniques of knowledge and strategies of power, there is no exteriority, even if they have specific roles and are linked together on the basis of their difference. We will start, therefore, from what might be called "local centers" of power-knowledge: for example, the relations that obtain between penitents and confessors, or the faithful and their directors of conscience. Here, guided by the theme of the "flesh" that must be mastered, different forms of discourse – self-examination, questionings, admissions, interpretations, interviews – were the vehicle of a kind of incessant back-and-forth movement of forms of subjugation and schemas of knowledge. Similarly, the body of the child, under surveillance, surrounded in his cradle, his bed, or his room by an entire watch-crew of parents, nurses, servants, educators, and doctors, all attentive to the least manifestations of his sex, has constituted, particularly since the eighteenth century, another "local center" of power-knowledge.

2 Rules of continual variations

We must not look for who has the power in the order of sexuality (men, adults, parents, doctors) and who is deprived of it (women, adolescents, children, patients); nor for who has the right to know and who is forced to remain ignorant. We must seek rather the pattern of the modifications which the relationships of force imply by the very nature of their process. The "distributions of power" and the "appropriations of knowledge" never represent only instantaneous slices taken from processes involving, for example, a cumulative reinforcement of the strongest factor, or a reversal of relationship, or again, a simultaneous increase of two terms. Relations of power-knowledge are not static forms of distribution, they are "matrices of transformations." The nineteenth-century grouping made up of the father, the mother, the educator, and the doctor, around the child and his sex, was subjected to constant modifications, continual shifts. One of the more spectacular results of the latter was a strange reversal: whereas to begin with the child's sexuality had been problematized within the relationship established between doctor and parents (in the form of advice, or recommendations to keep the child under observation, or warnings of future dangers), ultimately it was in the relationship of the psychiatrist to the child that the sexuality of adults themselves was called into question.

3 Rule of double conditioning

No "local center," no "pattern of transformation" could function if, through a series of sequences, it did not eventually enter into an overall strategy. And inversely, no strategy could achieve comprehensive effects if did not gain support from precise and tenuous relations serving, not as its point of application or final outcome, but as its prop and anchor point. There is no discontinuity between them, as if one were dealing with two different levels (one microscopic and the other macroscopic); but neither is there homogeneity (as if the one were only the enlarged projection or the miniaturization of the other); rather, one must conceive of the double conditioning of a strategy by the specificity of possible tactics, and of tactics by the strategic envelope that makes them work. Thus the father in the family is not the "representative" of the sovereign or the state; and the latter are not projections of the father on a different scale. The family does not duplicate society, just as society does not imitate the family. But the family organization, precisely to the extent that it was insular and heteromorphous with respect to the other power mechanisms, was used to support the great "maneuvers" employed for the Malthusian control of the birthrate, for the populationist incitements, for the medicalization of sex and the psychiatrization of its nongenital forms.

4 Rule of the tactical polyvalence of discourses

What is said about sex must not be analyzed simply as the surface of projection of these power mechanisms. Indeed, it is in discourse that power and knowledge are joined together. And for this very reason, we must conceive discourse as a series of discontinuous segments whose tactical function is neither uniform nor stable. To be more precise, we must not imagine a world of discourse divided between accepted discourse and excluded discourse, or between the dominant discourse and the dominated one; but as a multiplicity of discursive elements that can come into play in various strategies. It is this distribution that we must reconstruct, with the things said and those concealed, the enunciations required and those forbidden, that it comprises; with the variants and different effects – according to who is speaking, his position of power, the institutional context in which he happens to be situated – that it implies; and with the shifts and reutilizations of identical formulas for contrary objectives that it also includes. Discourses are not once and for all subservient to power or raised up against it, any more than silences are. We must make allowance for the complex and unstable process whereby discourse can be both an instrument and an effect of power, but also a hindrance, a stumbling-block, a point of resistance and a starting point for an opposing strategy. Discourse transmits and produces power; it reinforces it, but also undermines and exposes it, renders it fragile and makes it possible to thwart it. In like manner, silence and secrecy are a shelter for power, anchoring its prohibitions; but they also loosen its holds and provide for relatively obscure areas of tolerance. Consider for example the history of what was once "the" great sin against nature. The extreme discretion of the texts dealing with sodomy – that utterly confused category – and the nearly universal reticence in talking about it made possible a twofold operation: on the one hand, there was an extreme severity (punishment by fire was meted out well into the eighteenth century, without there being any substantial protest expressed before the middle of the century), and on the other hand, a tolerance that must have been widespread (which one can deduce indirectly from the infrequency of judicial sentences, and which one glimpses more directly through certain statements concerning societies of men that were thought to exist in the army or in the courts). There is no question that the appearance in nineteenth-century psychiatry, jurisprudence, and literature of a whole series of discourses on the species and subspecies of homosexuality, inversion, pederasty, and "psychic hermaphrodism" made possible a strong advance of social controls into this area of "perversity"; but it also made possible the formation of a "reverse" discourse: homosexuality began to speak in its own behalf, to demand that its legitimacy or "naturality" be acknowledged, often in the same vocabulary, using the same categories by which it was medically disqualified. There is not, on the one side, a discourse of power, and opposite it, another discourse that runs counter to it. Discourses are tactical elements or blocks operating in the field of force relations; there can exist different and even contradictory discourses within the same strategy; they can, on the contrary, circulate without changing their form from one strategy to another, opposing strategy. We must not expect the discourses on sex to tell us, above all, what strategy they derive from, or what moral divisions they accompany, or what ideology – dominant or dominated –

they represent; rather we must question them on the two levels of their tactical productivity (what reciprocal effects of power and knowledge they ensure) and their strategical integration (what conjunction and what force relationship make their utilization necessary in a given episode of the various confrontations that occur).

In short, it is a question of orienting ourselves to a conception of power which replaces the privilege of the law with the viewpoint of the objective, the privilege of prohibition with the viewpoint of tactical efficacy, the privilege of sovereignty with the analysis of a multiple and mobile field of force relations, wherein far-reaching, but never completely stable, effects of domination are produced. The strategical model, rather than the model based on law. And this, not out of a speculative choice or theoretical preference, but because in fact it is one of the essential traits of Western societies that the force relationships which for a long time had found expression in war, in every form of warfare, gradually became invested in the order of political power.

Sexuality must not be described as a stubborn drive, by nature alien and of necessity disobedient to a power which exhausts itself trying to subdue it and often fails to control it entirely. It appears rather as an especially dense transfer point for relations of power: between men and women, young people and old people, parents and offspring, teachers and students, priests and laity, an administration and a population. Sexuality is not the most intractable element in power relations, but rather one of those endowed with the greatest instrumentality: useful for the greatest number of maneuvers and capable of serving as a point of support, as a linchpin, for the most varied strategies.

There is no single, all-encompassing strategy, valid for all of society and uniformly bearing on all the manifestations of sex. For example, the idea that there have been repeated attempts, by various means, to reduce all of sex to its reproductive function, its heterosexual and adult form, and its matrimonial legitimacy fails to take into account the manifold objectives aimed for, the manifold means employed in the different sexual politics concerned with the two sexes, the different age groups and social classes.

In a first approach to the problem, it seems that we can distinguish four great strategic unities which, beginning in the eighteenth century, formed specific mechanisms of knowledge and power centering on sex. These did not come into being fully developed at that time; but it was then that they took on a consistency and gained an effectiveness in the order of power, as well as a productivity in the order of knowledge, so that it is possible to describe them in their relative autonomy.

1. *A hysterization of women's bodies*: a threefold process whereby the feminine body was analyzed – qualified and disqualified – as being thoroughly saturated with sexuality; whereby it was integrated into the sphere of medical practices, by

reason of a pathology intrinsic to it; whereby, finally, it was placed in organic communication with the social body (whose regulated fecundity it was supposed to ensure), the family space (of which it had to be a substantial and functional element), and the life of children (which it produced and had to guarantee, by virtue of a biologico-moral responsibility lasting through the entire period of the children's education): the Mother, with her negative image of "nervous woman," constituted the most visible form of this hysterization.

2. *A pedagogization of children's sex*: a double assertion that practically all children indulge or are prone to indulge in sexual activity; and that, being unwarranted, at the same time "natural" and "contrary to nature," this sexual activity posed physical and moral, individual and collective dangers; children were defined as "preliminary" sexual beings, on this side of sex, yet within it, astride a dangerous dividing line. Parents, families, educators, doctors, and eventually psychologists would have to take charge, in a continuous way, of this precious and perilous, dangerous and endangered sexual potential: this pedagogization was especially evident in the war against onanism, which in the West lasted nearly two centuries.

3. *A socialization of procreative behavior*: an economic socialization via all the incitements and restrictions, the "social" and fiscal measures brought to bear on the fertility of couples; a political socialization achieved through the "responsibilization" of couples with regard to the social body as a whole (which had to be limited or on the contrary reinvigorated), and a medical socialization carried out by attributing a pathogenic value – for the individual and the species – to birth-control practices.

4. *A psychiatrization of perverse pleasure*: the sexual instinct was isolated as a separate biological and psychical instinct; a clinical analysis was made of all the forms of anomalies by which it could be afflicted; it was assigned a role of normalization or pathologization with respect to all behavior; and finally, a corrective technology was sought for these anomalies.

Four figures emerged from this preoccupation with sex, which mounted throughout the nineteenth century – four privileged objects of knowledge, which were also targets and anchorage points for the ventures of knowledge: the hysterical woman, the masturbating child, the Malthusian couple, and the perverse adult. Each of them corresponded to one of these strategies which, each in its own way, invested and made use of the sex of women, children, and men.

What was at issue in these strategies? A struggle against sexuality? Or were they part of an effort to gain control of it? An attempt to regulate it more effectively and mask its more indiscreet, conspicuous, and intractable aspects? A way of formulating only that measure of knowledge about it that was acceptable or useful? In actual fact, what was involved, rather, was the very production of sexuality. Sexuality must not be thought of as a kind of natural given which power tries to hold in check, or as an obscure domain which knowledge tries gradually to uncover. It is the name that can be given to a historical construct: not a furtive reality that is difficult to grasp, but a great surface network in which the stimulation of bodies, the intensification of pleasures, the incitement to discourse, the formation of special knowledges, the strengthening of controls and resistances, are linked to one another, in accordance with a few major strategies of knowledge and power.

It will be granted no doubt that relations of sex gave rise, in every society, to a *deployment of alliance*: a system of marriage, of fixation and development of kinship ties, of transmission of names and possessions. This deployment of alliance, with the mechanisms of constraint that ensured its existence and the complex knowledge it often required, lost some of its importance as economic processes and political structures could no longer rely on it as an adequate instrument or sufficient support. Particularly from the eighteenth century onward, Western societies created and deployed a new apparatus which was superimposed on the previous one, and which, without completely supplanting the latter, helped to reduce its importance. I am speaking of the *deployment of sexuality*: like the *deployment of alliance*, it connects up with the circuit of sexual partners, but in a completely different way. The two systems can be contrasted term by term. The deployment of alliance is built around a system of rules defining the permitted and the forbidden, the licit and the illicit, whereas the deployment of sexuality operates according to mobile, polymorphous, and contingent techniques of power. The deployment of alliance has as one of its chief objectives to reproduce the interplay of relations and maintain the law that governs them; the deployment of sexuality, on the other hand, engenders a continual extension of areas and forms of control. For the first, what is pertinent is the link between partners and definite statutes; the second is concerned with the sensations of the body, the quality of pleasures, and the nature of impressions, however tenuous or imperceptible these may be. Lastly, if the deployment of alliance is firmly tied to the economy due to the role it can play in the transmission or circulation of wealth, the deployment of sexuality is linked to the economy through numerous and subtle relays, the main one of which, however, is the body – the body that produces and consumes. In a word, the deployment of alliance is attuned to a homeostasis of the social body, which it has the function of maintaining; whence its privileged link with the law; whence too the fact that the important phase for it is "reproduction." The deployment of sexuality has its reason for being, not in reproducing itself, but in proliferating, innovating, annexing, creating, and penetrating bodies in an increasingly detailed way, and in controlling populations in an increasingly comprehensive way. We are compelled, then, to accept three or four hypotheses which run counter to the one on which the theme of a sexuality repressed by the modern forms of society is based: sexuality is tied to recent devices of power; it has been expanding at an increasing rate since the seventeenth century; the arrangement that has sustained it is not governed by reproduction; it has been linked from the outset with an intensification of the body – with its exploitation as an object of knowledge and an element in relations of power.

It is not exact to say that the deployment of sexuality supplanted the deployment of alliance. One can imagine that one day it will have replaced it. But as things stand at present, while it does tend to cover up the deployment of alliance, it has neither obliterated the latter nor rendered it useless. Moreover, historically it was around and on the basis of the deployment of alliance that the deployment of sexuality was constructed. First the practice of penance, then that of the examination of conscience and spiritual direction, was the formative nucleus: as we have seen, what was at issue to begin with at the tribunal of penance was sex insofar as it was the basis of relations; the questions posed had to do with the commerce allowed or forbidden (adultery, extramarital relations, relations with a person prohibited by blood or statute, the legitimate or illegitimate character of the act of sexual congress) then, coinciding with the new pastoral and its application in seminaries, secondary schools, and convents, there was a gradual progression away from the problematic of relations toward a problematic of the "flesh," that is, of the body, sensation, the nature of pleasure, the more secret forms of enjoyment or acquiescence. "Sexuality" was taking shape, born of a technology of power that was originally focused on alliance. Since then, it has not ceased to operate in conjunction with a system of alliance on which it has depended for support. The family cell, in the form in which it came to be valued in the course of the eighteenth century, made it possible for the main elements of the deployment of sexuality (the feminine body, infantile precocity, the regulation of births, and to a lesser extent no doubt, the specification of the perverted) to develop along its two primary dimensions: the husband–wife axis and the parents–children axis. The family, in its contemporary form, must not be understood as a social, economic, and political structure of alliance that excludes or at least restrains sexuality, that diminishes it as much as possible, preserving only its useful functions. On the contrary, its role is to anchor sexuality and provide it with a permanent support. It ensures the production of a sexuality that is not homogeneous with the privileges of alliance, while making it possible for the systems of alliance to be imbued with a new tactic of power which they would otherwise be impervious to. The family is the interchange of sexuality and alliance: it conveys the law and the juridical dimension in the deployment of sexuality; and it conveys the economy of pleasure and the intensity of sensations in the regime of alliance.

Notes

1   The success of the Prussian troops can only be attributed to the "excellence of their discipline and their exercise; the choice of exercise is not therefore a matter of indifference; in Prussia the subject has been studied for forty years with unremitting application" (Saxe, II, 249).

2   Writing exercise: ". . . 9: Hands on the knees. This command is conveyed by one ring on the bell; 10: hands on the table, head up; 11: clean the slates: everyone cleans his slate with a little saliva, or better still with a piece of rag; 12: show the slates; 13: monitors, inspect. They inspect the slates with their assistants and then those of their own bench. The assistants inspect those of their own bench and everyone returns to his own place."

3   H. Bonnet and J. Bulard, *Rapport médico-légal sur l'état mental de Ch.-J. Jouy*, January 4, 1968.

4   Jouy sounds like the past participle of *jouir*, the French verb meaning to enjoy, to delight in (something), but also to have an orgasm, to come. (Translator's note)

References

Amboise, projet de règlement pour l'aciérie d', Archives nationales, f. 12, 1301.

Beccaria, C. de, *Traité des délits et des peines*, 1764, ed. 1856.

Bernard, Samuel, *Rapport du 30 octobre 1816 à la société de l'enseignement mutuel*.

Bonnet, H. and Bulard, J. *Rapport médico-légal sur l'état mental de Ch.-J. Jouy*, January 4, 1968.

Boussanelle, L. de, *Le Bon Militaire*, 1770.

Faucher, L., *De la Réforme des prisons*, 1838.

Foucault, Michel, *Discipline and Punish*, trans. Alan Sheridan, New York: Vintage Books, 1979.

—— *The History of Sexuality*, vol. 1, *An Introduction*, trans. Robert Hurley, New York: Vintage Books, 1980.

Guibert, J. A. de, "Discours préliminaire," *Essai général de tactique*, I, 1772.

La Salle, J.-B. de, *Conduite des écoles chrétiennes*, B.N. MS. 11759.

Montgommery, J. de, *La Milice française*, ed. 1636.

Oppenheim, *Règlement provisoire pour la fabrique de M.S.*, 1809, in J. Hayem, *Mémoires et documents pour revenir à l'histoire du commerce*, 1911.

"Ordonnace du 1er janvier 1766, pour régler l'exercise de l'infanterie."

Réal, A., *Arch. parl.*, 2e série, LXXII, December 1, 1831.

"Saint-Maur, Règlement de la fabrique de," B. N. MS. Coll. Delamare, Manufactures III.

Saxe, Maréchal de, *Les Rêveries*, 1756.

Schummel, Johann Gottlieb, *Fritzens Reise nach Dessau* (1776), cited by Auguste Pinloche, *La Réforme de l'education en Allemagne au XVIIIe siècle* (1889).

Swedish Discipline, The, London, 1632 (anon.).

Teeters, N. K., *The Cradle of the Penitentiary*, 1935.

—— *They Were in Prison*, 1937.

Tronchot, R. R., *L'Enseignement mutuel en France*, I (unpublished thesis).

Van Meenen, P., "Congrès pénitentiaire de Bruxelles," in *Annales de la charité*, 1847.

Zevaes, A. L., *Damiens le régicide*, 1937.

12

THE SUBJECTIFICATION OF THE BODY

Alphonso Lingis

Foucault's history is a materialist history, a history of inventions that mark discontinuities, for which, once put forth in the public space, different uses are found, about them different couplings of power are set up, different elaborations of discourse become possible. Inventions invest those who seize hold of them with new powers, technological as well as social powers, powers over others; they produce new forms of identity and new forms of competence. The inventions spread laterally; new uses for them are found in different sectors of social space. The resultant of multiple centers of power functioning in different directions becomes visible, not as the finality conceived by the inventors, but as a movement that functions in certain directions, toward certain ends, producing certain effects, which were perhaps not the efficacious intention of anyone. Bodies that are forcibly subjected produce power in their turn, devise their evasions, resistances, snares, ambushes, ruses, and mockeries; they signal, feint, and delude.

It is as a sensitive substance, a substance that produces pain and pleasures in itself, that a body is a subject of and subjected to power and discourse. Pain and pleasure are not just ineffable states of transitive impotence; they incite the power operations and discourse of others, they afflict the susceptible bodies of others. It is as a painful and voluptuous substance that a body attracts forces and gets inserted into the organized channels in which capacities are imprinted on it. With these capacities it not only manipulates material things, but inflicts pleasure and pain on others. It is not just inasmuch as its musculature and nervous circuitry can materialize a gesture, a perceptible signifier, that a body makes itself a subject that issues statements and has actions ascribed to it. The body that speaks is not a tabula rasa upon which its own gestures draw signs. In speaking its substance is relieved and wounded, is gratified and excites pleasure, troubles

Alphonso Lingis, "The Subjectification of the Body," *Foreign Bodies* (New York: Routledge, 1994), pp. 53–73 and torments. It is as a painful and voluptuous substance that its muscular and nervous circuitry attracts forces and get coded with blazons, signs, functional identities, and gets inserted into the grammar and rhetoric of kinship relations, the distribution of resources, and the communication of directives.

The cartography[1] that maps out the distances and directions across which we identify and constrain one another maps out the ways we torment and gratify one another.

The Pain of Identity

A body as a substance susceptible to pain can be tortured, can be punished, can be disciplined, can be made delinquent. These operations characterize distinctive periods of modern Western socialization, and make the corporeal substance significant and functional in quite different ways.

The blazon of the tortured body

The ancien régime in Europe made bodies substances subject to torture and correlatively made bodies sacred. Coronation, the ceremonies of subjection and obeisance, and the royal iconography were operations of power and of discourse by which the body of the ruler was doubled up with the very substance of the body politic. And the sacred rites which consecrated his body made it the terrestrial double of the King of Heavens, the body of Jesus doubled up with eternal godhead.[2]

It was in the name of the sovereign that the body of the malefactor was subjected to torture,[3] and it was tortured for an attack on the person or the personage of the king – that is, on the sovereign double of the ruler's body. The malefactor was denounced as an insurgent, a regicide; every criminal tortured was tortured for lese majesty. Torture was a raid during the time of political armistice, an operation of the king wreaking vengeance on the enemies of his sacralized body.

Here truth was determined, not by empirical assemblage of disparate data and critical evaluation of them, but by the torture that produced confession. The truth of the crime was concealed in the entrails and by the body of the accused; it had to be made manifest on his body.[4] The tongues of avowed blasphemers were pierced, the throats of conspirators seared with acid, the hands of armed aggressors cut off with their own weapons, the bodies of arsonists burnt with their own torches. The scaffold was a public theater of royal power; torture, a liturgy. Raised before the gates and under the eyes of the heavens, the flames of its fury rising from infernal depths, the scaffold situated the regicide body of the captive and the sovereign body of the ruler on cosmic axes. In the mutilation, castration, and quartering of the body of the captive, the spectators were shown the absolute character of the outrage done to the body of the king. The body of the captive was reduced to a substance that produces nothing but pain, a pain that was branded not with ciphers and messages but with horror and infamy.

The scaffold was a theater, the victim was also an actor. On his or her flesh being scorched the crowd saw the flames of eternal damnation rising to envelop him – but this same agony may also make visible the pain that redeems and that consumes the guilt. As the torture produced the confession, it delivered from guilt and delivered to glory – or it produced the oaths, outcries, and blasphemies with which the victim cursed irrevocably his judges, the king, and his God, and turned the theater of sovereignty into a saturnalia in which the transcendental order was inverted and criminals transformed into heroes and legends.

The eventuality of such a denouement, provoking fear in the minds of monarchs – and not some contagion of compassion arising out of recognition of common corporeality – was what led to a decreasing incidence of torture, in the measure that absolute monarchy found itself the more threatened.

Punishment and the body of signs

The theorists who drew up a program of punishment for modern Republican Europe were concerned to deliver the criminal from the hands of the crowd that had massed about the king's scaffold, spectators of the royal action and depositories of the insurrectional legends, into the hands of a citizenry actively united by social contract and subjected to the non-arbitrary decrees of rational law. Torture is spectacular, it is a theater of glory, whether for the monarch or for his enemy. The punishment they planned was a program of calculated and limited operations on members of the body politic, pedagogical rather than dramatic and terrorizing – essentially inglorious.

As the extremities to which torture went resulted from the transcendent nature of the sovereign's body that was being shown forth and not from the rage of the ruler, so the differentiations, degrees, and limits of intensity in punishment they argued for did not result from compassion in the hearts of the Republican penologists. The torture of the ancien régime was an operation on the body of a subject unlimited in intensity but limited to transgressions perceived as lese majesty; the punishment of the Republican regime is limited and graded in intensity in order to be virtually unlimited in extension.

The development of production, the amassing of wealth, the rapid increase in property holdings – which characterized the epoch – motivated the will to extend penalization into zones where, previously, the identification of offense as offense against the body of the sovereign had left certain activities unlegislated or had tolerated certain illegalities. Privately capitalized industries and commercial hold-ings became too extensive for the owner himself to maintain his domination throughout them; the previously tolerated zones of production unregulated by guilds and corporations, or of production of new and illegal substances, or of smuggling had become too extensive, regional protectionism and extortions too consolidated not to attract the legislating and penalizing will of the citizens' Republic. Soon the industrial slums and proletarian and subproletarian family housing, health, and property transfers would also attract this will.

The punishment must become differentiated and graded because it is conceived, not as an act of branding on the body as a substance of pain, but as a mechanical operation on representations – the representations of advantage that activate the body's powers. The penologists must draw up an ideally complete table of transgressions, and conceive for each an injury contrived to invert the specific advantage the transgressor represents himself or herself as gaining from the transgression. The policed Republic will be one in which those who abuse public liberty are deprived of their own, those who abuse the privilege of public office are stripped of their civil rights, speculators and usurers are subjected to fines, thieves have their assets confiscated, murderers are executed. The complete table of punishments, each conformed to the nature of the offense, will make the law appear to be in the nature of things.

The punishment will come to an end when the reform of the representational faculty is brought about and this reform verified. The sentence meted out is thus to fit not only the nature of the specific transgression, but the attitude of the criminal, his past, his way of life, his nature, his rate of transformation. The masses, whose functional identities in the agrarian, manufacturing, military, and ecclesiastical hierarchies were dissolved in the collapse of the feudal order, have a new kind of identity produced for them in the penal practices which the Republican order set out to extend throughout society.

Through punishment the body-mechanics of the offender is being made into a place where the representations it produces for itself are inverted, by outside intervention, and also where they are exteriorized, where *signs* are being produced. These signs will designate to others the identity of the ordinance violated, and associate the specific transgression with a representation of disadvantage. Punishment will turn the social space into a pedagogical tableau in which the public which judges and sentences also reads the logic of the civil code in the mortified figures of its transgressors. In quarries being worked, along roads being repaired and bridges being built, in workshops and mines open to the public, everyone will see the civil code being inscribed on the bodies of citizens.

Discipline: the body individuated as a value

The industrial, mercantile, and colonialist bourgeoisie who had enlisted the masses, produced by the dissolution of the feudal order, in the struggle to overthrow the monarchies, had no intention of giving power to "the people." The new juridical order – representative government – was soon to show itself to be a coalition of the most powerful special-interest groups. The ideology of government by law, devised as a weapon in the conflict against the monarchies, would henceforth serve to mask new structures of power. For this period was not only a period of inventions of industrial and military technology, but also of social technology. The invention of those distinctively modern apparatuses of subjection, which were the barracks, the factory, the public school, the hospital, and the asylum, was to completely restructure modern social space. These structures were the decisive means by which the unleashed forces of the masses were not simply segregated, neutralized, and controlled, but made productive. Foucault identifies with the term "discipline" the new social technologies devised in them.

Barracks, factories, and public schools are spaces enclosed, and then partitioned. The bodies to be disciplined are distributed in the gridded space as interchangeable elements in a table of ranked subordinations.

Each maneuver to be performed in the assigned site is broken down analytically. The limbs of the body are separately assigned positions and directions; the position and movement of each limb or organ are fixed in relationship with the assigned overall position of the body. Each position and movement is then correlated with an object – a weapon, a tool, a machine, a notebook, a medication. The duration of the movements is calculated and timed. The timetable will make possible an exhaustive usage of each segment of time.

The multiple activities of a factory, a barracks, or a school are broken down into specific operations. They are not performed as organic and reciprocally coordinated aspects of a common team project, but are executed as preprogrammed and timed exercises. This new methodology of power is, Foucault suggests,[5] the source of the new concept of a linear and progressive kind of time which now begins to dominate in modern society. In the enclosures of disciplinary society time figures, no longer as a field which is punctuated by events and feats, but as the linear dimension of the continuous execution of successive and parallel operations.

The exercises, each determined as a performance in an assigned place and taking a determined time, distributed in gridded space and in linear time, are combined so as to produce composite results, calculable in advance. The composite operation will not be simply the additive sum of massed agents nor the synthetic momentum of a reciprocally coordinating team. The instance that commands these docile bodies is then not, as in slavery or servitude, the individual will of the master, the individuality, charisma, or caprice of the power that wills, but the tactical calculus of the headmaster, the foreman, the coach, the lieutenant, or the administrator.

Disciplining is a technical operation designed to form and to fix aptitudes in a body, thus augmenting the body's powers, increasing its functional efficacy. It also dissociates those aptitudes from the power of the body in which they are seated; they are powers in the body over which that body does not exert power.[6] The capacities that are developed in the individual body do not result in its acceding to dominion over segments of the social field; the new aptitudes are loci of subjection in the body. Disciplining makes bodies docile – adapted to instrumental layouts and productive, and also tractable. It makes bodies function as elements that can be programmed and maneuvered.

Confinement first appeared in Europe in the setting up of leper colonies. Walls of exclusion were devised for lepers; when leprosy subsided in Europe, the walls remained and the spaces they excluded were filled with beggars, vagabonds, sociopaths, and madmen.

When, in the wake of leprosy, the plague spread across Europe, the social space outside the walls of exclusion came to be partitioned, internally gridded, for the ordered distribution of bodies and movements. The advance of the plague called up not the thaumaturgic powers of medical authorities, which proved in fact impotent, but the segregating methods of the civic authorities. They acted to halt behind multiple barriers the movements of the disease whose contagion spread in the commingling of bodies, but also in order to halt the spread of the moral evil of plague times – the frenzy of lifetimes cut short, the consorting of bodies without respect for civic status and identity, the indifference to laws and prohibitions. The institution of a power that assigns to each individual his place and fixes each individual in the capacities and malady of his body, first appeared in Europe in the methods of force the public authorities marshaled to deal with the plague.

In the eighteenth century the masses threatened the cities from within; they were confined in barracks, factories, schools, penal colonies, hospitals, and psychiatric asylums, where the walls of exclusion were compounded with internal partitioning. Individuals were distributed, each at his post, in a social space become a disciplinary archipelago. The social technology of disciplining is the use of procedures of individualization to mark the confined: disciplining post-feudal mass society consisted, Foucault says, in treating lepers as plague victims.[7]

Surveillance registers the transgression as soon as it is initiated, indeed observes every possibility of transgression and every temptation to transgress, and neutralizes them in advance. It differentiates individuals, makes comparison possible between the levels, abilities, and performances of different individuals, and between the different stages in the evolution of an individual. The individual is constituted as a describable, analyzable object through a set of procedures for identification, codification, narration, and induction. Examination procedures maintain the individual exposed and visible. The disciplined body is individual in his or her school record, examination results, aptitude tests, military record, employment record, prison record, and medical file.

Surveillance and examinations make possible the establishing, for each individual, of a minimum to maintain and an optimum to strive for, and counteract deviations from this optimum. Norms are produced by the comparison surveillance makes possible between the levels, abilities, and performances of different individuals. Individuality is the zone of intersection of several such extensive classes. The abnormalities with which the individual is individuated define a fixed range of other individuals with which he or she is equivalent and interchangeable.

The individuality of the individual then does not consist in the autonomy of a singular set of powers and a singular sensibility within him or her. Nor does it consist in signifying a transcendental referent – an ideal category to which he or she would belong, or an ideal individual that his or her own individuality would reflect, in the measure that he or she participates through his or her own function in the scope of power of that ideal individual. For him or her to identify himself or herself is not to declare that he or she is a priest of a great God or a knight or servant of a great lord.

Ferdinand de Saussure differentiated between the *meaning* and the *value* of a term in a semiotic system. Inasmuch as a term in language has a meaning, it designates a referent. Inasmuch as a term in language has a value, it is defined and delimited by the set of other terms with which it can be exchanged, and those with which it contrasts. In the disciplinary regime, the individuality of the individual is marked by a degree of approximation to the norm, but the norm itself is nothing but the measure of the mean range of variations. In de Saussure's terminology we could say that the individuality of the individual has no meaning. Maintained visible in its post, comparable with the constellation of other individuals with which it can be substituted, the individuated disciplined body has, or is, a value.[8]

The uses of the delinquent body

The penology conceived by the theorists of Republican Europe was short-lived. Almost at once the concept of the prison was adopted, and incarceration replaced the table of fines, confiscations, sequesterings, divestment of civil rights, and the forced labor in public works that penologists had elaborated, to become the uniform chastisement for all offenses.

The prisons built were not a simple return of the dungeons of the ancien régime; its dungeons were for interrogation and for the neutralization of political prisoners, rather than themselves the penalty. The prison, as conceived by the theorists of the Walnut Street Prison and the Ghent Workhouse,[9] was the architecture of a project aimed at the nature of the felon. His transgression was perceived to issue, not simply from a representation, but from an antisocial nature. He was to be born again through a technological reconstruction of his physical nature. The Quaker theorists of the Walnut Street Prison and the Enlightenment theorists of the Ghent Workhouse conceived the prison as a model institution of the Christian utopia of the reborn or as a model of the Rousseauist city of citizens whose eyes are open only to the whole. But what they assembled within prison walls were the new methods of human engineering contrived to produce disciplined bodies.

The prison individuates – isolates the convict from the exterior world, from what motivates the offenses of which he was charged, from other prisoners. It subjects his past, his proclivities, his aptitudes, his habits, and his speech to incessant surveillance, and builds up for him an individual prison file. It imposes labor not for production, but in order to bend bodies to regular movements, to exclude agitation and distraction, and to subject them to hierarchy and to imperatives. It regulates the form and the duration of the sentence to effect a technical transformation of the body of the convict.

The inventors of the prison heralded it as an apparatus to effect reform, the reconstruction of the nature of the bodies isolated from the social space – and thus as the most effective protection of society. Within twenty years after it was instituted in Republican France, a parliamentary commission set up to report on its functioning already reported[10] what subsequent investigations of the penitentiary system to our day have continued to report: penitentiary procedures produce different effects on the inmates they mark and individuate. For, Norman Mailer writes, "it is that not only the worst of the young are sent to prison, but the best – that is, the proudest, the bravest, the most daring, the most enterprising, and the most undefeated of the poor, ... those who are drawn to crime as a positive experience – because it is more exciting, more meaningful, more mysterious, more transcendental, more religious than any other experience they have known...."[11] Studies of the results of the prison system show that one part of the prison material will be made functional in other disciplinary apparatuses – factories, military barracks. One part will be marked and individuated to the point that they will be unable to function outside prison; these are the punks that will get themselves rounded up again as soon as they are released. Another part – the statistically largest part – will be made into delinquents, offenders schooled in the methods of crime within the prison and who, when released, enter into careers in illegal activities. Finally, one part will make careers of being convicts within the prison, "annealed until they are harder than the steel that encloses them"[12] and, if released, make themselves outlaws, pursuing not the efficacy of rebel commandants but the glory of bandits.

In the United States at this writing there are 628,000 convicted criminals in prisons, a number double that of ten years ago; 150,000 await trial in jails. There are, in addition, six million jail admissions of arrested people each year; a million are on parole. Nearly two-thirds of all convicts are rearrested within three years of their release. Federal penitentiaries (for non-white-collar offenders) house secret societies of convicts, bandits and killers; they are, in Jack Abbott's words, schools for gladiators. Yet legislators, penal officials, and public agree to build more prisons.

It is then that these factories producing delinquents and these schools for gladiators are judged better than the alternative: treaties negotiated among urban and rural zones held by undisciplined masses,[13] or street war against urban guerrillas;[14] an ecology maintaining zones outside the disciplinary archipelago for those who are drawn to crime as a positive experience – because it is more exciting, more meaningful, more mysterious, more transcendental, more religious than any other experience they have known[15] – or campaigns to exterminate them.[16]

The forty-five-year-old alcoholic imprisoned for robbery has, when released, the range of alternatives drastically reduced. The eighteen-year-old Black adolescent who is released on parole in the ghetto with a prison record has few alternatives to theft and drug dealing. The range of alternatives is reduced already with each truancy from school being recorded, each defective report card. In multiple penitentiary enclosures – foster homes, public assistance institutions, social workers with their disciplining of space, public schools, residential apprenticeships, juvenile homes, disciplinary regiments in the army and the marines, prisons, hospitals, asylums – delinquents are being progressively manufactured.[17] Delinquents are not outlaws, nomads prowling about the confines of the docile and frightened citizenry; delinquency is not constituted through successive exclusions from the social order, but through successive inclusions under ever more insistent surveillance.

In fact delinquents do not constitute a multitude of individuals upon whom the technology of the disciplinary archipelago has proven ineffective, and who are at large conducting a guerrilla war on its institutions. They are an identified, documented group, maintained under surveillance outside and used by the forces of order to maintain under surveillance the whole network of their contacts and their milieux. They are recruited and put to use. It is not the prostitute who lives off renting her body for pay who threatens the disciplinary structure of society, but the possibility of women generally going to singles bars for casual adventure and occasional supplementary income. The prostitutes are quickly identified by the police for whom they are needed as available forced informers; they are used by the molders of public opinion to justify the power and discourse that maintains the disciplinary structure of the family and the posts in the coded social space.

The prison precipitates the organization of a delinquent population, closed in upon itself, in relations of hostility and mutual suspicion with the strata of

society from which the delinquents come. It extends its surveillance and supervision to delinquents when they are released and to the milieux into which they
are released, making possible the recruiting of informers and stool
pigeons. Through prohibitions on residence, probation control, and unemploy-
ment, delinquents are induced to carry out the tasks of infiltrating, rendering
disreputable, and provoking into adventurism other segments of the
population involved in unrest, dissidence, or illegalities. Delinquents are
not only the objects of the policing of society, but its accomplices and double
agents.

What about the proud and brave who are convicts, those of whom
Mailer wrote that prison can only anneal them until they are harder than the
steel that encloses them? It was because the monarchy that tortures shares
the exhilaration of torturing with the public it assembles as, today, the
legislature that decrees capital punishment shares the pleasure of exterminating
with readers of newspapers and spectators of television,[18] that it makes itself
accepted.

Prisons are both the failure of the disciplinary archipelago and its loci of
concentration. Today the prisons, ever multiplying, are not enough. Torture is
being reinvented everywhere, and in republican societies (the incarceration of
drug addicts is torture; high-tech maximum security federal prisons such as
Marion are listed by Amnesty International as loci of torture). The methods
advocated by eighteenth-century penologists – sequestrations, seizures of all
personal property, forced denunciations and entrapment – are being added to
incarceration.

Suffering is not simply debilitation; there rises up, in the substance of the
body that suffers, a power of endurance, which can generate powers to devise
mockeries, evasions, ruses, and even posthumous subversions. The suffering of
the torture victim delivered him or her from guilt and delivered him or her to
glory, or produced the strength to blaspheme and curse his or her judges, king,
and God. In quarries and mines being dynamited, along roads being repaired
and bridges being built worked with forced labor, bodies which were sentenced
to write large the civil code in social space are inscribing another deposition.
The travail of the schooled, barracked, proletarianized, hospitalized, and insti-
tutionalized can make intractability a pleasure and give rise to disciplined
sedition. Prisons can anneal the bodies of convicts until they are harder than
the steel that encloses them.

Endurance is not simply the passivity of a material organism; it slowly
generates a skill or an art of endurance. When it functions as a skill in subversion
of the disciplinary archipelago, it also confirms and reinforces that disciplinary
archipelago: delinquents are its accomplices and double agents. Can it become
an art of creating a space outside the disciplinary archipelago? Who is there to
teach such an art?

The Voluptuous Subjection

Our bodies, substances of pain which can be marked and utilized, are also substances of pleasures. Mechanisms of power are contrived and fastened onto these voluptuous substances, mechanisms that produce power and knowledge. The voluptuous emotion that simmers in these substances is itself a power, a power exercised on those substances themselves as well as on other such substances.

Sexualized natures

Foucault finds that, at the end of the eighteenth century, four new strategic areas were isolated and specific power-knowledge apparatuses were contrived on them.[19]

The bodies of women were qualified, and disqualified, as substances wholly saturated with hysteric sexuality. Wholly *hysterike*, that is, a womb (*hystera*) – and hysterical, that is, subject to dislocations and shiftings of the womb, for the womb from Hippocratic times was taken to be a mobile organ whose displacements in the space of the female abdomen were taken to be the cause of female psychoneurological excitability and of disturbances of the sensory, vasomotor, and visceral functions. In conception, clothing, and practice, while the expanses, nipples, orifices of the virile body were desensitized, anaesthetized, and male orgasmicity was wholly located in the erected penis, all the expanses and pulp of the female body about the womb were saturated with sexual excitability. Female nature became unsettled, irresolute, neurasthenic, pathogenic. The instability and corruptibility of female nature made its forces without force, reliable for nothing but generation; its materiality was maternity. It was set under the family alliance as a material substrate of a set of power relationships.

The pharmacist and the surgeon were displaced by the family doctor, set up as the ultimate instance of decision about maternity and childbearing, and about the specifically maternal weaknesses and liabilities. By her susceptibility to vapors, fevers, miasmas, her fainting spells, her long bouts of bedriddenness, her enigmatic female ailments, the spouse withdrew from her subjection to her husband to subject her body to the knowledge and powers of the doctor. As such she was individuated in her nature; medicine was set up scientifically at the end of the eighteenth century as the first science of the individual. The agitations that the diagnostic eye scrutinized in this maternal substance were the individuating signs – more exactly, the *indexes* – about which this science elaborated its theoretical generalizations and its individuating praxes.

A second strategic area was the onanistic body of children. Childhood was subjected now to perpetual surveillance, not as the time of emergence of manual, intellectual, and economic powers and responsibilities, but as the age of masturbatory discharges. The infantile body was constituted as a substance that is a constant temptation for itself, a volume of pleasures ever on hand but in which vigor and future are being undermined. The masturbating child was taken to be wasting his substance and permanently prejudicing his physical growth, his nervous stability, his future sexual competence and potency, his mental alertness, his moral will. In the name of these dangers, the child was delivered over to the authority and power of governesses, pastors, headmasters, and educators. The pedagogical institutions which confined the child and subjected him to surveillance, also owed their authority and their power to this substance constituted as masturbatory. The pedagogical powers adjusted upon the body of the child functioned to intensify the sensations of onanism, and to invest the child with knowledge and counter-powers that locked into the adult powers set up over his so portentous compulsions.[20]

A third strategic area was the procreative performance of the couple. For a mercantilist directorate, population was wealth; for an imperialist politics, population was arms. Specific agencies for investigation, for planning, for financing, for verification, and for control were set up about projects to regulate the birthrate, the contraceptive practices, abortions, public housing, paternity responsibilities and childcare payments. They were set up not only to incite fertility, but also to administer the methods and devices that would sterilize bad blood, criminal inheritance, precocious and devitalized, senile, reproductive organs, and degenerate genes. The reproductive organs were isolated, subjected to examination, surveillance, and to economic, racist, imperialist finalities.

As geneticists conceived of the organism, not as a system endowed with, as one of its peculiarities, a reproductive capacity, but instead as the sustaining hull, itself perishable, about the genetic code for which it exists, so for the new complexes of power-knowledge agencies the reproductive organs and the genetic code of the couple were the ultimate substrate and interpretand beneath all the codes of kinship alliance, domesticity, romance, and leisure.

Finally, the whole field of sexual practices that had fallen outside of the codes and mechanisms that regulated the family structure became in the eighteenth and nineteenth centuries the concern of new mechanisms of power.[21] The prostitute, an amasser of wealth in a time when economic upheavals and imperialist adventures populated cities and ports with men far from their families, became, with her or his clients, the focus of power operations on the part of innkeepers, procurers, police, blackmailers, and protectors in high places; in addition, as a woman who refused maternity, an unnatural woman, the female prostitute and, as a man that gives himself over to the desires of others, the male prostitute were subjected to the new scrutiny and authority of the psychiatrist.

Psychiatry separated itself from general medicine by postulating a specific pathology of the sexual instinct. Debauchery, a phenomenon of excess or of libertinage, was reformulated as perversion. Wantonness was now changed from an act into a nature. Debauchery, in the Renaissance understanding, was done out of libertinage; it was an act of domination and a pleasure that one gave oneself once one had willfully determined to disobey the law for the sake of disobeying the law and to posit oneself as sovereign. For Sade, sodomy was the supreme libertine act, for he interpreted it biblically, as the use of the erected male organ not for pleasure bonding nor for the reproduction of the race, but to gore and disembowel one's partner and release the germ of the race only in its excrement. It was an act directed, then, against the human genus as such, the ultimate substrate for all the generality of discourse and of norms; it was the act by which one posited oneself in sovereign singularity. If sodomy became a mania for the libertine, the same act continually reiterated without modification or development, this was not the sign that it issued blindly from a bound instinct; it was repeated out of lucid and free decision, out of a willed asceticism of apathy, in order to free one's acts from the inconstant suggestions of pleasure.[22] The psychiatry of the nineteenth century substantized this act of transgression into a nature; there were homosexuals – the species was named in 1870 – who rarely or never perform an act of sodomy, but who had a distinctive past, childhood, history, way of life, character, also a specific anatomy and nervous system which was manifested in the style of movements, tics, and gestures, in intonations of voice, in taste in colors and in artistic styles, and in certain kinds of ideas. The famous sexologists of the nineteenth century, Havelock Ellis, Krafft-Ebbing, and Rohleder, identified as many species of pervert as there are nonreproductive libidinal acts – mixoscopophiles, presbytophiles, necrophiliacs, copraphagists, zoophiles, and so on. Psychiatry gave itself importance by tracking down these strange breeds in schools, in monasteries, in isolated farms, in the clubs and mansions of the aristocrats, in ships at sea, in prisons, and in the undergrounds of cities. It drew up methods to identify them, procedures to entrap them – methods and procedures used by a vice police in blackmailing them and the espionage services in using them. Psychiatric literature also gave them a notoriety which would be profitable to owners of cabarets and publishers of illustrated magazines, and finally to themselves.

The agencies constructed about the arena of pleasures and practices outside of the family constituted a new archipelago of power that succeeded the power system set up to regulate marriage as alliance. But the new agencies of sexuality – the family doctor, the pedagogues, the social workers, and the psychiatrist – were called upon to resolve problems within marriage; the result was a sexual individuation of figures in the husband–wife, parents–children axes of the family. There now appeared the unsatisfiable wife, the frigid spouse, the indifferent mother or the mother with murderous obsessions, the impotent, sadistic, perverted husband, the hysterical or neurasthenic daughter, the precocious and already exhausted child, the homosexual who refuses marriage or neglects his wife. The axes of the family were henceforth not only relationships of economic and political commitment and nutritive and protective support; the personages of the family institution became individuated through sexual practices and pleasures identified and culpabilized. The family space became an arena where sexually individuating pleasures and practices were implanted in its members by experts, but subjected to the laws of alliance; the family became incestuous.[23]

Aristocratic blood, bourgeois semen

The place of this newly circumscribed domain of sexual identities, open to the power and delineated by the discourse of doctors, pedagogues, social workers, and psychiatrists, was the bourgeois family; it was itself that the bourgeoisie first organized with these agencies and these discourses. The feudal aristocracy had looked back to its ancestry, its bloodlines, for the authentification of its power; the bourgeoisie, a class with a future, looked instead to its descendence. The scientifico-technological preoccupation with sexualities, coded medically, was, positively, a concern for progeny. The thrust of power was not, negatively, on the repression of gratuitous pleasures, but, positively, on maximizing wholesome reproductive vigor.

The aristocracy had affirmed the specificity of their bodies; nobility is first a vital, corporeal characteristic. Blood took on distinctive value in a society where power was monopolized power to put to death, to shed blood; where sovereignty was transmitted through bloodlines; where the orders of society are hereditary castes; and where famine, epidemics, and wars were the principal concerns of power.[24] For the bourgeoisie the distinctive value of sex will replace that of blood. The bourgeois affirmed the political value of their bodies in ensuring the health and vigor of their sexual practices. They set forth longevity and auspicious progeny as the authentification of their right to rule. Wholesome sexuality in a body became the publicness or sociality of the corporeal substance, not as a meaning, a telos, or a sign, but as a certification, a seal.

Disciplinary biopolitics

Disciplinary apparatuses – schools, barracks, factories, prisons, hospitals – in which our bodies are inserted, which technologically increase the utility of our individuated bodies and increase knowledge – proliferate; the bourgeois family as the matrix of truth and power continually depreciates. The individuating technologies of the disparate agencies of sexuality are relayed by those of the diverse sectors of the disciplinary archipelago. Inserted into disciplinary spaces, women, children, couples, and deviants can be made into tractable

substances of pain-pleasure susceptibility. Their individuated powers and discourses can enter into the strategic policies of biological management. The
twentieth century has seen the micro-agencies set up for the management of
population, race, and the species integrated into the overall policies of the
contemporary state.

The circuits of state power connect the large number of mechanisms that
have been devised to inquire into – to subject to observation and regulation –
the birth rate and the childbearing age, birth prevention and abortions, the
genetic coding of progeny; to subject to documentation and control the migra-
tions of populations; to supervise health and aging. This biopolitics is being
formulated in the archaic terminology of rights – the right to life, to health, to
the management of one's body, to happiness, to the satisfaction of needs. But in
reality its campaigns are conducted in view of the appropriation of the positive
forces of life by power and by knowledge, conducted in view of the incitement,
reinforcement, surveillance, and management of forces, the increase of potenti-
alities and of results.

A confessional science of sex

Discourse proliferates about the four kinds of sexually individuated bodies that
got identified, compounded, and fixed at the end of the eighteenth century.
This discourse is not that of an *ars erotica* such as that which great civilizations in
India, in China, in Persia, produced: a magisterial and initiatory teaching of the
varieties, specific kinds, durations, and reverberations of pleasure, a teaching
designed to extend and intensify the realm of pleasures and thereby to produce
absolute mastery of the body, unique enjoyment, an oblivion of time and its
threats.

The truth of sex in the West in modern times was produced, not in sexual
pedagogy, which was virtually nonexistent, nor in initiation, usually silent or
accompanied with laughter and derision, but in the formulations of confessional
literature. The first specifically Western form of discourse about sexuality was
confession – first, sacramental confession, then a desacralized and commercial
literature of confession.[25] In its monastic usage confession meant an explicit
report of one's acts, impulses, thoughts, desires, and feelings. In medieval civil
society the term "confession" had meant a testification of status, identity, value,
a certification of one's family, allegiance, and protection, which was made to
authenticate what one said. It meant in the torture of the ancien régime the
forcing out into the open of one's inner insurgent and regicide nature. The
production of truth by confession, which ceased to be the fundamental method
to produce truth in penal institutions during the age of the Republican refor-
mers, found a whole new region in which to invest, that of the practices and
pleasures of sexualized individuals. The doctor assigned to the mother, the

pedagogue to the child, the social worker to the couple, and the psychiatrist to the pervert subject these individuals to interrogations, confrontations, hypnosis, and free-association sessions.

The West also produced forms of public discourse about sexual practices. It produced economic and political discussions about population, a rational and technical discourse designed for the administration of sexual practices by specific public agencies. It produced a silent discourse about sexual pleasures in the architecture of school buildings, hospitals, and prisons and the layout of desks, recreational spaces, and dormitories. It produced medical, psychiatric, and penal discourses about the kinds of sexually individuated bodies. Interrogations, questionnaires, interviews, biographies, and surveys supplied the data which these various kinds of public discourse organized, coded in rational and calculative vocabularies and grammar, recast in the pseudo-scientific form of medicine, and worked into legislative decrees.

The secret of sex that is confessed has to be interpreted by another. Sexual practices will be interpreted no longer in the register of fault and sin, excess or transgression, but according to the axes of the normal and the pathological. The hermeneutics of sexual data will delineate a pathology of instincts behind unhealthy tendencies, images, pleasures, and practices – abnormal and pathogenic, in turn, of physical and psychic maladies.

The truth confessed produces power effects. The pastoral practice of confession was designed to produce specific effects on the desire that is formulated in discourse – mastery of and detachment from desire, spiritual conversion toward God; it was designed to intensify the identifying signs of temptation and of the solicitations of grace. In the laicized forms of confession, the specific effects of confession are therapeutic, not only in that the conclusions gleaned prescribe medical treatments, but in that the truth itself produced confessionally is now taken to *heal*.

But the effects of the truth produced by confession are multiple. The confessional subjugation intensifies the depths of sexual inclinations and obsessions in the one confessing, electrifies the surfaces of contact and of sexual inscription, and dramatizes the troubled moments and the phantasms. And the powers that subjugate in these apparatuses give themselves a dividend of pleasure – the pleasures of subjecting to interrogation, of pursuit, of espionage, of maintaining surveillance, the pleasures of surprising and exasperating and provoking betrayal. And these pleasures of knowledge and power induce new pleasures in those subjected to them – pleasures of defying, of scandalizing, of parodying, of shamming, pleasures of captivating and seducing in turn. The power maneuvers between parents and children, adults and adolescents, educators and students, doctors and patients, psychiatrists and perverts, social workers and parents turn in reinforcing spirals of pleasure.

Confession is a procedure of truth-production; it is also a procedure of individuation. The injunction to confess, issuing from multiple mechanisms of power, postulates lines of consequences to be tracked down, a clandestine causality of the sexual drive. Sexual conduct is sought out as the cause of bad behavior in children, phthisis in adults, apoplexy in the aged, nervous illness, the degeneration of the racial stock. The confessional imperative identifies a general and concealed sexual causality as the principle of individual significations, values, and tastes in the subject of attribution. In the end nothing will be more individual than our sexual tastes and our sexual penchants, and our discourse, our interests, our conducts, and our commitments, with which we figure as moments of the common discourse of a society and as supports of common projects and undertakings, are singularized inasmuch as they also refer to, and are interpretable as symptoms of, our sexual tastes and appetites.

Conspiratorial strategies of dismemberment

The sexual liberation movements of recent times have taken the form of a struggle of the representatives of sexuality to emancipate themselves from the law of alliance. Women assert their sexual identity and struggle to liberate themselves from the patriarchical law. Children and adolescents finance cults to youth folk heroes who sing the pleasures of premarital sexual gratification. Couples claim the right to birth control practices and the legitimacy of a couple that aborts its offspring. "Perverts" set up their own clubs, places of encounter and dens of pleasure, and fight the police, the courts, and public opinion for the protection of their combat zones.

The sexual liberation advanced is that of hystericized women, narcissistic adolescents, sterile couples, and proud perverts struggling to assert their identities, to valorize them by founding and protecting institutions, spaces, and organs of power and of knowledge for themselves. They take themselves to be repressed, subjugated to the laws of the family, the laws of the sovereign patriarch, reinforced by a patriarchical state apparatus. But in reality, today the enclosed spaces of disciplining, the panoptical surveillance, and the individuation by disciplinary examinations and norms transmogrify our bodies as the old laws of alliance no longer do. The school system is far more effective than the family in its capillary application of power; it succeeds in making public accountants and junior executives – whose body parts are distributed in cellularized space, whose body movements are meticulously regulated by timetables, whose bodies are permeable to the impersonal surveillance of corporate bodies, and whose operations are responsive to the signals of programs – of those that the family apparatus proved impotent to transform into responsible fathers, faithful wives, or respectful children. The army and the transnational corporation are far more effective mechanisms to render bodies compliant and effica-cious at a time when the family demonstrates its impotence to make women mothers, adolescents self-controlled, couples fertile and home-oriented, and perverts straight.

These individuated figures of sexuality are not natural species which a monolithic culture represses and a politico-economic authority oppresses. It is the medicalization of the body of the woman and the elevation of the figure of the doctor into the authority, power, and wealth he manipulates today that has made the woman know herself as a sexually saturated substance. The incarcera-tion of infancy in the power systems of pedagogy has constituted the child's body as vulnerable and an object of power operations by reason of a narcissist and onanist sensuality diffused throughout it. The network of social-work programs, fiscal systems, and population management has made the heterosexual couple into responsible or delinquent biopolitical agents. The sado-masochist, pederast, gerontophile, homosexual, fetishist, etc. are made by the psychiatrists and by their accomplices – the pastors, the pedagogues, the police – just as the delinquent is produced by the penitentiary archipelago and pursues a career within it which feeds its knowledge and serves its power. The psychiatrists, along with the priests, the pedagogues, the police, the advertisers, and the stockholders constitute, produce, and regulate the pervert, and organize and augment his forces for the production of their power and their riches, as well as of their forms of cognition and their pleasures.

The sexual revolution is proclaimed in the name of "sex." What is this new concept now taken to be fundamental, the source, the cause, and the secret, the generating source of each one's nature and the principle of his or her intellig-ibility? It is, Foucault says, an artificial compound of anatomical elements, biological functions, behaviors, sensations, and pleasures set up as a causal principle.[26] It is set up as the formula that gives us access to an understanding of our identity, our behavior, the totality of our bodies. In reality this "sex" is a construct formed in the practice and the discourse that sexualizes bodies – as hystericized mother, masturbating child, Malthusian couple, and pervert; it is reified as the causal and intelligible principle of which hysteria, onanism, coitus interruptus, and fetishism are taken to be the symptoms.

Will these personages – the hystericized woman, the narcissist child, the Malthusian couple, and the pervert – succeed in emancipating themselves from the codes and power mechanisms of the patriarchical family? Will they emerge as the dominant forms in which we are subjects of sexuality and subjected to sexuality? Will they in turn be subjected to the multiplying mechanisms of discipline, and the global strategies of biopolitics?

Foucault does invoke a possible counter-strategy, in the name of bodies and pleasures and knowledges, in their multiplicity and in their disparate possibilities of resistance. "Mastery and awareness of one's own body can be acquired only through the effect of an investment of power in the body: gymnastics, exercises, muscle-building, nudism, glorification of the body beautiful." Insistent, persistent, meticulous work of power on bodies leads to desiring one's own body. "But once power produces this effect, there inevitably emerge the responding claims and affirmations, those of one's own body against power, of health against the economic system, of pleasure against the moral norms of sexuality, marriage, decency. Suddenly, what had made power strong becomes used to attack it. Power, after investing itself in the body, finds itself exposed to a counter-attack in that same body."[27]

In the first volume of *The History of Sexuality*, Foucault wrote of an *ars erotica*, like that which other civilizations — China, India, Persia — produced, a magisterial art and teaching of pleasures and of their powers. In different interviews during the last years of his life, he spoke of the artist-ideal — not only of the art of knowing how to multiply and intensify pleasures and powers, but also of an art that would make of those pleasures and powers an artwork. "What strikes me is the fact that in our society, art has become something which is related only to objects and not to individuals, or to life. That art is something which is specialized or which is done by experts who are artists. But couldn't everyone's life become a work of art? Why could the lamp or the house be an art object, but not our life?"[28] An *ars erotica*, then, which would teach, not only skills in obtaining pleasures and acceding to their powers, but an aesthetics of bodies and of pleasures and of their powers.

What could such an art be, in an age of biopolitical administration? Can an *ars erotica* be an epic or heroic art? Would it be but a minor art — flower arranging of tropical orchids, after the swords have been melted into the transistor circuitry that is programming the final epidemic and the unending nuclear winter? Where is there the master that could tell?

Notes

1   Gilles Deleuze, "Ecrivain non: un nouveau cartographe," *Critique*, 369 (décembre 1975): pp. 1207–1227. Gilles Deleuze: *Foucault* (Paris: Editions de Minuit, 1986).
2   Ernst Kantorowicz, *The King's Two Bodies* (Princeton: Princeton University Press, 1957).
3   Not all crimes come under the royal order: guilds, chartered cities, feudal lords, town councils, and the Church all had spheres of jurisdiction.
4   Michel Foucault, *Discipline and Punish*, trans. Alan Sheridan (New York: Vintage, 1979), pp. 40–47.
5   Ibid., pp. 160–61.
6   Ibid., p. 138.
7   Ibid., p. 199.

8   The value of a student, as measured by examinations, identifies him by the percentile of other students who have performed a set of exercises established as normal for that group. His individuality is neither that of an individual essence nor that of the index of a transcendent referent. He is identified neither by a singular sensibility and individual genius, an autonomous mind, nor by identifying the transcendent figure of the sage or the intellectual in him.

Similarly, compare the soldier with the knight or the guerrilla, the worker with the craftsman, the student with the apprentice, the sufferer with the patient, the one marked with a singular destiny – zealot, shaman, or possessed – with the mentally ill, the entertainer with the visionary, etc. See John Berger, *Pig Earth* (New York: Pantheon, 1979), pp. 195–213.

9   The published reports on the Rasphuis of Amsterdam, the Maison de force at Ghent, and the Walnut Street Prison were the models used throughout a Europe that, twenty years after the Constituent Assembly adopted a penal code elaborated by the theorists of penology, would be covered with prisons.

10   Report by G. de Rouchefoucauld during the parliamentary debate on the penal code, 1831. Foucault, *Discipline and Punish*, p. 265.

11   Norman Mailer, introduction to Jack Abbott, *In the Belly of the Beast* (New York: Random House, 1982), pp. xii-xiv.

12   Ibid., p. xii.

13   See the social pact with drug users in Holland; drug addiction has been decriminalized; free needles and methadone treatment are supplied.

14   Proposals are made to shut down immigration and deport illegal aliens, perceived as an undisciplined sector responsible for most crimes.

15   "If you can conceive of a society (it is very difficult these days) that is more concerned with the creative potential of violent young men than with the threat they pose to the suburbs, then a few solutions for future prisons may be there. Somewhere between the French Foreign Legion and some prodigious extension of Outward Bound may lie the answer, at least for all those juvenile delinquents who are drawn to crime as a positive experience." Norman Mailer, *In the Belly of the Beast*, p. xii.

16   In the United States capital punishment is being reintroduced in more and more states and for more and more offenses. Capital punishment has now been decreed for juveniles and the mentally retarded.

17   "Half Irish, half Chinese, Jack Abbott was born January 21, 1944, in Oscoda, Michigan. He spent his childhood in foster homes throughout the Midwest. At the age of twelve he was committed to a juvenile penal institution – the Utah State Industrial School for Boys – for 'failure to adjust to foster homes,' and was released five years later. At eighteen he was convicted of 'issuing a check against insufficient funds,' and was incarcerated in the Utah State Penitentiary on a sentence of up to five years. By the age of twenty-nine Abbott had killed an inmate and wounded another in a fight behind bars, had escaped from maximum security, had committed bank robbery as a fugitive, and had served time in such federal penitentiaries as Leavenworth, Atlanta, and Marion. Since the age of twelve Jack Abbott has been free a total of only nine and a half months. He has served a total of more

than fourteen years in solitary confinement." (Biographical notice on the jacket of the book of Jack Abbott, *In the Belly of the Beast*.)

18 And with delinquents themselves. Prisons, whose entrances lie beyond the corridors of detectives with the instincts of hunters, campaigning prosecuting attorneys, politically ambitious judges, sadistic and cowardly guards, are hardly places where impartial and dispassionate justice is inculcated. Prison populations divide into the "normal" – who accept all the structures of policed and mercantile society and judge themselves framed, betrayed, or stupid – and the "creeps" – sexual offenders, immigrant minorities, and the mentally retarded or disturbed, whose punishment decreed by the courts is daily supplemented by torments inflicted by the "normal" prisoners. Four convicts a day are executed in the penitentiaries of the United States, with the complicity of the guards, who often lock in the same cell prisoners they expect will batter or kill one another. Prisoners do not leave prison revolutionaries for a new social order, but bandits.

19 Michel Foucault, *History of Sexuality*, trans. Robert Hurley (New York: Vintage, 1990), vol. I., pp. 103–5.

20 Demetrius Zambaco, "Onanism and Nervous Disorders in Two Little Girls," *Semiotext(e)*, IV, no. 1 (1981), *Polysexuality*, pp. 22–36.

21 Foucault, *The History of Sexuality*, vol. I, pp. 38ff.

22 Pierre Klossowski, *Sade My Neighbor*, trans. Alphonso Lingis (Evanston: Northwestern University Press, 1991), pp. 28–33.

23 Foucault, *The History of Sexuality*, vol. I, pp. 108–9.

24 Ibid., pp. 124, 147.

25 Ibid., pp. 18ff.

26 Ibid., p. 154.

27 Michel Foucault, *Power/Knowledge: Selected Interviews and Other Writings*, trans. Colin Gordon (New York: Pantheon Books, 1980), p. 56.

28 Hubert Dreyfus and Paul Rabinow, *Michel Foucault: Beyond Structuralism and Hermeneutics* (University of Chicago Press, 1982), p. 236.

13

FOUCAULT AND THE PARADOX OF BODILY INSCRIPTIONS

Judith Butler

The position that the body is constructed is one that is surely, if not immediately, associated with Michel Foucault. The body is a site where regimes of discourse and power inscribe themselves, a nodal point or nexus for relations of juridical and productive power. And, yet, to speak in this way invariably suggests that there is a body that is in some sense there, pregiven, existentially available to become the site of its own ostensible construction. What is it that circumscribes this site called "the body"? How is this delimitation made, and who makes it? Which body qualifies as "the" body? What establishes the "the," the existential status of this body? Does the existent body in its anonymous universality have a gender, an unspoken one? What shape does this body have, and how is it to be known? Where did "the body" come from? To claim that "the body is culturally constructed" is, on the one hand, to assert that whatever meanings or attributes the body acquires are in fact culturally constituted and variable. But note that the very construction of the sentence confounds the meaning of "construction" itself. Is "the body" ontologically distinct from the process of construction it undergoes? If that is the case, then it would appear that "the body," which is the object or surface on which construction occurs, is itself prior to construction. In other words, "the body" would not be constructed, strictly considered, but would be the occasion, the site, or the condition of a process of construction only externally related to the body that is its object. In effect, the statement, "the body is constructed," refuses to allow that the indefinite article is itself a construction that calls for a genealogical account. But perhaps the referential claim of the statement is rhetorical, that is, treating the body named within the sentence not as an object that receives a construction, i.e., as a substantive thing that might take on a contingent attribution.

Judith Butler, "Foucault and the Paradox of Bodily Inscriptions," *The Journal of Philosophy*, 86 (November, 1989), 601–7

Perhaps instead it is necessary to read the statement in a self-referential way, that is, as asserting that any reference to "the" body in its indefiniteness is of necessity a construction, one that is open to a genealogical critique.

Within a number of texts, Foucault clearly questions whether there is a "materiality" to bodies which is in any sense separable from the ideational or cultural meanings that constitute bodies within specific social fields. In *The History of Sexuality: Vol. I*,[1] he claims that the body is a site of culturally contested meanings, and that "sex," what we might be tempted to rank among the most factic aspects of bodily life, is itself an "imaginary point," the consequence of a materiality fully "invested" with ideas. In "Nietzsche, Genealogy, History,"[2] Foucault clearly writes. ". . . nothing in man (sic) – not even his body – is sufficiently stable to serve as the basis for self-recognition or for understanding other men (sic)" (*ibid.*, p. 153). Foucault's efforts to describe the mechanism by which bodies are constituted as cultural constructions, however, raises the question of whether there is in fact a body which is external to its construction, invariant in some of its structures, and which, in fact, represents a dynamic locus of resistance to culture per se.

This last claim is no doubt surprising for anyone who has read Foucault's critique of the twin evils of liberationist sexuality and psychoanalytic theory in *The History of Sexuality: vol. I*. In that text Foucault claimed quite clearly that there could be no body before the law, no sexuality freed from relations of power. If the body in its indefinite generality, however, proves to be a point of dynamic resistance to culture per se, then this body is not culturally constructed, but is, in fact, the inevitable limit and failure of cultural construction. I shall argue in the following that, whereas Foucault wants to argue – and does claim – that bodies are constituted within the specific nexus of culture or discourse/power regimes, and that there is no materiality or ontological independence of the body outside of any one of those specific regimes, his theory nevertheless relies on a notion of genealogy, appropriated from Nietzsche, which conceives the body as a surface and a set of subterranean "forces" that are, indeed, repressed and transmuted by a mechanism of cultural construction external to that body. Further, this mechanism of cultural construction is understood as "history," and the specific operation of "history" is understood, and understood problematically, as inscription. Indeed, I shall try to show that, for Foucault, not unlike for Kafka in *The Penal Colony*, the cultural construction of the body is effected through the figuration of "history" as a writing instrument that produces cultural significations – language – through the disfiguration and distortion of the body, where the body is figured as a ready surface or blank page available for inscription, awaiting the "imprint" (*ibid.*, 148) of history itself. Although Foucault appears to argue that the body does not exist outside the terms of its cultural inscription, it seems that the very mechanism of "inscription" implies a power that is necessarily external to the body itself. The critical question that emerges from these considerations is whether the understanding of the process of cultural construction on the model of "inscription" – a logocentric move if ever there was one – entails that the "constructed" or "inscribed" body have an ontological status apart from that inscription, precisely the claim that Foucault wants to refute.

Within "Nietzsche, Genealogy, History," Foucault describes the body through a series of metaphors and figures, yet predominantly as a "surface," a set of multidirectional "forces," and as the scene or site of a cultural inscription. He writes: "the body is the inscribed surface of events" (*ibid*.). The task of genealogy, he claims, is "to expose a body totally imprinted by history" (*ibid*.). His sentence continues, however, by referring to the goal of "history" as the "destruction of the body" (*ibid*.). This remark paradoxically recalls Freud's description of "civilization," that juridical structure of power exercised through the repression and sublimation of primary drives that Foucault seeks to criticize in *The History of Sexuality: vol. I.* Forces and impulses with multiple directionalities are precisely what "history" both destroys and preserves through the *Entstehung* (historical emergence) of inscription. As "a volume in perpetual disintegration," Foucault writes, the body is always under seige, suffering destruction by the very terms of history. History is understood as that creator of values and meanings, that signifying practice, which requires the subjection of the body in order to produce the speaking subject and its significations. Described through the language of surface and force, this is a body weakened through what Foucault in a radically ahistorical way terms the "single drama" of history, a drama or a structure of repressive signification which requires a subjugation and inscription of the body for the creation of new values (*ibid*., p. 150). This is not the modus vivendi of one kind of history rather than another, but rather "history" (*ibid*., p. 148) in its essential repressive/generative gesture.

Although Foucault writes that the body is not stable and cannot serve as a common identity among individuals cross-culturally or transhistorically, he nevertheless points to the constancy of cultural inscription as a "single drama," suggesting that this drama of historical "inscription" enjoys the very universality denied to the body per se. If the creation of values, that signifying practice of history, requires the destruction of the body, much as the instrument of torture in Kafka's *Penal Colony* destroys the body on which it writes, then there must be a body prior to that inscription, stable and self-identical, subject to and capable of that sacrificial destruction. In a sense, for Foucault, as for Nietzsche, cultural values emerge as the result of an inscription *on* the body, where the body is understood as a medium, indeed, a blank page, an unusual one, to be sure, for it appears to bleed and suffer under the pressure of a writing instrument. In order for this inscription to signify, however, the body-as-medium must itself be destroyed and transvaluated into a sublimated (to use Freud's language) or "transvaluated" (to use Nietzsche's language) domain of values.

Implicit to this description of the creation of cultural values is the notion of history as a relentless writing instrument, and the body as the medium that must be destroyed and transfigured in order for "culture" to emerge.

By maintaining a body prior to its cultural inscription, Foucault appears to assume a materiality to the body prior to its signification and form. In separate contexts, Foucault appears paradoxically to criticize both Freud and Nietzsche for assuming a prediscursive ontology of the body and its drives. In *The History of Sexuality: vol. I*, he argues that desires that psychoanalysis claims are repressed are, in fact, produced by psychoanalysis as a juridical practice. Indeed, "repressed desire," he appears to suggest, is a consequence of psychoanalytic discourse, a delectable discursive production, a contemporary fabrication and organization of sexuality. Quite directly, in fact, he argues against the conceptualization of a juridical and repressive law that presumes that there is a "rebellious energy" (p. 81) that temporally and ontologically precedes repression. The effect of his genealogical critique of the repressive hypothesis is to conceive the discursive figuration of drives and/or desires as simultaneous with or consequent to the law, rather than its antecedent presupposition. Interestingly, Foucault provides, in *Discipline and Punish: The Birth of the Prison*,[3] an implicit yet parallel critique of Nietzsche's presumption of a prediscursive instinctuality. In *The Genealogy of Morals* (section II), Nietzsche argues that the multiplicitous and life-affirming instincts are negated and internalized through the prohibitive effects of slave-morality. Foucault, however, challenges the language of internalization and the distinction between inner psychic and external social space which that language implies.

Foucault objected to what he understood to be the psychoanalytic belief in the "inner" truth of sex in *The History of Sexuality: vol. I*. In *Discipline and Punish*, he similarly refuses the doctrine of internalization in his account of the subjection and subjectivation of criminals. The prohibitive law is not taken into the body, internalized or incorporated, but rather is written *on* the body, the structuring principle of its very shape, style, and exterior signification. Consider the generative play of surface significations and the refusal to engage a concept of interior psychic space in the following quotation: "the body is . . . directly involved in a political field: power-relations have an immediate hold on it; they invest it, mark it, train it, torture it, force it to carry out tasks, to perform ceremonies, to emit signs" (*ibid.*, p. 25).

In a sense, *Discipline and Punish* can be read as Foucault's effort to reconceive Nietzsche's doctrine of internalization as a language of inscription. In the context of prisoners, Foucault writes, the strategy has not been to enforce a repression of their criminal impulse, but to compel their bodies to signify the prohibitive law as their manifest essence, style, and necessity. That law is not literally internalized, but incorporated *on* bodies; there the law is manifest as a sign of the essence of their selves, the meaning of their soul, their conscience, the law of their desire. In effect, the law is fully dissimulated into the body as such; it is the principle that confers intelligibility on that body, the sign by which it is socially known. The juridical law no longer appears external to the bodies it subjects and subjectivates. "It would be wrong," Foucault writes, "to say that the soul is an illusion, or an ideological effect. On the contrary, it exists, it has a reality, it is produced permanently *around, on, within,* the body by the functioning of a power that is exercised on those that are punished . . ." (*ibid.,* p. 29; my italics). The figure of the interior soul understood as "within" the body is produced through its inscription *on* the body; indeed, the soul is inscribed on the surface, a signification that produces on the flesh the illusion of an ineffable depth. The soul as a structuring invisibility is produced in and by signs that are visible and the corporeal. Indeed, the soul requires the body for its signification, and requires also that the body signify its own limit and depth through corporeal means. Furthermore, the body must signify in a way that conceals the very fact of that signifying, indeed that makes that signifying practice appear only as its reified "effect," that is, as the ontological necessity of a defining and immaterial internality and depth.

The effect of the soul as a structuring inner space is produced through the signification of a body as a vital and sacred enclosure. The soul is precisely what the body lacks; hence, the body presents itself as a signifying lack. That lack which *is* the body signifies the soul as that which cannot show. In this sense, then, the soul is a surface signification that contests and displaces the inner/outer distinction itself, a figure of interior psychic space inscribed *on* the body as a social signification that perpetually conceals itself as such. In Foucault's terms, the soul is not imprisoned by or within the body but, inversely, "the soul is the prison of the body" (*ibid.,* p. 30).

The critical power of Foucault's analysis assumes that only under certain conditions of power and discourse do bodies get signified and regulated in the ways that he describes in *Discipline and Punish* and in *The History of Sexuality: vol. I.* In "Nietzsche, Genealogy, History," however, Foucault "confesses" his metaphysical commitments in such a way that the critical power of his genealogical critique is severely undermined. In that essay, he makes clear that "subjection," though historically specific in its modalities, is also the essential and transhistorical precondition of "history" writ large; indeed, he makes clear that this significatory or generative subjection is the essential gesture of a singular history, its one infinitely repeatable "drama."

In the introduction to *The Order of Things,*[4] Foucault rather defensively suggests that, although structuralism exists as the reigning philosophical ethos of his time, and his own work invariably engages the philosophical vocabulary of structuralism, he nevertheless does not feel constrained by its terms. Although I would not want to reduce Foucault's work to a structuralist position, I would argue that the notion of signification as a universal cultural law that produces meanings through the subjection and disfiguration of the materiality of bodies seems fully derivable from Claude Lévi-Strauss's analysis of the structure of kinship exchange. For Lévi-Strauss, the incest taboo institutes identities along the axis of sexual difference and, hence, represses bodies in order to produce highly structured kinship relations. The materiality of "bodies" for Lévi-Strauss constitutes "nature" or "the raw," whereas the prohibitions that repress sexuality and create social organization are "culture" and the "cooked." Whereas Foucault appears to criticize precisely those binary oppositions encoded by structuralism as the universal tensions of anthropology, he appears to reengage those oppositions in his own descriptions of how historical meanings come into being. That history is "inscribed" or "imprinted" onto a body that is not history suggests not only that the body constitutes the material surface preconditional to history, but that the deregulation and subversion of given regimes of power are effected by the body's resistance against the workings of history itself. In other words, Foucault appears to have identified in a prediscursive and prehistorical "body" a source of resistance to history and to culture, where history and culture are finally and paradoxically conceived in juridical terms. That this is contrary to Foucault's stated program to formulate power in its generative as well as juridical modes seems clear. Yet his statements on "history" appear to undermine precisely the insight into the constructed status of the body which his studies on sexuality and criminality were supposed to establish.

Because the distinction between the historical act of inscription and the body as surface and resistance is presupposed in the task of genealogy as he defines it, the distinction itself is precluded as an object of genealogical investigation. Indeed, the distinction not only operates as an uncritically accepted and implicitly formulated premise of his argument, but it ends up undermining the central point that his argument concerning the constructed status of bodies was supposed to prove. Occasionally, in his *The History of Sexuality: vol. I*, or in his brief introduction to the journals of Herculine Barbin, the nineteenth-century hermaphrodite, Foucault seeks recourse to a prediscursive multiplicity of bodily forces that break through the surface of the body to disrupt the regulating practices of cultural coherence imposed upon that body by a regulatory regime, understood as some vicissitude of "history." If the presumption of a source of potential precategorial disruption is refused, and if the very notion of the body as surface externally related to the act of inscription is subjected to a genealogical critique, would it be possible to give a Foucaultian account of the demarcation of bodies as such as a signifying practice? How would "the" body as cultural or discursive practice be described?

What is clear is that inscription would be neither an act initiated by a reified history nor the performative accomplishment of a master historian who produces history as he writes it. The culturally constructed body would be the result of a diffuse and active structuring of the social field with no magical or ontotheological origins, structuralist distinctions, or fictions of bodies, subversive or otherwise, ontologically intact before the law.

Notes

1   Robert Hurley, trans. (New York: Vintage, 1980).
2   In *Language, Counter-Memory, Practice: Selected Essays and Interviews by Michel Foucault*, Donald F. Bouchard, trans., Sherry Simon and Donald F. Bouchard, eds (Ithaca: Cornell, 1977).
3   Alan Sheridan, trans. (New York: Vintage, 1979).
4   New York: Random, 1971.

PART III

TOWARDS A SEMIOTICS OF THE GENDERED BODY

Julia Kristeva

Subject and Body

The phenomenological subject of enunciation

We must specify, first and foremost, what we mean by the *signifying process* vis-à-vis general theories of meaning, theories of language, and theories of the subject.

Despite their variations, all modern linguistic theories consider language a strictly "formal" object – one that involves syntax or mathematicization. Within this perspective, such theories generally accept the following notion of language. For Zellig Harris, language is defined by: (1) the arbitrary relation between signifier and signified, (2) the acceptance of the sign as a substitute for the extra-linguistic, (3) its discrete elements, and (4) its denumerable, or even finite, nature.[1] But with the development of Chomskyan generative grammar and the logico-semantic research that was articulated around and in response to it, problems arose that were generally believed to fall within the province of "semantics" or even "pragmatics," and raised the awkward question of the *extra-linguistic*. But language [*langage*] – modern linguistics' self-assigned object[2] – lacks a subject or tolerates one only as a *transcendental ego* (in Husserl's sense or in Benveniste's more specifically linguistic sense),[3] and defers any interrogation of its (always already dialectical because trans-linguistic) "externality."

Two trends in current linguistic research do attend to this "externality" in the belief that failure to elucidate it will hinder the development of linguistic theory itself. Although such a lacuna poses problems (which we will later specify) for "formal" linguistics, it has always been a particular problem for semiotics, which is concerned with specifying the functioning of signifying practices such as art, poetry, and myth that are irreducible to the "language" object.

From Julia Kristeva, *Revolutions in Poetic Language*, trans. by Margaret Waller (New York: Columbia University Press, 1984), pp. 21–30, 43–5, 167–70.

1. The first of these two trends addresses the question of the so-called "arbitrary" relation between signifier and signified by examining signifying systems in which this relation is presented as "motivated." It seeks the principle of this motivation in the Freudian notion of the unconscious insofar as the theories of drives [*pulsions*] and primary processes (displacement and condensation) can connect "empty signifiers" to psychosomatic functionings, or can at least link them in a sequence of metaphors and metonymies; though undecidable, such a sequence replaces "arbitrariness" with "articulation." The discourse of analysands, language "pathologies," and artistic, particularly poetic, systems are especially suited to such an exploration.[4] Formal linguistic relations are thus connected to an "externality" in the psychosomatic realm, which is ultimately reduced to a fragmented substance [*substance morcelée*] (the body divided into erogenous zones) and articulated by the developing ego's connections to the three points of the family triangle. Such a linguistic theory, clearly indebted to the positions of the psychoanalytic school of London and Melanie Klein in particular, restores to formal linguistic relations the dimensions (instinctual drives) and operations (displacement, condensation, vocalic and intonational differentiation) that formalistic theory excludes. Yet for want of a dialectical notion of the *signifying process* as a whole, in which significance puts the subject in process/on trial [*en procès*], such considerations, no matter how astute, fail to take into account the syntactico-semantic functioning of language. Although they rehabilitate the notion of the fragmented body – pre-Oedipal but always already invested with semiosis – these linguistic theories fail to articulate its transitional link to the post-Oedipal subject and his always symbolic and/or syntactic language. (We shall return to this point.)

2. The second trend, more recent and widespread, introduces within theory's own formalism a "layer" of *semiosis*, which had been strictly relegated to pragmatics and semantics. By positing a *subject of enunciation* (in the sense of Benveniste, Culioli, etc.), this theory places logical modal relations, relations of presupposition, and other relations between interlocutors within the speech act, in a very deep "deep structure." This *subject of enunciation*, which comes directly from Husserl and Benveniste (see n. 3), introduces, through categorial intuition, both *semantic fields* and *logical* – but also *intersubjective* – *relations*, which prove to be both intra- and trans-linguistic.[5]

To the extent it is assumed by a subject who "means" (*bedeuten*), language has "deep structures" that articulate *categories*. These categories are semantic (as in the semantic fields introduced by recent developments in generative grammar), logical (modality relations, etc.), and intercommunicational (those which Searle called "speech acts" seen as bestowers of meaning).[6] But they may also be related to historical linguistic changes, thereby joining diachrony with synchrony.[7] In this way, through the subject who "means," linguistics is opened up to all possible categories and thus to philosophy, which linguistics had thought it would be able to escape.

In a similar perspective, certain linguists, interested in explaining semantic constraints, distinguish between different types of *styles* depending on the speaking subject's position vis-à-vis the utterance. Even when such research thereby introduces stylistics into semantics, its aim is to study the workings of signification, taking into account the subject of enunciation, which always proves to be the phenomenological subject.[8] Some linguistic research goes even further: starting from the subject of enunciation/transcendental ego, and prompted by the opening of linguistics onto semantics and logic, it views signification as an ideological and therefore historical production.[9]

We shall not be able to discuss the various advantages and drawbacks of this second trend in modern linguistics except to say that it is still evolving, and that although its conclusions are only tentative, its epistemological bases lead us to the heart of the debate on phenomenology which we can only touch on here – and only insofar as the specific research we are presently undertaking allows.[10]

To summarize briefly what we shall elucidate later, the two trends just mentioned designate *two modalities* of what is, for us, the same signifying process. We shall call the first "*the semiotic*" and the second "*the symbolic.*" These two modalities are inseparable within the *signifying process* that constitutes language, and the dialectic between them determines the type of discourse (narrative, metalanguage, theory, poetry, etc.) involved; in other words, so-called "natural" language allows for different modes of articulation of the semiotic and the symbolic. On the other hand, there are nonverbal signifying systems that are constructed exclusively on the basis of the semiotic (music, for example). But, as we shall see, this exclusivity is relative, precisely because of the necessary dialectic between the two modalities of the signifying process, which is constitutive of the subject. Because the subject is always *both* semiotic *and* symbolic, no signifying system he produces can be either "exclusively" semiotic or "exclusively" symbolic, and is instead necessarily marked by an indebtedness to both.

The semiotic chora ordering the drives

We understand the term "semiotic" in its Greek sense: σημεῖον=distinctive mark, trace, index, precursory sign, proof, engraved or written sign, imprint, trace, figuration. This etymological reminder would be a mere archaeological embellishment (and an unconvincing one at that, since the term ultimately encompasses such disparate meanings), were it not for the fact that the preponderant etymological use of the word, the one that implies a *distinctiveness*, allows us to connect it to a precise modality in the signifying process. This modality is the one Freudian psychoanalysis points to in postulating not only the *facilitation* and the structuring *disposition* of drives, but also the so-called *primary processes* which displace and condense both energies and their inscription. Discrete quantities of energy move through the body of the subject who is not yet constituted as such and, in the course of his development, they are arranged according to the various constraints imposed on this body – always already involved in a semiotic process – by family and social structures. In this way the drives, which are "energy" charges as well as "psychical" marks, articulate what we call a *chora*: a nonexpressive totality formed by the drives and their stases in a motility that is as full of movement as it is regulated.

We borrow the term *chora*[11] from Plato's *Timaeus* to denote an essentially mobile and extremely provisional articulation constituted by movements and their ephemeral stases. We differentiate this uncertain and indeterminate *articulation* from a *disposition* that already depends on representation, lends itself to phenomenological, spatial intuition, and gives rise to a geometry. Although our theoretical description of the *chora* is itself part of the discourse of representation that offers it as evidence, the *chora*, as rupture and articulations (rhythm), precedes evidence, verisimilitude, spatiality, and temporality. Our discourse – all discourse – moves with and against the *chora* in the sense that it simultaneously depends upon and refuses it. Although the *chora* can be designated and regulated, it can never be definitively posited: as a result, one can situate the *chora* and, if necessary, lend it a topology, but one can never give it axiomatic form.[12]

The *chora* is not yet a position that represents something for someone (i.e., it is not a sign); nor is it a *position* that represents someone for another position (i.e., it is not yet a signifier either); it is, however, generated in order to attain to this signifying position. Neither model nor copy, the *chora* precedes and underlies figuration and thus specularization, and is analogous only to vocal or kinetic rhythm. We must restore this motility's gestural and vocal play (to mention only the aspect relevant to language) on the level of the socialized body in order to remove motility from ontology and amorphousness[13] where Plato confines it in an apparent attempt to conceal it from Democritean rhythm. The theory of the subject proposed by the theory of the unconscious will allow us to read in this rhythmic space, which has no thesis and no position, the process by which significance is constituted. Plato himself leads us to such a process when he calls this receptacle or *chora* nourishing and maternal,[14] not yet unified in an ordered whole because deity is absent from it. Though deprived of unity, identity, or deity, the *chora* is nevertheless subject to a regulating process [*réglementation*], which is different from that of symbolic law but nevertheless effectuates discontinuities by temporarily articulating them and then starting over, again and again.

The *chora* is a modality of significance in which the linguistic sign is not yet articulated as the absence of an object and as the distinction between real and symbolic. We emphasize the regulated aspect of the *chora*: its vocal and gestural organization is subject to what we shall call an objective *ordering* [*ordonnance-ment*], which is dictated by natural or socio-historical constraints such as the biological difference between the sexes or family structure. We may therefore posit that social organization, always already symbolic, imprints its constraint in a mediated form which organizes the *chora* not according to a *law* (a term we reserve for the symbolic) but through an *ordering*.[15] What is this mediation?

According to a number of psycholinguists, "concrete operations" precede the acquisition of language, and organize preverbal semiotic space according to logical categories, which are thereby shown to precede or transcend language. From their research we shall retain not the principle of an operational state[16] but that of a preverbal functional state that governs the connections between the body (in the process of constituting itself as a body proper), objects, and the protagonists of family structure.[17] But we shall distinguish this functioning from symbolic operations that depend on language as a sign system – whether the language [*langue*] is vocalized or gestural (as with deaf-mutes). The kinetic functional stage of the *semiotic* precedes the establishment of the sign; it is not, therefore, cognitive in the sense of being assumed by a knowing, already constituted subject. The genesis of the *functions*[18] organizing the semiotic process can be accurately elucidated only within a theory of the subject that does not reduce the subject to one of understanding, but instead opens up within the subject this other scene of pre-symbolic functions. The Kleinian theory expanding upon Freud's positions on the drives will momentarily serve as a guide.

Drives involve pre-Oedipal semiotic functions and energy discharges that connect and orient the body to the mother. We must emphasize that "drives" are always already ambiguous, simultaneously assimilating and destructive; this dualism, which has been represented as a tetrad[19] or as a double helix, as in the configuration of the DNA and RNA molecule,[20] makes the semiotized body a place of permanent scission. The oral and anal drives, both of which are oriented and structured around the mother's body,[21] dominate this sensorimotor organization. The mother's body is therefore what mediates the symbolic law organizing social relations and becomes the ordering principle of the semiotic *chora*,[22] which is on the path of destruction, aggressivity, and death. For although drives have been described as disunited or contradictory structures, simultaneously "positive" and "negative," this doubling is said to generate a dominant "destructive wave" that is drive's most characteristic trait: Freud notes that the most instinctual drive is the death drive.[23] In this way, the term "drive" denotes waves of attack against stases, which are themselves constituted by the repetition of these charges; together, charges and stases lead to no identity (not even that of the "body proper") that could be seen as a result of their functioning. This is to say that the semiotic *chora* is no more than the place where the subject is both generated and negated, the place where his unity succumbs before the process of charges and stases that produce him. We shall call this process of charges and stases a *negativity* to distinguish it from negation, which is the act of a judging subject (see below, part II).

Checked by the constraints of biological and social structures, the drive charge thus undergoes stases. Drive facilitation, temporarily arrested, marks *discontinuities* in what may be called the various material supports [*matériaux*] susceptible to semiotization: voice, gesture, colors. Phonic (later phonemic), kinetic, or chromatic units and differences are the marks of these stases in the drives. Connections or *functions* are thereby established between these discrete marks which are based on drives and articulated according to their resemblance or opposition, either by slippage or by condensation. Here we find the principles of metonymy and metaphor indissociable from the drive economy underlying them.

Although we recognize the vital role played by the processes of displacement and condensation in the organization of the semiotic, we must also add to these processes the relations (eventually representable as topological spaces) that connect the zones of the fragmented body to each other and also to "external" "objects" and "subjects," which are not yet constituted as such. This type of relation makes it possible to specify the *semiotic* as a psychosomatic modality of the signifying process; in other words, not a symbolic modality but one articulating (in the largest sense of the word) a continuum: the connections between the (glottal and anal) sphincters in (rhythmic and intonational) vocal modulations, or those between the sphincters and family protagonists, for example.

All these various processes and relations, anterior to sign and syntax, have just been identified from a genetic perspective as previous and necessary to the acquisition of language, but not identical to language. Theory can "situate" such processes and relations diachronically within the process of the constitution of the subject precisely because *they function synchronically within the signifying process of the subject himself*, i.e., the subject of *cogitatio*. Only in *dream* logic, however, have they attracted attention, and only in certain signifying practices, such as the *text*, do they dominate the signifying process.

It may be hypothesized that certain semiotic articulations are transmitted through the biological code or physiological "memory" and thus form the inborn bases of the symbolic function. Indeed, one branch of generative linguistics asserts the principle of innate language universals. As it will become apparent in what follows, however, the *symbolic* – and therefore syntax and all linguistic categories – is a social effect of the relation to the other, established through the objective constraints of biological (including sexual) differences and concrete, historical family structures. Genetic programmings are necessarily semiotic: they include the primary processes such as displacement and condensation, absorption and repulsion, rejection and stasis, all of which function as innate preconditions, "memorizable" by the species, for language acquisition.

Mallarmé calls attention to the semiotic rhythm within language when he speaks of "The Mystery in Literature" ["Le Mystère dans les lettres"]. Indifferent to language, enigmatic and feminine, this space underlying the written is rhythmic, unfettered, irreducible to its intelligible verbal translation; it is musical, anterior to judgment, but restrained by a single guarantee: syntax. As evidence, we could cite "The Mystery in Literature" in its entirety.[24] For now, however, we shall quote only those passages that ally the functioning of that "air or song beneath the text" with woman:

> And the instrument of Darkness, whom they have designated, will not set down a word from then on except to deny that she must have been the enigma; lest she settle matters with a wisk of her skirts: "I don't get it!"

> – They [the critics] play their parts disinterestedly or for a minor gain: leaving our Lady and Patroness exposed to show her dehiscence or lacuna, with respect to certain dreams, as though this were the standard to which everything is reduced.[25]

To these passages we add others that point to the "mysterious" functioning of literature as a rhythm made intelligible by syntax: "Following the instinct for rhythms that has chosen him, the poet does not deny seeing a lack of proportion between the means let loose and the result." "I know that there are those who would restrict Mystery to Music's domain; when writing aspires to it."[26]

> What pivot is there, I mean within these contrasts, for intelligibility? a guarantee is needed –
>   Syntax –
>   ...an extraordinary appropriation of structure, limpid, to the primitive lightning bolts of logic. A stammering, what the sentence seems, here repressed [...]

> The debate – whether necessary average clarity deviates in a detail – remains one for grammarians.[27]

Our positing of the semiotic is obviously inseparable from a theory of the subject that takes into account the Freudian positing of the unconscious. We view the subject in language as decentering the transcendental ego, cutting through it, and opening it up to a dialectic in which its syntactic and categorical understanding is merely the liminary moment of the process, which is itself always acted upon by the relation to the other dominated by the death drive and its productive reiteration of the "signifier." We will be attempting to formulate the distinction between *semiotic* and *symbolic* within this perspective, which was introduced by Lacanian analysis, but also within the constraints of a practice – the *text* – which is only of secondary interest to psychoanalysis....

The thetic: rupture and/or boundary

We shall distinguish the semiotic (drives and their articulations) from the realm of signification, which is always that of a proposition or judgment, in other words, a realm of *positions*. This positionality, which Husserlian phenomenology orchestrates through the concepts of *doxa, position,* and *thesis,* is structured as a break in the signifying process, establishing the *identification* of the subject and its object as preconditions of propositionality. We shall call this break, which produces the positing of signification, a *thetic* phase. All enunciation, whether of a word or of a sentence, is thetic. It requires an identification; in other words, the subject must separate from and through his image, from and through his objects. This image and objects must first be posited in a space that becomes symbolic because it connects the two separated positions, recording them or redistributing them in an open combinatorial system.

The child's first so-called holophrastic enunciations include gesture, the object, and vocal emission. Because they are perhaps not yet sentences (NP-VP), generative grammar is not readily equipped to account for them. Nevertheless, they are already thetic in the sense that they separate an object from the subject, and attribute to it a semiotic fragment, which thereby becomes a signifier. That this attribution is either metaphoric or metonymic ("woof-woof" says the dog, and all animals become "woof-woof") is logically secondary to the fact that it constitutes an *attribution*, which is to say, a positing of identity or difference, and that it represents the nucleus of judgment or proposition.

We shall say that the thetic phase of the signifying process is the "deepest structure" of the possibility of enunciation, in other words, of signification and the proposition. Husserl theologizes this deep logic of signification by making it a productive *origin* of the "free spontaneity" of the Ego:

> Its *free spontaneity and activity* consists in positing, positing on the strength of this or that, positing as an antecedent or a consequent, and so forth; it does not live within the theses as a passive indweller; the theses radiate from it as from a primary source of generation [*Erzeugungen*]. Every thesis begins with a *point of insertion* [*Einsatzpunkt*] with a point at which *the positing has its origin* [*Ursprungssetzung*]; so it is with the first thesis and with each further one in the synthetic nexus. This "inserting" even belongs to the thesis as such, as a remarkable modus of original actuality. It somewhat resembles the *fiat*, the point of insertion of will and action.[28]

In this sense, *there exists only one signification*, that of the thetic phase, which contains the object as well as the proposition, and the complicity between them.[29] There is no sign that is not thetic and every sign is already the germ of a "sentence," attributing a signifier to an object through a "copula" that will function as a signified.[30] Stoic semiology, which was the first to formulate the matrix of the sign, had already established *this complicity between sign and sentence*, making them proofs of each other.

Modern philosophy recognizes that the right to represent the founding *thesis* of signification (sign and/or proposition) devolves upon the transcendental ego. But only since Freud have we been able to raise the question not of the origin of this thesis but rather of the process of its production. To brand the thetic as the foundation of metaphysics is to risk serving as an antechamber for metaphysics – unless, that is, we specify the way the thetic is produced. In our view, the Freudian theory of the unconscious and its Lacanian development show, precisely, that thetic signification is a stage attained under certain precise conditions during the signifying process, and that it constitutes the subject without being reduced to his process precisely because it is the threshold of language. Such a standpoint constitutes neither a reduction of the subject to the transcendental ego, nor a denial [*dénégation*] of the thetic phase that establishes signification.

On the Meaning of Drives

The dichotomy and heteronomy of drives

The Freudian theory of drives may be viewed as a transition from the psychical to the somatic, as a bridge between the biological foundation of signifying functioning and its determination by the family and society. Alongside this *heteronomy*, Freud maintains the fundamental *dichotomy* of drives as contradictory forces (life drives/death drives, ego drives/sexual drives), which are opposed and in conflict. He thus makes drives the shattered and doubly differentiated site of conflict and rejection. What interests us is the materialist dialectic he thereby establishes, hence, the heteronomy of drives – not their dichotomy. Drives are material, but they are not solely biological since they both connect and differentiate the biological and symbolic within the dialectic of the signifying body invested in a practice. Neither inside nor outside, drives are neither the ideational interior of a subject of understanding, nor the exteriority of the Hegelian Force. Drives are, instead, the repeated scission of matter that generates significance, the place where an always absent subject is produced.

Freud's fundamental insight into the heterogeneity of drives reveals drive activity's signifying and signifiable conflictual materiality. In a moment that constitutes a *leap* and a *rupture* – *separation* and *absence* – the successive shocks of drive activity produce the signifying function. Post-Freudian theories,

From Julia Kristeva, *New Maladies of the Soul*, trans. by Ross Buberman (New York: Columbia University Press, 1995) pp. 27–35 however, generally seem to place much more emphasis on the neurobiological aspect of drives, particularly the division inherent in drive movement.

Constantin von Monakow and Raoul Mourgue propose the term *diaschisis* (from διασχίζω, meaning "I split, tear") to denote "a special kind of trauma, which usually but not necessarily arises suddenly and originates in a local lesion." [The extent of the "separation" corresponds to the severity of the trauma and literally] "extends along the fibers that originate in and around the focal point of the lesion." They call the splitting tendency of nerve tissue *horme* (from ὁρμή, meaning "impulse" or "impetus"): the *horme* is the "matrix of instincts, ... indeed, it was originally a property of living protoplasm." "For organisms that have a nervous system, we can define instinct as a latent propelling force stemming from the *horme*. The instinct synthesizes excitations within the protoplasm (introceptivity) with those acting from the outside (extroceptivity) to realize a process that will ensure, with adapted behavior, the vital interests of both the individual and the species."[31] In cases of schizophrenia, they write, the instincts are polarized: a unifying tendency (*klisis*) is overshadowed by a defense tendency (*ekklisis*) which is directed outside. This brings about a fragmentation of nervous energy (*diaspasis*), a "piecemeal" deconstruction of the nervous system that is reflected in changes in the verbal element itself, which is disturbed as if to deaden diaspasis and protect the organism from it. This biologism is provided with a teleology that is not radically different from Hans Driesch's vitalism.[32] It hastily erases the boundaries between the realms of biology and social practice, and encompasses them both within a notion of biological energy. The transcendental nature of this notion can be seen in this theory's presentation of religion as the supreme form of "syneidesis," i.e., "the mediating force of nature," a "regulating and compensatory principle."

Lipot Szondi also stresses the conflictual aspect of drives whose matrix proves to have four components (the result of the doubling of the two genes making up the heterozygote): "the source of all drives lies in the genes." "In Freud's words, 'a drive is the inherent impulsion of a living organism towards restoration of an earlier state.' Freud has, however, neglected to explain why the drives behave in this manner. Only the theory of genes can supply an adequate answer."[33] The amount of drive pressure (*Triebdrang*) depends on the extent of the contrast between the genes that condition the whole. Modern genetic theory has confirmed this doubling and its repetition and has made it more precise by positing the reversed selection of doubles in the constitution of new structures.[34] Yet this substantialism, removed from the field of social practice (such as it is taken into account by Freudian theory), confines the theory of drives to a mechanistic and transcendental arena, as seen in Szondi's crude and naive definitions of psychopathological types, and in the inability of contemporary authors to specify what they mean by their vague but constant reference to the impact of the "social factor" on psychosis.

It is nevertheless likely, as André Green reminds us, that "the genetic code functions as a copula between sexuality and the phenomenon of memory."[35] Similarly, processes germane to these genetic codes – notably the reproduction of nucleic acids patterned on the model of the double helix[36] – indicate the operation, which is always already doubled, shattered, and reversed (as in a film negative), of what will become a subjective and signifying "unity." The division, indeed the multiplication, of matter is thus shown as *one of the foundations* of the signifying function. This foundation will be repressed or reorganized by the constraints imposed by signifying social reality, but will nevertheless return, *projecting itself* onto the structured surface – disturbing and reorganizing it (as "poetry"), or piercing and annihilating it (in "madness").

This duality (both heterogeneity and the doubling of the drives) allows us to account for a heteronomous conflictual process; without it, we would be unable to situate psychotic experience or any kind of renewable practice. To preserve this duality is to obey a materialist methodological requirement that Freud always stressed:

> *Our views have from the very first been dualistic, and to-day they are even more definitely dualistic than before* – now that we describe the opposition as being, not between ego drives and sexual drives but between life drives and death drives. Jung's libido theory is on the contrary *monistic*; the fact that he has called his one instinctual force "libido" is bound to cause confusion, but need not affect us otherwise.[37]

But Freudian theory is more than a theory of dualism, it is a theory of *contradiction* and of *struggle*: "These speculations seek to solve the riddle of life by supposing that these two drives [the life drive and death drive] were struggling with each other from the very first."[38]

Genetic biological rejection suffuses the organic body with motility and imprints on it a "gesturality" that social needs and constraints will then structure. The Freudian *fort-da* reveals that the return of instinctual rejection is already kinetic and gestural and that it projects biological material rejection onto a rejection that constitutes a signifying space and/or a space of practice. It separates the object and constitutes the real and *absence* and, through absence, by means of repeated rejection, the unstable engram of the primary vocalic, gestural, and signifying stases. The instability and mobility of engrams can be seen during language acquisition, in the engendering of the holophrastic, fluctuating lexical system that grammar has yet to grasp or master. In the already constituted subject, the constant return of this mobility will make the linguistic texture [*tissu*] paragrammatic (see n. 85, part II, supra), indicating its "piecemeal dispersal" where the renewal of rejection looms up through the engram:

> Feelings are nothing,
> nor are ideas,
> everything lies in motility
> from which, like the rest, humanity has taken
> nothing but a ghost.[39]

Psychoanalysis and normalization

I am picturing a sprawling metropolis with glass and steel buildings that reach to the sky, reflect it, reflect each other, and reflect you – a city filled with people steeped in their own image who rush about with overdone make-up on and who are cloaked in gold, pearls, and fine leather, while in the next street over, heaps of filth abound and drugs accompany the sleep or the fury of the social outcasts.

This city could be New York; it could be any future metropolis, even your own.

What might one do in such a city? Nothing but buy and sell goods and images, which amounts to the same thing, since they both are dull, shallow symbols. Those who can or wish to preserve a lifestyle that downplays opulence as well as misery will need to create a space for an "inner zone" – a secret garden, an intimate quarter, or more simply and ambitiously, a psychic life.

Yet that is where the story gets complicated. The West has been crafting this inner life since the beginning of the Christian era, when Plotinus transformed a Janus-faced Narcissus into two hands joined in prayer. Inner life has been reinforced by the spiritual path and carnival of the Middle Ages, and it has been shaped by Montaigne's fragile ego, Diderot's passions, and the meditations of Hegel and Kant. It has since become a psychic drama, a psychodrama.

Plotinus has degenerated into . . . Dallas. Indeed, the residents of this steel city are not in want of inner drama – in fact, they are as anxious, depressed, neurotic, and psychotic as the Freudian unconscious would wish them to be. If we believe, however, that we can escape from the surface value of our actions, we fall into the trap of psychology. Therefore, psychoanalysis has some work ahead of it, since Freud's doctrine seeks precisely to free us from this suppressed space of psychological ill-being.

The city that I chose as an image of contemporary life encourages us to include *social history* as one of the elements of organization and permanency that constitute psychic life. Using the terminology of our industrial society, one could say that psychoanalysis turns money into time and joins painful affect with language – language that may be listless or indecipherable, but that is always directed toward other people. Such an extraordinary metamorphosis, which goes against the tide of the market economy as well as the neurosis that it patterns, may also shed light on psychosis. Two thousand years of inner experience have built this prison of the soul, a prison that offers psychoanalysis an innocent vulnerability in which it can pierce a hole that will serve to resound the polyphony of our motives.

Proust has accorded us the finest summary of what is becoming (or will soon become) the Freudian psyche: "Those who suffer feel closer to their soul."[40] Or perhaps:

> For even if we have the sensation of being always enveloped in, surrounded by our own soul, still it does not seem a fixed and immovable prison; rather do we seem to be borne away with it, and perpetually struggling to transcend it, to break out into the world, with a perpetual discouragement as we hear endlessly all around us that unvarying sound which is not an echo from without, but the resonance of a vibration from within.[41]

Here, Proust evokes the permanency of the psyche and offers a glimpse of its limits. Freud has provided us with a preliminary method for achieving this sort of listening, but we still need to elaborate our approach. Our empathy and familiarity with the malady of the soul will enable us to transcend the psyche – forever.

The psychic realm may be the place where somatic symptoms and delirious fantasies can be worked through and thus eliminated: as long as we avoid becoming trapped inside it, the psychic realm protects us. Yet we must transform it through *linguistic activity* into a form of sublimation or into an intellectual, interpretive, or transformational activity. At the same time, we must conceive of the "psychic realm" as a *speech act*, that is, neither an acting–out nor a psychological rumination within an imaginary crypt, but the link between this inevitable and necessary rumination and its potential for verbal expression.

For this reason, the current onslaught of psychological illness, which takes the form of "soap operas" that inevitably cater to the other side of the society of performance and stress, seems to call out to psychoanalysis. "Tell us the meaning of our inner turmoil, show us a way out of it." – such is the cry of psychological helplessness, of the *alter ego* of the society of the spectacle. As a result, psychoanalysis wagers to modify the prison of the soul that the West has made into a means of survival and protection, although this prison has recently been revealing our failings. This wager is therapeutic as well as ethical, and incidentally, political. Yet although we may seek the acceptance and even expansion of psychoanalysis, our wish is coming up against some substantial barriers.

I am not referring to the ever-present danger of transforming psychoanalysis into a normalization that would guide patients toward social success. Such a deterioration of psychoanalytic treatment, traditionally American, is widely known and denounced, and even if it remains a threat, resisting it was primarily a matter for the past that we still must keep in mind.

In my view, psychoanalysis will soon be confronted with two major issues that concern the problem of the organization and permanency of the psyche. The first issue pertains to its competition with the neurosciences. From now on, "take a pill or talk" may replace "to be or not to be." The second issue regards the challenge to which psychoanalysis is subject as a result of our desire to *remain in ignorance*, a desire that is in harmony with the apparent simplicity that pharmacology offers, and that also reflects the negative narcissism of modern man.[42]

Biology and language: Freudian drives and the imaginary

The analytic position could be briefly outlined as follows: an unconscious psychic life is governed by determinants and restrictions that can be described and modified through an interpretation of the transference relation.

Some of these determinants and restrictions are *biological* in nature: recent advances in neurobiology and pharmacology have had an impact on our *behavior* and have enabled us to modify certain *fragments* of psychic life. The connection between analytic treatment and these interventions is more topical than ever, and this link is attracting the attention of analysts – who consider each concrete situation to be a singular experience.

The "attack" of the neurosciences is not making psychoanalysis defunct, but it is encouraging us to reconsider the Freudian concept of the *drive*. The drive is a pivot between "soma" and "psyche," between biology and representation – the highest level of organization and permanency to which Freudian listening and theory can aspire – that is, to which analytic construction (or imagination) can aspire. For what we understand by biology is – drives and energy, if you wish, but always already a "carrier of meaning" and a "relation" to another person, even though this person may be yourself.

Owing to its dual nature (biological and energetic/semiotic), the drive is also a structure. Within the space between its source (an organ) and its aim (satisfaction), its strength or weakness governs the restrictions placed on each subject. These restrictions circumscribe relationships that are among the most stubborn, because they are the most archaic (onto- and phylogenetically speaking), and the most discordant in terms of linguistic expression. In addition, the ego and its object relation are shaped within this drive framework.

The structure of the subject bases itself upon the different positions of the ego with respect to the different modalities of the object, and we must underscore that egos as well as the types of objects formed within the space between drives and language are *diverse in nature*. Nevertheless, any Freudian analyst would know that these subjective structures are charged with both the fate of drives and their dual nature (one that stems from biology and *non*linguistic representation).

For example, the fantasy, which could be considered a result of the eruption of the drive into the dispassionate logic of judgment – a logic that consequently finds itself transformed into a hallucination or a fit of delirium, reminds us that drives (and by implication, affects) form not only a myth, but also an element of organization and permanency that incites changes in the activity of thinking (as well as of judging and speaking). We also need to analyze the intermingling of drives and language with respect to the dulling of affects, to the disavowal of the object, and to the lifeless speech that characterizes those who suffer from depression.

That depression denies the meaning of discourse – which is to escort eros to the object – implies that the aggressive (or death) drive prevents a separation between the ego and the object. In its place, the death drive ushers in a melancholic subject – a negative Narcissus, an absolute master not of an object, but of a deadly *Thing* that must never be lost.[43]

In short, if we take the "myth" of the drive seriously, we must realize that an *imaginary deployment* reconstructs the logic of the drive in order to free up the linguistic restrictions that ultimately govern our capacities as speaking beings. It does so to show that this element of organization and permanency (discourse) consists not only of myriad significations and logical implications or presuppositions, but also of an interruption of the ability to produce speech (which can be schizophrenic or depressive – the figures vary). This imaginary deployment thereby reveals itself as a privileged witness to the *meaning* of the drive that joins the *signification* of speech.

Once fascinated by linguistics, contemporary psychoanalysis has a growing interest in drives, an interest that stems from Freud's legacy as well as from the daunting impact of the neurosciences. As a result, contemporary psychoanalysis has been attempting to decode the drama of drives while going beyond the *signification of language* that conceals the *meaning of drives*.

Traces of the meaning of drives can be translinguistic. Let us take the example of the voice: vocal stresses and rhythms often harbor the secret eroticism of depressed people who have severed the bond between language and the other, but who have nevertheless buried their affects in the hidden code of their vocalizations – in which the analyst may discover a desire that is not as dead as it may seem.

This brings me to the elements of organization and permanency that are the immediate object of analytic interpretation, insofar as they stem from our relation with others and are manifested through language. In light of what I have said concerning the primacy of drive destiny, these restrictions on signification would appear to constitute a complex, *heterogeneous* structure that is formed from the first years of our lives, grows and develops alongside us, and ultimately determines our symbolic destiny.

As a result of the growth of linguistics and of the other "human sciences" during the 1960s, the notion of *structure* in psychoanalysis (for which we are primarily indebted to Jacques Lacan) has enabled us to surmise more accurately than ever the organization of this *symbolic destiny*, this "being of language" that governs psychic life. Freudian analysts will agree that a discourse or symptom with which someone entrusts us can be taken as a whole, whose parts can only acquire meaning through the relationship between speaking subjects and their addressee, notably their analyst.

What is more, Freudian analyses have already noted that while this network of signifying relations that characterize symptoms, discourses, transference, and subjects is a *theoretical construction*, it is nevertheless the only *reality* in which psychic life can be manifested and developed. *A fortiori*, it constitutes the sole reality that offers the analyst – to whom someone has made a direct request – the possibility of intervening and modifying it. This aspect of analysis brings up three pressing questions:

1 Can we reduce the fate of speaking beings to *language* and *speech*, or do other *systems of representation* have a bearing on their logical features and on the actual psychic level that encompasses meaning for the subject?
2 Which characteristics of *interpretive language* are able to echo the symbolic fate of subjects, and thus affect and modify their biological substratum?
3 If analytic treatment is capable of such modifications, how might we define its boundaries and its *ethics*?

• The growth of semiology, which has encouraged us to contemplate various signifying systems (the iconic code, the musical code, and so forth) that are irreducible to language (whether language is considered as a specific language or a discourse, a structure or a grammar, an utterance or an enunciation), has shattered "linguistic imperialism." In like manner, the return to Freud, and more specifically to his conception of *representation*, has acknowledged the diversity of psychic representatives: thing-presentation, word-presentation, drive representative, affect representation. This has resulted in a "multi-layered" model of psychic *signifiance*, one that incorporates heterogeneous *marks* and *signs*. Analysts must be aware of this polyphony if they wish to approach the discourse that is addressed to them from different linguistic and translinguistic levels (the voice, movement, and so forth) as well as to identify the levels that reveal the significance that discourse has for transference.

• In an ideal situation, interpretive silence would make these different structures of meaning, which shelter the subject's symptom, reverberate into his conscious. More directly and more frequently, however, analytic *interpretation* is what reveals the diverse linguistic and translinguistic expressions of ill-being and restores them to the subject. How does it do this? By giving a name to the familial determinants that have tainted sexual development with a given symptom or structure. What is more important, though, is that interpretation offers an *appropriate formulation* that is expressed in elliptical, metaphorical, or condensed terms, and has a bearing on both the analyst's affects and its own series of psychic representatives (of words, things, and drives).

A veritable poiesis comes into play here, one that includes the musical qualities of the voice as well as tropes and the rhetorical analysis of mental functioning. As the ultimate reality of transference and countertransference, this poiesis has an effect on conscious listening and exerts an influence on the patient's unconscious psychic representatives, which can be assumed to be closely related to the flux of the neurons that make up subcortical, "electrical," or "humoral" systems. Perhaps there is nothing that would form links between unconscious psychic representatives or separate them from the realm of neurobiology. Yet, while theoreticians and scientists are pondering the relationship between psychoanalysis and neurobiology, interpretive language is producing its own psychosomatic effects.

● If we take this to be true, we cannot help being struck by the violence of analytic interpretation. The mere fact that patients ask us to fulfill their request does not seem to justify such violence. Does their request not constitute an integral part of the symptom as well as the onset of its excess? Consequently, the ethics of psychoanalysis might base itself on two requirements that are characteristic of the Western rationalism from which it stems:

● On the one hand, there is a need to uphold a *single* meaning, a *single* truth that is valid and demonstrable in a given situation. This is the "normative" side of psychoanalysis. Indeed, the norm is dictated by the state of psychoanalytic theory and by any given analyst's position within it.

● On the other hand, there is a need to preserve respect (by way of freedom) for the patient's desire and jouissance, which are what determine his ability to accept our interpretation (since the structure of the patient emerges out of his particular resistance to our interpretation). At the same time, the validity of interpretation itself is challenged, for the analyst's jouissance is revealed, although it is clouded by the "truth" of his interpretive construction.

No other discourse in the history of Western rationalism has wagered to counterbalance truth and jouissance, authority and transgression. The ensuing equilibrium preserves the vitality of this discourse, a vitality that grows out of the immanence of death (the discourse of knowledge) and resurrection (the discourse of desire). As a result, psychoanalysis upsets the social contract, which is founded, according to Freud, on an act of murder. Analysts do not shy away from being dead fathers of knowledge, but they are also subjects of affect, desire, and jouissance. Consequently, they are distanced from schools and institutions and concentrate instead on restructuring other people's psyches.

Notes

1 See Zellig Harris, *Mathematical Structures of Language* (New York: Interscience Publishers, 1968). See also Maurice Gross and André Lentin, *Introduction to Formal Grammars*, M. Salkoff, tr. (Berlin: Springer-Verlag, 1970); M.-C. Barbault and J.-P. Desclés, *Transformations formelles et théories linguistiques*, Documents de linguistique quantitative, no. 11 (Paris: Dunod, 1972).

2 On this "object" see *Langages* (December 1971), vol. 24, and, for a didactic, popularized account, see Julia Kristeva, *Le Langage cet inconnu* (Paris: Seuil, 1981).

3 Edmund Husserl, in *Ideas: General Introduction to Pure Phenomenology*, W. R. Boyce Gibson, tr. (London: Allen & Unwin, 1969), posits this subject as a subject of intuition, sure of this universally valid unity [of consciousness], a unity that is provided in *categories* itself, since transcendence is precisely the immanence of this "Ego," which is an expansion of the Cartesian *cogito*. "We shall consider conscious experiences," Husserl writes, "*in the concrete fullness and entirety* with which they figure in their concrete context – the *stream of experience* – and to which they are closely attached through their own proper essence. It then becomes evident that every experience in the stream which our reflexion can lay hold on has *its own essence open to intuition*, a 'content' which can be considered in its *singularity in and for itself*. We shall be concerned to grasp this individual content of the *cogitatio* in its *pure* singularity, and to describe it in its general features, excluding everything which is not to be found in the *cogitatio* as it is in itself. We must likewise describe the *unity of consciousness* which is demanded *by the intrinsic nature of the cogitationes*, and so necessarily demanded that they could not be without this unity" (p. 116). From a similar perspective, Benveniste emphasizes language's dialogical character, as well as its role in Freud's discovery. Discussing the I/you polarity, he writes: "This polarity does not mean either equality or symmetry: 'ego' always has a position of transcendence with regard to *you*." In Benveniste, "Subjectivity in Language," *Problems in General Linguistics*, Miami Linguistics Series, no. 8, Mary Elizabeth Meek, tr. (Coral Gables, Fla.: University of Miami Press, 1971), p. 225. In Chomsky, the subject-bearer of syntactic synthesis is clearly shown to stem from the Cartesian *cogito*. See his *Cartesian Linguistics: A Chapter in the History of Rationalist Thought* (New York: Harper & Row, 1966). Despite the difference between this Cartesian-Chomskyan subject and the transcendental ego outlined by Benveniste and others in a more clearly phenomenological sense, both these notions of the act of understanding (or the linguistic act) rest on a common metaphysical foundation: consciousness as a synthesizing unity and the sole guarantee of Being. Moreover, several scholars – without renouncing the Cartesian principles that governed the first syntactic descriptions – have recently pointed out that Husserlian phenomenology is a more explicit and more rigorously detailed basis for such description than the Cartesian method. See Roman Jakobson, who recalls Husserl's role in the establishment of modern linguistics, "Linguistics in

Relation to Other Sciences," in *Selected Writings*, 2 vols. (The Hague: Mouton, 1971), 2:655–696; and S.-Y. Kuroda, "The Categorical and the Thetic Judgment: Evidence from Japanese Syntax," *Foundations of Language* (November 1972), 9(2): 153–185.

4   See the work of Ivan Fónagy, particularly "Bases pulsionnelles de la phonation," *Revue Française de Psychanalyse* (January 1970), 34(1): 101–136, and (July 1971), 35(4):543–591.

5   On the "subject of enunciation," see Tzvetan Todorov, spec. ed., *Langages* (March 1970), vol. 17. Formulated in linguistics by Benveniste ("The Correlations of Tense in the French Verb" and "Subjectivity in Language," in *Problems*, pp. 205–216 and 223–230), the notion is used by many linguists, notably Antoine Culioli, "A propos d'opérations intervenant dans le traitement formel des langues naturelles." *Mathématiques et Sciences Humaines* (Summer 1971), 9(34):7–15; and Oswald Ducrot, "Les Indéfinis et l'énonciation," *Langages* (March 1970), 5(17):91–111. Chomsky's "extended standard theory" makes use of categorial intuition but does not refer to the subject of enunciation, even though the latter has been implicit in his theory ever since *Cartesian Linguistics* (1966); see his *Studies on Semantics in Generative Grammar*, Janua Linguarum, series minor, no. 107 (The Hague: Mouton, 1972).

6   See John R. Searle, *Speech Acts: An Essay on the Philosophy of Language* (London: Cambridge University Press, 1969).

7   See Robert D. King, *Historical Linguistics and Generative Grammar* (Englewood Cliffs, NJ: Prentice-Hall, 1969); Paul Kiparsky, "Linguistic Universals and Linguistic Change," in *Universals of Linguistic Theory*, Emmon Bach and Robert T. Harms, eds. (New York: Holt, Rinehart and Winston, 1968), pp. 170–202; and Kiparsky, "How Abstract Is Phonology?" mimeograph reproduced by Indiana University Linguistics Club, October 1968.

8   S.-Y. Kuroda distinguishes between two styles, "reportive" and "non-reportive." "Reportive" includes first-person narratives as well as those in the second and third person in which the narrator is "effaced"; "non-reportive" involves an omniscient narrator or "multi-consciousness." This distinction explains certain anomalies in the distribution of the adjective and verb of sensation in Japanese. (Common usage requires that the adjective be used with the first person but it can also refer to the third person. When it does, this agrammaticality signals another "grammatical style": an omniscient narrator is speaking in the name of a character, or the utterance expresses a character's point of view.) No matter what its subject of enunciation, the utterance, Kuroda writes, is described as representing that subject's "*Erlebnis*" ("experience"), in the sense Husserl uses the term in *Ideas*. See Kuroda, "Where Epistemology, Style, and Grammar Meet," mimeographed, University of California, San Diego, 1971.

9   Even the categories of dialectical materialism introduced to designate a discourse's conditions of production as essential bestowers of its signification are based on a "subject-bearer" whose logical positing is no different from that found in Husserl (see above, n. 3). For example, Cl. Haroche, P. Henry, and Michel Pêcheux stress "the importance of linguistic studies on the relation between utterance and

enunciation, by which the 'speaking subject' situates himself with respect to the representations he *bears* – representations that are put together by means of the linguistically analyzable 'pre-constructed.'" They conclude that "it is undoubtedly on this point – together with that of the syntagmatization of the characteristic substitutions of a discursive formation – that the contribution of the theory of discourse to the study of ideological formation (and the theory of ideologies) can now be most fruitfully developed." "La Sémantique et la coupure saussurienne: Langue, langage, discours," *Langages* (December 1971), 24:106. This notion of the subject as always already there on the basis of a "pre-constructed" language (but how is it constructed? and what about the subject *who constructs* before *bearing* what has been constructed?) has even been preserved under a Freudian cover. As a case in point, Michel Tort questions the relation between psychoanalysis and historical materialism by placing a subject-bearer between "ideological agency" and "unconscious formations." He defines this subject-bearer as "the biological specificity of individuals (individuality as a biological concept), inasmuch as it is the material basis upon which individuals are called to function by social relations." "La Psychanalyse dans le matérialisme historique," *Nouvelle Revue de Psychanalyse* (Spring 1970), 1:154. But this theory provides only a hazy view of how this subject-bearer is produced through the unconscious and within the "ideological" signifier, and does not allow us to see this production's investment in ideological representations themselves. From this perspective, the only thing one can say about "arts" or "religions," for example, is that they are "relics." On language and history, see also Jean-Claude Chevalier, "Langage et histoire," *Langue Française* (September 1972), 15:3–17.

10   On the phenomenological bases of modern linguistics, see Kristeva, "Les Epistémologies de la linguistique," *Langages* (December 1971), 24:11; and especially: Jacques Derrida, "The Supplement of Copula: Philosophy Before Linguistics," Josué V. Harari, tr., *Textual Strategies*, Josué V. Harari, ed. (Ithaca, NY: Cornell University Press, 1979), pp. 82–120; *Of Grammatology*, Gayatri Chakravorty Spivak, tr. (Baltimore: Johns Hopkins University Press, 1976), pp. 27–73; and *Speech and Phenomena, and Other Essays on Husserl's Theory of Signs*, David B. Allison, introd. and tr. (Evanston, Ill.: Northwestern University Press, 1973).

11   The term "*chora*" has recently been criticized for its ontological essence by Jacques Derrida, *Positions*, Alan Bass, annotator and tr. (Chicago: University of Chicago Press, 1981), pp. 75 and 106, n. 39.

12   Plato emphasizes that the receptacle (ὑποδοχεῖον), which is also called space (χώρα) vis-à-vis reason, is necessary – but not divine since it is unstable, uncertain, ever changing and becoming; it is even unnameable, improbable, bastard: "Space, which is everlasting, not admitting destruction; providing a situation for all things that come into being, but itself apprehended without the senses by a sort of bastard reasoning, and hardly an object of belief. This, indeed, is that which we look upon as in a dream and say that anything that is must needs be in some place and occupy some room …" (*Timaeus*, Francis M. Cornford, tr., 52a–52b). Is the receptacle a "thing" or a mode of language? Plato's hesitation between the two gives the receptacle an even more uncertain status. It is one of the elements that antedate

not only the *universe* but also *names* and even *syllables*: "We speak ... positing them as original principles, elements (as it were, letters) of the universe; whereas one who has ever so little intelligence should not rank them in this analogy even so low as syllables" (*ibid.*, 48b). "It is hard to say, with respect to any one of these, which we ought to call really water rather than fire, or indeed which we should call by any given name rather than by all the names together or by each severally, so as to use language in a sound and trustworthy way. ... Since, then, in this way no one of these things ever makes its appearance as the *same* thing, which of them can we steadfastly affirm to be *this* – whatever it may be – and not something else, without blushing for ourselves? It cannot be done" (*ibid.*, 49b–d).

13   There is a fundamental ambiguity: on the one hand, the receptacle is mobile and even contradictory, without unity, separable and divisible: pre-syllable, pre-word. Yet, on the other hand, because this separability and divisibility antecede numbers and forms, the space or receptacle is called *amorphous*; thus its suggested rhythmicity will in a certain sense be erased, for how can one think an articulation of what is not yet singular but is nevertheless necessary? All we may say of it, then, to make it intelligible, is that it is amorphous but that it "is of such and such a quality," not even an index or something in particular ("this" or "that"). Once named, it immediately becomes a container that takes the place of infinitely repeatable separability. This amounts to saying that this repeated separability is "ontologized" the moment a *name* or a *word* replaces it, making it intelligible: "Are we talking idly whenever we say that there is such a thing as an intelligible Form of anything? Is this nothing more than a word?" (*ibid.*, 51c). Is the Platonic *chora* the "nominability" of rhythm (of repeated separation)?

Why then borrow an ontologized term in order to designate an articulation that antecedes positing? First, the Platonic term makes explicit an insurmountable problem for discourse: once it has been named, that functioning, even if it is pre-symbolic, is brought back into a symbolic position. All discourse can do is differentiate, by means of a "bastard reasoning," the receptacle from the motility, which, by contrast, is not posited as being "a *certain* something" ["une *telle*"]. Second, this motility is the precondition for symbolicity, heterogeneous to it, yet indispensable. Therefore what needs to be done is to try and differentiate, always through a "bastard reasoning," the specific arrangements of this motility, without seeing them as recipients of accidental singularities, or a *Being* always posited in itself, or a projection of the *One*. Moreover, Plato invites us to differentiate in this fashion when he describes this motility, while gathering it into the receiving membrane: "But because it was filled with powers that were neither alike nor evenly balanced, there was no equipoise in any region of it; but it was everywhere swayed unevenly and shaken by these things, and by its motion shook them in turn. And they, being thus moved, were perpetually being separated and carried in different directions; just as when things are shaken and winnowed by means of winnowing baskets and other instruments for cleaning corn ... it separated the most unlike kinds farthest apart from one another, and thrust the most alike closest together; whereby the different kinds came to have different regions, even before the ordered whole consisting of them came to be ... but were altogether in such a condition as we should expect for anything when deity is absent from it" (*ibid.*, 52d–53b). Indefinite "conjunctions" and "disjunctions" (functioning, devoid of Meaning), the *chora* is governed by a necessity that is not God's law.

14 The Platonic space or receptacle is a mother and wet nurse: "Indeed we may fittingly compare the Recipient to a mother, the model to a father, and the nature that arises between them to their offspring" (*ibid.*, 50d); "Now the wet nurse of Becoming was made watery and fiery, received the characters of earth and air, and was qualified by all the other affections that go with these …" Ibid., 52d; translation modified.

15 "Law," which derives etymologically from *lex*, necessarily implies the act of judgment whose role in safeguarding society was first developed by the Roman law courts. "Ordering," on the other hand, is closer to the series "rule," "norm" (from the Greek γνώμων meaning "discerning" [adj.], "carpenter's square" [noun]), etc., which implies a numerical or geometrical necessity. On normativity in linguistics, see Alain Rey, "Usages, jugements et prescriptions linquistiques," *Langue Française* (December 1972), 16:5. But the temporary ordering of the *chora* is not yet even a *rule*: the arsenal of geometry is posterior to the *chora*'s motility; it fixes the *chora* in place and reduces it.

16 Operations are, rather, an act of the subject of understanding. [Hans G. Furth, in *Piaget and Knowledge: Theoretical Foundations* (Englewood Cliffs, NJ: Prentice-Hall, 1969), offers the following definition of "concrete operations": "Characteristic of the first stage of operational intelligence. A concrete operation implies underlying general systems or 'groupings' such as classification, seriation, number. Its applicability is limited to objects considered as real (concrete)" (p. 260). – Trans.]

17 Piaget stresses that the roots of sensorimotor operations precede language and that the acquisition of thought is due to the symbolic function, which, for him, is a notion separate from that of language per se. See Jean Piaget, "Language and Symbolic Operations," in *Piaget and Knowledge*, pp. 121–130.

18 By "function" we mean a dependent variable determined each time the independent variables with which it is associated are determined. For our purposes, a function is what links stases within the process of semiotic facilitation.

19 Such a position has been formulated by Lipot Szondi, *Experimental Diagnostic of Drives*, Gertrude Aull, tr. (New York: Grune & Stratton, 1952).

20 See James D. Watson, *The Double Helix: A Personal Account of the Discovery of the Structure of DNA* (London: Weidenfeld & Nicolson, 1968).

21 Throughout her writings, Melanie Klein emphasizes the "pre-Oedipal" phase, i.e., a period of the subject's development that precedes the "discovery" of castration and the positing of the superego, which itself is subject to (paternal) Law. The processes she describes for this phase correspond, *but on a genetic level*, to what we call the semiotic, as opposed to the symbolic, which underlies and conditions the semiotic. Significantly, these pre-Oedipal processes are organized through projection onto the mother's body, for girls as well as for boys: "at this stage of development children of both sexes believe that it is the body of their mother which contains all that is desirable, especially their father's penis." *The Psychoanalysis of Children*, Alix Strachey, tr. (London: Hogarth Press, 1932), p. 269. Our

own view of this stage is as follows: Without "believing" or "desiring" any "object" whatsoever, the subject is in the process of constituting himself vis-à-vis a non-object. He is in the process of separating from this non-object so as to make that non-object "one" and posit himself as "other": the mother's body is the not-yet-one that the believing and desiring subject will imagine as a "receptacle."

22   As for what situates the mother in symbolic space, we find the phallus again (see Jacques Lacan, "La Relation d'objet et les structures freudiennes," *Bulletin de Psychologie*, April 1957, pp. 426–430), represented by the mother's father, i.e., the subject's maternal grandfather (see Marie-Claire Boons, "Le Meurtre du Père chez Freud," *L'Inconscient*, January – March 1968, 5:101–129).

23   Though disputed and inconsistent, the Freudian theory of drives is of interest here because of the predominance Freud gives to the death drive in both "living matter" and the "human being." The death drive is transversal to identity and tends to disperse "narcissisms" whose constitution ensures the link between structures and, by extension, life. But at the same time and conversely, narcissism and pleasure are only temporary positions from which the death drive blazes new paths [*se fraye de nouveaux passages*]. Narcissism and pleasure are therefore inveiglings and realizations of the death drive. The semiotic *chora*, converting drive discharges into stases, can be thought of both as a delaying of the death drive and as a possible realization of this drive, which tends to return to a homeostatic state. This hypothesis is consistent with the following remark: "at the beginning of mental life," writes Freud, "the struggle for pleasure was far more intense than later but not so unrestricted: it had to submit to frequent interruptions." *Beyond the Pleasure Principle*, in *The Standard Edition of the Works of Sigmund Freud*, James Strachey, ed. (London: Hogarth Press and the Institute of Psychoanalysis, 1953), 18:63.

24   Mallarmé, *Œuvres complètes* (Paris: Gallimard, 1945), pp. 382–387.

25   *Ibid.*, p. 383.

26   *Ibid.*, pp. 383 and 385.

27   *Ibid.*, pp. 385–386.

28   Husserl, *Ideas*, p. 342.

29   In *Ideas*, posited meaning is "the unity of meaning and thetic character." "The concept of proposition (*Satz*)," Husserl writes, "is certainly extended thereby in an exceptional way that may alienate sympathy, yet it remains within the limits of an important unity of essence. We must constantly bear in mind that for us the concepts of meaning (*Sinn*) and posited meaning (or position) (*Satz*) contain nothing of the nature of expression and conceptual meaning, but on the other hand include all explicit propositions and all propositional meanings" (*Ideas*, p. 369). Further on, the inseparability of posited meaning, meaning, and the object is even more clearly indicated: "According to our analyses these concepts indicate an abstract stratum belonging to the *full tissue of all noemata* [emphasis added]. To grasp this stratum in its all-enveloping generality, and thus to realize that it is represented in *all act-spheres*, has a wide bearing on our way of knowledge. Even in the plain and simple *intuitions* the concepts meaning (*Sinn*) and posited meaning (*Satz*)

which belong inseparably to the concept of object (*Gegenstand*) have their necessary application ... (pp. 369–370).

30   On the matrix of the sign as the structure of a logical proof, see Emile Bréhier, *La Théorie des incorporels dans l'ancien stoicisme* (Paris: J. Vrin, 1970).

31   Von Monakow and Mourgue, *Introduction biologique à l'étude de la neurologie et de la psychologie* (Paris: F. Alcan, 1928), pp. 87, 33, and 38.

32   Driesch, *The Science and Philosophy of the Organism*, 2 vols. (London: Adam and Charles Black, 1908).

33   Szondi, *Experimental Diagnostic of Drives*, Gertrude Aull, tr. (New York: Grune & Stratton, 1952), pp. 6 and 7.

34   Thus, certain modern psychiatric and biological theories of schizophrenia maintain that this is "basically caused by major gene differences which express themselves regularly in homozygotes (i.e., in a recessive manner) and occasionally in heterozygotes (i.e., in a dominant manner)." Jan A. Böök, "Genetical Aspects of Schizophrenic Psychoses," in *The Etiology of Schizophrenia*, Don D. Jackson, ed. (New York: Basic Books, 1960), p. 29.

35   André Green, "Répétition, différence, réplication," *Revue Française de Psychanalyse* (May 1970), 34:479.

36   See James D. Watson, *The Double Helix: A Personal Account of the Discovery of the Structure of DNA* (London: Weidenfeld & Nicolson, 1968).

37   "Beyond the Pleasure Principle," in *The Standard Edition of the Works of Sigmund Freud*, James Strachey, ed., 24 vols. (London: Hogarth Press and the Institute of Psychoanalysis, 1953), 18:53; emphasis added; translation modified.

38   *Ibid.*, p. 61; translation modified.

39   Antonin Artaud, "Notes pour une 'Lettre aux Balinais,'" *Tel Quel* (Summer 1971), 46:10.

40   Marcel Proust, "Les Plaisirs et les jours," *Jean Santeuil* (Paris: Bibliothèque de La Pléiade, 1971), p. 6.

41   Marcel Proust, *Swann's Way*, in *Remembrance of Things Past*, vol. I, C. K. Scott Moncrieff and Terence Kilmartin, trs. (New York: Random House, 1981), p. 93.

42   André Green, *Narcissisme de vie, narcissisme de mort* (Paris: Editions de Minuit, 1983).

43   Julia Kristeva, *Black Sun: Depression and Melancholia*, Léon S. Roudiez, tr. (New York: Columbia University Press, 1989).

15

THE FLESH BECOME WORD: THE BODY IN KRISTEVA'S THEORY

Kelly Oliver

One of Kristeva's most important contributions to contemporary theory is her attempt to bring the speaking body back into the discourses of the human sciences.[1] Her writing challenges theories that rely on unified, fixed, stagnant theories of subjectivity; she insists on semiotic negativity, which produces a dynamic subjectivity. Yet, she challenges theories that would reduce subjectivity to chaotic flux; she also insists on symbolic stasis and identity. Her writing stages the oscillation between what she calls the *semiotic* and *symbolic* elements in signification. In order to bring the body back into theories of language, she develops a science that she calls "semanalysis," which is a combination of semiotics, taken from Charles Pierce and Ferdinand de Saussure, and psychoanalysis, taken from Sigmund Freud, Jacques Lacan, and Melanie Klein.

Following Lacan, Kristeva maintains that subjectivity is formed in conjunction with language acquisition and use. All of Kristeva's writing has addressed the relationship between language and subjectivity. Kristeva is concerned with the places where self-identity is threatened, the limits of language. As a result, her work is focused between the two poles of language acquisition and psychotic babble. She is interested both in how the subject is constituted through language acquisition and how the subject is demolished with the psychotic breakdown of language. These limits of language point to the delicate balance between semiotic and symbolic, between affects and words. The motility of the subject and the subject's ability to change are the result of the interplay of semiotic drive force and symbolic stasis. Because of the relationship between language and subjectivity, the psychoanalyst can work backwards from language in order to diagnose the analysand's problems with self-image. Freud called psychoanalysis the "talking cure" because the analysand's articulation of his or her malaise is the fulcrum of clinical practice.

Kristeva attempts to bring the speaking body back into discourse by arguing both that the logic of language is already operating at the material level of bodily processes and that bodily drives make their way into language. She postulates that signifying practices are the result of material bodily processes. Drives make their way into language through the semiotic element of signification, which does not represent bodily drives but discharges them. In this way, all signification has material motivation. All signification discharges bodily drives. Drives move between *soma* and *psyche*, and the evidence of this movement is manifest in signification.

Kristeva takes up Freud's theory of drives as instinctual energies that operate between biology and culture. Drives have their source in organic tissue and aim at psychological satisfaction. Drives are heterogeneous; that is, there are several different drives that can conflict with each other. In *Revolution*, Kristeva describes drives as "material, but they are not solely biological since they both connect and differentiate the biological and symbolic within the dialectic of the signifying body invested in practice" (RPL 167). Nearly two decades later, Kristeva emphasizes the same dialectical relationship between the two spheres – biological and social – across which the drives operate. In *New Maladies of the Soul* (NM), she describes the drives as "a pivot between 'soma' and 'psyche', between biology and representation" (NM 30).[2] Drives can be reduced neither to the biological nor to the social; they operate in between these two realms and bring one realm into the other. Drives are energies or forces that move between the body and representation. This notion of drives challenges the traditional dualism between the biological and the social, the body and the mind. Kristeva's attempts to bring the body back to theory also challenge traditional notions of the body; for her, the body is more than material.[3]

By insisting that language expresses bodily drives through its semiotic element, Kristeva's articulation of the relationship between language and the body circumvents the traditional problems of representation. The tones and rhythms of language, the materiality of language, is bodily. Traditional theories which postulate that language represents bodily experience fall into an impossible situation by presupposing that the body and language are distinct, even opposites. Some traditional theories purport that language is an instrument that captures, mirrors, or copies bodily experience. The problem, then, becomes how to explain the connection between these two distinct realms of language, on the one hand, and material, on the other.[4]

Since traditional theories have not been able to explain adequately how language is related to the material world, some contemporary theorists have proposed that language does not refer to some extralinguistic material world; rather, language refers only to itself. Words have their meaning in relation to other words and not in relation to things in the world. We can discern the meaning of words by analyzing the structures within which words operate rather than examining the correspondence between words and things. Whereas Husserlian phenomenology describes words as windows onto the meaning constituted by the transcendental subject, structuralism describes words as elements operating within systems that constitute their meanings, and poststructuralism describes words as traces of the processes of difference and deferral that constitute the illusion of their stable meaning and determinant references, Kristeva describes the meaning of words as combinations of dynamic *semiotic* bodily drive force or affect and stable *symbolic* grammar.

Kristeva maintains that all signification is composed of these two elements, the symbolic and the semiotic. The symbolic element is what philosophers might think of as meaning proper. That is, the symbolic is the element of signification that sets up the structures by which symbols operate. The symbolic is the structure or grammar that governs the ways in which symbols can refer. The semiotic element, on the other hand, is the organization of drives in language. It is associated with rhythms and tones that are meaningful parts of language and yet do not represent or signify something. In *Revolution in Poetic Language* (1974), Kristeva maintains that rhythms and tones do not *represent* bodily drives; rather bodily drives are *discharged* through rhythms and tones. In *New Maladies of the Soul* (1993), she discusses different ways of representing that are not linguistic in a traditional sense. There, Kristeva says that the meaning of the semiotic element of language is "translinguistic" or "nonlinguistic" (NM 32–3; 31); she explains this by describing these semiotic elements as irreducible to language because they "turn toward language even though they are irreducible to its grammatical and logical structures" (NM 35). This is to say that they are irreducible to the *symbolic element* of language. The symbolic element of language is the domain of position and judgment. It is associated with the grammar or structure of language that enables it to signify something.

The symbolic element of language should not, however, be confused with Lacan's notion of the Symbolic. Lacan's notion of the Symbolic includes the entire realm of signification, while Kristeva's symbolic is one element of that realm. Whereas Lacan's Symbolic refers to signification in the broadest possible sense, including culture in general, Kristeva's symbolic is a technical term that delimits one element of language associated with syntax. In addition, Kristeva's semiotic element (*le sémiotique*) should not be confused with semiotics (*la sémiotique*), the science of signs.

The dialectical oscillation between the semiotic and the symbolic is what makes signification possible. Without the symbolic element of signification, we have only sounds or delirious babble. But without the semiotic element of signification, signification would be empty and we would not speak; for the semiotic provides the motivation for engaging in signifying processes. We have a bodily need to communicate. The symbolic provides the structure necessary to communicate. Both elements are essential to signification. And it is the tension between them that makes signification dynamic. The semiotic both motivates signification and threatens the symbolic element. The semiotic provides the movement or negativity and the symbolic provides the stasis or stability that keeps signification both dynamic and structured.

Kristeva compares her dialectic between semiotic and symbolic, or negativity and stasis, to Hegel's dialectic. For Kristeva, unlike Hegel, there is no synthesis of the two elements, no *Aufhebung* (sublation or cancellation with preservation). In *Revolution*, she maintains that negativity is not merely the operator of the dialectic, but the fourth term of the dialectic.[5] There, she replaces the Hegelian term "negativity" with the psychoanalytic term "rejection," which adds the connotation of a connection to bodily drive force. Because they indicate the drive force in excess of conscious thought, Kristeva prefers the terms *expenditure* or *rejection* "for the movement of material contradictions that generate the semiotic function" (RPL 119). For Kristeva, unlike Hegel, negativity is never canceled and the contradiction between the semiotic and symbolic is never overcome.

While the symbolic element gives signification its meaning in the strict sense of reference, the semiotic element gives signification meaning in a broader sense. That is, the semiotic element makes symbols matter; by discharging drive force in symbols, it makes them significant. Even though the semiotic challenges meaning in the strict sense, meaning in the terms of the symbolic, it gives symbols their meaning for our lives. Signification makes our lives meaningful, in both senses of meaning – signifying something and having significance – through its symbolic and semiotic elements. The interdependence of the symbolic and semiotic elements of signification guarantees a relationship between language and life, signification and experience; the interdependence between the symbolic and semiotic guarantees a relationship between body (*soma*) and soul (*psyche*).[6]

Kristeva maintains that any theory of language is also a theory of the subject. In "From One Identity to An Other," and *Revolution*, against Husserl's transcendental ego, Kristeva postulates her notion of a subject-in-process/on trial (*le sujet en procès*). Taking poetic language as emblematic, Kristeva argues that signification is "an undecidable process between sense and nonsense, between *language* and *rhythm*" (DL 135). The Husserlian transcendental ego cannot account for nonsense or rhythm within signification; it cannot account for the unconscious. But heterogeneity within signification points to heterogeneity within the speaking subject; if language is a dynamic process then the subject is a dynamic process. Like signification, the subject is always in a constant process of oscillation between instability and stability or negativity and stasis. The subject is continually being constituted within this oscillation between conscious and unconscious as an open system, subject to infinite analysis. The Cartesian *cogito* and Husserlian transcendental ego, then, are only moments in this process; they are neither chronologically nor logically primary.

Kristeva criticizes Husserlian phenomenology for taking one stage of the process of subjectivity and fetishizing it. The stasis and stability of the transcendental ego is but one element of subjectivity. In addition, for Kristeva meaning is not the unified product of a unified subject; rather, meaning is Other and as such makes the subject other to itself. Meaning is not constituted by a transcendental ego; meaning is constituted within a bio-social situation. Infants are born into a world where words already have meanings. Meaning is constituted through an embodied relation with another person. In this sense, meaning is Other; it is constituted in relation to an other and it is beyond any individual subjectivity. Insofar as meaning is constituted in relationships – relationships with others, relationships with signification, relationships with our own bodies and desires – it is fluid. And, the subject for whom there is meaning is also fluid and relational.

Although structuralism does not posit a Husserlian transcendental ego, it does silence the speaking body in favor of bloodless structures. Kristeva describes these theories as necrophiliac. She begins *Revolution in Poetic Language*:

> ... our philosophies of language, embodiments of the Idea, are nothing more than the thoughts of archivists, archaeologists, and necrophiliacs. Fascinated by the remains of a process which is partly discursive, they substitute this fetish for what actually produced it. ... These static thoughts, products of a leisurely cognition removed from historical turmoil, persist in seeking the truth of language by formalizing utterances that hang in midair, and the truth of the subject by listening to the narrative of a sleeping body – a body in repose, withdrawn from its socio-historical imbrication, removed from direct experience. (RPL 13)

Feminism has levied similar criticisms against ahistorical theories that ignore or silence the body, particularly women's bodies. Some feminists have been concerned to articulate a feminine sexuality and subjectivity. Luce Irigaray maintains that feminine sexuality and women's bodies have been defined as the other of masculine sexuality and men's bodies. So too, women are not subjects; rather, they are the others against which men become subjects. Many feminists argue that women's experiences have been silenced by cultures whose governments and intellectual lives have been controlled by men. Conceptions of subjectivity that once were thought to apply universally – the Cartesian *cogito*, the Kantian autonomous subject, the Husserlian transcendental ego – have been challenged as gender-specific conceptions of man.[7] Feminists have rejected ahistorical notions of subjectivity, which privilege characteristics historically associated with men and masculinity.

While poststructuralist theories generally do not propose formalizing utterances or subjectivity in terms of ahistorical structures or concepts, few of them suggest ways to articulate the body. Kristeva's most well-known poststructuralist colleague, Jacques Derrida, struggles with the relationship between language and the living, speaking body. On the most reductionistic and hostile readings, Derrida's critics take the phrase from *Of Grammatology*, "there is nothing outside of the text," out of context to claim that Derrida is a linguistic monist or a nominalist who does not believe in the reality of anything other than language itself (OG 158). A careful reading of Derrida makes this position difficult to defend. As Derrida says in an interview: "It is totally false to suggest that deconstruction is a suspension of reference. Deconstruction is always deeply concerned with the 'other' of language. I never cease to be surprised by critics who see my work as a declaration that there is nothing beyond language, that we are imprisoned in language; it is, in fact, saying the exact opposite"(RK 123).

Derrida's work is a continual struggle to articulate the "other" of language, which, as he reminds us, is impossible (see Psyche 60). The other of language is antithetical to language even if it is the call from this other that gives language its meaning. Still, language always only points to that which is absent; it is this absence that makes signification possible. Words can do no more than point to, or conjure, the absence of that about which they speak. That about which they speak – life, love, the material world – is other to language.

On Derrida's account, language does violence to this other (OG 135). At best, language gives us traces of something beyond language, homicidal traces that turn life into death. Although in "Circumfessions" Derrida dreams of a writing that could directly express the living body without violence, for him, language is always the dead remains of a living body:

> If I compare the pen to a syringe, and I always dream of a pen that would be a syringe, a suction point rather than that very hard weapon with which one must inscribe, incise, choose, calculate, take ink before filtering the inscribable, playing the keyboard on the screen, whereas here, once the right vein has been found, no more toil, no responsibility, no risk of bad taste nor of violence, the blood delivers itself all alone, the inside gives itself up. (C 12)

Even as Derrida imagines writing that is like a transfusion of the living body into language, he resigns himself to the violence of trying to inscribe the uninscribable.[8] The living body is this uninscribable.

Kristeva's theory more optimistically addresses the problem of the relationship between language and bodily experience by postulating that, through the semiotic element, bodily drives manifest themselves in language. Instead of lamenting what is lost, absent, or impossible in language, Kristeva marvels at this other realm that makes its way into language. The force of language is living drive force transferred into language. Signification is like a transfusion of the living body into language. This is why psychoanalysis can be effective; the analyst can diagnose the active drive force as it is manifest in the analysand's language. Language is not cut off from the body. And, while, for Kristeva, bodily drives involve a type of violence, negation, or force, this process does not merely necessitate sacrifice and loss. The drives are not sacrificed to signification; rather bodily drives are an essential semiotic element of signification.

In addition to proposing that bodily drives make their way into language, Kristeva maintains that the logic of signification is already present in the material of the body. Once again combining psychoanalytic theory and linguistics, Kristeva relies on both Lacan's account of the infant's entrance into language and Saussure's account of the play of signifiers. Lacan points out that the entrance into language requires separation, particularly from the maternal body. Saussure maintains that signifiers signify in relation to one another through their differences. Combining these two theses, it seems that language operates according to principles of separation and difference, as well as identification and incorporation. Kristeva argues that the principles or structures of separation and difference are operating in the body even before the infant begins to use language.

In *Revolution in Poetic Language* Kristeva proposes that the processes of identification or incorporation, and differentiation or rejection, that make language use possible are operating within the material of the body. She maintains that before the infant passes through what Freud calls the Oedipal situation, or what Lacan calls the Mirror Stage, the patterns and logic of language are already operating in a preoedipal situation. In *Revolution* she focuses on differentiation or rejection and the oscillation between identification and differentiation. She analyzes how material rejection (for example the expulsion of waste from the body) is part of the process that sets up the possibility of signification.[9]

She calls the bodily structures of separation the "logic of rejection." For Kristeva the body, like signification, operates according to an oscillation between instability and stability, or negativity and stases. For example, the process of metabolization is a process that oscillates between instability and stability: food is taken into the body and metabolized and expelled from the body. Because the structure of separation is bodily, these bodily operations prepare us for our entrance into language. From the time of birth, the infant's body is engaging in processes of separation; anality is the prime example. Birth itself is also an experience of separation, one body separated from another.

Part of Kristeva's motivation for emphasizing these bodily separations and privations is to provide an alternative to the Lacanian model of language acquisition. Lacan's account of signification and self-consciousness begins with the mirror stage and the paternal metaphor's substitution of the law of the father for the desire of the mother. On the traditional psychoanalytic model of both Freud and Lacan, the child enters the social or language out of fear of castration. The child experiences its separation from the maternal body as a tragic loss and consoles itself with words instead. Paternal threats make words the only, if inadequate, alternative to psychosis. Kristeva insists, however, that separation begins prior to the mirror stage or Oedipal situation and that this separation is not only painful but also pleasurable. She insists that the child enters the social and language not just due to paternal threats but also because of paternal love.

At bottom, Kristeva criticizes the traditional account because it cannot adequately explain the child's move to signification. If what motivates the move to signification are threats and the pain of separation, then why would anyone make this move? Why not remain in the safe haven of the maternal body and refuse the social and signification with its threats? Kristeva suggests that if the accounts of Freud and Lacan were correct, then more people would be psychotic (see RPL 132; TL 30, 31, 125). The logic of signification is already operating in the body and therefore the transition to language is not as dramatic and mysterious as traditional psychoanalytic theory makes it out to be.

Reconnecting bodily drives to language is not only the project of her theoretical work but also the project of her clinical psychoanalytic practice and one aspect of her fiction. Since *Tales of Love* (1983) Kristeva has been including notes from analytic sessions in her theory and fiction. In her theory she uses these notes to further substantiate her diagnosis of literary texts and culture. She often diagnoses a gap between her analysand's words and his or her affects. Affects are physical and psychic manifestations of drive energy; recall that drive energy has its source in bodily organs and its aim in satisfaction of desires. Kristeva describes a phenomenon whereby it seems that words become detached from their affects and the corresponding drive energy, and the job of the analyst is to try to help the analysand put them back together again.

There is a fragile connection between words and affects that is set up during a child's acquisition of language and simultaneous acquisition of a sense of self or subjectivity. If this connection between words and affects is broken or never established, then borderline psychosis can be the result. Kristeva suggests that in contemporary culture there seems to be more slippage, or a different kind of slippage, than in the past between words and affects, between who we say we are and our experience of ourselves. Perhaps the abyss between our fragmented language and our fragmented sense of ourselves is the empty soul or psyche of the postmodern world. Kristeva's writing attempts to negotiate this impasse by bringing the body back into language and bringing language back into the body, by reconnecting bodily drives to language.

Her discussion of the need to reconnect words and affects, language and the body, is punctuated with quotations from her analysands' speech. This strategy not only addresses the absence of the speaking body from traditional theoretical discourse, but also the transcripts stand as examples of the practical consequences of traditional dualistic theoretical positions on the relationship between language and life, symbols and experience, mind and body. Her strategy of including her notes from analytic sessions, peppered with the words of her analysands, brings the speaking body into theoretical discourse.[10] These speaking bodies are articulating the pain of living in worlds where symbols have been detached from affect, where the meaning of words has been detached from the meaning of life, from what matters.

The affective or semiotic element of language matters in the double sense of giving language its *raison d'etre* and its material element. Recall that in *New Maladies of the Soul* Kristeva suggests that the loss of meaning and emptiness of contemporary life is related to an uncoupling of affect and language which is encouraged by the very remedies that contemporary society proposes for dealing with the problem. Contemporary society offers two primary ways of addressing the malaise caused by the disconnection of affect and language: drugs (narcotics, psychotropic drugs, and anti-depressants) and media images. Kristeva suggests that both drugs and media images do nothing to treat the cause of our malaise; rather, they could be seen as symptoms of the problem itself. The problem, as she articulates it in *New Maladies of the Soul*, is that contemporary culture has left behind the psyche or soul. The soul is empty or nonexistent, and without it our lives, our words, have no meaning.

Kristeva suggests that our souls (*psyche*) have been flattened and emptied by the rhythms and images of our culture, which are two-dimensional. Life takes place on the screen, movie screens, TV screens, computer screens. Yet these media images merely cover over the surface of the emptiness that we feel facing the loss of meaning. Psychotropic drugs and anti-depressants flatten the psyche. They relieve the feeling of crisis caused by a loss of meaning at the expense of a feeling of emptiness; they flatten or empty the patient's affects. Both drugs and media images provide only false or artificial selves which only temporarily smooth over the surface of an otherwise empty psyche. By substituting surface images for psychic depth, drugs and media images close psychic space.

Psychic space is the space between the human organism and its aims; it is the space between the biological and the social. It is the space of drives which move energy between these two interconnected spheres. It is within this psychic space that affects materialize between bodily organs and social customs. Our emotional lives depend on this space. Meaning is constituted in this space between the body and culture. Our words and our lives have meaning by virtue of their connection to affect. The meaning of words (in the narrow sense of the symbolic element of language) is charged with affective meaning (in the broader sense of the semiotic element of language) through the movement of drive energy within psychic space.

As Kristeva says in *Tales of Love*, we are extraterrestrials wandering and lost without meaning due to this abolition of psychic space: "What analysands are henceforth suffering from is *the abolition of psychic space*. Narcissus in want of light as much as of a spring allowing him to capture his true image, Narcissus drowning in a cascade of false images (from social roles to the *media*), hence deprived of substance or place" (TL 373). We experience somatic symptoms cut off from their psychic or affective meaning. The goal of the analyst, then, is to reconnect *soma* and *psyche*, body and soul. The "talking cure" involves giving meaning to language by reconnecting words and affects, and thereby giving meaning to life. Psychoanalysis is unique in that it tries to open up psychic space and provide various interpretations with which to give meaning to both language and life.

In *Tales of Love* Kristeva identifies meaning, in both senses, with love. "Today Narcissus is an exile, deprived of his psychic space, an extraterrestrial with a prehistory bearing, wanting for love. An uneasy child, all scratched up, some-what disgusting, an alien in a world of desire and power, he longs only to reinvent love" (TL 382–3). The analysand is a child with no adequate images of a loving mother or a loving father. Kristeva suggests that (in the West) tradi-tionally Christianity has provided images of a loving mother and a loving father, as problematic as those images might be. But with contemporary suspicions of religion, she seems to ask, where can we find images of loving mothers and fathers? And without images of loving mothers and fathers, how can we love ourselves?

For Kristeva, love provides the support for fragmented meanings and frag-mented subjectivities. Love provides the support to reconnect words and affects. She says that "*love is something spoken, and it is only that*" (TL 277). Our lives have meaning for us, we have a sense of ourselves, through the narratives which we prepare to tell others about our experience. Even if we do not tell our stories, we live our experience through the stories that we construct in order to "tell ourselves" to another, a loved one. As we wander through our days, an event takes on its significance in the narrative that we construct for an imaginary conversation with a loved one as we are living it. The living body is a loving body, and the loving body is a speaking body. Without love we are nothing but walking corpses. Love is essential to the living body and it is essential in bringing the living body to life in language.

Notes

1   A different version of this essay appears in the introduction to *The Portable Kristeva*,
     edited by Kelly Oliver, Columbia University Press: New York, 1997.
2   For a more developed account of Kristeva's theory of drives, see chapter six of my
     Womanizing Nietzsche: Philosophy's Relation to the "Feminine" (New York: Routle-
     dge, 1995).
3   Kristeva's theory also challenges the narrow conception of material as it is opposed
     to social or linguistic.

4   Traditional theories have tried to address these problems in various ways. Referential theories of meaning have held that the meaning of a word is its reference to
something extralinguistic, something in the world. The meaning of a word is
either what it refers to (some thing) or the relationship between the word and its
referent. But as Frege pointed out, meaning and reference are not the same since
there are many different ways of referring to the same thing; and not all of these
linguistic expressions necessarily have the same meaning even if they have the
same referent. The most famous example is the reference to Venus as both the
morning star and the evening star. Some theorists (e.g., Locke, Husserl, Saussure)
have tried to avoid some of the problems of referential theories by supposing that
the meaning of a word is determined by the thought that corresponds to that
word. The referent in this case becomes an idea or concept and not a material
thing in the world. These theories, however, merely displace the problems of
reference from the material world to the world of ideas. All of the problems of
correspondence still obtain. Some contemporary theorists (Austin, Wittgenstein,
Searle) propose that meaning is determined by the use of words and that the use of
words must be analyzed as a type of activity with certain rules and regulations. The
way in which words are used, however, varies as much as the thoughts or ideas
associated with them and their possible material referents.

5   The three terms of the Hegelian dialectic are commonly referred to as thesis,
antithesis, and synthesis, which correspond to Universal, Particular, Individual.

6   In the history of philosophy, the distinction between body and soul has also been
discussed as a distinction between body and mind, or the mind-body problem.

7   For example, for a feminist criticism of Descartes, see Susan Bordo, *The Flight to
Objectivity* (Albany: SUNY, 1987). For a feminist criticism of Kant, see Robin
Schott, *Cognition and Eros: A Critique of the Kantian Paradigm* (Boston: Beacon
Press, 1988). Kristeva's relationship to feminism is complex. For a discussion of
Kristeva's relationship to these issues, see Kelly Oliver, *Reading Kristeva: Unraveling
the Doublebind* (Bloomington: Indiana University Press, 1993).

8   For a detailed analysis of the relationship between language and the living body in
Derrida's "Circumfessions," see my article "The Maternal Operation" in Raw-
linson et. al. (eds) *Derrida and Feminism* (New York: Routledge, 1996).

9   Kristeva's writings themselves can be read as an oscillation between an emphasis on
separation and rejection and an emphasis on identification and incorporation. In
Revolution (1974) and *Powers of Horror* (1980) she focuses on separation and
rejection; in *Tales of Love* (1983) and *Black Sun* (1987) she focuses on identification
and incorporation. In *Strangers to Ourselves* (1989) she again analyzes separation and
rejection. And in *New Maladies of the Soul* (1993) she again analyzes identification
and incorporation. In an interview with Rosalind Coward in 1984 at the Institute
of Contemporary Arts, Kristeva claims that for this reason, *Powers of Horror* and
Tales of Love should be read together; alone each provides only half of the story.

10   Starting with *Tales of Love* and continuing through *New Maladies of the Soul*
Kristeva begins to insert what appear as her notes from analytic sessions into her
texts.

References

Derrida, Jacques (1976) *Of Grammatology*, trans. Gayatri Spivak (Baltimore: Johns Hopkins University Press). Cited as OG.

—— (1984) Interview with Richard Kearney, in Richard Kearney (ed.) *Dialogues with Contemporary Continental Thinkers* (Manchester: Manchester University Press). Cited as RK.

—— (1989) "Psyche: Inventions of the Other," in L. Waters and W. Godzich (eds) *Reading DeMan Reading*, trans. Catherine Porter (Minneapolis: University of Minnesota Press). Cited as Psyche.

—— (1993) "Circumfessions," in *Jacques Derrida*, trans. Geoffrey Bennington (Chicago: University of Chicago Press). Cited as C.

Kristeva, Julia (1974) *La Révolution du langage poétique*, Paris: Seuil. Translated as *Revolution in Poetic Language*, by Margaret Waller (New York: Columbia University Press, 1984). Cited as RPL.

—— (1977) "*D'un château l'autre*," in *Polylogue*, Paris: Seuil, 1977, translated as "From One Identity to an Other," by Gora, Jardine and Roudiez in *Desire in Language*, Roudiez (ed.) (New York: Columbia University Press, 1980). Cited as DL.

—— (1983) *Histoires d'amour*, Paris: Edtions Denoël. Translated as *Tales of Love* by Leon Roudiez (New York: Columbia University Press, 1987). Cited as TL.

—— (1987) *Soleil noir: Depression et mélancolie*, Paris: Gallimard. Translated as *Black Sun* by Leon Roudiez (New York: Columbia University Press, 1989).

—— (1989) *Etrangers à nous-mêmes*, Paris: Fayard. Translated as *Strangers to Ourselves* by Leon Roudiez (New York: Columbia University Press, 1991).

—— (1990) *Nations Without Nationalisms*, partially translated from *Lettre ouverte à Harlem Désir* by Leon Roudiez (New York: Columbia University Press, 1993).

—— (1993) *Les Nouvelles maladies de l'ame*, Paris: Libraire Artheme Fayard. Translated as *New Maladies of the Soul* by Ross Guberman (New York: Columbia University Press, 1995). Cited as NM.

LUCE IRIGARAY

Female Desire

Female sexuality has always been conceptualized on the basis of masculine parameters. Thus the opposition between "masculine" clitoral activity and "feminine" vaginal passivity, an opposition which Freud – and many others – saw as stages, or alternatives, in the development of a sexually "normal" woman, seems rather too clearly required by the practice of male sexuality. For the clitoris is conceived as a little penis pleasant to masturbate so long as castration anxiety does not exist (for the boy child), and the vagina is valued for the "lodging" it offers the male organ when the forbidden hand has to find a replacement for pleasure-giving.

In these terms, woman's erogenous zones never amount to anything but a clitoris-sex that is not comparable to the noble phallic organ, or a hole-envelope that serves to sheathe and massage the penis in intercourse: a non-sex, or a masculine organ turned back upon itself, self-embracing.

About woman and her pleasure, this view of the sexual relation has nothing to say. Her lot is that of "lack," "atrophy" (of the sexual organ), and "penis envy," the penis being the only sexual organ of recognized value. Thus she attempts by every means available to appropriate that organ for herself: through her some-what servile love of the father-husband capable of giving her one, through her desire for a child-penis, preferably a boy, through access to the cultural values still reserved by right to males alone and therefore always masculine, and so on. Woman lives her own desire only as the expectation that she may at last come to possess an equivalent of the male organ.

Yet all this appears quite foreign to her own pleasure, unless it remains within the dominant phallic economy. Thus, for example, woman's autoeroticism is

From Luce Irigaray, *This Sex Which is Not One*. (Ithaca, New York: Cornell), pp. 23–33 very different from man's. In order to touch himself, man needs an instrument: his hand, a woman's body, language . . . And this self-caressing requires at least a minimum of activity. As for woman, she touches herself in and of herself without any need for mediation, and before there is any way to distinguish activity from passivity. Woman "touches herself" all the time, and moreover no one can forbid her to do so, for her genitals are formed of two lips in continuous contact. Thus, within herself, she is already two – but not divisible into one(s) – that caress each other.

This autoeroticism is disrupted by a violent break-in: the brutal separation of the two lips by a violating penis, an intrusion that distracts and deflects the woman from this "self-caressing" she needs if she is not to incur the disappearance of her own pleasure in sexual relations. If the vagina is to serve *also*, but *not only*, to take over for the little boy's hand in order to assure an articulation between auto-eroticism and heteroeroticism in intercourse (the encounter with the totally other always signifying death), how, in the classic representation of sexuality, can the perpetuation of autoeroticism for woman be managed? Will woman not be left with the impossible alternative between a defensive virginity, fiercely turned in upon itself, and a body open to penetration that no longer knows, in this "hole" that constitutes its sex, the pleasure of its own touch? The more or less exclusive – and highly anxious – attention paid to erection in Western sexuality proves to what extent the imaginary that governs it is foreign to the feminine. For the most part, this sexuality offers nothing but imperatives dictated by male rivalry: the "strongest" being the one who has the best "hard-on," the longest, the biggest, the stiffest penis, or even the one who "pees the farthest" (as in little boys' contests). Or else one finds imperatives dictated by the enactment of sadomasochistic fantasies, these in turn governed by man's relation to his mother: the desire to force entry, to penetrate, to appropriate for himself the mystery of this womb where he has been conceived, the secret of his begetting, of his "origin." Desire/need, also to make blood flow again in order to revive a very old relationship – intrauterine, to be sure, but also prehistoric – to the maternal.

Woman, in this sexual imaginary, is only a more or less obliging prop for the enactment of man's fantasies. That she may find pleasure there in that role, by proxy, is possible, even certain. But such pleasure is above all a masochistic prostitution of her body to a desire that is not her own, and it leaves her in a familiar state of dependency upon man. Not knowing what she wants, ready for anything, even asking for more, so long as he will "take" her as his "object" when he seeks his own pleasure. Thus she will not say what she herself wants; moreover, she does not know, or no longer knows, what she wants. As Freud admits, the beginnings of the sexual life of a girl child are so "obscure," so "faded with time," that one would have to dig down very deep indeed to discover beneath the traces of this civilization, of this history, the vestiges of a more archaic civilization that might give some clue to woman's sexuality. That extremely ancient civilization would undoubtedly have a different alphabet, a different language . . . Woman's desire would not be expected to speak the same language as man's; woman's desire has doubtless been submerged by the logic that has dominated the West since the time of the Greeks.

Within this logic, the predominance of the visual, and of the discrimination and individualization of form, is particularly foreign to female eroticism. Woman takes pleasure more from touching than from looking, and her entry into a dominant scopic economy signifies, again, her consignment to passivity: she is to be the beautiful object of contemplation. While her body finds itself thus eroticized, and called to a double movement of exhibition and of chaste retreat in order to stimulate the drives of the "subject," her sexual organ represents *the horror of nothing to see*. A defect in this systematics of representation and desire. A "hole" in its scoptophilic lens. It is already evident in Greek statuary that this nothing-to-see has to be excluded, rejected, from such a scene of representation. Woman's genitals are simply absent, masked, sewn back up inside their "crack."

This organ which has nothing to show for itself also lacks a form of its own. And if woman takes pleasure precisely from this incompleteness of form which allows her organ to touch itself over and over again, indefinitely, by itself, that pleasure is denied by a civilization that privileges phallomorphism. The value granted to the only definable form excludes the one that is in play in female autoeroticism. The *one* of form, of the individual, of the (male) sexual organ, of the proper name, of the proper meaning . . . supplants, while separating and dividing, that contact of *at least two* (lips) which keeps woman in touch with herself, but without any possibility of distinguishing what is touching from what is touched.

Whence the mystery that woman represents in a culture claiming to count everything, to number everything by units, to inventory everything as individualities. *She is neither one nor two.* Rigorously speaking, she cannot be identified either as one person, or as two. She resists all adequate definition. Further, she has no "proper" name. And her sexual organ, which is not *one* organ, is counted as *none*. The negative, the underside, the reverse of the only visible and morphologically designatable organ (even if the passage from erection to detumescence does pose some problems): the penis.

But the "thickness" of that "form," the layering of its volume, its expansions and contractions and even the spacing of the moments in which it produces itself as form – all this the feminine keeps secret. Without knowing it. And if woman is asked to sustain, to revive, man's desire, the request neglects to spell out what it implies as to the value of her own desire. A desire of which she is not aware, moreover, at least not explicitly. But one whose force and continuity are capable of nurturing repeatedly and at length all the masquerades of "femininity" that are expected of her.

It is true that she still has the child, in relation to whom her appetite for touch, for contact, has free rein, unless it is already lost, alienated by the taboo against touching of a highly obsessive civilization. Otherwise her pleasure will find, in the child, compensations for and diversions from the frustrations that she too often encounters in sexual relations per se. Thus maternity fills the gaps in a repressed female sexuality. Perhaps man and woman no longer caress each other except through that mediation between them that the child – preferably a boy – represents? Man, identified with his son, rediscovers the pleasure of maternal fondling; woman touches herself again by caressing that part of her body: her baby-penis-clitoris.

What this entails for the amorous trio is well known. But the Oedipal interdiction seems to be a somewhat categorical and factitious law – although it does provide the means for perpetuating the authoritarian discourse of fathers – when it is promulgated in a culture in which sexual relations are impracticable because man's desire and woman's are strangers to each other. And in which the two desires have to try to meet through indirect means, whether the archaic one of a sense-relation to the mother's body, or the present one of active or passive extension of the law of the father. These are regressive emotional behaviors, exchanges of words too detached from the sexual arena not to constitute an exile with respect to it: "mother" and "father" dominate the interactions of the couple, but as social roles. The division of labor prevents them from making love. They produce or reproduce. Without quite knowing how to use their leisure. Such little as they have, such little indeed as they wish to have. For what are they to do with leisure? What substitute for amorous resource are they to invent? Still . . .

Perhaps it is time to return to that repressed entity, the female imaginary. So woman does not have a sex organ? She has at least two of them, but they are not identifiable as ones. Indeed, she has many more. Her sexuality, always at least double, goes even further: it is *plural*. Is this the way culture is seeking to characterize itself now? Is this the way texts write themselves/are written now? Without quite knowing what censorship they are evading? Indeed, woman's pleasure does not have to choose between clitoral activity and vaginal passivity, for example. The pleasure of the vaginal caress does not have to be substituted for that of the clitoral caress. They each contribute, irreplaceable, to woman's pleasure. Among other caresses... Fondling the breasts, touching the vulva, spreading the lips, stroking the posterior wall of the vagina, brushing against the mouth of the uterus, and so on. To evoke only a few of the most specifically female pleasures. Pleasures which are somewhat misunderstood in sexual difference as it is imagined – or not imagined, the other sex being only the indispensable complement to the only sex.

But *woman has sex organs more or less everywhere.* She finds pleasure almost anywhere. Even if we refrain from invoking the hystericization of her entire body, the geography of her pleasure is far more diversified, more multiple in its differences, more complex, more subtle, than is commonly imagined – in an imaginary rather too narrowly focused on sameness.

"She" is indefinitely other in herself. This is doubtless why she is said to be whimsical, incomprehensible, agitated, capricious... not to mention her language, in which "she" sets off in all directions leaving "him" unable to discern the coherence of any meaning. Hers are contradictory words, somewhat mad from the standpoint of reason, inaudible for whoever listens to them with ready-made grids, with a fully elaborated code in hand. For in what she says, too, at least when she dares, woman is constantly touching herself. She steps ever so slightly aside from herself with a murmur, an exclamation, a whisper, a sentence left unfinished... When she returns, it is to set off again from elsewhere. From another point of pleasure, or of pain. One would have to listen with another ear, as if hearing *an "other meaning" always in the process of weaving itself, of embracing itself with words, but also of getting rid of words in order not to become fixed, congealed in them.* For if "she" says something, it is not, it is already no longer, identical with what she means. What she says is never identical with anything, moreover; rather, it is contiguous. *It touches (upon).* And when it strays too far from that proximity, she breaks off and starts over at "zero": her body-sex.

It is useless, then, to trap women in the exact definition of what they mean, to make them repeat (themselves) so that it will be clear; they are already elsewhere in that discursive machinery where you expected to surprise them. They have returned within themselves. Which must not be understood in the same way as within yourself. They do not have the interiority that you have, the one you perhaps suppose they have. Within themselves means *within the intimacy of that silent, multiple, diffuse touch.* And if you ask them insistently what they are thinking about, they can only reply: Nothing. Everything.

Thus what they desire is precisely nothing, and at the same time everything. Always something more and something else besides that *one* – sexual organ, for example – that you give them, attribute to them. Their desire is often interpreted, and feared, as a sort of insatiable hunger, a voracity that will swallow you whole. Whereas it really involves a different economy more than anything else, one that upsets the linearity of a project, undermines the goal-object of a desire, diffuses the polarization toward a single pleasure, disconcerts fidelity to a single discourse...

Must this multiplicity of female desire and female language be understood as
shards, scattered remnants of a violated sexuality? A sexuality denied? The
question has no simple answer. The rejection, the exclusion of a female imaginary certainly puts woman in the position of experiencing herself only frag-
mentarily, in the little-structured margins of a dominant ideology, as waste, or
excess, what is left of a mirror invested by the (masculine) "subject" to reflect
himself, to copy himself. Moreover, the role of "femininity" is prescribed by this
masculine specula(riza)tion and corresponds scarcely at all to woman's desire,
which may be recovered only in secret, in hiding, with anxiety and guilt.

But if the female imaginary were to deploy itself, if it could bring itself into
play otherwise than as scraps, uncollected debris, would it represent itself, even
so, in the form of *one* universe? Would it even be volume instead of surface? No.
Not unless it were understood, yet again, as a privileging of the maternal over
the feminine. Of a phallic maternal, at that. Closed in upon the jealous possession of its valued product. Rivaling man in his esteem for productive excess. In
such a race for power, woman loses the uniqueness of her pleasure. By closing
herself off as volume, she renounces the pleasure that she gets from the *nonsuture
of her lips*: she is undoubtedly a mother, but a virgin mother; the role was
assigned to her by mythologies long ago. Granting her a certain social power
to the extent that she is reduced, with her own complicity, to sexual impotence.

(Re-)discovering herself, for a woman, thus could only signify the possibility of
sacrificing no one of her pleasures to another, of identifying herself with none of
them in particular, *of never being simply one*. A sort of expanding universe to
which no limits could be fixed and which would not be incoherence nonetheless – nor that polymorphous perversion of the child in which the erogenous
zones would lie waiting to be regrouped under the primacy of the phallus.

Woman always remains several, but she is kept from dispersion because the
other is already within her and is autoerotically familiar to her. Which is not to
say that she appropriates the other for herself, that she reduces it to her own
property. Ownership and property are doubtless quite foreign to the feminine.
At least sexually. But not *nearness*. Nearness so pronounced that it makes all
discrimination of identity, and thus all forms of property, impossible. Woman
derives pleasure from what is *so near that she cannot have it, nor have herself*. She
herself enters into a ceaseless exchange of herself with the other without any
possibility of identifying either. This puts into question all prevailing economies:
their calculations are irremediably stymied by woman's pleasure, as it increases
indefinitely from its passage in and through the other.

However, in order for woman to reach the place where she takes pleasure as
woman, a long detour by way of the analysis of the various systems of oppres-
sion brought to bear upon her is assuredly necessary. And claiming to fall back

on the single solution of pleasure risks making her miss the process of going back through a social practice that *her* enjoyment requires.

For woman is traditionally a use-value for man, an exchange value among men; in other words, a commodity. As such, she remains the guardian of material substance, whose price will be established, in terms of the standard of their work and of their need/desire, by "subjects": workers, merchants, consumers. Women are marked phallicly by their fathers, husbands, procurers. And this branding determines their value in sexual commerce. Woman is never anything but the locus of a more or less competitive exchange between two men, including the competition for the possession of mother earth.

How can this object of transaction claim a right to pleasure without removing her/itself from established commerce? With respect to other merchandise in the marketplace, how could this commodity maintain a relationship other than one of aggressive jealousy? How could material substance enjoy her/itself without provoking the consumer's anxiety over the disappearance of his nurturing ground? How could that exchange – which can in no way be defined in terms "proper" to woman's desire – appear as anything but a pure mirage, mere foolishness, all too readily obscured by a more sensible discourse and by a system of apparently more tangible values?

A woman's development, however radical it may seek to be, would thus not suffice to liberate woman's desire. And to date no political theory or political practice has resolved, or sufficiently taken into consideration, this historical problem, even though Marxism has proclaimed its importance. But women do not constitute, strictly speaking, a class, and their dispersion among several classes makes their political struggle complex, their demands sometimes contradictory.

There remains, however, the condition of underdevelopment arising from women's submission by and to a culture that oppresses them, uses them, makes of them a medium of exchange, with very little profit to them. Except in the quasi-monopolies of masochistic pleasure, the domestic labor force, and reproduction. The powers of slaves? Which are not negligible powers, moreover. For where pleasure is concerned, the master is not necessarily well served. Thus to reverse the relation, especially in the economy of sexuality, does not seem a desirable objective.

But if women are to preserve and expand their autoeroticism, their homosexuality, might not the renunciation of heterosexual pleasure correspond once again to that disconnection from power that is traditionally theirs? Would it not involve a new prison, a new cloister, built of their own accord? For women to undertake tactical strikes, to keep themselves apart from men long enough to learn to defend their desire, especially through speech, to discover the love of other women while sheltered from men's imperious choices that put them in the position of rival commodities, to forge for themselves a social status that compels recognition, to earn their living in order to escape from the condition of prostitute... these are certainly indispensable stages in the escape from their proletarization on the exchange market. But if their aim were simply to reverse the order of things, even supposing this to be possible, history would repeat itself in the long run, would revert to sameness: to phallocratism. It would leave room neither for women's sexuality, nor for women's imaginary, nor for women's language to take (their) place.

BEYOND SEX AND GENDER: ON LUCE IRIGARAY'S *THIS SEX WHICH IS NOT ONE*

Tina Chanter

Luce Irigaray, along with other feminists and philosophers, has been influenced by Jacques Lacan's return to Freud. Inflected through the equally influential texts of figures such as Derrida, Heidegger, Levinas, and Merleau-Ponty, Irigaray's engagement with Freud's account of femininity takes shape as a critical interrogation. Taking on the familiar Oedipal configurations of the Freudian story about how male and female desire are constructed, how they differ from one another, and what problems are characteristic of both sexes, Irigaray shows how Freud's project is embedded in a set of unexamined presuppositions. By rendering these assumptions explicit, and exposing the mechanics which inform them, she demonstrates how Freud's representation of women repeats a pattern that can be found throughout the history of Western metaphysics.[1] Thus Freud's account often unwittingly replicates the dichotomies on which philosophers have depended since the ancient Greeks, consigning women to passivity, while men take on the active role of subjects, treating women as deviating from or falling short of a male norm, and assigning to men a flourishing sexuality, while conceding only grudgingly women's sexuality. This series of oppositions – Active/passive, Subject/object, Sexual/asexual – line up with a host of other fundamental divisions which orchestrate the discourse of Western philosophy.

The first part of this essay will interact with Irigaray's essay *This Sex Which Is Not One*[2] as a loose commentary. In the second part I will situate Irigaray's work in the context of recent feminist ideas by highlighting the distinction between sex and gender that has orchestrated so much of feminist thought during the past 30 years, and showing how this is now giving way to discourses exploring sexed bodies, and sexual difference. I will suggest that Irigaray's interrogation of sexual difference moves beyond the impasses of positing a rigid distinction between sex and gender, enabling us to see how neither term can properly be understood in abstraction from one of the central ideas to which Irigaray appeals, the female, or feminine imaginary. The imaginary body is formulated in culturally specific terms, and as such it is variable and historical. Body images are produced, received and manipulated according to the symbolic values that attach to ideals and images of femininity. There is no simple one-way mechanism that can explain gendered identities – they cannot be reduced to behavior which is caused by sex, nor can they be adequately explained independently of sexed bodies. The female imaginary constitutes a background which both informs and constitutes subjects, but which can also be made available for rearticulation and revision. Similarities can be found between Irigaray's elaboration of the feminine imaginary, and the body-image or corporeal schema that informs Merleau-Ponty's phenomenology of the body, and Lacan's psychoanalytic theory of the body (both of which draw on the work of Paul Schilder). Irigaray appropriates both phenomenology and psychoanalysis, and fuses their insights with a thoroughgoing analysis of bodies as sexed and gendered. By unravelling the ways in which our bodies are immersed in cultural and normative presuppositions, and our genders are created in relation to behavior inscribed through a habituated and coded sexuality, she shows how we cannot afford to assume that the sexes are symmetrical or equivalent. Analyzing the ways in which bodies and cultures operate along the axes of sexual difference, she calls for a re-examination of female sexuality.

1 Material Women, Formal Men

If Aristotle was the first to identify the formal principle as masculine, and the material cause as feminine, he was not the last. The idea of man as a spiritual force, breathing life into matter, and of woman as incubator and receptacle, providing the material support for the masculine initiative, seems to be built into the very fabric of our thought. Man is the instigator, the creative force, the inspiration, and woman is the material substrate, the bodily support, the provider of sustenance. Freud is only following a well-established tradition when he discovers penis-envy in girls, or when he envisages the clitoris as a "little penis," a tradition that is silently arranged according to what Irigaray calls the "Blind spot of an old dream of symmetry."[3] The blind spot marks what is missing – the hole, the lack, the negativity or non-sex that constitutes women's place, or non-place, in the phallic economy; the dream of symmetry consists of the myth that women must be represented as if they were essentially the same as, or parallel to, men.

The dark continent of women's sexuality is subjected to the same laws of masculine sexuality – and if no exact equivalence can be found, a symbolic equivalence is constructed. If female sexuality is found wanting, if the clitoris is not as large, or active, or visible as the penis – this can be explained away by women's inherent inferiority, her essential asexuality, her tendency towards passivity, her imperfection. Women are partial men – they are defined in relation to, as secondary to, as answerable to, men.

2 Invisible Sex

Women's sexuality is defined by an absence, because it is already decided in advance that in order for women's sex to exist, it must conform to parameters that turn out to be laid down by male sexuality. Hence the title *This Sex Which Is Not One* – a sex that is not one judged by male parameters, a sex found wanting in comparison to the virile presence of a visible, erect, penis, a sex which appears to consist of nothing, a sex which is no sex at all. If it is not comparable to male anatomy, it doesn't count, it can't signify. No means of representation can be found for it, no language can capture it. It is not a thing, it defies appearance, it evades scrutiny, eludes examination. It is not a phenomenon, it is not a being – therefore its existence is in question, it cannot be. It must not be.

Since no other terms of judgment are available than those of masculine appearance, the female sex cannot be, it does not exist. It is pure lack, negativity, absence – a black hole, a lost continent, mysterious, foreign, other. It is an enigma, a riddle, impenetrable. Yet riddles are for solving, and to posit femininity as beyond solution would be to set a limit on the tools of rationality. If femininity is outside the purview of masculine understanding, if it defies reason, if it is unrepresentable, this implies the finitude of masculine logic. Therefore a solution must be found, this enigma must be solved. If female sexuality offers no direct equivalent to the penis, then an indirect equivalent must be found. Something else must be assigned the value of a penis, must stand in for the penis, signify the penis. An inferior-penis-substitute must be located on the female body. The clitoris must represent the penis. Similarities are found, established, chronicled. Analogies are drawn, elaborated, qualified.

Freud does not stop to ask what informs the assumption that women's sexuality is examined through the lens of the male sexologist, it does not occur to him to ask why the definition of the female sex organs is automatically a matter of identifying a body part that approximates to the penis. He does not wonder about the privilege of the specular economy that guides his analysis, and he is untroubled by any suggestion that his quest for a substitute penis might be misdirected. All this is taken for granted, taken on faith, beyond question.

The only question is – clitoris or vagina? Which female body part best approximates to the male penis? Clearly, it must be the clitoris. The clitoris is more visible, it can be manipulated more or less like a penis, it can become erect, and in this sense it is active – it therefore qualifies as a "little penis." It is obviously much more suitable as a penis-substitute than the passive, invisible, all but absent vagina. In so far as it is conceptualized at all, the dark hole that constitutes the specific domain of female sexuality is recognized only as a place colonized by others. "The vagina is valued for the 'lodging' it offers the male organ" says Irigaray. The woman as mother has always been seen as provider and giver, in some form or other. She shelters, offers a dwelling, an abode, a home. For the child, the mother represents a guardian, a protector, a sanctuary. Nurturing and caring, the maternal figure gives food, warmth, milk, and wipes away tears. Could it be that the cultural role of nurturer and caregiver has surreptitiously crept into Freud's account of female sexuality? Could Freud have inadvertently allowed the societal expectations that demand of women that they fulfill the role of good mother, wife, and housemaker to instruct his account of their "natural" sexual disposition as passive? In his attempt to account for female development, has he done anything other than read back into their sexual constitution – which he was supposed to explain – a cultural expectation? Has the acquiescence, the modesty, the compliance that has been traditionally expected of women, simply been presupposed by Freud, whose descriptions are in the service of the myth of the eternal feminine? Is his account of the female body merely a prescriptive account of ideal femininity, an exemplar of the perfect mother? Passive, receptive, accepting, and caring. The contours of this shadowy, marginal, maternal figure, hovering in the wings, are blurred, her sexuality is obscured. She is peripheral, playing only a supporting role, filling in the background – part of the scenery. Irigaray says "Woman, in this sexual imaginary, is only a more or less obliging prop for the enactment of man's fantasies."

3 An Economy of the Same

Whence the impetus to produce an image of the clitoris as "little penis" or the woman as inferior man? Why must there be a single identity, a singular narrative? Why only one? Is the privilege of masculinity orchestrated by a metaphysical quest for univocity and monism? Is the plural outlawed from the beginning? When Irigaray insists on the multiple and diffuse character of female sexuality, she is not merely pointing out that Freud's account is teleologically oriented towards male desire, or that this account represents women's sexuality as if it were homologous to male penile activity; she is also showing that the very idea of having to choose between the vagina and the clitoris as the true or original site of female pleasure reflects a phallic privilege. Only one account must be true, and it is the one that approximates to male morphology. If Freud's account is thoroughly permeated by the masculine trajectory of erection, and climax, directed by a single dominant end, Irigaray's description of female desire resists definition – it is always elsewhere. It cannot be pinned down, or counted. "Her sexuality, always at least double, goes even further: it is plural." As Irigaray has already announced in the title *This Sex Which Is Not One* – this sex is not reducible to one, cannot be distributed numerically, and lacks any fixed boundaries. The contours of women's sexuality are difficult to distinguish. They cannot be easily enumerated: "she is already two – but not divisible into one(s) – that caress each other." The ideas of separation and cleavage are not privileged by women's anatomy. Instead, we find an uneven morphology of indistinguishable layers, layer on layer, a lack of linearity, an uncertain continuity, a contiguity, confusion, multiplicity, a touching-touched, a chiasmic self-caressing movement that cannot be relegated to passivity, nor defined simply as activity. Women's bodies mix up male categories. Form and definition, enumeration and classification, first and second, inner and outer, upper and lower – these levels and hierarchies no longer make much sense. The female body parts of sexuality are not easily viewed, resisting scrutiny, and they do not easily divide into discretely named or numbered organs. Could this be because categories themselves are drawn from and imbued with male experience?

Whence the need to number, to count, to individuate, to classify, to identify from, to distinguish one from the other? Does this urge to numerically quantify derive from the need to possess, to subordinate, to value, to assess one commodity as worth more than another? To assign a use-value, to define and determine and circumscribe what a thing is for, and how it might best serve its purpose? To lay down the law, create an economy in which one thing is equivalent to another? And would women escape such evaluation? Or are we just so many commodities, objects, goods to go on the market, up for sale? Who then determines our value? What rules of commerce establish the price, and what authority measures the goods? Who guarantees the market? What dictates the exchange-value?

If women are to be passed between men, from one to the other, if they are to pass inspection, to be marketable, so many goods going to the market, of what can our desire consist? Only in being desirable, saleable, goods? In meeting the requirements of the buyers? And who sets these standards, if not those with purchasing power? Isn't there a sense in which women's desire is subsumed by male desire? Is there any possibility of a female desire?

If desire itself consists of a competition among women to be desirable to men, then not only can women be said to lack any desire of their own – they haven't even begun to ask what they want. If women are busy keeping up appearances, maintaining a pretense of their sexuality for men, maintaining their part in the circulation of women between men, this economy would be dictated by the desires of men alone. And the objects of exchange – women – are substitutes not only for male desire, but also for one another. Irigaray says "With respect to other merchandise in the marketplace, how could this commodity maintain a relationship other than one of aggressive jealousy?" Women are in competition with each other for male attention, a competition set in motion by male desire. In this limited sense, the heterosexuality of this economy becomes a homosexual economy – only one sex counts, only one desire signifies. There is no space, or value, allotted to desire among women. Women become mere tokens of exchange, repositories of male desire. The man who accrues the most wealth can acquire the most desirable female. And the most desirable female is defined by her place as the property or acquisition of the most wealthy male. The circularity of this economy is as evident as the singularity of desire. And women's bodies constitute the sites at which this economy reproduces itself.

4 Women as Unrepresentable Other

If women are the receptacles, the vessels, the incubators, of male desire – first they house the penis, then the child (at least if things go as the phallic economy dictates) – they also facilitate the representation of the male subjects, whose actions they reflect, and whose identities they consolidate. Women themselves are excluded from the "scene of representation" that they facilitate for men. If women are envisaged in the specular economy as inferior copies of men, this mimesis and replication is also a means of assuring the centrality, the value, the mastery of the dominant subjects. If there were no women to compare themselves to, if the weaker sex and its manifest inadequacies did not provide an anchoring point from which the male gaze could orient itself, steadying its own perspective, finding something against which to counterpoise itself, how would the process of constituting an identity be altered?

How could Freud fail to see that his account, which purports to explain the nature of female sexuality, in fact merely plays a part in extending and elaborating a cultural myth that is already in place? Perhaps it is in his interests to keep up the pretense, the belief in a mysterious femininity, an indefinable aura that resists analysis. It resists analysis, it is coy, shy, modest. And yet it must be conquered, reined in, harnessed to reason, related to truth, revealed in the light of day. It must conform to the myth of male desire, it must be shaped to the male pattern of development.

A woman is not simply a woman (as if to be a woman were simple). Irigaray says "women do not constitute, strictly speaking, a class, and their dispersion among several classes makes their political struggle complex, their demands sometimes contradictory." None of the available discourses, political narratives, or analyses are adequate to women's sometimes contradictory struggle, because none of them speak to the question of what it means to be a woman. Either the question of sexuality is elided into the supposition that women are basically the same as men – in which case the issue of sexual difference is obliterated, displaced by a demand for equality – or women's differences from men are taken as given and used as a platform from which to argue women's alleged inferiority. In both cases, the meaning of sexual difference is negated, obscured, or defused before it has even been properly posed as a question. Hence Irigaray declares that the question of sexual difference is the epochal question of our age. The urgency of posing this question resides in the fact that it is in danger of becoming a meaningless question because it has taken on the appearance of irrelevance even for many feminists. Since traditionally the differences between women and men – often signaled by their sexuality – have been used as an excuse to prevent women from being treated as equal to men, sexual difference has become a symbol of danger. Rather than draw attention to their differences from men, women have been encouraged to play down these differences, for fear that they will be disqualified from the realm of public discourse.

What does it mean to assert that women are different from men? In order to answer this question, and in order to situate Irigaray's intervention into feminist and philosophical discourses, I am going to tell a partial story about the recent history of feminism that highlights the concept of sex and gender.

5 Problems with the Typical Formulation of Sex/Gender

The language of sex and gender caught on in the 1970s, and came to be a useful distinction for feminists who were still trying to make the case that Simone de Beauvoir had couched in the existentialist language of "One is not born, one becomes a woman."[4] Beauvoir focused on woman as the other of man, woman as the second sex, defined in relation to, and as subordinate to, man – who was tacitly assumed to be the subject of discourse when it came to discussions of human nature, humanity in general, or even existentialist reformulations of the more traditional metaphysical notion of mankind – in terms of transcendence, becoming, change. As Beauvoir delineated it, the problem for women was an over-identification with our bodies, and the answer was a repudiation of our bodily existence, as mothers, as caregivers, and as nurturers – in short as unrewarded reproducers of material existence. What women needed was to realize their freedom, to overcome the limitations of their situation, to transcend their immanence. Not to put too fine a point on it – what women needed was to become more like men. Women needed to find paid work, and so not be financially dependent on men, they needed to realize their projects, enacting their freedom, and so not be metaphysically dependent on men.

The concept of gender, borrowed from psychology, and filtered through the lens of sociology, neatly fitted into Beauvoir's scheme of things. Gender took on the burden of the feminist argument for changing women's situation. With the help of gender, mothering and caregiving were seen as activities that were encouraged by the social norms of a particular society, located in a specific historical epoch, with no necessity bolstering them up. Rather than being a bastion of nature, assumed to be part of the myth of the eternal feminine, written in the stars as woman's destiny, being a mother could now be identified with a cultural expectation, rather than a natural and determinative force. As such, motherhood, and other traditional forms of institutionalizing femininity, were seen as capable of change.

If the label of gender took on the mantle of change, precisely how gender worked was left rather vague. It was assumed to be somewhat congruent with amorphous categories such as culture, society, or history, and these terms themselves – different as they are – were (as Butler suggests)[5] left unarticulated, as were the mechanics of their operation. Just how does gender take effect, how does it produce identity? Insofar as gender is equated with a social force, understood as social conditioning, the assumption is that society, or culture, tells girls to act in a feminine way and boys to act in a masculine way. But this obviously cannot be the whole story, since what we end up with is not a battery of identical barbie-doll chorus girls, all wearing pink, and embodying the feminine ideal. So, we have to ask ourselves, why is this? First, and most obviously, it is because we cannot – even if we wanted to – all be blonde blue-eyed beauties because of bodily constraints. Our bodies intervene. To illustrate both the ideals for which we strive, despite our failures to embody them, let me present two fictional aspirations to achieve a culturally specific ideal of femininity.

In Barbara Kingsolver's *Pigs in Heaven*[6] a waitress has had her name legally changed to Barbie, owns "probably the largest personal collection of Barbie-related items in the entire world," knows every Barbie model on the market, and dresses in Barbie doll look-alike ensembles. She is also wanted for counterfeiting money and robbing a casino.

In Toni Morrison's *The Bluest Eye*[7] Pecola Breedlove presents Elihue Michah Whitcomb, who is regarded by the women of the town as having supernatural powers, with a request to change the color of her eyes: "I want them blue" she tells him – "Like she was buying shoes." Summing up the situation, the narrator observes, "A little black girl yearns for the blue eyes of a little white girl, and the horror at the heart of her yearning is exceeded only by the evil of fulfillment."

If bodies irreducibly complicate the picture of sex and gender as one of cause and effect, as a matter of social conditioning, there are other factors that intervene – among them our choices, wishes, and desires which can transform and challenge gender ideals through subversion, rebellion, and transgression. Not all girls or women accept the feminine ideal. Many of us reject it as inappropriate for us. Society holds up certain ideals for us in the form of advertisement, a constant barrage of media images, pornography, and so on, but we don't all react by acquiescing to these images – precisely because we make choices as to how to present ourselves through our bodies, and even if those choices are always relative to the images society holds up for us to imitate, there are ways of refashioning these images, ways of rejecting, reshaping, transfiguring what it means to be a woman according to prevailing cultural norms. We don't all hear the social message of how to be feminine and masculine and react by conforming. Through practices such as body-building, cross-dressing, and so on, we resculpt our bodies, and our body images.

At a third, more theoretical level, what is unsatisfactory about the vision of gender affecting everyone in an identical way is that it construes gender as a monolithic force, and individuals as passive and unsuspecting victims of its wicked ways. At a theoretical level, then, we have to conceive of the relation between gender and sex not as a replaying of the Cartesian mind/body dichotomy, where we react as passive recipients of social lessons that are inscribed through our bodies in a way that presupposes an uneasy relation between our physical existence and the message that society sends our way to tell us how to be. We are not at the mercy of society, but neither are we entirely in charge of our gendered fate. We are neither entirely determined by gender, nor do we entirely determine it. We need a model of gender that can accommodate the fact that gender doesn't happen in a vacuum – it is enacted against the background of a particular body. Equally, the body plays itself out in relation to cultural scripts that we find ourselves inserted into, even as we try to rewrite them. A girl gets treated like a girl because she has a girl's body. Bodies are already culturally encoded – as soon as we are born we are fitted into a binary scheme of coordinated opposites (either male or female). But bodies also offer resources to subjects to reshape and recode culture. Although bodies are not stable or fixed, but are themselves the site of instability at a number of different levels (biological, psychological, technological) they nonetheless offer opportunities of bodily resistance to cultural shaping.

There are medical maps that force bodies into the mold of male and female, refusing the ambiguity of hermaphrodites, for example, checking that all the "right" parts are there, and that no extraneous parts confuse the picture. There are also ways in which the body disrupts and intrudes into the cultural maps that heterosexual and binary gender imperatives demand of them.

6 Why We Need to Talk About Sex, and Not Just Gender

One helpful way of thinking the relation of gender to sex is to posit two extremes which need avoiding. The body – sex – is not simply the cause of gender, gender does not simply follow from sex – one does not have to be feminine in all (or indeed any) respect, just because one is a woman. Nor is sex merely irrelevant to gender. The fact that one might be feminine in some, or indeed many, respects, is not entirely incidental to one's femaleness. One is brought up to do the things that girls do, because of, not irrespective of, one's female sex. Sex is neither the single cause of gender, neither completely determinative of gender, nor an arbitrary factor in relation to gender. The chances of one's being feminine in this culture if one is female are good – but this relation between being female and feminine carries no overriding necessity with it. It is neither a necessary, nor an arbitrary relation, but rather a contingent one. Here I am drawing on the work of Moira Gatens.[8]

Once it is seen that even if sex is not completely determinative of gender, sex is not entirely irrelevant to gender either, then bodies have to be taken seriously. They are the background against which gender is played out, just as culture is the informative and creative background on which sex is enacted in its various performative modes. One cannot afford to dispense with sex, any more than one can afford to dispense with gender. Bodies, far from being put out of play – as early feminist articulations of gender tended to do – need to be brought back into the picture. Sexual difference constitutes an important part of understanding gender. The point can be made very simply. For a boy to dress up in girls' clothes means something different from a girl dressing in girls' clothes. The male body registers differently than the female body precisely in relation to gender.

Hence it is no surprise that the 1990s have seen an infusion of interest in sexual difference, deviant bodies,[9] posthuman bodies,[10] cyborgs,[11] bodies that matter,[12] volatile bodies,[13] nomadic subjects,[14] to mention just a few topics. As if to make up for the deficit, bodies have come back into play. One thing that is being rethought from a number of different angles is the refusal of bodies to keep to any fixed boundaries, the impossibility of fixing boundaries between nature and culture, or bodies and technology. Advances in medical technology, the increasing availability and popularity of procedures such as in-vitro fertilization are challenging what it has meant up until fairly recently to be a woman, what it has meant to have the capacity to reproduce, and how female bodies are defined. Technology is quite literally reorganizing what it means to be a woman, what it means to be pregnant, and what it means to be capable of reproduction. Not only have cultural and political redefinitions occurred through single women and lesbian couples having children, but also one of the defining characteristics of being a woman is undergoing radical change.

7 Hasn't Foucault Taught Us to be Suspicious of Talking about Sex All the Time?

Let's step back a moment from all this talk about sex, bodies, and crossing or transgressing boundaries, and ask ourselves a Foucault-inspired question.[15] Isn't this just another instantiation of imagining we are engaging in some kind of self-liberating gesture, when in fact all we are doing is continuing our submission to the will to truth? Aren't we just reacting to some external compulsion to admit the truth of our sexuality, haven't we simply shifted from the confessional box to the psychoanalyst's couch, don't we keep on acting out the same role vis-à-vis authority, substituting the analyst for the priest, paying our fees instead of our tithes? Has anything really changed? Are we just imagining that there is some emancipatory aspect to our apparent transgressions of gender, isn't this emancipatory force illusory? In fact aren't we continuing to labor under the weight of social dictates, which only reinforce new dogmatic codes, rather than freeing us from their authority? Shouldn't we be suspicious of this call to talk about sex and bodies, and physicality, as just another ruse of authority to distract our attention from any really effective social change?

We would have no hesitation in answering these questions in the affirmative, were it not for the fact that the subject position of women and men are not symmetrically arranged around the axes of sexuality and power. But representation for women and men has been far from equal. Talk about sex has been primarily about male sex. Read Freud. As we saw, Irigaray shows that women may have been seen as the dark continent, the mysterious other, the enigmatic riddle – but they have also been made to conform to the male pattern of development. Men have castration complexes, so we have penis envy; men have an Oedipus complex, so we have a retarded, undeveloped Oedipus complex. Men have superegos, but we are still trying to find ours.

When Foucault bemoans the prolixity of talk about sex, we need to see how much this talk has been biased from the start. Women need to begin to develop a vocabulary, a lexicon, an iconology to begin to talk about sex. We need to notice and appreciate the irony that just when women are beginning to talk about sex, we apparently learn from Foucault that this is a misplaced wish.

A parallel development can be seen in the apparently poststructuralist dismissal of authorial intentions – and therefore histories, biographies, social locations, politics – that allegedly follows from Foucault's "Death of an Author." Just at the time when African-American women were beginning to document their lives, and stop being invisible, or rather make the whiteness of feminism visible, deconstruction comes along and says that none of that matters anyway.

The oversimplification of both cases needs correction. Foucault doesn't advocate preventing talk about sex, any more than he throws into disrepute any talk about the politics of location – precisely the opposite. What he does is issue warnings that we need to ask about what authority is in play, and whether there isn't a danger of simply reinventing or replicating the power dynamics we seek to avoid. And this warning seems to me valid enough when I look around and see feminism unwittingly reproducing many of the same problems of patriarchy, albeit in different guises, instead of being self-critical enough to distance itself from its abuses. As long as feminism contents itself with celebrating the success of token women, it will celebrate that success at the expense of other women – feminism's others.

To return to Irigaray and her call for feminism to develop a female imaginary, let me leave you with an image, which may explain why women need to figure themselves in new ways that do not replicate male desire, why we need to overcome the feminine ideal that still haunts us of barbie-doll, artificial beauty.

8 The Female Imaginary

The anorexic subject has a complex relationship to her body that cannot be cashed out without taking into account the body image, or the "imaginary body."[16] The illusory gross distension of the stomach that the subject sees when she steps in front of the mirror can only be explained with the help of an account of the relation between cultural ideals of femininity on the one hand, and the empirical reality of the anorexic body on the other hand.

> Sixty-nine and a half pounds! I've gained a pound and a half in three days (not counting the five glasses of water I drank before being wheeled here: half a pound perhaps?) My belly feels tight to bursting and suddenly looks obscenely round; reflexively, I press it with my palm, resolving not to eat again today.
> I have a rule when I weigh myself: if I've gained weight, I starve for the rest of the day. But if I've lost weight, I starve too.[17]

The distorted and bloated image that confronts the anorexic after she has eaten food that represents only a few calories is real enough for her, but its lack of fit with what an impartial observer would see – an emaciated and under-nourished body – must be explained.

Irigaray calls for a female imaginary, in which the question of women's desire could be posed for the first time, where body-images are not constrained by male desire. Women would no longer be restricted to their fragmentary roles of giving pleasure to their male lovers, securing the identity of their masters, or of preserving and safeguarding their children – all of which require the submergence of female desire in the other-oriented, caring, maternal provider.

The very idea that a desire for a child would be a substitute for penis envy reflects a logic of substitution that could only make sense if value accrued to a singular object. If there is only one value, then in order for other values to be generated, a process of substitution must be instituted. In order for an exchange to take place, for intercourse of any type to occur – economic, sexual, communicative – one object must be judged the equivalent of another. Such equivalence must be kept in order, overseen, controlled, monitored. Inflation must be channeled in a direction that allows the benefits to be reaped by those who administer the controls.

Displacing the hierarchy that dictates that there can be only one sign of value, upsetting the discourse that circulates around the phallus will do little to change things unless another way of thinking the system is also embraced. Simply replacing the mastery of one sex for another does nothing to change the system. Thus Irigaray says if we aim "to reverse the order of things, even supposing this to be possible, history would repeat itself in the long run, would revert to sameness; to phallocratism." What is needed in order for women to invent a female imaginary is to find a way of "*never being simply one*" – of never sacrificing one pleasure for another. We have to abandon the goal of discovering one true pleasure, of defining woman according to a single essence, of reducing multiplicity to singularity, and plurality to monism. We have to stop thinking in terms of reducing one to another, subsuming a person to the whole, extrapolating from me to the others, giving priority to the system at the expense of the individual. In order for difference not to be extinguished, we cannot always have decided in advance on a quantifiable ordering in which one counts for more or is better according to a standard that is apparently abstract, but is in fact based in concrete privileges dictated by dominant social groups, and rendered invisible in and through the mechanisms which maintain dominance and privilege.

What would it mean to create genuine alternatives, not to have always decided in advance, not to repress alterity by taming it with familiarity? How could we move beyond the matrix of mastery and slavery? How could we avoid building new prisons, and new cloisters in which to manufacture new desires according to the old regimes? If one thing is clear, it is that there can be no single answer, for to imagine that there is one answer for everyone, that everyone must follow the same route, is to invoke a single definition of what it means to be a woman, and to act as if we are all essentially the same. This would be to forget that no woman is ever simply one. Her pleasures are neither singular, nor reducible to one.

Like female bodies and sexuality, Irigaray's texts are not easily summed up. The insistent descriptions of female sexuality challenge the taboos which surround and repress women's expression of their desire. They contain a certain relentless excess, betray an irritability. There is both a proximity to the male tradition, and a distance from it. At times Irigaray's flirtation with the philosophers borders on the parasitical – a mimicry, a parody, an irony in relation to the masters. There is a lyrical, elliptical tone to Irigaray's writing. Reflective, rather than argumentative, Irigaray writes in styles other than and irreducible to that of the dominant philosophical voice. Putting into question the neutral, objective, impartial tone of the male philosophers, Irigaray exposes the prejudices and biases underlying the apparently rigorous and logical. She points to the ellipses, the blanks, the unthought, the repression that marks the underside of Western metaphysics, and shows how women have become the trope of the mysterious other – outside the system, unacknowledged and unrepresented, yet anchoring and informing its structure in multiple, subterranean and labyrinthine ways.

Notes

1   Sigmund Freud (1951–73) *The Standard Edition of the Complete Psychological Works of Sigmund Freud*, trans. James Strachey, ed. James Strachey in collaboration with Anna Freud (London: Hogarth Press and the Institute of Psycho-analysis). See especially Sigmund Freud, "Femininity" SE, XXII pp. 112–35, and "Three Essays on the Theory of Sexuality," SE, VII.

2   Luce Irigaray (1985) *This Sex Which Is Not One*, tr. Catherine Porter with Carolyn Burke (New York: Cornell University Press), pp. 23–33; *Ce sexe qui n'en est pas un* (Paris: Minuit, 1977), pp. 23–32.

3   Luce Irigaray (1985) "The Blind Spot of an Old Dream of Symmetry," *Speculum of the Other Woman*, trans. Gillian C. Gill (Ithaca, NY: Cornell University Press, 1985), pp. 11–129; *Speculum de l'autre femme* (Paris: Editions Minuit, 1974), pp. 9–162.

4   Simone de Beauvoir (1954) *The Second Sex*, trans. H. M. Parshley (New York: Knopf).

5   Judith Butler (1990) *Gender Trouble: Feminism and the Subversion of Identity* (New York: Routledge).

6   Barbara Kingsolver (1993) *Pigs in Heaven* (New York: HarperCollins).

7   Toni Morrison (1994) *The Bluest Eye* (New York: Plume).

8   Moira Gatens (1991) "A Critique of the Sex/Gender Distinction," *A Reader in Feminist Knowledge*, ed. Sneja Gunew (London: Routledge), pp. 139–57, reprinted in *Imaginary Bodies* (New York: Routledge, 1996), pp. 3–20, originally published in *Beyond Marxism? Interventions After Marx*, ed. J. Allen and P. Patton (NSW: Intervention Publications, 1983), pp. 143–60.

9   Jennifer Terry and Jacqueline Urla (eds) (1995) *Deviant Bodies: Critical Perspectives on Difference in Science and Popular Culture* (Bloomington and Indianapolis: Indiana University Press).

10   Judith Halberstam and Ira Livingston (eds) (1995) *Posthuman Bodies* (Indianapolis and Bloomington: Indiana University Press).

11   Donna J. Haraway (1991) *Simians, Cyborgs, and Women: The Reinvention of Nature* (New York: Routledge).

12   Judith Butler (1993) *Bodies That Matter* (New York: Routledge).

13   Elizabeth Grosz (1994) *Volatile Bodies: Toward a Corporeal Feminism* (Bloomington and Indianapolis: Indiana University Press).

14   Rosi Braidotti (1994) *Nomadic Subjects: Embodiment and Sexual Difference in Contemporary Feminist Theory* (New York: Columbia University Press).

15   See Michel Foucault (1980) *History of Sexuality*, vol. 1, trans. Robert Hurley (New York: Vintage); *Histoire de la sexualité 1: La volonté de savoir* (Paris: Gallimard, 1978).

16   Gatens uses this term, and her analysis is influenced by M. Merleau-Ponty's account of the phantom limb in *Phenomenology of Perception*, trans. Colin Smith (London: Routledge & Kegan Paul, 1962).

17   Jenefer Shute (1992) *Life-size* (London: Martin Secker and Warburg), p. 19.